Architectural Drafting

# JOHN E. BALL

Northeast Louisiana University

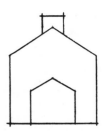

RESTON PUBLISHING COMPANY, INC.
*A Prentice-Hall Company*
Reston, Virginia 22090

# Architectural Drafting

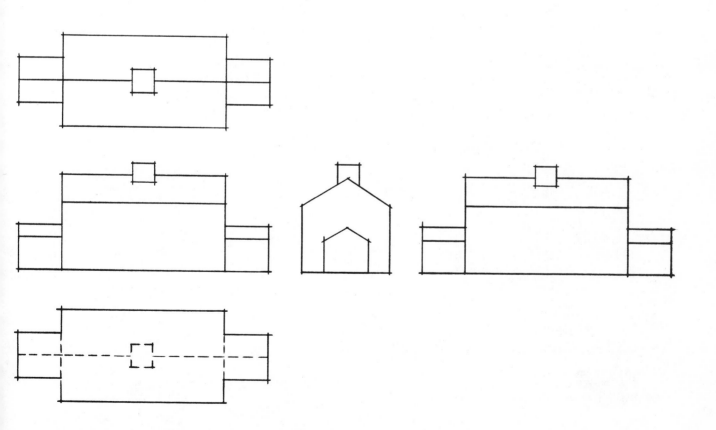

*Dedicated to my loving wife,*
*ALICE*

*Library of Congress Cataloging in Publication Data*

BALL, JOHN E
Architectural drafting.

Includes index.
1. Architectural drawing.   I.  Title.
NA2700.B27      720'.28'4      80-13940
ISBN 0-8359-0255-2

*Architectural Drafting,* by John E. Ball
© 1981 by Reston Publishing Company, Inc.
*A Prentice-Hall Company*
Reston, Virginia 22090

10   9   8   7   6   5   4   3   2   1

PRINTED IN THE UNITED STATES OF AMERICA

# PREFACE

*Architectural Drafting* is a textbook for use as an introductory course in architectural drafting. It is designed to be used at the secondary, technical, junior college, and college levels.

Included in the text is a review of basic technical drafting for students who have no experience in drafting; for those who do have a background in technical drafting, it serves as a brief refresher.

The remainder of the book is arranged in chapters each of which is directly related to a particular architectural phase. Some of these chapters are: Floor Plans, Elevations, Details, Schedules, Perspectives, The Plot Plan, Sketching, The Foundation Plan, The Plumbing Plan, and The Heating and Air Conditioning Plan. This particular feature sets the text aside from most other architectural drafting texts, because it breaks the text into related chapters that correspond to a typical set of plans.

The text also has numerous illustrations that are drawn as they would appear on a set of architectural drawings.

---

The author is grateful to the following sources for illustrations and tables:

Alpine Engineered Products, Inc. (Tables A6 and A8)

American Plywood Association (Tables 8-1, 8-2, 9-1, 9-2, and A10 through A18)

American Standard, Inc. (Tables A42 through A46)

Andersen Corporation (Figures 9-37 through 9-41)

*Architectural Graphic Standards* (New York: John Wiley & Sons, Inc.) (Tables 9-3, 16-3, and 16-6)

Asphalt Roofing Manufacturing Association (Tables A19 through A23)

Canadian Wood Council (Tables A26 through A31)

Conestage (Table A50)

Connor Forest Industries (Tables A47 and A48)

Construction Specifications Institute, Inc. (Figure 19-2)

Conweb Corporation (Tables A35 through A41)

William Cavit Cookson III (Figures 9-42, 9-43, 10-36, 14-1, 14-6, and 15-1)

Dietzgen Corporation (Figure 1-6)

House Beautiful Special Publications (Figure 18-7)

House of Plans (Figures 7-1, 8-31, 11-9, 13-30, 13-31, 15-19, and 19-3)

House Plans Department, Building Manual (P.O. Box 1701, Sandusky, Ohio 44870) (Figures 17-1, 18-1, and 18-2)

Hudson Home Publications (Figures 18-4 and 18-5)

Keuffel & Esser Company (Figures 1-1, 1-5, 1-8, 1-10, 1-11, 1-13, 1-17, 1-27, 1-32, 2-8, and 2-15)

W.A. Lawrence Drafting Service (Figures 10-5 and 10-33)

*Light Frame House Construction* (U.S. Department of Health, Education and Welfare) (Table 16-4)

Manas Publications (Tables 13-4 and 13-5)

Mega Corporation (Figures 9-2, 9-3, 10-1, 11-1, 15-16, and 15-17)

Mississippi Louisiana Brick Manufacturing Association (Figure 9-55)

National Forest Products Association (Tables A7 and A32)

National Lumber Manufacturers Association (Figures 5-2 through 5-7 and Tables A33 and A34)

National Plumber's Code (Tables 13-1 through 13-3)

Red Cedar Shingle and Handsplit Shake Bureau (Figure 10-11 and Tables A24 and A25)

Stanley Hardware (Table A9)

*State of Louisiana Manual of Practice, Individual Sewerage Disposal*, Bureau of Environmental Health, Division of Engineering (Table 13-6)

Timely Products Company (Figure 2-14)

U.S. Department of Housing and Urban Development, Federal Housing Administration (Figure 19-1)

Western Wood Products Association (Tables A1 through A5 and A49)

# CONTENTS

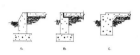

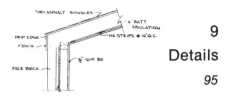

To produce a quality drawing, the drafts-person must have certain drafting equipment. The amount of equipment varies with different draftspersons and their experience, but it should all be of good quality. Catalogs of drafting tools and equipment are helpful to the beginner in the selection of supplies.

## Drawing Boards

Drawing boards (see Fig. 1-1) vary in size from small, 12″ × 15″, to as long as 12′. Most students, however, find that a board measuring 18″ × 24″ or 24″ × 36″ is a suitable and convenient size. Drawing boards are usually made from soft white pine or basswood. Some are lined with an aluminum or steel strip to provide a true edge. If a metal strip is not placed along the drawing board edge, a wooden cleat is usually fastened to the edge by a tongue-and-groove joint.

To improve the resiliency of the drawing surface, many draftspersons prefer to cover their boards with a cover paper or a vinyl top. The paper top is moisture-proof, cleans easily, and is available in plain or gridded sheets. A vinyl top has excellent resiliency and will not show instrument holes and dents in the drawing board.

## Drafting Tables and Chairs

There are many kinds of drafting tables (see Fig. 1-2). Some can be adjusted for varying heights from 32 to 42″. Many students prefer to have portable drafting tables at home. These can be easily picked up and moved from one location to another. Some portable drafting tables are bolted, but can be easily disassembled. Others can be folded together for easy storage. For classroom and office use large, stationary drafting tables are popular, and can be purchased with roomy plan drawers, drawers for equipment, or no drawers at all.

There are also many kinds of drafting chairs and stools (see Fig. 1-3). Some draftspersons prefer to use a stool because they do quite a bit of their work standing and a stool is more convenient. Others prefer to use a drafting chair. Most of the chairs can be adjusted from 22 to 32″.

1

# 1

# Drafting
# Equipment

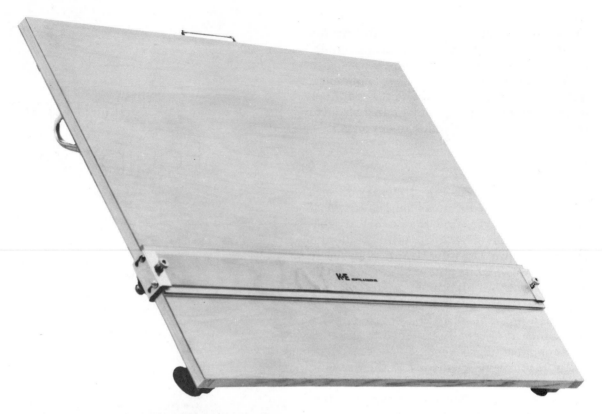

FIGURE 1-1 (above)    Typical drawing board

FIGURE 1-2 (left)    Drafting table

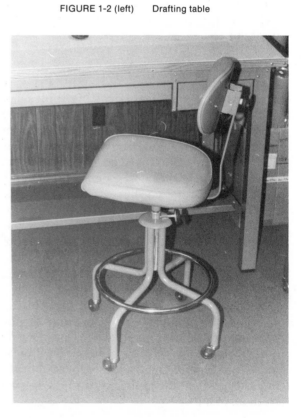

FIGURE 1-3 (right)    Drafting chair

FIGURE 1-4 (below)    T-square

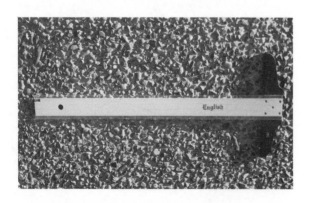

FIGURE 1-5    Parallel straightedge

## The T-square

The T-square (see Fig. 1-4) is used to draw horizontal lines and can be used, in conjunction with a triangle, to draw vertical lines. The instrument has two primary parts—the head and the blade. The blade serves as a guide for drawing all horizontal lines and should be kept free of any defects. The head is attached to the blade with screws and glue. If it ever becomes loose it should be reglued and screwed to the blade. The size of a T-square can vary in length from 12 to 60″, but the most popular lengths are 24 and 36″.

A right-handed draftsperson should place the head of the T-square along the left edge of the drawing board and apply slight pressure to the head and blade with the left hand. For a left-handed draftsperson, the procedure is reversed. When a line is drawn, pressure on the T-square should remain constant as the pencil is drawn along the top (working) edge of the T-square.

## The Parallel Straightedge

Many architects and architectural draftspersons prefer a parallel straightedge to a T-square (see Fig. 1-5). A parallel straightedge operates on cords or wires that run through the tool and are attached to the board at each of the four corners.

A parallel straightedge is available in many different lengths. It can be fastened to a drawing board, or it can be mounted to a drafting table. This tool has the advantage of automatically maintaining its parallel motion regardless of the amount of applied pressure. A disadvantage, however, is that it can come loose and get out of proper alignment. To properly use a parallel straightedge, first correctly position it; then apply pressure with the right or left hand and draw a pencil along the top edge.

## The Drafting Machine

The drafting machine is becoming more and more popular in architects' and engineers' offices. It is used in place of a parallel straightedge or a T-square (see Fig. 1-6). A drafting machine can replace scale, triangles, and adjustable triangle, and it can be used to lay out and measure angles. The desired angle is achieved by depressing a control button and shifting the blades to an angle on the protractor. To speed the setting of a drafting machine, most scale assemblies can be automatically snapped into any unit multiple of 15 degrees. The blades on a drafting machine can be interchanged with either an architect's or engineer's scale.

## Pencils and Leads

There are special types of pencils and leads that are used in architectural drafting. Some draftspersons prefer to use a mechanical holder for their lead; others prefer a traditional wooden pencil. The lead of a wooden pencil should be sharpened on the end away from the hardness symbol. About ⅜″ of lead should be exposed and formed into a conical point; this can be achieved by rotating the lead back and forth on a sandpaper pad (see Fig. 1-7). The sandpaper pad is quite messy and should never be used over a drawing. When it is not in use it should be stored in an envelope.

Because it offers the advantage of speed and neatness, a mechanical lead holder is popular in most architectural offices (see Fig. 1-8). It is relatively clean, easy to use, and can provide varying degrees of sharpness for the lead.

Lead can range from the hardest, 9H, to the softest, 7B (see Fig. 1-9). The harder leads are used for preliminary layout work and to draw fine light lines. The harder the lead, the lighter the line will appear. The softer leads

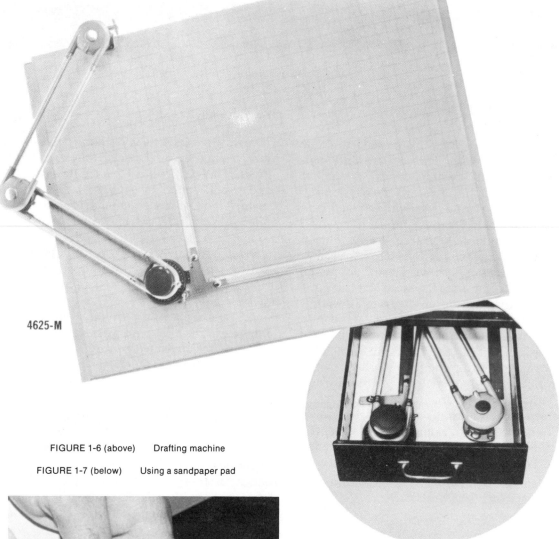

4625-M

FIGURE 1-6 (above)        Drafting machine

FIGURE 1-7 (below)        Using a sandpaper pad

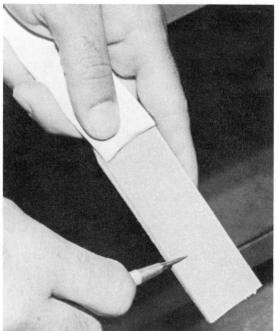

are used to darken the drawing, as well as for lettering, sketching, and rendering. Each lead is designed for a specific purpose, and the beginning draftsperson should be aware of the varying hardnesses and pressures required to use them.

In many cases it will be necessary to experiment with the lead to find one that meets personal needs. Different brands of lead vary in hardness, even though they may carry the same hardness symbol. For this reason it is advisable to use only one brand of lead. Beginning draftspersons should experiment with the various leads before making a definite choice. A 4H is usually used for preliminary layout work, and an H or 2H for lettering and to darken the drawing.

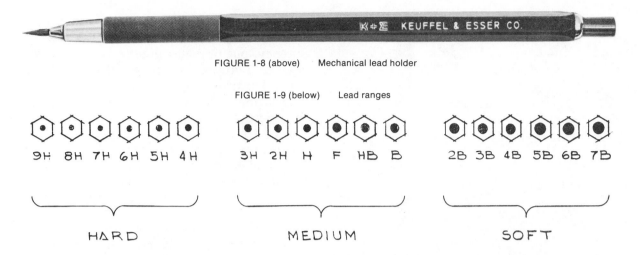

FIGURE 1-8 (above)    Mechanical lead holder

FIGURE 1-9 (below)    Lead ranges

9H 8H 7H 6H 5H 4H        3H 2H H F HB B        2B 3B 4B 5B 6B 7B

HARD                    MEDIUM                    SOFT

There are also leads that can be used that do not reproduce on prints. A lead of this type is usually used for preliminary layout work and is available with a diameter of 0.5 mm.

A specially formulated lead is available for use on drafting film; it produces a dark inklike line that reproduces well even when microfilming is a factor. The lines don't easily smudge, but can be erased. This type is available in three degrees of hardness and diameters of 0.5 mm, 0.7 mm, and 0.9 mm.

### Lead Pointers

There are many kinds of lead pointers. One popular variety has a sandpaper drum; the lead holder and lead are placed in the pointer and turned clockwise to produce a fine point. Some pointers also have variable tapers (see Fig. 1-10) to produce varying types of lead points.

Some lead pointers have a case-hardened tool steel cutting wheel (see Fig. 1-11); in these, the wheel never needs to be replaced. The inexpensive pocket model shown in Fig. 1-12 has four small blades that are used to point the lead. The lead holder and lead are placed in the holder and rotated between thumb and forefinger.

### Drafting Media and Tape

There are three basic types of drafting media—cloth, film, and paper. Each has certain advantages and disadvantages. Cloth is transparent, with good surface quality, strength,

and permanence. This medium is made from cotton fibers that are sized with starch. Water will spot tracing cloth and if any moisture leaches the starch out, the cloth will shrink.

Polyester film has great tearing strength, is highly transparent, and is age- and heat-resistant, nonsoluble, and waterproof. Both pencil and ink "take" superbly on film. Plastic pencils can also be used on polyester film to produce crisp, clean, smudge-proof tracings.

Tracing papers that are used in architectural drafting are available in a wide range of transparencies. In most cases, however, thinner papers are more transparent and are

FIGURE 1-10    Lead pointer

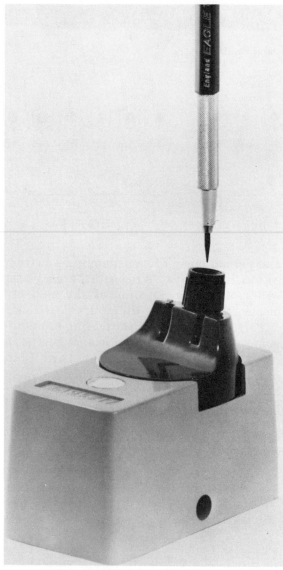

FIGURE 1-11 (above)    Lead pointer, with steel
                        cutting wheel

FIGURE 1—12 (below)    Pocket-model lead pointer

primarily used for preliminary sketching. Heavier paper offers slightly less transparency, but provides greater strength and erasing qualities and is suitable for most general drafting applications.

Drafting paper is available in 100 percent rag or no-rag content. The 100 percent rag papers are a lot more durable, and do not become brittle with age; they resist discoloration and are extremely durable. Papers with no rag are economical, but not very durable. They are usually used for preliminary layouts.

A paper that has been treated with oil is called *vellum* and is used by some architectural firms. Vellum offers the strength and drafting qualities of the finest drawing papers with the transparency of the thinnest tracing paper. The biggest disadvantage, however, is its cost—it is slightly more expensive than regular tracing paper.

Drafting media are available in cut sheets or rolls, but for the beginning draftsperson an 18″ × 24″ or 24″ × 36″ cut sheet is the most popular and convenient size. The drafting medium is secured to the drawing board with ⅝ or ¾″ drafting tape, torn in small pieces and placed on the four corners of the medium. Precut tape is also available; this is peeled from a backing paper and then placed on the drafting medium. Transparent mending tape and masking tape should not be used, because they can leave a gum residue on the completed drawing.

## Technical Fountain Pens

Technical fountain pens are sometimes used in detail work, general drafting work, lettering, and template work. They are as easy to use as pencils, provide even lines, and make excellent blueprints. They are available in varying line widths (see Fig. 1-13). Most technical fountain pens have color-coded caps and rings for quick identification. Ink is becoming quite popular in architectural and engineering offices; it erases easily from polyester paper.

## Erasers

Some popular erasers are the: *Pink Pearl, artgum,* and *vinyl* eraser (see Fig. 1-14). Pink

FIGURE 1-13 (above)    Technical fountain pens

FIGURE 1-14 (right)    Erasers: Pink Pearl, Artgum, and vinyl

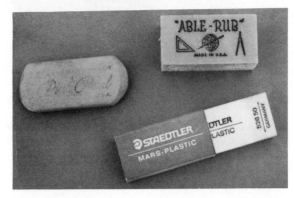

Pearl is available in different sizes and shapes and is used to remove darkened lines. Artgum is used for pencil and smudge erasures. When an area needs to be erased, slight pressure should be applied with the fingertips near the area to be erased; if the drawing is not held in place the drawing could be torn. Once pressure has been applied, the mark can be removed safely.

A vinyl eraser is used to remove any smudges and unwanted lines from film. Such an eraser should first be slightly moistened and then drawn over any inked lines that are not wanted. The lines will erase quickly without leaving "ghosts."

Erasing machines are often used to speed the erasing process and increase erasing accuracy (see Fig. 1-15). These machines are lightweight and hold a long eraser by a screw-type collet. To minimize damage to a drawing, most such machines are designed to stall when excessive pressure is applied.

An erasing shield is often used when it is necessary to remove lines in a confined area (see Fig. 1-16). This device is a thin sheet of metal with holes of varying shapes and sizes. It is placed over the area to be erased; when it is positioned it should be held firmly in place until the erasure has been completed.

Drawing cleaners are made of a soft, granular material that provides a protective coating over the drawing. They are available in powder form or in a pad (see Fig. 1-17). The cleaner is sprinkled over the drawing to pick up any loose lead dust, dirt, or body oil that might interfere with a quality drawing. The material also acts as small ball bearings between the instruments and the drafting medium, producing a much cleaner drawing.

## The Drafting Brush

A drafting brush is used to remove any loose graphite and eraser dust from the drawing

FIGURE 1-15 (left)    Erasing machine

FIGURE 1-16 (below)    Erasing shield

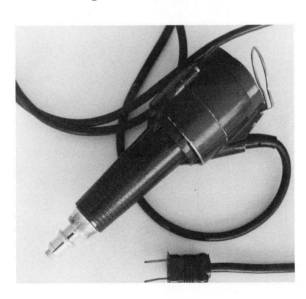

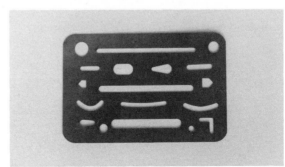

FIGURE 1-17 (left)   Drawing cleaner

FIGURE 1-18 (above)   Drafting brush

(see Fig. 1-18). The brush is used with quick wrist snaps to clean the drawing without smudging the linework.

## The 30/60-Degree Triangle

A 30/60-degree triangle, usually made of clear plastic, has angles of 90 degrees, 30 degrees, and 60 degrees. When it is held in a position as shown in Fig. 1-19, a 30-degree line to the horizontal can be drawn. If it is repositioned as shown in Fig. 1-20, a 60-degree line to the horizontal can be drawn. To use a 30/60-degree triangle, place the base of the triangle against the T-square blade. Hold the triangle in place with the fingertips, with the palm of the hand positioned on the T-square blade; then pass the drafting pencil along the edge of the triangle. As the line is being drawn, incline the pencil in the direction in which the line is being drawn.

## The 45-Degree Triangle

To draw vertical or inclined lines, a 45-degree triangle can be used in combination with a parallel-ruling straightedge or T-square (see Fig. 1-21). The 45-degree triangle has two 45-degree angles and one 90-degree angle. To properly use the triangle, place the vertical edge to the left side of the drawing board. Then place the pencil next to the triangle and draw along the edge of it. As the pencil is moved, it should be rotated between the thumb and forefinger; this maintains an even point on the lead.

The 45- and 30/60-degree triangles can be used separately or in combination for drawing 15-degree increments (see Fig. 1-22).

FIGURE 1-19 (below)   Drawing a 30-degree line to the horizontal

FIGURE 1-20 (right)   Drawing a 60-degree line to the horizontal

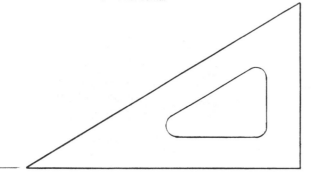

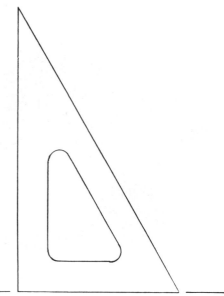

FIGURE 1-21      The 45-degree triangle

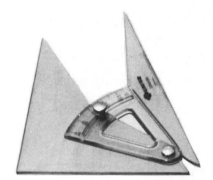

FIGURE 1-23 (above left)      The adjustable triangle

FIGURE 1-24 (below right)      The protractor

## The Adjustable Triangle

An adjustable triangle has a protractor scale that permits the measuring of an angle between 0 and 90 degrees and can take the place of a 45- or 30/60-degree triangle, (see Fig. 1-23). The protractor has two rows of graduations—an outer and an inner. The outer row is used to measure angles from 0 to 45 degrees, while the inner row is used to measure angles from 45 to 90 degrees. When the triangle has been adjusted to the desired angle it is secured and held in place by a thumbscrew.

## The Protractor

A protractor is usually a circular or semicircular drafting tool with moulded graduations, usually of half-degrees (see Fig. 1-24). It is used to lay out angles that cannot normally be laid out with the 45- or 30/60-degree triangle. To use a protractor, first place the apex over the point to be measured. Then mark the desired angle along the curvature of

FIGURE 1-22      Triangle summary

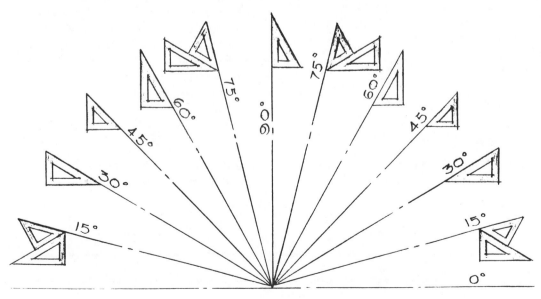

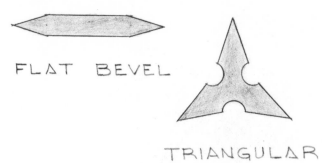

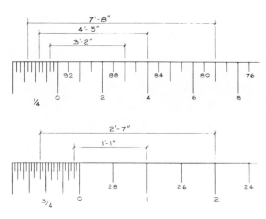

FIGURE 1-25     The architect's scale

FIGURE 1-26     Reading the architect's scale

the protractor. The apex is the tip of the angle—the point where the two inclined lines meet.

### The Architect's Scale

Most of the drawings in a typical set of plans are drawn to scale. A scale drawing is a drawing made to a size other than the actual size of the object represented. To convert the large dimensions to a smaller scale, an architect's scale is used. This is made from boxwood or plastic, and is available in a flat bevel or a triangular style (see Fig. 1-25). For a beginning student in architectural drafting, the triangular style is usually the most popular. A triangular scale has ten different scales: full scale ($\frac{1}{16}''$ graduations); and $\frac{1}{8}''$, $\frac{3}{4}''$, $\frac{1}{2}''$, $1''$, $3''$, $\frac{3}{32}''$, $\frac{3}{16}''$, $\frac{3}{8}''$, and $1\frac{1}{2}''$—all of these equal to $1'0''$. Each scale has several divisions representing feet, and one division at the end of the scale that is divided into inches and fractions. The dimension of feet is read from the zero out and the dimension in inches is read from the zero in (see Fig. 1-26).

To properly use the scale, turn it so it is parallel with the line to be measured, and place it away from the body. Then mark the correct dimension with a sharp pencil held in a vertical position.

### The Engineer's Scale

The engineer's scale is used in architectural drafting primarily for the construction of plot plans. The engineer's scale is also available in a bevel or triangular style, but the scale is graduated into decimal parts of a foot, rather than in inches (see Fig. 1-27). There are six different scales, each representing an inch that is divided into 10, 20, 30, 40, 50, and 60 equal parts. If the 10 scale is used it can represent $1'' = 10'$, $1'' = 100'$, or $1'' = 1000'$. Other scales are used to represent $1'' = 20'$, $1'' = 30'$, $1'' = 40'$, etc.

### The French Curve

It is often necessary to draw a curve other than a circle or arc. To accomplish this, a French curve, or irregular curve, is used. This instrument is made of transparent plastic and has many different curves built into its shape (see Fig. 1-28). Once the French curve has been correctly positioned, the curve or a portion of the curve can be drawn in. If it is necessary to reposition the French curve, it should be allowed to overlap a portion of the previously drawn line and a minimum of two points. In this way, a smooth line is achieved.

### Adjustable Curves

An adjustable curve is an instrument that has a flexible metal core covered by a plastic,

FIGURE 1-27     The engineer's scale

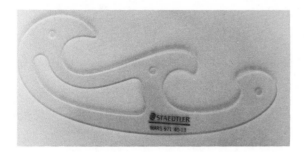

FIGURE 1-28    French curve

rubber, or metal ruling edge. It is used to draw long, uninterrupted curves, such as highway curves and contour lines. The curve can be bent to any shape and is held in place by metal weights or "ducks." When it is in position an entire curve can be drawn in one smooth motion.

## Case Instruments

A "set" of drawing instruments (see Fig. 1-29) is not essential in architectural drafting, although it is sometimes used. There are varying degrees of quality in such a set, as well as a varying number of instruments included. A case set that meets most needs consists of a compass, divider, and ruling pen. The compass and divider are used occasionally, but the ruling pen has now been replaced by the technical fountain pen.

For proper use, the needle point of the compass should be adjusted so that it projects slightly past the point of the lead. Then it is possible to set the radius of the compass by adjusting the thumbscrew. The compass

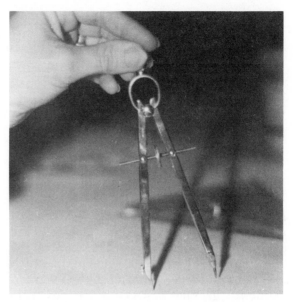

FIGURE 1-30    Using the compass

must be positioned so the needle point is correctly located. With the compass leaning forward, a line is started in a clockwise direction (see Fig. 1-30). As the compass is turning, the handle should be rotated between the thumb and forefinger.

Dividers are used to separate a line into equal parts, to transfer dimensions, or to transfer measurements from one location to another. To properly use the divider to divide a line, hold the handle between the thumb and forefinger and rotate the divider, alternating from clockwise to counter-clockwise (see Fig. 1-31).

FIGURE 1-31    Using the dividers

FIGURE 1-29    Case instruments

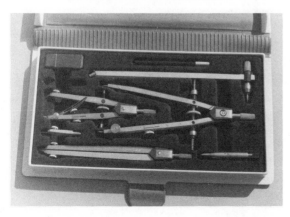

FIGURE 1-32     Proportional dividers

## Proportional Dividers

A proportional divider (see Fig. 1-32) can be used to give the ratio of the diameter to the circumference of a circle. The legs of the divider are divided into 100 equal parts, which are further subdivided into tenths by a vernier. Using the graduations as a guide, any ratio between 1:1 and 1:10 may be indicated. When the instrument is set, the opening at one end will give the diameter of a circle, and the distance between points on the other end will give the circumference reduced to lineal measure.

## Drafting Templates

A drafting template is made from a thin sheet of plastic and is often used to save the draftsperson time (see Fig. 1-33). Symbols for such things as doors, water closets, tubs, ranges, roof pitch, stair design, and circles are all included on a standard architectural template. Circle templates and plumbing templates are also used. A template should be held firmly in place and the symbol drawn to the correct line

weight on the first setting. Repositioning the template over the first setting makes it difficult to achieve complete accuracy.

## Lighting

Proper lighting of a drafting surface is very important and is a feature that is often overlooked. A soft, natural light usually provides the best type of lighting. Direct sunlight and bright lights can cause blind spots on the drafting surface and strain the eyes. Fluorescent lighting is usually used to achieve a subdued light. One popular drafting fixture has two 15″ fluorescent tubes in a reflector head that is mounted on an arm that swivels at the slightest touch (see Fig. 1-34). The base is equipped with a clamp that can be fastened to the drawing board. Other models use incandescent bulbs and a reflector, or an incandescent bulb in a circular fluorescent tube.

## Optional Equipment

Carrying tubes should always be used to protect tracing paper or drawings. Without

FIGURE 1-33     Drafting template

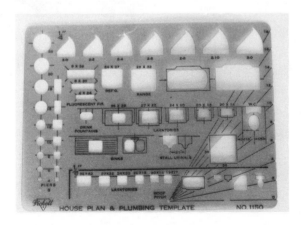

FIGURE 1-34     Lighting fixture

them, the paper may become spoiled, creased, or damaged, and these areas could be transferred to the reproduction. Carrying tubes with screw-on tops are available in most drafting supply outlets.

Paper scissors are indispensable to the draftsperson. They are used primarily to trim and cut paper, but are also useful for model building and various other activities.

Mending tape may be necessary to repair small tears in drawings. The tape, usually ¾″ wide, is bonded to the tracing paper by heat and pressure. Once in place, mending tape can be drawn over with a pencil or ink. It should never be used to repair a drawing.

A drafting cover is made of a pliable green fabric and is used to protect drawings left on the board from dust and damage. When the cover is not in use it is rolled to the back or side of the table.

A tool holder, to keep tools within convenient reach, is sometimes used to hold pencils, circles, and angles. It is most helpful when the board is used in a vertical position.

## Assignment:

The following drafting problems should first be drawn with a 4H lead, then darkened with an H or 2H lead. If the construction lines are drawn lightly it is not necessary to erase them. To accent the corners, the object lines can cross each other. Lead should be kept sharp to produce dark, sharp, crisp lines.

1. Using the scale ¾″ = 1′0″, draw a door that is 3′0″ × 6′8″. Include the panels, as shown in Fig. 1-35.

FIGURE 1-35    Panel door

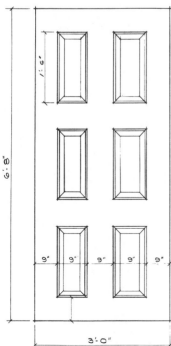

2. Using the scale 1″ = 1′0″, draw the asphalt strip shingle shown in Fig. 1-36.

FIGURE 1-36    Asphalt strip shingle

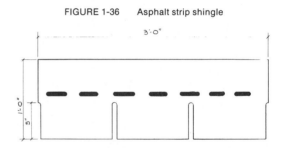

3. Using the scale 3″ = 1′0″, reproduce the pattern of the resilient flooring shown in Fig. 1-37.

FIGURE 1-37    Resilient flooring

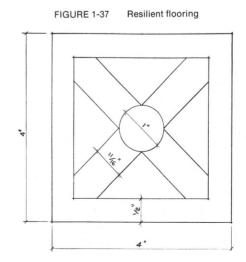

4. Using the scale ½″ = 1′0″, draw the single hung window in Fig. 1-38.

FIGURE 1-38    Single-hung window

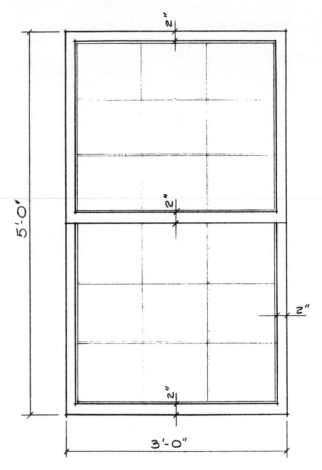

# 2

# Lettering

The lettering found on any architectural drawing is extremely important, for without legible notes and dimensions the plans are useless. Lettering is used to convey a message on a drawing that cannot be shown by graphic shapes and symbols and should complement the graphic shapes.

## Lettering Styles

There are many different lettering styles used today, but most are a variation or offshoot of the single-stroke Gothic style, in which each letter is formed by a series of single strokes of even width (see Fig. 2-1).

Roman-style lettering (see Fig. 2-2) is achieved by thin and thick strokes, but is not used much in standard practice. If lettering of this nature is needed, commercially prepared "rub-on" type is usually used—they are transferred to the drawing by application of pressure.

Text letters include all styles of Old English and German Text (see Fig. 2-3)—like the Roman style, they are not often used today. Letters of this nature are usually found on formal documents such as diplomas.

## Letter Strokes

The skill to execute good lettering requires practice and is not usually obtained overnight. But, by constant experimentation with different leads and techniques, an adequate lettering style can usually be developed. Individual strokes are usually considered to be one of the most important aspects of good lettering and should be studied carefully. The number and direction of strokes vary with each letter, but most draftspersons follow the strokes shown in Fig. 2-4. Individual vertical strokes are made in a downward direction, while horizontal strokes are made from left to right—whether the letterer is right- or left-handed. Using strokes of this nature a draftsperson can develop a natural flow of lines with a minimum change of pencil direction.

As the letters are formed, even pressure should be exerted on the pencil, which should be rotated every few strokes to achieve uniformity of line. The letters must be darkened in with each stroke; poor lettering will be the

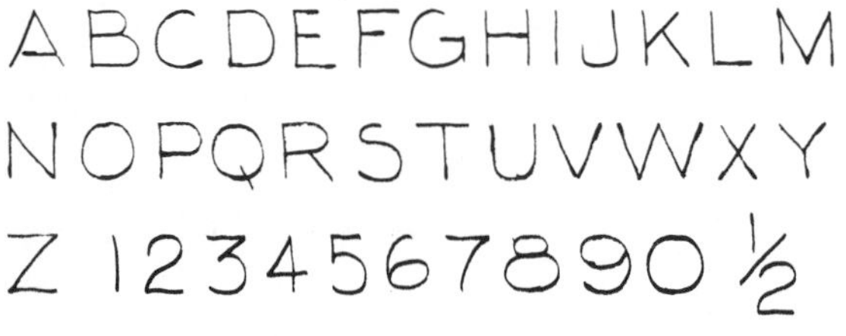

A B C D E F G H I J K L M
N O P Q R S T U V W X Y
Z 1 2 3 4 5 6 7 8 9 0 ½

# ROMAN
# LETTERING

FIGURE 2-1 (left)      Single-stroke Gothic lettering
FIGURE 2-2 (above)     Roman lettering
FIGURE 2-3 (below)     Old English lettering

𝕬𝕭𝕮𝕯𝕰𝕱𝕲𝕳𝕴𝕵𝕶𝕷𝕸𝕹𝕺𝕻𝕼𝕽𝕾𝕿
𝖀𝖁𝖂𝖃𝖄𝖅 &'-:,!? $ 0 1 2 3 4 5 6 7 8 9
a b c d e f g h i j k l m n o p q r s t u v w x y z

result of lightly forming the letters and then darkening them in.

## Uniformity

One of the most important aspects of good lettering is uniformity; without it, the effect is visually distracting. Letters should all be the correct height, spaced correctly, with individual strokes that are uniform in thickness.

Proper uniformity in letter height can be obtained by the use of guidelines (see below). The thickness of the individual strokes can be controlled by the proper lead selection and by rotation of the pencil after each stroke. The correct spacing of letters and words can also be achieved by the use of guidelines, but in most cases this skill comes with practice. Letters are not spaced an equal distance apart, but in such a way that the areas of white spaces between them are approximately equal. The general rule of thumb for

spacing two words is to leave a space between them that is equal to the height of the letters. The distance between two sentences, however, is equal to twice the height of a letter.

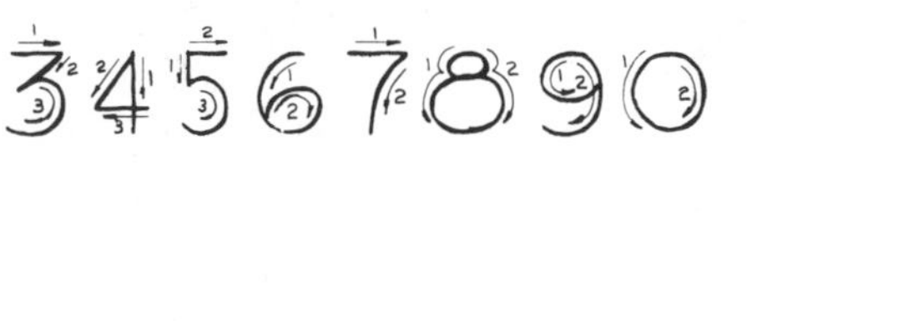

## Stability

In addition to being uniform, the letters must also have stability—this means that they do not have a top-heavy appearance. To avoid a top-heavy look in letters such as A, B, E, F, and H, place the horizontal crossbar slightly above or below center (see Fig. 2-5). For correct balance, the white area in the upper portion of a letter should be slightly smaller than the white space in the lower portion. Make the base of letters such as S, K, R, X, and Z a bit wider than the top to provide a stable effect (see Fig. 2-6).

## Guidelines

Guidelines are permanent but extremely light lines that are used to maintain the correct height for any letters or numerals. They are usually drawn with a hard lead such as 4H or 6H. As guidelines are drawn, only slight pressure should be placed on the pencil.

The Braddock-Rowe Lettering Triangle or the Ames Lettering Instrument can be used to

FIGURE 2-4      Letter strokes

A B C D E F G H I J
K L M N O P Q R S
T U V W X Y Z 1 2
3 4 5 6 7 8 9 0

FIGURE 2-5 (left)      Placement of horizontal
                       crossbar in letter
FIGURE 2-6 (right)     Stabilizing the letters "S," "K,"
                       "R," and "Z"

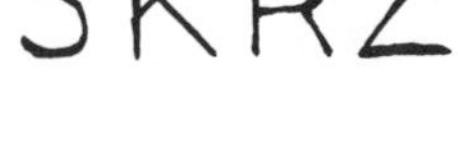

A B E F H     S K R Z

FIGURE 2-7    Braddock-Rowe lettering triangle

lower case lettering is seldom used

b d f h k l    p q g y  ─ CAP LINE / ─ BASE LINE / ─ DROP LINE

## SOME PEOPLE USE INCLINED LETTERS

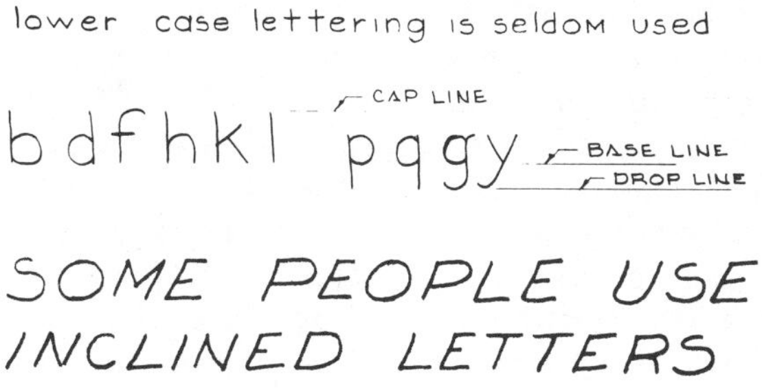

FIGURE 2-9 (top)    Lower-case lettering
FIGURE 2-10 (center)    Placement of ascenders
and descenders
FIGURE 2-11 (bottom)    Inclined letters

aid the draftsperson in drawing guidelines. The Braddock-Rowe Lettering Triangle (see Fig. 2-7) has a series of holes; a drafting pencil is inserted in one of the holes, and then the pencil and triangle gently slid across the paper. The holes in the triangle are uniformly spaced, but the number at the base of the triangle indicates the correct spacing of the lines in 32nds of an inch. Thus if No. 4 holes are used, the guidelines will be ⅛″ apart, and if No. 6 holes are used they will be 3⁄16″ apart.

The Ames Lettering Instrument (see Fig. 2-8) is used in a similar manner, but the height of the guidelines is controlled by turning a disk to a desired setting. The setting is made by selecting a number at the bottom of the disk and aligning it with an inscription on the disk frame. The number indicates the height of the guidelines in 32nds of an inch. For instance, to draw guidelines 3⁄16″ apart the disk would be set at No. 6.

### Lowercase Letters

Lowercase letters are not usually used in architectural drafting, but when they are, the

FIGURE 2-8    Ames lettering guide

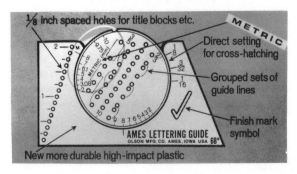

bodies are drawn two-thirds the height of the capitals (see Fig. 2-9). The ascenders extend to the cap line and the descenders extend an equal distance below the bottom guideline (see Fig. 2-10). Lowercase letters are based on a combination of circles, curves, and straight lines. Becoming proficient in lowercase lettering requires many hours of practice.

### Inclined Letters

Inclined letters are sometimes used on architectural drawings (see Fig. 2-11). For some, this style is easier to master than the vertical. In drawing inclined letters, a uniform slope should be maintained and the curves of the rounded letters should be of the correct shape. The vertical guidelines for the letters are usually drawn at 67½ degrees and can be drawn with the aid of a lettering guide.

### Lettering with a Triangle

To make letters larger than ¼″ in height, some draftspersons prefer to use an aid such as a triangle. The triangle is slid along the parallel straightedge and is used as an aid in drawing all vertical lines. All the other lines are drawn freehand. A blunt conical point or a chisel point produces a distinct and unique lettering style. This technique should not replace freehand lettering, however, and should only be used for drawing large letters, such as titles.

### Lettering Pencils

Most draftspersons prefer an F, H, or 2H lead with a conical point, although other leads and points can be used. The specific grade of pencil can vary with the brand name used or with the amount of pressure applied. To correctly use a lettering pencil, sharpen it to a needle point, then dull it slightly by marking on a scratch pad. As the pencil is used, enough pressure should be exerted to produce jet-black lettering. For a black line, the lead needs to be fairly soft, but hard enough to prevent excessive wearing down of the point.

### Lettering with Ink

Sometimes it is necessary to letter a drawing in ink. There are three different inking devices that can be used: (1) a speedball pen, (2) a technical fountain pen, or (3) a lettering device or guide. A speedball pen is usually used only for wide-stroke letters. Technical fountain pens use India ink to produce a variety of line widths, depending on the size. Lettering guides are used to produce uniform lettering for both vertical and inclined letters.

### Letter Size

There is no absolute rule that dictates the height of letters, because the size of lettering is dependent upon the size of the drawing. But in most cases letters are made ⅛ or ³⁄₃₂″ high, with titles and important words lettered much larger. The numerator or denominator of a fraction should be two-thirds the height of a whole number (see Fig. 2-12).

### Dry-Transfer Lettering

Dry-transfer lettering is a technique that is used primarily for illustrations or for title sheets. The individual letters are available on a transparent plastic sheet and are transferred by being rubbed with a smooth instrument (see Fig. 2-13). The sheet is then lifted away, and the letter is left on the drafting medium. If the drawing is to be reproduced, the letters should be heat-resistant—if they

# DRY TRANSFER LETTERING
## $ &!?85

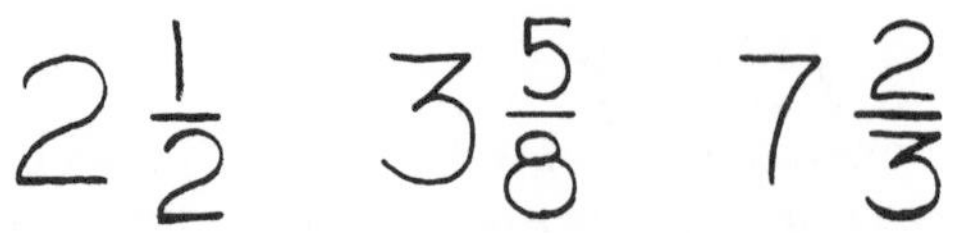

FIGURE 2-13     Dry-transfer lettering

are not, they can peel off during reproduction. If the drafting medium is to be handled extensively, it may be necessary to bind the letters with a clear acrylic spray.

### Stencil Lettering Guides

A stencil lettering guide (see Fig. 2-14) is used in the same manner as a template, but is not usually recommended for standard lettering. The template provides uniformity, but it is slow and prevents development of an individual lettering style. Another disadvantage is that some of the letters are not completely formed, and this sometimes causes confusion for the print user. Stencil lettering guides are usually used for titles, or in other special situations.

### Lettering Device

The Leroy Lettering Instrument (see Fig. 2-15) is used to accomplish uniform letters, and is becoming quite popular in architectural and engineering offices. It consists of a template and an instrument that follows grooved letters in the template. A guide pin is placed in a grooved letter on the template and the letter

FIGURE 2-14     Stencil lettering guides

FIGURE 2-12     Sizing fractions

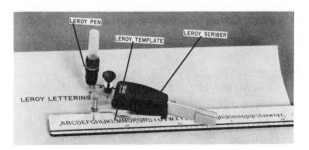

FIGURE 2-15    Leroy lettering instrument

is traced to reproduce the same letter on the drafting medium. The arm of the instrument can be adjusted to reproduce either vertical or inclined letters. There are a number of different templates that can be used, and the letters can be produced in either ink or pencil. But, because of the time involved in its use, this device is usually used only for inking purposes.

## Title Blocks

A title block or title strip (see Fig. 2-16) should always accompany a drawing. It should be easy to read and contain information such as (1) the name and address of the architectural firm, (2) the date, (3) the sheet number, (4) the draftsperson's name, and (5) the title of the sheet.

Some firms use a rectangular title block placed in the lower right-hand corner of the sheet; others use a title strip that extends across the bottom or end of the sheet.

## Repetitive Title Block Layouts

In some cases it may be necessary to lay out the same title block on several sheets of tracing paper. For speed and ease of application, there are several techniques that can be used to transfer a standard title block to multiple sheets. Sometimes a standard title block is laid out and placed under the corner or edge of a piece of tracing paper that has been previously taped to the drawing board. The title block is then traced and removed for future use. Some title blocks are reproduced on rubber stamps, which are coated with ink and pressed on the tracing paper.

## Lettering Titles

The size of the title will vary, depending on its importance. Additional emphasis can be achieved by the use of broad strokes or one or several underlines. The title is usually centered directly below the drawing (see Fig. 2-17). To get the title to fall within a given space, the lettering can first be placed on a scrap of overlay, which is then slipped under the drafting medium and traced. Large titles are sometimes lettered with the aid of instruments such as triangles, compasses, French curves, circle templates, and parallel straightedges. Lettering devices, stencils and rub-on letters, however, are preferred.

## Developing an Architectural Lettering Style

Many architects and draftspersons have developed distinct architectural lettering styles

FIGURE 2-16    Title block

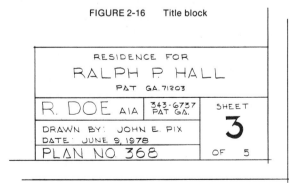

FIGURE 2-17    Lettering a title

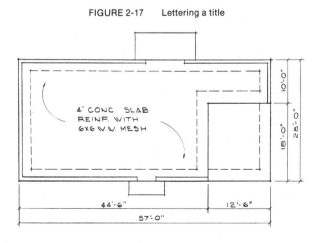

*FANCY LETTERING IS HARD TO READ.*

FIGURE 2-18    Fancy lettering

that are the result of years of practice. It is usually best for the beginning draftsperson to use the traditional single-stroke lettering style until it is perfected, and only then experiment with different lettering styles. A draftsperson should never get too fancy with lettering (see Fig. 2-18)—this can make the drawing hard to read and confuse the print reader.

In some architectural or drafting service offices, one particular lettering style may be standard, and all lettering must conform to that style.

## Lettering Rules

Listed below are several rules that should be followed if good lettering is to be achieved:
- ☐ Always use guidelines
- ☐ Make all letters dark and bold
- ☐ Make each stroke quickly, but take your time.
- ☐ Rotate your pencil with each stroke
- ☐ Use a soft pencil, such as an F or H
- ☐ PRACTICE!

## Assignment:

1. On an 8½″ × 11″ sheet of drafting medium, lay out a ½″ border and title block. Draw a series of guidelines ⅛″ apart. (They should be drawn with a 4H lead and should be light, permanent lines.) Using an H or 2H lead, letter the following:

   a. GOOD LETTERING REQUIRES PRACTICE.
   b. ALL LETTERS SHOULD BE DARK AND BOLD.
   c. ALWAYS USE GUIDELINES.
   d. ROTATE THE PENCIL WITH EACH STROKE.

2. On an 8½″ × 11″ sheet of drafting medium, lay out a ½″ border and title block. Draw a series of guidelines ⅜″ apart. (They should be light, permanent lines drawn with a 4H lead.) Using an H or 2H lead, letter the following:

   a. FRONT ELEVATION
   b. SECTION A
   c. FLOOR PLAN
   d. TYPICAL WALL SECTION
   e. FOUNDATION PLAN

3. On an 8½″ × 11″ sheet of drafting medium, lay out a ½″ border and title block. Draw a series of guidelines. (They should be permanent lines drawn with a 4H lead.) Using a scrap piece of drafting medium, write:

   *The size of the title will vary, depending on its importance. Additional emphasis can be placed on the title by using broad strokes or underlining it with one or more lines.*

   Remember to use guidelines on the scrap piece of drafting medium. When the sentences are complete, slip them under the 8½″ sheet and trace them.

4. On an 8½″ × 11″ sheet of drafting medium, letter six sentences from the text. Remember to lay out the border and title block, and use guidelines. Do this exercise using single-stroke Gothic lettering, Roman, lower-case lettering, and inclined lettering.

Without an understanding of technical drawing, a draftsperson will have difficulty in architectural drafting, because geometric construction, orthographic projection, sectioning, and pictorial drawings are fundamental to architectural drafting. Geometric construction is used in the formulation of general shapes and line intersections; orthographic projection is a universal technique used to show the principal views of an object; sectioning is used for a wide variety of details; and pictorial drawings are used so the untrained eye can see a particular structure or detail more clearly.

## GEOMETRIC CONSTRUCTION

There are a variety of geometric shapes that are used in architectural drafting; the most common are angles, circles, plane figures, and solids.

### Angles

An angle is created by the intersection of two lines. Five types of angles are used in technical and architectural drafting (see Fig. 3-1): right angles, acute angles, straight angles, obtuse angles, and reflex angles. A right angle has an angle of 90 degrees; an acute angle is less than 90 degrees; a straight angle contains 180 degrees; an obtuse angle is greater than 90 degrees; and a reflex angle is greater than 180 degrees.

### Triangles

A triangle is a plane figure that has three sides (see Fig. 3-2). A scalene triangle has no equal sides; an equilateral triangle has three equal sides; an isosceles triangle has only two equal sides. If a triangle has one angle of 90 degrees and two acute angles, it is classified as a right triangle. An obtuse triangle has one angle greater than 90 degrees and two acute angles. An acute triangle has three angles less than 90 degrees.

### Drawing an Arc Tangent to Perpendicular Lines

When it is necessary to draw an arc tangent to two perpendicular lines (see Fig. 3-3), first set

# 3

# Basic Technical Drawing

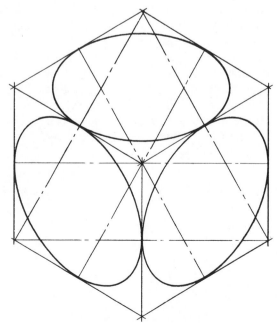

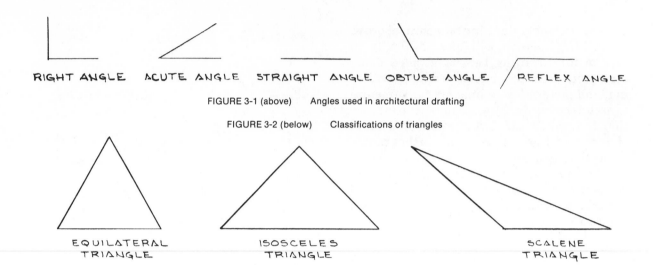

RIGHT ANGLE    ACUTE ANGLE    STRAIGHT ANGLE    OBTUSE ANGLE    REFLEX ANGLE

FIGURE 3-1 (above)      Angles used in architectural drafting

FIGURE 3-2 (below)      Classifications of triangles

EQUILATERAL          ISOSCELES          SCALENE
TRIANGLE             TRIANGLE           TRIANGLE

the compass to the desired radius. Then place the point of the compass at the intersection of the two lines and strike a short arc on each line. Place the compass point on the intersection of the line and the short arc, and strike two intersecting arcs to locate the center of the rounded corner. By placing the compass at the intersection of the two arcs, it is possible to strike an arc that is tangent to the perpendicular lines.

## Drawing an Arc Tangent to Lines That Are Not Perpendicular

To draw an arc tangent to two nonperpendicular lines (see Fig. 3-4), first draw two light construction lines parallel to the two lines. The distance from the line to the construction line should equal the radius of the arc. To locate the points of tangency, draw perpendicular construction lines from the intersection of the two construction lines. When the compass is placed at the intersection of these lines, an arc can be struck that is tangent to the two intersecting lines.

## Polygons

A polygon is a plane figure that has at least three angles and sides. Some of the more common polygons are triangles, squares, hexagons, and octagons.

An equilateral triangle is constructed by drawing two 60-degree angles on a horizontal line. A square can be drawn by first drawing a circle, then drawing 45-degree tangents to complete the square.

An octagon can be inscribed in a circle or a square (see Fig. 3-5). To draw an octagon within a circle, first inscribe center lines through the circle. Then draw 45-degree diagonals through the center point. To complete the octagon, draw lines from the intersection of the center lines and the circumference of the circle. To draw an octagon within a square, place a compass on each corner and pass an arc through the center of the square. Then draw the sides of the octagon by connecting the intersection of the two arcs.

A hexagon can be drawn either inside or

FIGURE 3-3      Drawing an arc tangent to perpendicular lines

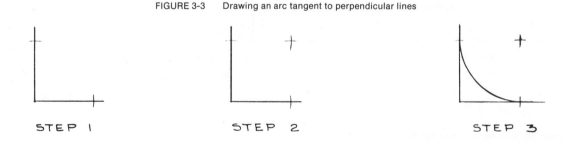

STEP 1                    STEP 2                    STEP 3

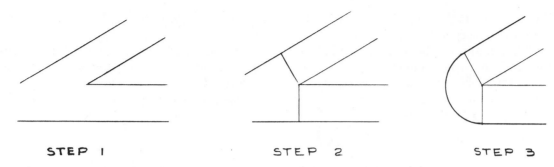

STEP 1                                STEP 2                                STEP 3

FIGURE 3-4 (above)          Drawing an arc tangent to lines that are not perpendicular

FIGURE 3-5 (below)      An octagon inscribed in          FIGURE 3-6 (below)      Drawing a hexagon inside or
a circle or square                                                outside a circle

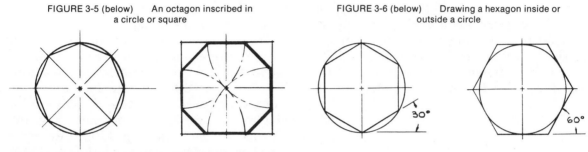

outside a circle (see Fig. 3-6). To draw a hexagon inside a circle, first inscribe 30-degree angles from the intersection of the vertical line and the circle. Then draw the vertical sides of the hexagon in at the intersection of the inclined lines and the circle.

To draw a hexagon on the outside of a circle, inscribe a top and bottom line tangent to the circle. Then use a 30/60 degree triangle to draw four sides tangent to the circle.

## Division Of a Line into Equal Parts

Frequently a line must be divided into several equal parts that cannot be readily divided by a scale (see Fig. 3-7). One of the easiest techniques for doing this can best be described in a series of steps:

□ Draw a perpendicular line at the end of the line that is to be divided.

FIGURE 3-7      Division of a line into equal parts

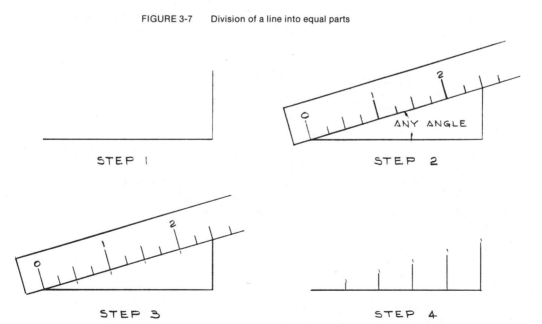

STEP 1                                          STEP 2

STEP 3                                          STEP 4

□ Place a scale at the end of the line and adjust it to the perpendicular line until the required divisions fall between the end of the line and the perpendicular line (it does not matter what size divisions are used, as long as they are all equal distances).

□ At each equal interval, mark the division.

□ From each division mark, draw a line perpendicular to the line to be divided. Equal divisions are created where the perpendicular lines intersect the line.

## ORTHOGRAPHIC PROJECTION

In technical drawings most objects are described by two or more views, usually the top view, front view, and right side view (see Fig. 3-8). If necessary, additional views such as the left side, back, and bottom view, can also be used to describe an object (see Fig. 3-9). The use of the different views is based on the principles of orthographic projection. In its

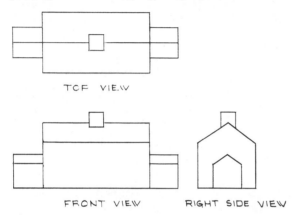

TOP VIEW

FRONT VIEW          RIGHT SIDE VIEW

FIGURE 3-8 (above)        Basic shape description: top, front, and right side view

FIGURE 3-9 (below)        Six basic views: top, bottom, left, right, front, and rear views

simplest form, orthographic projection means that two or more views of an object can be drawn by projecting construction lines from one view to another.

The front view of an object appears as if an observer were looking directly at the object, his line of sight perpendicular to the object. When an object is looked at in this manner the front view reveals the true dimensions of height and width, but does not show the dimension of depth (see Fig. 3-10). To draw the top view, the dimension of width is projected up from the front view and the dimension of depth is added to complete the view. When complete, the top view shows the dimensions of depth and width, but not the dimension of height. The right side view is also projected from the front view, showing the dimension of height and depth.

The three principal dimensions are height, width, and depth, but only two of the dimensions are common to one view. For example, the front view of an object has the dimensions of height and width, the top view the dimen-

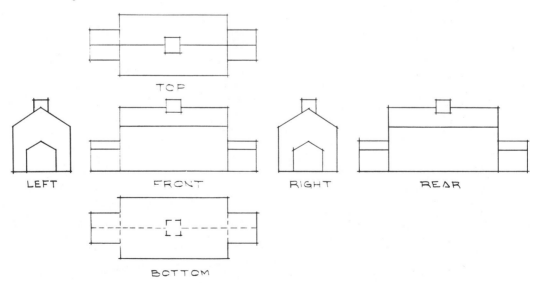

TOP

LEFT          FRONT          RIGHT          REAR

BOTTOM

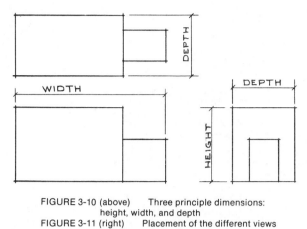

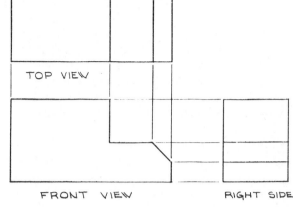

FIGURE 3-10 (above)    Three principle dimensions:
height, width, and depth
FIGURE 3-11 (right)    Placement of the different views

sions of depth and width, and the right side view the dimensions of depth and height.

One of the worst mistakes that can be made in technical drawing is to place the different views improperly; all the views must line up with each other. The top view should be directly over the front view, and the right side view should be aligned from the front view (see Fig. 3-11).

## Projection of Curved Surfaces

Cylinders and cones project as a circle in one view and a straight line in another (see Fig. 3-12). When the surface of the cylinder is parallel to a plane of projection, it will be projected as a circle; however, if the axis of the cylinder is parallel to a plane of projection, its

FIGURE 3-12    Projection of curved surfaces

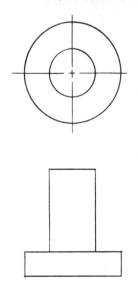

surface will be projected as a straight line. A sphere will be viewed as a circle in any view.

## Hidden Surfaces

In some cases when a three-view drawing is used, a surface cannot be seen in one of the principal views; for clarity, the surface needs to be shown. Surfaces that cannot be seen are represented by hidden lines (see Fig. 3-13), which are composed of short dashes approximately $\frac{1}{8}''$ in length with a $\frac{1}{32}''$ gap between them. (It isn't necessary to measure each dash, but only to give an approximation of the desired length.) The first dash of a hidden line should touch the object line, and if two hidden lines intersect, two dashes should touch at the corner. If a hidden line is a continuation of an object line, there should be a space between the two lines. The hidden line for an arc starts at the end of the tangent points. Parallel hidden lines should be drawn so the dashes are staggered and do not fall directly over each other.

FIGURE 3-13    Using hidden lines

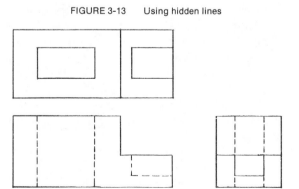

## SECTIONING

In many cases the addition of hidden lines to a view simply distorts the view and makes it confusing; therefore, to clarify a view, an imaginary portion of the object is removed to reveal the interior of the object. The resulting view is called a section (see Fig. 3-14). To obtain a sectional view, an imaginary cutting plane is drawn through an object. The cutting-plane line is indicated by a dark dashed line (see Fig. 3-15). The long dash is approximately ⅝″ long and the two short dashes are approximately ⅛″ in length. The dashes are separated by a short $\frac{1}{16}$″ gap. The ends of a cutting-plane line are terminated by arrowheads that indicate the direction in which the observer is looking at the object. (Placement of the cutting-plane line effects "removal" of a portion of the object, revealing the interior of the object.) The portion of the object touched by the imaginary cutting plane should then be cross-hatched with thin lines spaced approximately $\frac{1}{16}, \frac{3}{32}$, or ⅛″ apart (see Fig. 3-16). The spacing of the lines depends upon the size of the object. If the object is small, the lines are placed close together, but as the object gets larger the cross-hatching lines are spaced further apart. These lines are usually drawn at a 45-degree angle, but if there are three or more adjacent pieces in a section it may be necessary to place cross-hatching lines of one intersecting piece at a different angle (see Fig. 3-17).

### Full Sections

There are several different types of sections; one of the most common is a full section. To draw a full section, a cutting-plane line is passed entirely across and through the object; in this way half of the object is "removed" (see Fig. 3-18). The imaginary cutting plane can be placed parallel to the frontal plane, parallel to the profile, or parallel to the horizontal plane (see Fig. 3-19). The arrowheads on the cutting-plane line indicate the plane of projection to which the imaginary cutting plane will be parallel.

FIGURE 3-18 (right)        Full section

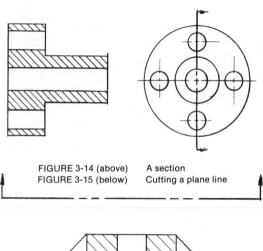

FIGURE 3-14 (above)        A section
FIGURE 3-15 (below)        Cutting a plane line

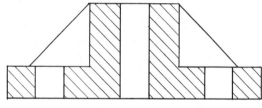

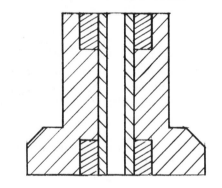

FIGURE 3-16 (above)        Crosshatching a section
FIGURE 3-17 (below)        Placement of section lines if there
are three or more adjacent pieces

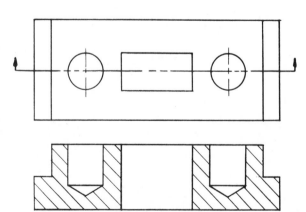

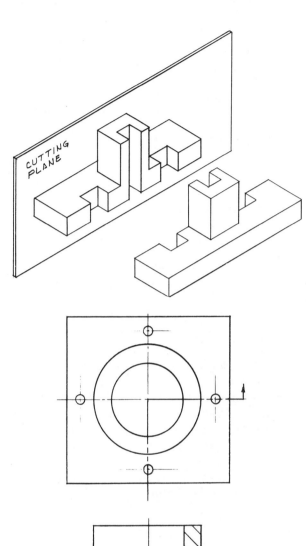

## Half-Sections

If the cutting plane passes through only half of an object and a quarter of the object is "removed," the section is called a half-section (see Fig. 3-20). A section of this type has the advantage of showing both the inside and outside of an object and is usually used when the object is symmetrical. To indicate the direction of sight, the cutting-plane line is terminated by only one arrowhead. Unless hidden lines are needed for clarity, they are usually omitted from the sectioned view.

## Removed Sections

A removed section is one that has been, in a sense, lifted out of the object and placed at a convenient location on the drawing (see Fig. 3-21). A section of this type is used to clarify a particular detail and can be drawn to a larger scale. A removed section should not be revolved on the paper, but should be drawn with its lines parallel or perpendicular to the correct plane of projection. Because a portion of the object is removed, it is necessary to label the cutting-plane line and the section. The cutting-plane line is usually labeled A-A, B-B, C-C, etc. and the removed section is labeled to correspond to a given cutting-plane line.

## Revolved Sections

Revolved sections are drawn by passing a cutting plane through an object and rotating the section on an imaginary vertical axis for 90 degrees (see Fig. 3-22). The revolved section can be placed between two break-lines, or it can be revolved to fit directly on the elevation. If break-lines are used, the object can be shortened, but the full length should be indicated by the correct dimension.

FIGURE 3-19 (top)    Placement of the cutting plane line
FIGURE 3-20 (above)    Half section

FIGURE 3-21 (left and below)    Removed section

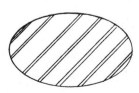

SECTION A-A

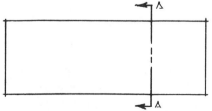

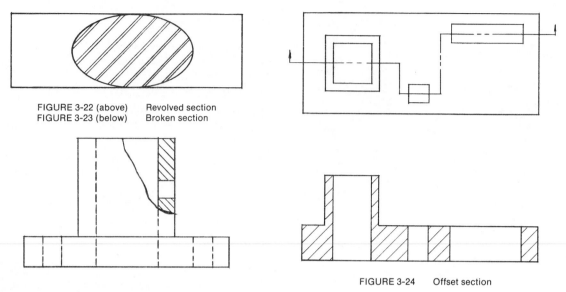

FIGURE 3-22 (above)      Revolved section
FIGURE 3-23 (below)      Broken section

FIGURE 3-24      Offset section

## Broken-Out Sections

Often it is necessary to show only a small sectioned part of a particular object. When this is the case, a broken-out section is sometimes used (see Fig. 3-23). A section of this type is made by constructing a freehand break-line for the portion to be removed. Cross-hatching lines are then placed to indicate the passage of the imaginary cutting plane. Since the placement of the cutting plane is obvious, it is not necessary to show a cutting-plane line.

## Offset Sections

In some cases desired features do not appear in a straight line and cannot be sectioned by a conventional cutting plane. To include some of the features that might not appear in a straight line, the cutting-plane line can be bent or "offset" so that it can pass through each feature (see Fig. 3-24). Although the cutting plane is bent, the offset in the sectional view will not show.

# PICTORIAL DRAWINGS

A pictorial drawing is used to show the dimensions of height, width, and depth from a single view and is especially helpful to people who cannot read orthographic projection. The three common types of pictorial drawings are isometrics, obliques, and perspectives.

FIGURE 3-25      Skeleton of three lines for isometric drawing

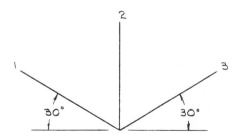

## Isometric Drawing

An isometric drawing (isometric means "equal measure") is based on revolution and is built on a skeleton of three lines (see Fig. 3-25). An object drawn isometrically is shown as rotated about a vertical axis 45 degrees and tilted forward 35 degrees and 16 minutes. In such a position, the three principal dimensions of height, width, and depth can be seen in a single view. The three-line skeleton consists of a vertical line and two other lines drawn at an angle of 30 degrees from the horizontal.

There are definite rules to follow in preparing an isometric drawing:

□ Hidden lines are not shown unless they are needed to clarify the object.

□ Center lines are used to show symmetry, or they can be used for dimensioning purposes (see Fig. 3-26).

□ Only lines parallel to one of the three axes will project as isometric lines.

□ If a line is not parallel to one of the three axes it is a nonisometric line and cannot be set off directly with the scale (see Fig. 3-27).

□ An angle in an isometric drawing projects true size only when its plane is parallel to the plane of projection (see Fig. 3-28).

□ Curves in an isometric drawing are constructed by plotting a series of points on a number of construction lines (see Fig. 3-29).

□ A circle in an isometric drawing will appear as an ellipse and can be drawn with a compass from four centers of a parallelogram (see Fig. 3-30).

The diagonals that create the centers are horizontal or 60 degrees from the horizontal,

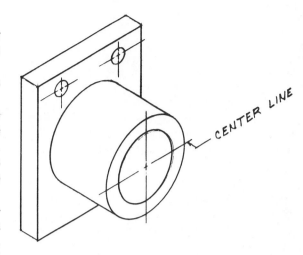

FIGURE 3-26     Use of center lines in an isometric drawing

and they all bisect one side of the parallelogram. Once the construction lines are drawn, a compass can be used to strike four individual arcs.

FIGURE 3-27 (upper left)        Non-isometric line
FIGURE 3-28 (upper right)       Projection of an angle
                               in isometrics
FIGURE 3-29 (lower left)        Curves in isometrics
FIGURE 3-30 (lower right)       Circles in isometrics

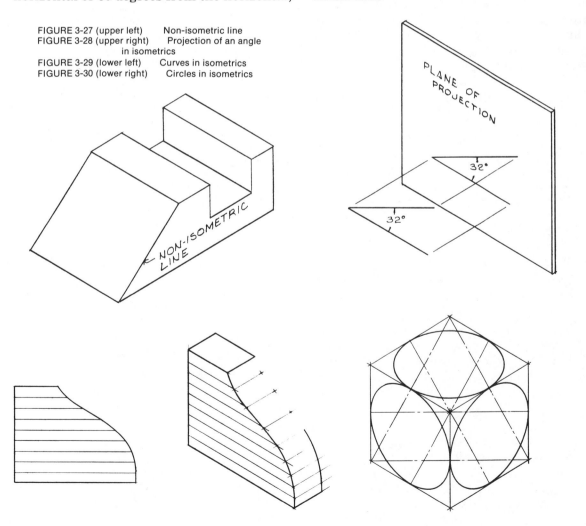

## Isometric Sections

It is often necessary to draw an isometric section to reveal the interior of an object that could not otherwise be seen (see Fig. 3-31). The section is usually taken on an "isometric plane" that can best describe the object. When the section has been made, section lines are drawn where the cutting-plane line passed through. The section lines are fine lines drawn with the 60-degree triangle in opposite directions on any two surfaces that are perpendicular to each other, and are usually placed about 1/16″ apart.

## Oblique Drawing

An oblique drawing is a form of a pictorial in which one surface is parallel to the frontal plane of projection (see Fig. 3-32). The other sides of the object are drawn at an angle to the frontal plane. Just like an isometric, an oblique is built around a skeleton of three lines, but two of the axes form a right angle, and the other angle is drawn at any convenient angle.

Some things to remember when preparing an oblique drawing are:

☐ The longest side of the object, or the side of the object that has the most irregular shapes, should be placed parallel to the frontal plane.
☐ Curves and circles on the front face of the drawing should appear in their true shape (see Fig. 3-33).
☐ An angle on the front face of the drawing should be drawn true to size, but an angle in a receding plane will not be in true size (see Fig. 3-34).
☐ When the projecting axis is at a 45-degree angle to the frontal plane of projection, the drawing is called a Cavalier projection (a type of oblique projection) (see Fig. 3-35).
☐ When the projecting axis is reduced in length by one-half, the drawing is called a cabinet drawing (a type of oblique drawing) (see Fig. 3-36).
☐ A line parallel to the frontal plane of projection should project in its true length.
☐ The face of an object should have the same appearance in both oblique and orthographic projection.

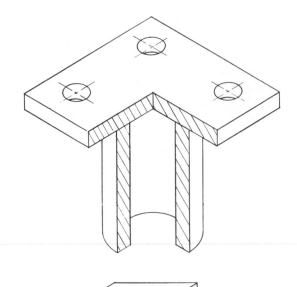

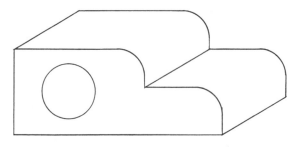

FIGURE 3-31 (top)        Isometric sections
FIGURE 3-32 (above)       Oblique drawing
FIGURE 3-33 (below)       Curves and circles in oblique drawing
FIGURE 3-34 (second below)       Angle development in oblique drawing

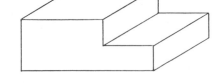

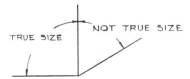

FIGURE 3-35    Cavalier projection

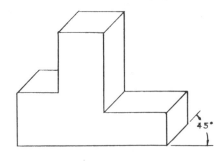

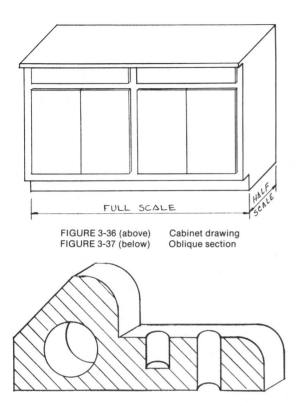

FULL SCALE

HALF SCALE

FIGURE 3-36 (above)     Cabinet drawing
FIGURE 3-37 (below)     Oblique section

## Oblique Sections

Oblique sections, like isometric sections, are used to better describe an oblique drawing, Fig. 3-37. When it is necessary to use an oblique section, the section is usually placed on the frontal plane. The section lines are usually placed at 45° angles, although other angles can be used.

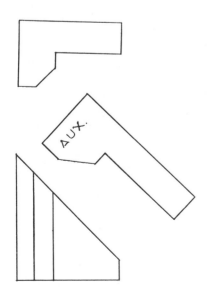

AUX.

## Auxiliary Views

When a surface of an object is not parallel to one of the three principal planes of projection, it is necessary to draw an auxiliary view to show the true shape of the surface (see Fig. 3-38). A left or right auxiliary view is drawn on a plane that is perpendicular to the vertical plane (see Fig. 3-39). A front and rear auxiliary view is drawn on a plane that is perpendicular to the profile plane of projection.

The first step in drawing an auxiliary view is to establish reference-plane lines. For symmetrical objects, a reference plane is usually passed through the center of one of the views. A second reference-plane line is then drawn parallel to the slanted surface. For a non-symmetrical object, the reference-plane line is usually placed on the edge of one of the views. The second reference-plane line is placed at a convenient location parallel to the slanted surface.

Next, a series of light construction lines should be projected from the slanted surface to the reference plane that is parallel to it. The construction lines should form a 90-degree

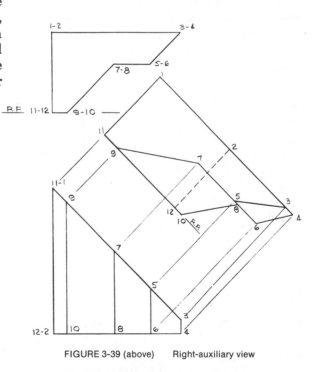

FIGURE 3-39 (above)     Right-auxiliary view

FIGURE 3-38 (left)     Auxiliary view

angle with the slanted surface. All points on the views should now be lettered. It is not necessary to letter the points, but doing so sometimes clears up questions about the location of points on the auxiliary view. With the reference planes as a guide, all the points can be transferred to the auxiliary view. A simple rule to remember when transferring the points is that all points will be the same distance from each of the reference planes. If a point falls on the reference-plane line in one of the principal views, it will also fall on the reference-plane line that is parallel to the slanted surface.

To complete the auxiliary view, the various points are then connected.

### Line Weights

The weight and consistency of a line used in architectural drafting are very important, for they can dictate the importance of the line. Lines usually considered to be less important are center lines and dimension lines. These lines are light, fine lines and have a definite contrast to a line that outlines an object. The center line is used to indicate an axis of symmetrical parts (see Fig. 3-40). It is composed of long and short dashes. The long dash is approximately ⅝″ long and the short dash is

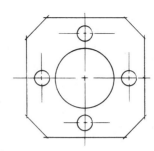

FIGURE 3-40    Indicating symmetrical parts with center lines

about ⅛″ in length. The long and short dashes are separated by a ¹⁄₁₆″ space. The short dashes should cross at the center of a circular view and the center line should project about ¼″ outside the view. A center line should always start and stop with a long dash.

A line that is used to outline an object should be dark, crisp, and call attention to itself. For additional emphasis a technical fountain pen can be used for important lines.

To maintain crisp, consistent lines the pencil should be kept sharp and various pressures used. A technique of applying more pressure on the beginning and end of a line eliminates the likelihood of fading at the beginning or end. The linework will also appear a bit more distinctive if the lines are allowed to extend slightly past the corners.

## DIMENSIONING

If a drawing is to be complete, and if it is intended that the object or structure will be built, a drawing must include dimensions and notes. Dimensions give particular sizes, and notes give related information. The correct dimensions are just as important, or perhaps even more important, than the views that describe the object.

### Extension and Dimension Lines

An extension line is a fine dark line that extends at a right angle from the object. It should be separated from the outline of the object by a ¹⁄₁₆″ gap and should extend ⅛″ past the last dimension line (see Fig. 3-41). The ¹⁄₁₆″ gap and the protrusion of the extension line past the dimension line are not measured, but

should be estimated. Care, however, should be taken to place them as accurately as possible. If extension lines are placed too close they will appear as overruns of the object, and if they are placed too far from the object, the connection may not be clear.

A dimension line is a fine dark line that is placed parallel to an object line and stretched between two extension lines. It is drawn as a

FIGURE 3-41    Placement of an extension line

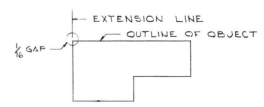

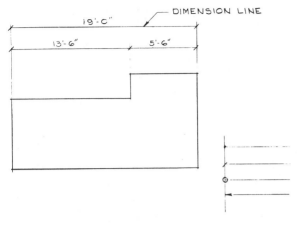

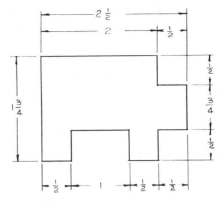

FIGURE 3-45    Unidirectional system of dimensioning

FIGURE 3-42 (left)    Placement of a dimension line
FIGURE 3-43 (right)    Terminating a dimension line

continuous line and is placed ⅜ to ½″ from the outline of the object (see Fig. 3-42). Any adjacent dimension lines are usually placed ¼ to ⅜″ apart. In architectural drafting dimension lines are usually terminated by a dot, slash, circle, or arrowhead (see Fig. 3-43). If an arrowhead is used to terminate the dimension line it should be approximately ⅛″ long and one-third that length in width.

## Dimensioning Systems

There are two ways to correctly dimension a drawing—the aligned system and the unidirectional system. In the aligned system, all the dimensions are placed in line with the dimension line (see Fig. 3-44). The unidirectional system of dimensioning, however, places the dimensions to read from the bottom of the drawing (see Fig. 3-45).

## Dimensioning Arcs, Circles, Rounds, Fillets, and Angles

The diameter of a circle is considered its dimension. This measurement can be given outside the circle or inside the circle, or a leader can be used (see Fig. 3-46). After the diameter of the circle is given, D or DIA is placed after the dimension.

The radius of an arc is its dimension. This measurement is usually placed on the inside of the arc, but if the arc is small it may be placed on the outside (see Fig. 3-47).

The dimensions of rounds and fillets are given in the same manner as for an arc, but if they are uniform only one or two dimensions are necessary, and in some cases a note is used to denote this size (see Fig. 3-48).

FIGURE 3-46 (below)    Dimensioning a circle
FIGURE 3-47 (bottom)    Dimensioning an arc

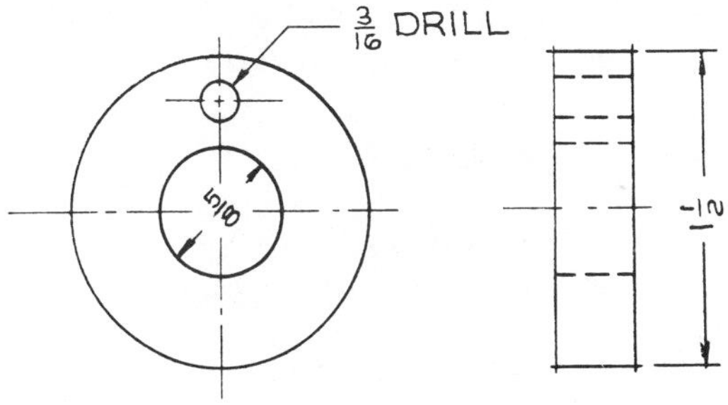

FIGURE 3-44    Aligned system of dimensioning

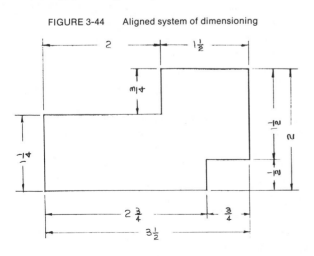

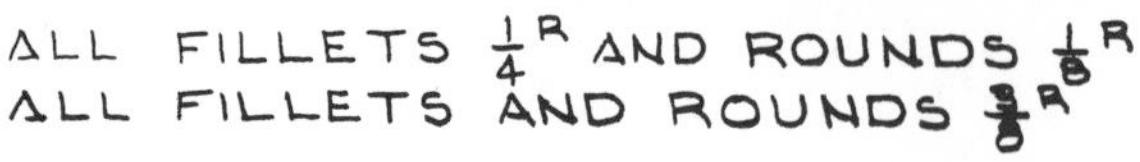

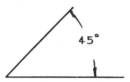

FIGURE 3-50     Use of a leader

FIGURE 3-48 (top)     Using a note for rounds and fillets
FIGURE 3-49 (above)     Dimensioning an angle

The dimension line for an angle is drawn as an arc. This measurement should be placed so it can be read from the bottom of the sheet (see Fig. 3-49).

## Leaders and Notes

A leader is a fine dark line that extends from a note or dimension to a particular detail (see Fig. 3-50). There are two basic types of leaders: one is drawn freehand, the other is drawn with instruments. A freehand leader is usually made with a zigzag motion and is terminated with an arrowhead. If instruments are used, a 45-degree triangle is usually used to draw the inclined portion of the leader. A leader drawn with instruments should have a shoulder and should terminate about ⅛″ from the note. There is no arrow on the end of the leader nearest the note.

Notes are used to clarify a particular detail and should be brief and worded clearly (see Fig. 3-51). Notes are usually drawn to a height of ⅛ to ³⁄₁₆″, but vary according to the size of the drawing. Light guidelines should be drawn for lettering the note, and there should be a space between the written lines.

## Dimensioning Rules

In the dimensioning process there are several rules that should be followed: Some of these rules are:

□ The actual size of the object should be shown, even though it may be drawn to scale.
□ An unbroken dimension line should be used, with the dimension placed slightly above the dimension line.
□ The dimension line should be approximately ½″ away from the outline of the object.
□ A ¹⁄₁₆″ gap should be left between the outline of the object and the extension line.
□ The dimensions should be placed so they can be read from the bottom or right side of the drawing.
□ Any distance over 12″ should be recorded in feet and inches; if the dimension does not contain any inches the representation should be the same—for example, 6′0″.
□ Complete dimensions must be given so it will not be necessary to scale the drawing.
□ Center lines should be placed through the centers of all circles, openings, and symmetrical drawings.
□ Dimension openings should be figured from their centers.
□ Dimensions should never be placed directly on the dimension line.
□ Care should be taken to avoid crossing extension and dimension lines by placing the longer dimensions farther away from the outline of the object.
□ Dimensions should not be crowded.
□ All obvious dimensions should be omitted—for example, a door placed at the corner of the room does not need to be located with a dimension.
□ The leaders should be made as short as possible.
□ Dimensions should not be duplicated.
□ A dimension line should never be drawn through a dimension figure.

FIGURE 3-51     A note

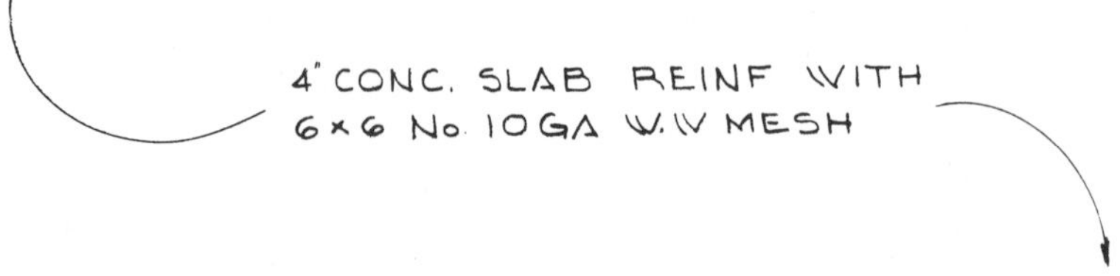

4″ CONC. SLAB REINF WITH
6×6 No. 10 GA W. W MESH

- When a dimension is not to scale, a note should be added that reads "NOT TO SCALE."
- The letter R should be placed after a radius dimension figure.
- Leaders should slope at 45, 30, or 60 degrees.
- The dimensions should always be checked by addition; if they do not check, there is an error.
- Dimension figures should be about ⅛" high.

## DRAFTING TECHNIQUES

The drafting paper should be kept as clean as possible. Listed below are various techniques that can be used to keep the drawing clean:

- Darken the drawing in from top to bottom and left to right. As the drawing is laid out, use light construction lines. A softer lead pencil can be used to darken the object lines. Darken in all the horizontal lines first, starting from the top and working down to the bottom of the drawing. Then, darken all vertical lines, starting from the left side of the drawing and working toward the right side. When such a systematic system is used, the various instruments will pass over the darkened lines a minimum amount of time, increasing the chance of a clean drawing.
- Use a dry cleaning pad to sprinkle a fine eraser powder on the drawing. The powder acts as small ball bearings between the triangles and parallel straightedge. As the instruments are moved, they glide with reduced friction across the drawing.
- Cover finished areas. A drawing is often large and it may be necessary to complete some areas before the entire sheet is complete. If this happens, the finished area can be covered with a sheet of typing paper, or a smaller sheet of tracing paper. The paper should be secured with drafting tape on all four corners.
- For small detail work, use small triangles. When it is necessary to do small detail work, these will eliminate the need of continuously passing a triangle over previously drawn lines that may not even be in the detail.
- Use clean instruments. All instruments should be cleaned periodically. This will remove any loose graphite and dirt that has accumulated. A clean cloth dampened with an approved cleaner should first be wiped over all the exposed surfaces of the equipment, then a clean dry cloth should be used to wipe them down.
- Remove any loose graphite from a sharpened pencil point by plunging it into a small piece of styrofoam and then removing it. Any size and shape of styrofoam can be used. There are some commercial models that are sold that fit around the pointer. A small paper towel or rag can also be used to wipe loose graphite from the lead. The pencil should never be sharpened over the drawing, because loose graphite may fall onto the drawing. The pencil pointer should never be carried in the same carrying case with the other drafting instruments; graphite will invariably spill and soil everything in the case.
- Use a drafting brush to remove any drafting powder or eraser crumbs. The drawing should never be brushed with the hand—it is very easy to smudge the lines.
- Wash hands before doing any drafting work. Talcum powder can be used to absorb any body oil that might be present on the hands. Dirty or oily hands will transfer the dirt and oil onto the drawing.

### Drawing Reproduction

Once a drawing has been completed it must be reproduced so the various crafts can have a copy. The ozalid (blueline) print is most often used; compared to other methods of reproduction, it is usually faster and more economical. The tracing is placed over a piece of paper that is light-sensitive on one side. The tracing and light-sensitive paper are then exposed to ultraviolet light. The light "burns out" any areas of the paper that is not covered by a line on the tracing. The paper is then exposed to chemical vapors, which turn all non-burned-out areas blue.

The equipment used to produce a blueline drawing is available in various styles, models, and prices (see Fig. 3-52).

A drawing can also be blueprinted to provide multiple drawings. This particular technique, however, has for the most part been replaced by the ozalid print. A blueprint is reproduced by exposure of sensitized paper and the drawing that has been placed on tracing paper to an ultraviolet light. Then the sensitized paper must be bathed in a chemical and water. A second bath in clear water follows, and then the prints are laid out to dry.

FIGURE 3-52     A blue-line printer

## Assignment:

1. On an 8½″ × 11″ sheet of drafting material, draw the following:
   a. An arc tangent to a perpendicular line.
   b. A hexagon inside a circle.
   c. A full section of Fig. 3-53.
   d. An oblique of Fig. 3-54.
   e. An auxiliary view of Fig. 3-55.
   f. An isometric of Fig. 3-56.
   g. The third view in Fig. 3-57.
   h. Three views of Fig. 3-58, adding the necessary dimensions.

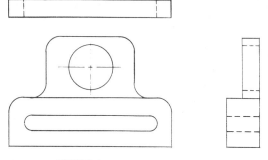

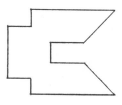

FIGURE 3-54 (above)     Draw an oblique

FIGURE 3-53     Draw a full section

FIGURE 3-55 (below)     Draw an auxiliary view

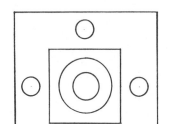

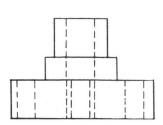

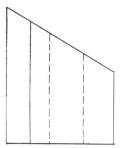

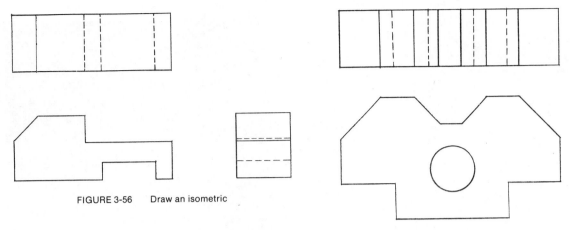

FIGURE 3-56      Draw an isometric

FIGURE 3-57      Draw a third view

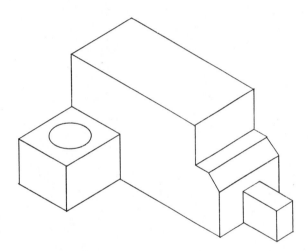

FIGURE 3-58      Draw three views; add dimensions

Architectural symbols are used on a set of plans to denote particular construction materials. The various symbols that are used are standardized, carrying the same meaning from one set of drawings to another. However, if a standard symbol is not used, a ledger should be placed in a convenient location on the drawing so that the various symbols can be described. Although symbols are standardized, they can look different depending on the situation in which they are used. For example, bricks on a floor plan are represented by cross-hatched lines, while bricks on an elevation are represented in an entirely different way.

On the following pages the most common symbols used in architectural drawing are depicted.

It is often standard practice to use architectural abbreviations rather than spelling out the word. Abbreviations save time, but they can be confusing and thus misinterpreted, so it is sometimes better not to use them. When they are used, they should be lettered in all caps with the period omitted.

Common abbreviations are listed at the end of this chapter.

# 4
# Architectural Symbols & Abbreviations

# LANDSCAPE

DECIDUOUS TREE

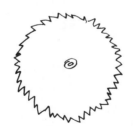

DECIDUOUS OR EVERGREEN TREE

EVERGREEN TREE

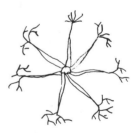

DECIDUOUS TREE

SMALL TREES AND SHRUBS

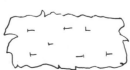 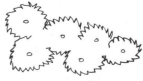

GROUND COVER & SMALL PLANTS

# CONSTRUCTION MATERIALS

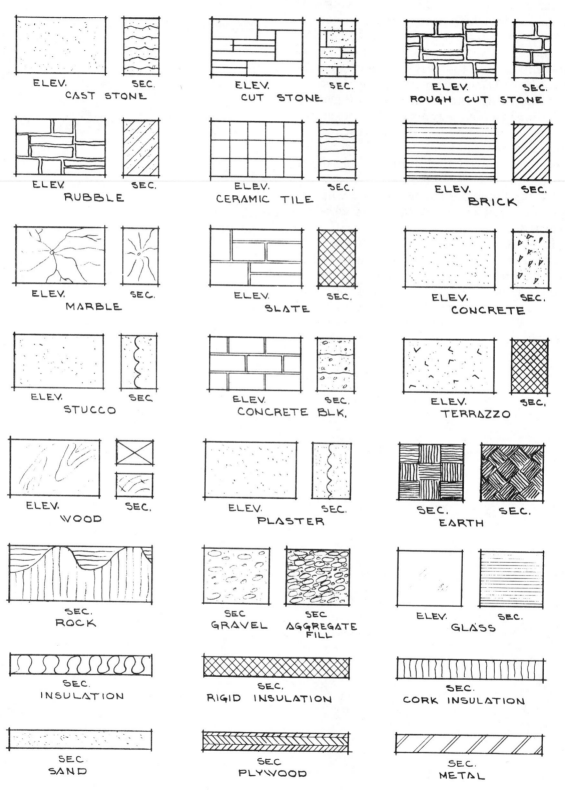

ELEV. SEC.
CAST STONE

ELEV. SEC.
CUT STONE

ELEV. SEC.
ROUGH CUT STONE

ELEV. SEC.
RUBBLE

ELEV. SEC.
CERAMIC TILE

ELEV. SEC.
BRICK

ELEV. SEC.
MARBLE

ELEV. SEC.
SLATE

ELEV. SEC.
CONCRETE

ELEV. SEC.
STUCCO

ELEV. SEC.
CONCRETE BLK.

ELEV. SEC.
TERRAZZO

ELEV. SEC.
WOOD

ELEV. SEC.
PLASTER

SEC. SEC.
EARTH

SEC.
ROCK

SEC. SEC.
GRAVEL AGGREGATE FILL

ELEV. SEC.
GLASS

SEC.
INSULATION

SEC.
RIGID INSULATION

SEC.
CORK INSULATION

SEC.
SAND

SEC.
PLYWOOD

SEC.
METAL

40

# DOORS

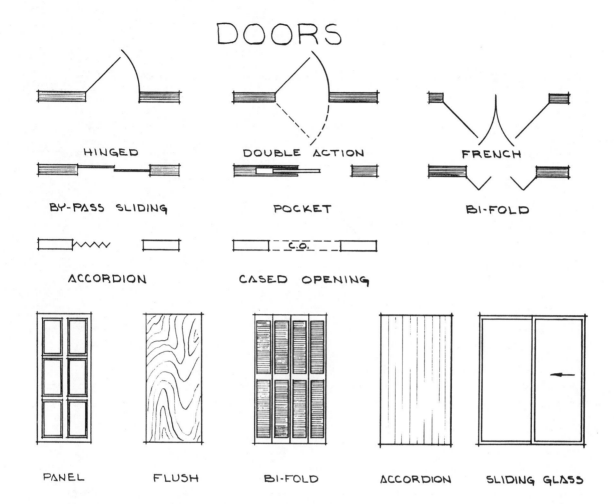

HINGED      DOUBLE ACTION      FRENCH

BY-PASS SLIDING      POCKET      BI-FOLD

ACCORDION      CASED OPENING

PANEL      FLUSH      BI-FOLD      ACCORDION      SLIDING GLASS

# WINDOWS

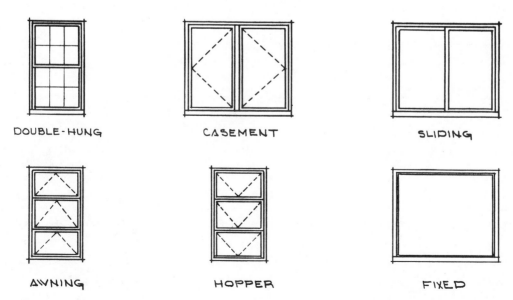

DOUBLE-HUNG      CASEMENT      SLIDING

AWNING      HOPPER      FIXED

# WINDOWS

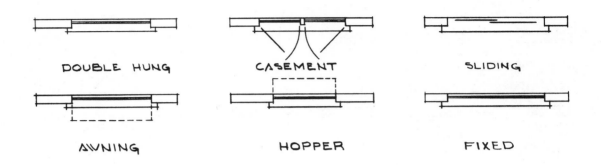

DOUBLE HUNG

CASEMENT

SLIDING

AWNING

HOPPER

FIXED

# PIPING

HOT WATER HEATING SUPPLY

HOT WATER HEATING SUPPLY

MEDIUM PRESSURE STEAM

LOW PRESSURE STEAM RETURN

HIGH PRESSURE STEAM

MEDIUM PRESSURE STEAM RETURN

LOW PRESSURE STEAM

HIGH PRESSURE STEAM RETURN

AIR RELIEF LINE

BOILER BLOW-OFF

———— FOF ———— FOF ————
FUEL OIL FLOW

———— FOR ———— FOR ——
FUEL OIL RETURN

———— FOV ———— FOV ————
FUEL OIL VENT

———— RD ———— RD —
REFRIGERANT DISCHARGE

———— RS ———— RS ——
REFRIGERANT SUCTION

—— C —— C ——
CONDENSER WATER FLOW

—— CR —— CR ——
CONDENSER WATER RETURN

———— CH ———— CH ————
CIRCULATING CHILLED OR HOT
WATER RETURN

MAKE-UP WATER

———— H —— · —— H —
HUMIDIFICATION LINE

# PIPING

——— D ——— D ———
DRAIN

——— B ——— B ———
BRIME SUPPLY

——— BR ——— BR ———
BRIME RETURN

——— V ——— V ———
VACUUM CLEANING

——— ACID ———
ACID WASTE

# PLUMBING

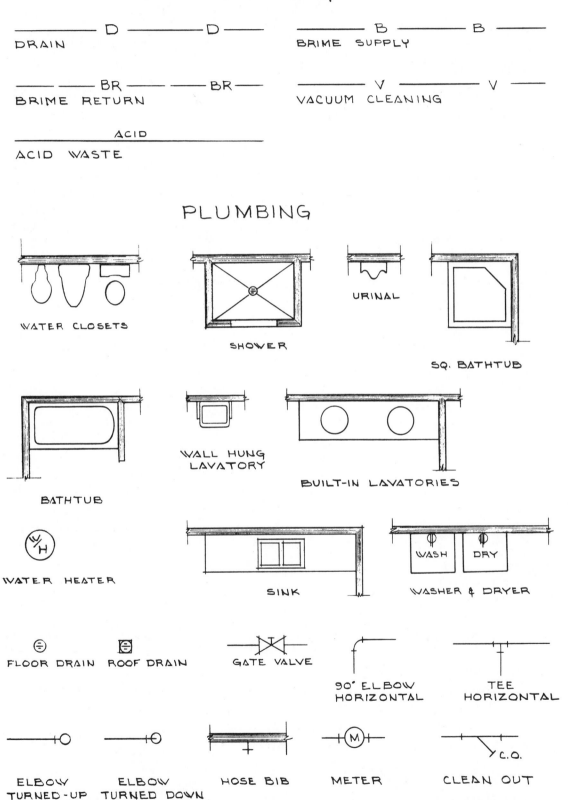

WATER CLOSETS

SHOWER

URINAL

SQ. BATHTUB

BATHTUB

WALL HUNG LAVATORY

BUILT-IN LAVATORIES

WATER HEATER

SINK

WASHER & DRYER

FLOOR DRAIN    ROOF DRAIN    GATE VALVE

90° ELBOW HORIZONTAL

TEE HORIZONTAL

ELBOW TURNED-UP    ELBOW TURNED DOWN    HOSE BIB    METER    CLEAN OUT

# PLUMBING

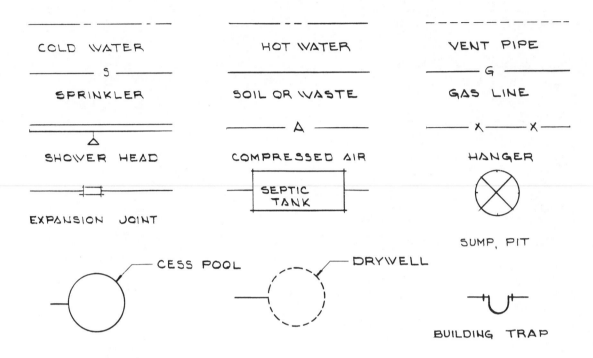

COLD WATER

SPRINKLER

SHOWER HEAD

EXPANSION JOINT

HOT WATER

SOIL OR WASTE

COMPRESSED AIR

SEPTIC TANK

VENT PIPE

GAS LINE

HANGER

SUMP PIT

BUILDING TRAP

CESS POOL

DRYWELL

# ELECTRICAL SYMBOLS

$S$

SINGLE POLE SWITCH

$S^4$

FOUR WAY SWITCH

$S^{WP}$

WEATHER PROOF SWITCH

DUPLEX CONVENIENCE OUTLET

WEATHER PROOF CONVENIENCE OUTLET

220 VOLT OUTLET

PULL SWITCH LIGHT

$S^2$

DOUBLE POLE SWITCH

$S^D$

AUTOMATIC DOOR SWITCH

$S$

SWITH-LOW VOLTAGE

SPLIT WIRED CONVENIENCE OUTLET

RECEPTACLE OUTLET WITH SWITCH

FLOOR OUTLET

FLUORESCENT LIGHT

$S^3$

THREE WAY SWITCH

$S^P$

SWITCH WITH PILOT LIGHT

$S^K$

KEY OPERATED SWITCH

GROUNDED DUPLEX CONVENIENCE OUTLET

RANGE OUTLET

CEILING FIXTURE

FAN

44

# ELECTRICAL SYMBOLS

FLOOR LIGHTING
OUTLET

EXIT LIGHT

BUZZER

BELL & BUZZER

BELL

ELEC. DOOR OPENER

CHIME

PUSH BUTTON

SPECIAL PURPOSE
OUTLET

MOTOR OUTLET

FLOODLITE

ANNUNCIATOR

TELEPHONE

INTER-OFFICE PHONE

T.V. OUTLET

MASTER POWER
SERVICE PANEL

LIGHTING
DISTRIBUTION PANEL

# SWITCHING ARRANGEMENTS

TWO STATIONS

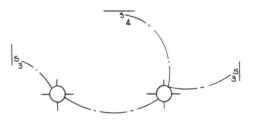

THREE STATIONS

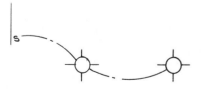

TWO OUTLETS

DUPLEX OUTLET

FLUORESCENT FIXTURE

# AIR DUCTS

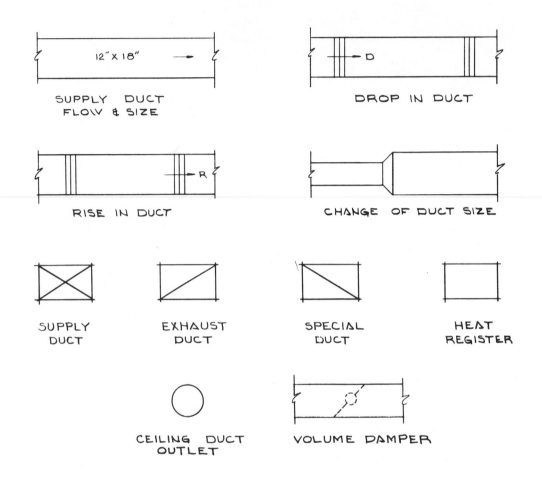

## ABBREVIATIONS

| access door | AD | asphalt tile | AT | built-in | BLT-IN | conductor | COND |
|---|---|---|---|---|---|---|---|
| access panel | AP | associate | ASSOC | | | construction | CONST |
| acoustic | ACST | at | @ | cabinet | CAB | copper | COP |
| acoustical | | avenue | AVE | calking | CLKG | coverplate | COV PL |
| tile | ACST | average | AVG | carpenter | CARP | cubic foot | CU FT |
| actual | ACT | | | cast iron | CI | | |
| addendum | ADD | bath tub | BT | ceiling | CLG | damp- | |
| air condi- | | beam | BM | cement | CEM | proofing | DP |
| tioning | AC | bedroom | BR | change | CHG | degree | DEG |
| alarm | ALM | bench mark | BM | closet | CLO | department | DEPT |
| alternating | | better | BTR | cold water | CW | diameter | DIA |
| current | AC | between | BET | column | COL | disconnect | DISC |
| aluminum | AL | beveled | BEV | common | COM | distance | DIST |
| approximate | APPROX | block | BLK | company | CO | ditto | DO |
| architect | ARCH | board feet | BD FT | compart- | | division | DIV |
| architectural | ARCH | bottom | BOT | ment | COMPT | double hung | |
| area drain | AD | british ther- | | concrete | CONC | window | DHW |
| article | ART | mal unit | BTU | concrete | | dowel | DWL |
| asphalt | ASPH | building | BLDG | floor | CONC FL | down | DN |

| | | | | | | | |
|---|---|---|---|---|---|---|---|
| downspout | DS | hardwood | HDWD | metal | MET | revision | REV |
| drawing | DWG | head | HD | minimum | MIN | riser | R |
| | | heater | HTR | miscel- | | road | RD |
| each | EA | height | HGT | laneous | MISC | roof drain | RD |
| edge | E | hollow metal | HM | molding | MLDG | roofing | RFG |
| electric | ELEC | hollow metal | | | | room | RM |
| elevation | EL | door | HMD | nail | N | rough | RGH |
| enclose | ENCL | horizon | H | not in | | round | RD |
| engineer | ENGR | horizontal | HOR | contract | NIC | | |
| entrance | ENT | hose bibb | HB | nominal | NOM | scale | SC |
| equipment | EQUIP | hospital | HOSP | north | N | schedule | SCH |
| estimate | EST | hot water | HW | number | NO | screw | SCR |
| expansion | | house | HSE | | | section | SECT |
| bolt | EXP BT | hundred | C | office | OFF | select | SEL |
| exterior | EXT | | | on center | OC | sewer | SEW |
| | | inch | IN | one thousand | | sheathing | SHTHG |
| fabricate | FAB | include | INCL | feet board | | sheet | SH |
| facing tile | FT | incorporated | INC | measure | MBM | shower | SH |
| feet | FT | information | INFO | opening | OPNG | siding | SDG |
| feet board | | inside | | ounce | OZ | sink | SK |
| measure | FBM | diameter | ID | out to out | O TO O | sink, service | SS |
| figure | FIG | inside pipe | | | | sleeve | SLV |
| finish | FIN | size | IPS | pair | PR | service sink | SS |
| finished | | insulation | INS | panel | PNL | soil pipe | SS |
| floor | FL | interior | INT | pantry | PAN | south | S |
| fire ex- | | | | penny | d | southwest | SW |
| tinguisher | F EXT | janitor's | | per | / | speaker | SPKR |
| fire place | FP | closet | J CL | percent | % | specifi- | |
| fireproof | FPRF | joint | JT | piece | PC | cations | SPEC |
| flange | FLG | | | plaster | PLAS | square | SQ |
| flashing | FL | kiln-dried | KD | plastic | PLASTC | square foot | SQ FT |
| floor | FL | kip | K | platform | PLAT | square inch | SQ IN |
| floor drain | FD | kitchen | KIT | plumbing | PLMB | stained | STN |
| fluorescent | FLUOR | knocked | | point | PT | staggered | STAG |
| foot | FT | down | KD | polished | | stained- | |
| footing | FTG | | | plate glass | PPGL | waxed | SW |
| foundation | FDN | laboratory | L | pound | LB | stainless | |
| frame | FR | ladder | LAD | pounds per | | steel | SST |
| framework | FRWK | left hand | LH | cubic foot | PCF | stairs | ST |
| full size | FS | length | LG | pounds per | | standard | STD |
| | | linear feet | LIN FT | square foot | PSF | standpipe | SP |
| gallery | GALL | liveload | LL | precast | PRCST | steel | STL |
| gallon | GAL | lumber | LBR | property | PROP | stirrup | STIR |
| galvanized | GALV | | | proposed | PROP | street | ST |
| gate value | GTV | | | pall chain | PC | structural | STR |
| general | | machine | MACH | | | substitute | SUB |
| contractor | GEN CON' | main | MN | quantity | QTY | super- | |
| glass | GL | manhole | MH | | | intendent | SUPT |
| government | GOVT | manufacture | MFR | radiator | RAD | supply | SUP |
| grade | GR | marble | MR | radius | RAD | surface | SUR |
| grade line | GL | masonry | | random | RDM | surfaced four | |
| granite | G | opening | MO | range | R | sides | S4S |
| gypsum | GYP | material | MATL | receptacle | RECP | suspended | |
| | | maximum | MAX | register | REG | ceiling | SUSP CEIL |
| hall | H | mechanical | MECH | reinforcing | | switch | SW |
| half-round | H RD | medium | MED | bar | REBAR | switchboard | SWBD |
| hardware | HDW | membrane | MEMB | required | REQD | symbol | SYM |

| telephone | TEL | unfinished | UNFIN | wall cabinet | W CAB | window | WDW |
| temperature | TEMP | | | water | W | wire glass | W GL |
| template | TEMP | vapor proof | VAP PRF | watercloset | WC | with | W/ |
| thermostat | THERMO | variable | VAR | weatherproof | WP | wood door | WD |
| thousand | M | ventilation | VENT | weather | | wood frame | WF |
| thousand | | vent stock | VS | stripping | WS | | |
| pounds | KIP | vertical | VERT | weight | WT | yard | YD |
| tongue and | | vestibule | VEST | wide flange | | yellow | YEL |
| groove | T&G | vitreous | VIT | (steel) | WF | yellow pine | YP |
| typical | TYP | volume | VOL | width | W | zinc | ZN |

## *Assignment:*

1. **Draw the symbols for the following materials:**
   a. Concrete
   b. Brick
   c. Wood
   d. Terrazzo
   e. Earth
   f. Hose bib
   g. Gate valve
   h. Water heater
   i. Building trap
   j. Bell and buzzer
   k. Floodlight
   l. Exhaust duct
   m. Deciduous tree
   n. Medium-pressure steam pipe
   o. Double-action door
   p. Double-hung window

2. **Identify the following symbols:**
   a.
   b.
   c.
   d.
   e.
   f.
   g.
   h.

Before the actual plans for a new house are drawn, several important factors should be considered:

- □ What are the price limits on the new home?
- □ What are the legal aspects and restrictions of the lot?
- □ What are the available facilities?
- □ What does the site look like?
- □ What are some preplanning considerations?
- □ What are some of the basic house types?
- □ What should the shape of the floor plan be?

These and many more questions should be dealt with before a set of plans is drawn. Once the questions have been satisfactorily answered, preliminary planning can begin.

## Price Limits of a New Home

One of the most important things to consider before a new home is purchased is the cost. If the price of a house does not fit into the family budget, there could be serious financial problems.

Most lending agencies base the amount of money they will lend an individual on his or her yearly income. As a general rule, it is suggested that the purchase price of a home should not exceed two-and-a-half times the yearly income of the head of the house. For example, if a person earns $25,000 a year, he or she should not pay more than $62,500 for a house. Another rule of thumb is not to spend more than 20 percent of the annual budget for shelter (figured on net, not gross income).

## LOANS

Once the cost limit of a house is decided upon, it is usually necessary to make arrangements for a loan. There are three basic types of loans: VA, FHA, and conventional loans.

## VA Loans

A VA loan is one that is guaranteed by the Veterans Administration up to a maximum cash amount of $17,500 or 60 percent of the loan amount, whichever is less. To be eligible for this loan a person must be an "eligible" veteran—that is, have an honorable discharge from one of the branches of the armed services, in which the time limitations are:

# 5
# Residential Planning

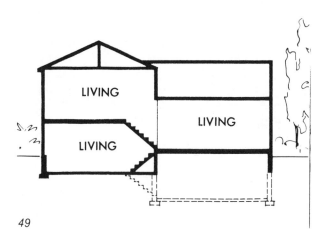

☐ 90 days or more of active duty, any part of which was between September 16, 1940 and July 25, 1957, or
☐ 180 days or more of active duty during the period from July 25, 1947 to July 27, 1950, or
☐ 90 days or more of active duty, any part of which was between June 27, 1950 and January 31, 1955, or
☐ 181 days or more of active duty, any part of which occurred after January 31, 1955.

When a veteran applies for a loan he or she usually must furnish the lender with four sets of plans and specifications. Each page of the plans and specifications should be signed or initialed by the builder and the veteran, and the plans must follow prescribed guidelines and meet certain minimum standards. The Veterans Administration publishes a booklet that outlines these standards; it can be obtained from a local VA office.

There are several advantages in using VA financing:

☐ VA appraisers usually give a full and fair value to a home.
☐ VA is one of the most liberal loan types in older and declining neighborhoods, and for properties in rural areas.
☐ VA is reasonable in income and credit underwriting.
☐ In most cases VA does not require a down payment.
☐ VA's monthly loan payments are usually less than any other type of financing.
☐ VA money is usually always available, even in periods of tight money.

## FHA Loans

The Federal Housing Administration was formed by an act of Congress in 1934. Its primary purpose was to promote home ownership by encouraging lenders to allow low down payments, and long-term loans. The FHA guarantees lenders against any loan loss due to default. In order for the FHA to guarantee the loan, an insurance premium of one-half of 1 percent of the loan balance each year must be paid by the buyer.

At one time FHA loans were designed primarily for moderate-income families. However, at the present time there are no restrictions on who may apply. When applying for a loan the applicant must be buying for his or her own occupancy. Applicants can borrow as much as 97 percent of their acquisition cost. The acquisition cost is the lesser of the FHA appraisal or sales price plus prepaid items.

There are several advantages in using FHA financing:

☐ Interest rates on FHA loans are often less than on other loan types.
☐ Money is usually available for FHA loans, even in times of tight money.
☐ In some cases FHA offers special programs to assist buyers.
☐ FHA financing is liberal in regard to income, credit, and length of employment.

## Conventional Loans

Conventional loans are usually for 95, 90, 80 percent, or lesser percentages of the sale price of the house. The choice depends on how much of a down payment the buyer is willing and can afford to pay. Some consideration should also be given to the monthly payment, which will go higher as the loan amount goes higher. Usually a 30-year loan is the most desirable, because the monthly payments are much lower than 10-, 15-, or 20-year loans. The monthly payment usually includes:

☐ *Principal and interest payment:* Derived from a standard rate book.
☐ *Escrow for hazard insurance:* Usually 1/12 of the annual hazard insurance premium.
☐ *Escrow for taxes:* Usually 1/12 of the estimated annual taxes.
☐ *Escrow of PMI (Private Mortgage Insurance) premium:* Half of 1% per year (1% of the loan amount is divided by 48 to find the exact amount).

## EXPENSES

There are certain expenses that a seller and a buyer will incur while processing a sale. The major ones will usually fall under the heading of discount, closing costs, or prepaid items:

☐ *Discount:* A percentage of the loan charged by the lender to increase the yield on the money he is lending.

☐ *Closing costs:* Costs that are usually associated with the closing of a loan, such as:

a. Attorney's fee: Includes the attorney's fee for checking the title to the property, for preparing documents, and for closing the sale. This fee can vary from area to area and attorney to attorney.

b. Title Insurance: Guards against the possibility of the attorney making a mistake, or not catching a defective title.

c. Survey: Should be made of each property to locate the property lines and servitudes.

d. Origination fee: A percentage charge on the loan amount by the mortgage banker for making the loan. The charge usually runs from 1 to 3%.

e. Private mortgage insurance (PMI): If a conventional loan is used and is in excess of 80% of the sale price the borrower is usually required to purchase PMI. This insures for the investor that amount of the loan that exceeds 80%. Part of the premium is paid at closing and the remainder is included in the monthly premiums.

f. Recording fees: Pays the Clerk of Court for the recording of the deed and mortgage. This is also paid for the certification of any necessary copies.

g. Miscellaneous fees: Can include items such as termite inspections, notary fee, photographs, and application fees.

☐ Prepaid items: Include such things as hazard insurance (usually the first year's), property taxes, and PMI.

## CONSTRUCTION CONTRACTS

A decision that often confronts a prospective homeowner concerns what type of contract to award for the construction of a new home. In most cases a single contract is used.

### Single contracts

This is a contract made with one contractor only. This person is responsible for the entire construction process. He must coordinate all the work with the subcontractors to see that their work is satisfactory and finished on schedule. Some of the most often used procedures for obtaining a single contract are:

☐ *Negotiation:* A negotiated contract is one in which the contractor agrees to build the structure for the construction cost plus a fee, which can be a percentage of the construction cost or a set fee. One or more contractors can be asked to negotiate for the contract.

☐ *Bidding* (with no subcontractors designated in the bid): Each contractor submits a bid that has been put together with the assistance of subcontractors of his choosing. But the contractor does not necessarily need to use the "subs" if he is the successful bidder.

☐ *Bidding* (with subcontractors designated in the bid): Each contractor submits a bid that designates specific subcontractors of his choosing. If the contractor is the successful bidder he must use those designated subcontractors unless a change is approved by the architect and/or owner for a good reason.

☐ *Bidding* (with subcontractors assigned): Each contractor submits a bid that has been assembled with the aid of various subcontractors. If awarded the contract, the contractor will assign the specialty work to the subcontractors who assisted in the assemblage of the bid.

## LEGAL ASPECTS AND RESTRICTIONS OF A LOT

Before a lot is purchased there are several factors that should be investigated, such as easements, location of property lines, zoning regulations, and building codes.

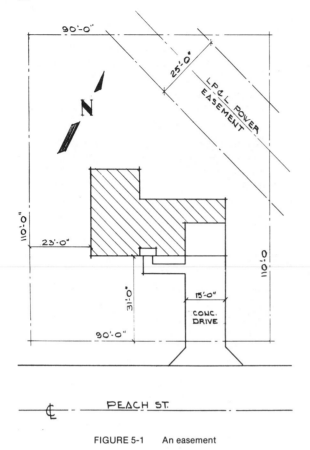

FIGURE 5-1    An easement

## Easement

An easement is a legal means for someone else other than the owner to have access to a piece of property. In some cases power lines, water lines, or sewer lines may run across the property and an easement is granted to these companies (see Fig. 5-1). An easement may not distract from the appearance of the

property, but it could prevent the owner from fencing the property, adding a storage shed on the easement, or perhaps adding a room.

### Location of the Property Lines

Property lines should always be located before the lot is purchased. Many people have bought land with the understanding the property lines were located in a specific place, only to find later that they were in another location. There have also been cases in which an individual has built a home only to find that it was built across the property line.

### Zoning regulations

Zoning regulations can influence an individual in the purchasing of a lot. Zoning regulations set guidelines for the type of structure that can be built in a certain location. Some dictate the minimum size of a home, cost, materials, and whether or not a detached building can be placed on the lot.

### Building Codes

Building codes can also influence the type of structure that can be built. These are legal specifications that govern how a building is constructed. Some cities write their own building codes, while other cities adopt a standard code. Most codes specify the type of material that can be used, how it is used, and where it can be used. Building codes will also specify whether or not a septic tank can be used.

## AVAILABLE FACILITIES

In choosing a location for a new home, there are many factors that the buyers must consider. For parents with small children, the location and quality of schools is important. Instead of choosing a location that will mean the children must ride a bus for an hour to get to school, the parents may well choose a location in an area that has a neighborhood school. The quality of the school is also very important. This can usually be checked by consulting with friends or neighbors in the area of the school. A visit to the school can

also be very helpful in making a decision about moving into a neighborhood.

Utilities and utility service is also an important consideration in the purchase of a property. Some areas may be serviced by public or private sewer systems, while in others it may be necessary to use a septic tank. This will add more to the initial cost of a home and in some cases the soil might not be suitable for the septic tank. Available energy sources and costs should also be investigated. If the cost of energy is excessive, alternate sources might be considered when planning the home.

The location of shopping centers, churches, medical facilities, grocery stores, and similar facilities is also an important consideration—most families want these facilities within easy reach so they can easily meet their everyday needs.

## PRELIMINARY SITE INVESTIGATION

Before a lot is purchased, a visit should be made to the site. The soil should be inspected and any trees noted. The type of soil on a lot can dictate what type of foundation can be used. If the soil is cohesive, problems could later arise that might affect the entire structure. If the area is extremely rocky or has large boulders, it may not be wise to plan a home with a basement—excavation might be virtually impossible or very expensive.

The location of trees could influence the location of the house, garage, patio, and other special features. Or an extra expense could be added to the total cost of the house if it is necessary to remove any trees.

The topography of the land should also be noted. It is extremely important to find out how the land slopes and in which direction. The slope and the amount of slope can determine whether fill is needed and whether there is a need to "cut" any of the lot. It can even dictate the type of foundation and the type of house that can be placed on the lot. Contour lines are uninterrupted lines that specify an elevation. They are usually spaced on 2-foot intervals, although other intervals can be used.

The shape and size of the lot is also an important factor that should be investigated. In many cases, these determine the style of home that can be built, as well as the location of drives and sidewalks.

## PLANNING THE HOUSE

Some type of preplanning should be done before the actual plans are drawn. During this stage, the style and shape of the house—one-story, two-story, split-level—should be considered. There are desirable features in any style, but things like the age and health of the family members should be considered. It is usually recommended that older people and children not live in homes that have stairs, which can present an obstacle and could cause serious accidents. If any family member is confined to a wheelchair, a home with stairs would be very inconvenient.

If possible, the house should be designed in relationship to the sun. It is usually recommended that the living areas have a southern exposure. However, most homes today are built in preplanned subdivisions that do not observe this factor.

Maximum use of trees should be made when planning the location of a house on a lot. Trees will provide shade during the hot summer months and can increase the price of the property.

The location of individual rooms should also be planned. Bedrooms should be placed away from the streets to avoid excessive noise. If there are young children in the house the kitchen should be placed overlooking the back yard, or the area where the children play. This makes it possible to observe the children while meals are being prepared. Family size and interest can dictate the location of other types of rooms in a home.

A home should be planned so that excessive excavation is not necessary. Most important, the house should be built to *fit* the site and not simply sit on a site.

## BASIC HOUSE TYPES

There are seven basic house styles considered to be standard. Most people can select one that is appropriate for both their lifestyle and the site.

### One-Story: Pitched Roof and Flat Ceiling

This one-story house (see Fig. 5-2) is the most popular style. More shapes, sizes, and designs can be achieved in a one-story house than in any of the other basic styles. Such a house is convenient for people of all ages and states of health.

### One-Story: Pitched Roof, Sloping Roof, Flat Roof

Houses of this type (see Fig. 5-3) often lend themselves to an exciting style of contemporary architecture. However, such houses are often more expensive than other styles. Because of the shape of the roof, conventional framing members cannot be used or fabricated. A built-up roof is often required and is usually more expensive.

### One-and-A-Half-Story: Two Living Levels, Varying Second-Floor Area and Ceiling

The traditional Cape Cod house (see Fig. 5-4) is typical of this house style. The basic shape provides a wide variety in designs, including traditional and contemporary. The half-story can be used as a multipurpose area or for sleeping. The area of the half-story depends upon the dimensions of the house and the use of dormers.

### Two-Story: Varying Roof and Ceiling Type

Two-story homes (see Fig. 5-5) can offer maximum living area at a lower cost than other house styles. One disadvantage, however, is that some living area is lost because of the stairs. When two-story house plans are drawn, great attention should be paid to the proportions of the design. The upper and lower exterior walls can be in the same plan, or the upper walls can be cantilevered out over the lower walls to provide more floor area in the second story.

FIGURES 5-2 (top right), 5-3 (upper middle right), 5-4 (lower middle right), and 5-5 (bottom right).   Various popular styles of residence

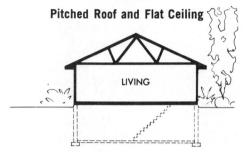

**ONE-STORY**
**Pitched Roof and Flat Ceiling**

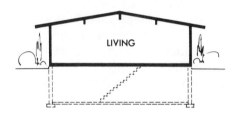

**ONE-STORY**
**Pitched Roof and Sloping Ceiling — Flat Roof**

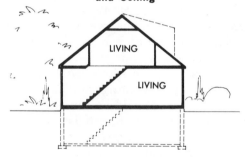

**1½-STORY**
**Two Living Levels — Varying Second Floor Area and Ceiling**

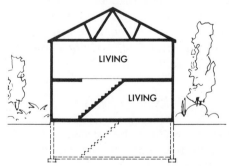

**TWO-STORY**
**Two Living Levels — Varying Roof and Ceiling Types**

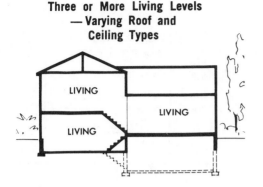

**SPLIT-LEVEL "A"**

**Three or More Living Levels — Varying Roof and Ceiling Types**

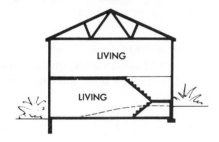

**BI-LEVEL "A"**

**Two Living Levels — Varying Roof and Ceiling Types — Split-Level Foyer**

## Trilevel: Three or More Living Levels

The most popular split-level house has three living areas connected by three segments of stairs (see Fig. 5-6). Each of the three living areas can be used for different functions. Split-level houses look better when they are designed around rolling hills, and the lower story has exposure to outdoor living. A trilevel can have varying roof and ceiling types, or it can have a continuous sloping roof and ceiling.

## Bilevel: Two Living Levels

A bilevel house has a split-level foyer between two full living areas (see Fig. 5-7). A house of this type could be identified as a finished one-story house with a finished basement. Room arrangement in this house style provides a wide variety of choices, just as the exterior offers a variety of design possibilities.

FIGURES 5-6 (upper left) and 5-7 (lower left)  Two more popular styles of residence

## SHAPE OF THE FLOOR PLAN

There are six basic shapes that are usually used for floor plans: the square, rectangle, L-shape, U-shape, T-shape, and H-shape (see Fig. 5-8). The square house plan is usually

FIGURE 5-8    Basic shapes for a floor plan

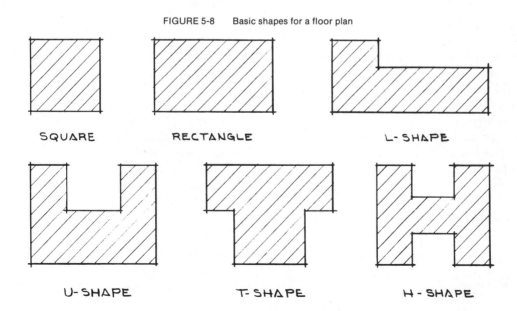

SQUARE          RECTANGLE          L-SHAPE

U-SHAPE          T-SHAPE          H-SHAPE

considered to be the most economical to build. One reason for this is that more space can be enclosed in a square than in any other geometric figure with the same lineal footage (see Fig. 5-9). This design, however, does not lend itself to producing many pleasing architectural variations.

The rectangle is probably one of the most widely used floor-plan shapes. It is economical to construct and is adaptable to varying roof styles. The L shape is also popular and can isolate areas into quiet zones without eliminating efficient traffic patterns. A T-shaped house has many corners that increase the cost. However, cross-ventilation can be achieved by isolating the various rooms in the wings of the T.

The U- and H-shaped house lends itself to private outdoor living with a minimum number of fences and hedges. Rooms can be built around open courtyards that provide this luxury. Cross-ventilation can also be obtained with these two floor-plan arrangements. Natural lighting is easily obtained with these styles. However, these styles have

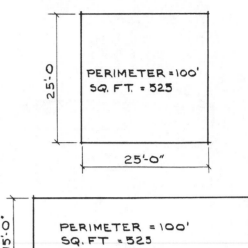

FIGURE 5-9    Comparison of a square floor plan with a rectangular one

a large gross area of exposed exterior walls, which increases the demands on heating and cooling units. Utility bills are then proportionally altered.

## CHECK LIST

Before a decision is made to locate, it is wise to make a thorough investigation of the area, using a checklist to determine the desirable and undesirable characteristics.

NEIGHBORHOOD CHARACTERISTICS    YES    NO

 1. Area in transition
 2. Average housing
 3. Below-average housing
 4. Above-average housing
 5. Developed areas
 6. Air pollution
 7. Good streets
 8. Area prone to flood
 9. Lot has been filled
10. Proper zoning
11. Excessive noise
12. Good drainage
13. Well-kept houses
14. Low crime rate

COMMUNITY FACILITIES NEARBY

 1. Good schools

 2. Churches
 3. Shopping centers
 4. Public transportation
 5. Recreational facilities
 6. Hospitals
 7. Place of work
 8. Pharmacy

PUBLIC UTILITIES

 1. Gas
 2. Electricity
 3. Water
 4. Telephone
 5. Fire protection
 6. Police protection
 7. Garbage pickup
 8. Streetlights
 9. Price of utilities

BUILDING PROTECTION

 1. Building codes
 2. Easements
 3. Good zoning laws

4. Restrictions of use of lot area
5. Adequate flood protection

HOUSE RELATIONSHIP TO SITE

1. House fits site
2. House can be properly orientated on site

3. Proper topographic features

PURCHASING TRANSACTION

1. Satisfactory appraisal
2. No lien on the property
3. Satisfactory tax base
4. Satisfactory title search

## Assignment:

1. What would be the advisable cost limit of a home for an individual who earned $33,000 a year?
2. What are three basic types of loans?
3. What is a single contract?
4. What are three basic house types?
5. Sketch the various shapes that can be used for a floor plan.

Sketching is an important means of communication, an effective way to get an idea across, and is a necessity in any type of drafting. Sketches are used for many reasons, but in most cases they are used to record and formulate ideas.

## Materials

The only materials needed for sketching are pencil, paper, and eraser. The pencil most often used is an H or F pencil that has a long tapered point (see Fig. 6-1). Before the pencil is used, however, the point should be worn down on fine sandpaper, with the pencil held at an approximate angle of 45 degrees. Then the point should be rubbed on scratch paper until each stroke gives a firm, even tone. When the lead has been properly sharpened, the flattened side can be used to make broad strokes, and fine lines can be drawn with the sharp edge. The paper can be either plain tracing paper, or it can be cross-sectioned. Cross-sectioned paper has light lines printed on one side, and is very beneficial for beginning students. The two erasers that are most often used are of two types: ruby for erasing dark lines and art gum for cleaning purposes.

## Methods

There are some basic guidelines you should follow in the development of a good sketch:

- □ Use a free arm motion rather than a tightly controlled finger motion.
- □ Use simple figures of people, trees, automobiles, and shrubs to add depth and scale to a drawing (see Fig. 6-2).
- □ Avoid a lot of detail in rough sketches.
- □ Try to obtain the correct proportion in the drawing.
- □ Make the sketches large enough so that they may be easily read.
- □ Don't spend a lot of time trying to correctly intersect the corners—let the lines intersect and pass each other slightly (see Fig. 6-3).
- □ Don't confine the drawing to single lines; use multiple lines to give the drawing character.
- □ Use standard symbols on the drawing.
- □ Practice the different techniques required for a good sketch.

# 6
# Sketching

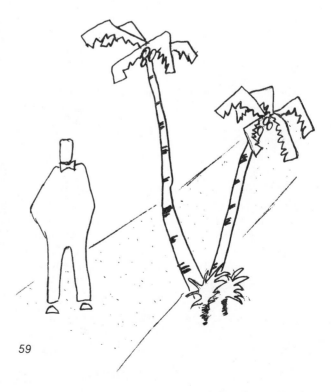

59

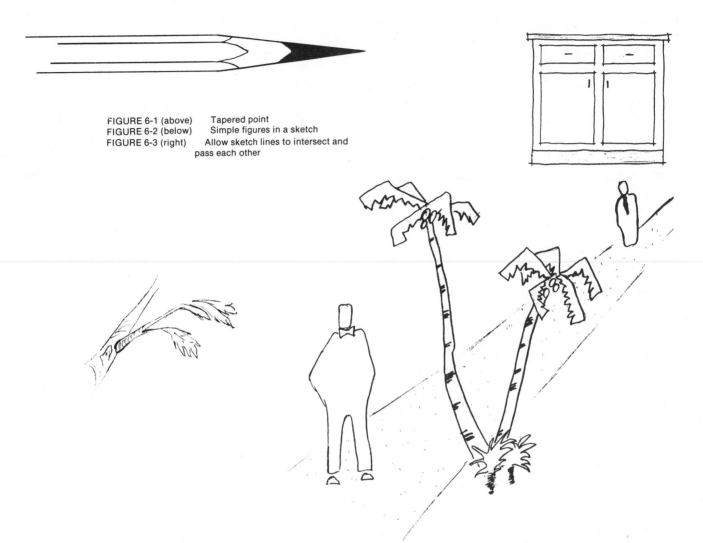

FIGURE 6-1 (above)      Tapered point
FIGURE 6-2 (below)      Simple figures in a sketch
FIGURE 6-3 (right)      Allow sketch lines to intersect and
pass each other

## Line Exercises

Before proficiency can be achieved in sketching, considerable time must be spent on line exercises. The first line exercise should involve lines placed horizontally and vertically, and lines placed in an inclined position (see Fig. 6-4).

Short lines are drawn by slightly moving the fingers and wrist, while longer lines are drawn as a series of short dashes. If a long line is drawn, the hand should be moved for each new dash. As the lines are being drawn, full pressure should be exerted so that most lines begin and end in a crisp "painted" stroke. But, to add definition to a line some strokes should be allowed to fade out gradually so that the ends of the line are lost in the tones of the paper (see Fig. 6-5). Other lines

can be accented by using extra pressure at their beginning and end.

A right-handed person should draw a horizontal line from left to right (right to left if left-handed) and a vertical line should be drawn from the top of the page down. To achieve a comfortable technique, the paper can be turned or positioned in various positions.

## Sketching Angles

When angles are sketched, the edges of the paper are often used as a reference line. For a 90-degree angle, the top and bottom line can be drawn by using the top and bottom edge of the paper as a guide. To complete the angle, a second line can be drawn parallel to the sides of the paper. If an angle less than 90 degrees is desired, it is drawn by visual comparison.

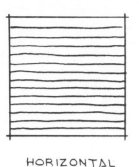

HORIZONTAL

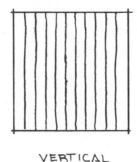

VERTICAL

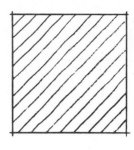

INCLINED

FIGURE 6-4    Exercise lines

## Sketching Circles

To sketch a circle, a square equal to the diameter of the desired circle must first be developed (see Fig. 6-6). Once the square has been drawn, horizontal and vertical center lines are drawn through the square so that it is divided into equal quadrants. Then, across the outside corner of each quadrant, a 45-degree line is sketched. Using the horizontal, vertical, and inclined lines as a guide, the circle is sketched in. The sketch should start at the intersection of the center line and the top of the square and proceed from left to right until half is complete. The pencil is then repositioned at the starting point and the procedure is repeated, only this time the line is sketched from right to left.

## Proportion

Proportion can be defined as the harmonious relation of parts. In sketching, correct pro-

portion is extremely important, and is usually acquired only through astute observation. When a sketch is made, close attention should be given to how the height relates to the width, width relates to depth, and how one particular feature is related to another.

If a sketch is made from a dimensioned drawing, the dimensions should be used to achieve correct proportion. For example: if a floor plan is $60' \times 30'$, the dimension of width can be drawn to any length; then the dimension of depth is sketched half the length of the previously drawn line. But if the object to be sketched has no dimensions, it can first be broken down into simple geometric shapes. For example, the front elevation of a house can be broken down into two rectangles that are complemented by smaller geometric shapes within the two large rectangles (see Fig. 6-7).

## Line Technique

When a sketch is first started, the object should be blocked in with light construction lines (see Fig. 6-8). Then heavy, deliberate lines should be used to cover the desired construction lines and to add detail to the

FIGURE 6-5    Definition is achieved by fading out some lines

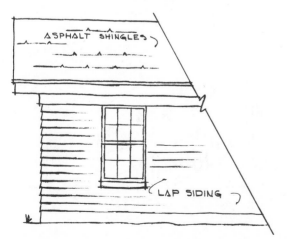

FIGURE 6-6    Sketching circles

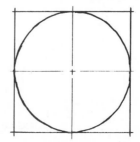

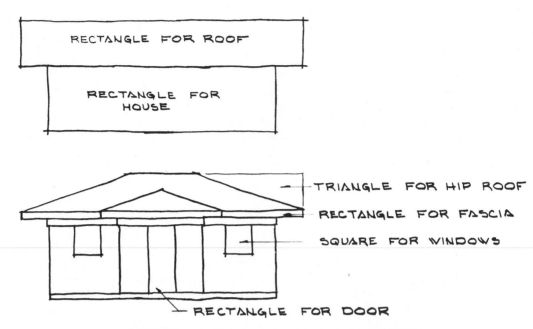

FIGURE 6-7     Breaking a house down into simple geometric shapes

sketch (see Fig. 6-9). As the lines are darkened in, their weight will vary with their importance. Object lines are made extremely dark and heavy, while less important lines are drawn much lighter.

## Pictorial Sketches

A pictorial sketch is a simple way of expressing an idea. There are several types of picto-

FIGURE 6-8 (left)     Using light construction lines to block in a sketch
FIGURE 6-9 (right)     Using heavy construction lines to add detail to the sketch

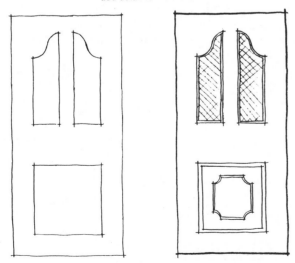

rials, but the one that is most often used is the isometric (see Fig. 6-10). An isometric sketch is drawn by rotating an object about a vertical axis and tilting it forward so that all three dimensions are represented. Height is represented by a vertical line and the dimensions of width and depth are represented by lines drawn at a 30-degree angle to the horizontal.

The first step in the construction of an isometric sketch is to lay out the axis (see Fig. 6-11). The dimensions of height, width, and depth are then placed on the three axes and the isometric shape is lightly blocked in (see Fig. 6-12). Once the outline of the figure is blocked in, details are added and the lines are darkened in (see Fig. 6-13). When the lines are

FIGURE 6-10     Pictorial sketch

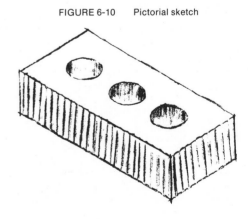

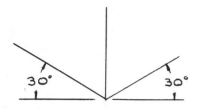

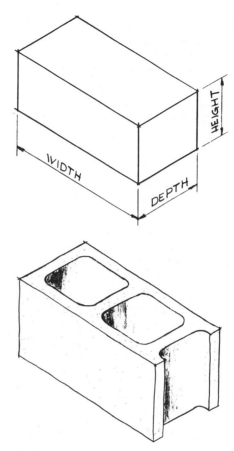

FIGURE 6-11 (above)      Isometric axis
FIGURE 6-12 (upper right)      Blocking in an isometric
FIGURE 6-13 (lower right)      Adding details to an
                              isometric sketch

drawn in, the corners need not meet precisely, but may pass each other slightly.

## Floor Plans

In developing a set of architectural floor plans, one of the first steps is to sketch tentative ideas on grid paper (see Fig. 6-14). The grid paper allows an expression of ideas to formulate in their proper scale; since the grids are to scale, it is not necessary to dimension the sketch. Even so, for later convenience, it is sometimes well to do this. When the first sketch is made it is usually made to about a ⅛″ scale. Some of the detail work, such as convenience outlets, lights, and

FIGURE 6-14      Floor-plan sketch

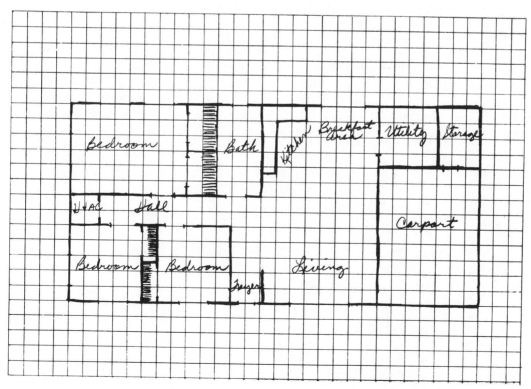

ceiling-joist direction are omitted from the sketch, but are later added to the floor plan. The exterior walls of the floor plan are heavy black lines that are usually drawn with an H or F pencil. The interior walls are drawn with a 2H pencil and are relatively light lines. The doors on the floor-plan sketch are often represented by only openings, but the direction of the door swing can be added if necessary. To complete the sketch, window symbols are added, kitchen cabinets and bathroom fixtures blocked in, and the closets are accented by means of a series of parallel lines perpendicular to the long dimension.

If a second-floor plan is needed, a sheet of tracing paper should be placed over the sketch of the first-floor plan. The exterior walls can then be sketched in, with the first-floor plan as a guide. The interior partitions are then added, placed over bearing walls whenever possible. When the second-floor plan is being developed, consideration should be given to the placement of the baths, stairwell, and fireplace; they should be placed over features of the same nature on the first floor.

## Elevations

Most sketches of elevations are begun by placing a clean sheet of tracing paper over the developed floor-plan sketch. The features are then transferred from the floor plan to the elevation. The features are projected by using light construction lines drawn perpendicular to the floor plan. When the features are projected, the dimension of width is shown, but the dimension of height and depth is not.

Height is later added to the projection lines in order that the elevation may be blocked in. The actual height of the building is determined by the particular architectural style and the size of structural members used. Once the outline of the elevation has been lightly sketched in, details such as windows and doors are added. Doors are sketched to a height of 6'8" and a width of 3'0", but the height and width of windows vary.

One of the most important points to remember in sketching an elevation is to maintain the correct proportions.

## Details

To sketch details, the main structural elements must first be blocked in. Then, other features such as exterior and interior wall coverings and moldings can be added (see Fig. 6-15). Object lines are dark and heavy, while the less important lines of the detail are drawn much lighter.

Details should be drawn large enough so the component parts are clear and their relationship to each other is distinct and drawn correctly to proportion.

## Perspective Sketches

There are two basic types of perspective sketches—a "parallel," or "one-point," perspective and a "two-point" perspective. A one-point perspective has one face parallel to the front plane, while a two-point perspective is turned at an angle (see Fig. 6-16).

FIGURE 6-15    Detail sketch

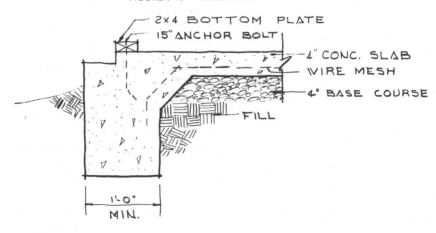

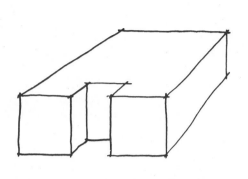

ONE-POINT PERSPECTIVE

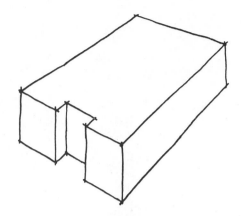

TWO-POINT PERSPECTIVE

FIGURE 6-16    Perspectives

For a one-point perspective, the front view of the object is first sketched in. A vanishing point is then located and all receding lines are projected toward it. The object should first be blocked in, with details added later. In this, too, it is important to keep the sketch in proportion. Regardless of how brilliant the technique is, if the proportions are wrong the sketch will be bad.

A two-point perspective depicts a more natural picture than the one-point perspective, but it requires more skill. The front corner of the object should first be located in its true height. A horizon line is then established. This line is usually placed at eye level. On the horizon line two vanishing points are located. With the lines projected to the vanishing points, the drawing is then blocked in and the drawing darkened. It should be noted that all parallel lines converge toward the same vanishing point. The outlines of the drawing should be thick and the inside lines thinner, especially when they are close together.

## Assignment:

1. Using an 8½″ × 11″ sheet of tracing paper, develop a sketch of the following items:

   a. Concrete block    b. Switchplate

   c. Light fixture    d. Tree
   e. Hand    f. Cap
   g. Bathroom    h. Car
   i. Truck    j. Shrub

The floor plan is an extension of the grid sketch with dimensions and details added (see Fig. 7-1). It is made up of individual components, with each playing a significant part in the total development of the plan.

# 7

# Floor Plans

## ROMS

For privacy, most homes are divided into individual rooms. A room can provide a retreat for an individual, an area for entertaining, a place for recreation, a place to sleep, and a place to prepare and eat meals. The size, location, and arrangement of rooms vary with individual taste, but there are some standards that are generally followed.

Typical rooms in a home usually include kitchen, bathroom, bedroom(s), dining and living room, and utility room.

### The Kitchen

A kitchen is divided into three main areas of activity: cooking, refrigeration, and sanitation (see Fig. 7-2). To maintain an efficient work area, each activity area should possess certain characteristics:

☐ The cooking area should have a working surface on both sides of the range plus working space near the double oven. This area should also have some storage space and should be located near the serving area. The area on both sides of the range should have heat-resistant counter-tops and the cooking area should be well ventilated.
☐ The sanitation area can include a dishwasher, sink, and garbage disposal. The sink should have a work area of 24″ on either side, with storage space provided for fruits, vegetables, and cooking utensils.
☐ The refrigerator area should be located near a service entrance and have at least 15″ of counter space adjacent to the refrigerator.

The three major work areas form a work triangle that determines how well a kitchen is planned. The work triangle is established by measuring from the center of the range to the center of the refrigerator to the center of the

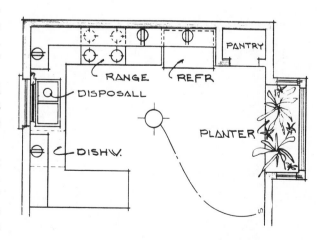

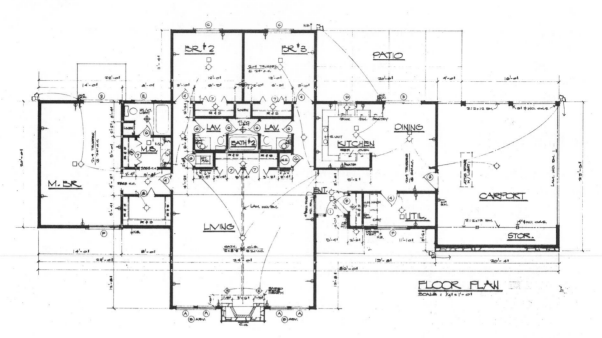

FIGURE 7-1    Floor plan

sink (see Fig. 7-3). The total length of the triangle should be less than 22' but more than 13'. The recommended distance, however, between the work areas are: sink to refrigerator—4 to 7'; sink to range—4 to 6'; and range to refrigerator—4 to 9'.

There are three basic types of kitchen plans: the U-shaped, the L-shaped, and the corridor kitchen (see Fig. 7-4). The U-shaped kitchen has the advantage of eliminating through traffic and can have a compact work triangle. The L-shaped kitchen has the cabinets along two adjacent walls and allows for a breakfast area without sacrificing space from the work

area. The corridor kitchen has the cabinets placed on two parallel walls and can serve as a passageway between other parts of the house. If this type of arrangement is used, the floor space between the two cabinets should be a minimum of 4 feet.

Regardless of the type of kitchen plan used,

FIGURE 7-3    Work triangle

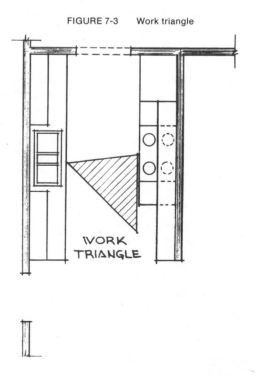

FIGURE 7-2    Activity areas in the kitchen

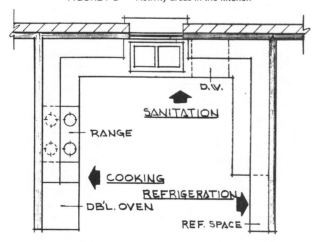

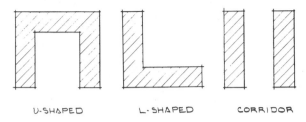

U-SHAPED    L-SHAPED    CORRIDOR

FIGURE 7-4    Basic types of kitchen plans

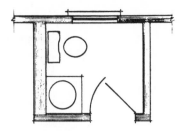

FIGURE 7-6    Full bath

there are certain minimum standards that should be met:

- The total shelving in the wall-hung and base cabinets should be at least 50 square feet.
- The minimum counter-top and drawer area should be a minimum of 11 square feet (the sink and cooking surface is not included in the counter-top area).

The cabinet counter-top should have a suitable surface—one that prevents any moisture penetration. Some recommended counter-tops are phenolic laminate, vinyl plastic, linoleum, ceramic tile, and stainless steel. In addition to the counter-top, a 3″ back- and endsplash should be provided.

For a healthful environment, proper ventilation, either natural or mechanical, is required for the kitchen. If natural ventilation is used, the opening should equal at least 5 percent of the total floor area. If mechanical ventilation is used, the air should be exhausted from the kitchen to the outdoors through a range hood, or through a ceiling or wall exhaust grille. This can be located in the ceiling or wall as long as it is not placed more than 4′ from the center line of the range; or it can be placed directly above the back of the range. If a range hood is used it should be as

wide as the range and at least 17″ deep. The range hood should also be a minimum of 30″ above the range top.

The range should not be located under a window, nor within 12″ of a window. If a cabinet is located above the range, there should be a minimum distance of 30″ between the two. There should also be a 9″ clearance from the edge of the range to an adjacent corner cabinet and a 15″ space between a refrigerator and an adjacent corner cabinet.

## The Bathroom

The bathroom is a private retreat and grooming center for all members of a family (see Fig. 7-5). The arrangement of the plumbing and bathrooms is one of the mechanical and design pivot points of a house and requires intelligent preplanning.

Every house is required to have at least one bath, but most have at least a bath and a half. A full bathroom has a tub, lavatory, and water closet, while a half-bath has only a water closet and lavatory (see Fig. 7-6). A full bathroom should be a minimum of 5′ × 8′ and located near the bedrooms, with its entry from the hall. When it is located in a two-story house it should be placed near the head of the stairs. A two-story house should have at least one and a half baths.

Bathrooms should also be supplied with the following accessories:

- Grab-bar and soap dish placed near the tub or shower
- Shower-curtain rod or tub enclosure
- Soap dish at lavatory (this can be built into the lavatory)
- Toilet paper holder placed near the water closet
- Towel bars
- Mirror and medicine cabinet

FIGURE 7-5    Bathroom

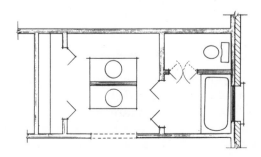

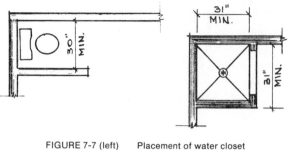

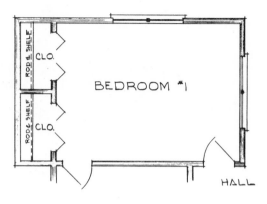

FIGURE 7-7 (left)     Placement of water closet
FIGURE 7-8 (right)    Shower

FIGURE 7-10     Bedroom

Each bath should be provided with a water closet that is not visible from other rooms. For proper placement, this requires a wall area of at least 30″ (see Fig. 7-7). A shower should contain a minimum of 8 square feet and a dimension of at least 31″ (see Fig. 7-8). The lavatory can be wall-hung or built-in, and in some cases a twin lavatory installation is used (see Fig. 7-9). Most bath tubs are 5′0″ × 2′6″ and are required to be enclosed on three sides.

The bathroom door should swing into the room, afford maximum privacy, and have a minimum width of 2′4″. The bathroom should be well lighted, heated, and ventilated. For proper ventilation, an exhaust fan or a window may be used.

## The Bedroom

A bedroom should contain a minimum of 100 square feet and should only be accessible to a hall and sometimes an outside patio door (see Fig. 7-10). In most cases, the bedroom should be located in a separate wing on the quiet side of the lot. Children's bedrooms should be adjacent to or near the master bedroom, but

there should be a buffer between the two, such as a closet or a bath.

If possible, there should be windows on two walls of each bedroom. The windows allow for cross-ventilation and should comprise at least 15 percent of the bedroom floor area. However, there should be a minimum of one uninterrupted wall, at least 10′ long.

The door to the bedroom should be a minimum of 2′6″ in width and should swing into the bedroom.

## The Dining and Living Rooms

The dining room should be located between the kitchen and the living area and can be designed from one of two basic plans. The plan that is most widely accepted is the living room/dining room combination (see Fig. 7-11). In this type of arrangement there are no walls to separate the two rooms. The other arrangement is to have the dining room and living room separate (see Fig. 7-12). In this case, they should be adjacent to each other, with a large opening between the two rooms. The living room should have direct access from the entry, and not provide passage to other parts of the house. The dining room and living room should have about 300 square feet, and should be isolated from the bedrooms.

## The Entrance and the Hall

The entrance of a house should lead to the central area and open into a hall (see Fig. 7-13). There is no standard size for an entry, but most are about 5′ × 6′. The entry door should be covered by a porch or overhang and

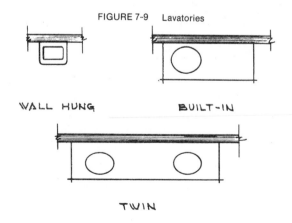

FIGURE 7-9     Lavatories

WALL HUNG          BUILT-IN

TWIN

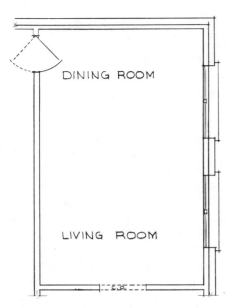

FIGURE 7-11     Living and dining room combination

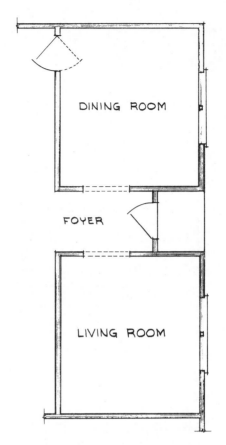

FIGURE 7-12 (above)      Dining room and living room
                                        separate
FIGURE 7-13 (below)      Main entrance to a house
FIGURE 7-14 (bottom)     Position of entry door

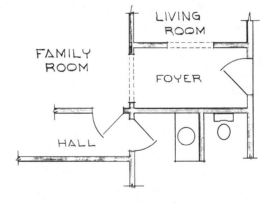

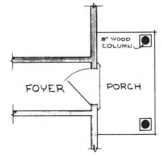

open into the house (see Fig. 7-14). The entry can be walled off, or it can be an extension of the living room. If it is an extension of the living room, a divider can be used to separate the two areas.

The recommended width of a hall is 3′6″. The minimum width, however, is 3′0″ and the maximum width is 4′0″. To maintain an efficient operation and to keep the cost to a minimum, it is best to make the total area of the hall as small as possible.

## Closets

Closets are used to store items that are not in use. There are three basic types: bedroom, coat, and linen (see Fig. 7-15).

A bedroom closet should have a minimum of 4 linear feet of closet-rod space and it should have a depth of 2′. There are many types of closet doors that can be used, but a bifold door provides the most accessibility (see Fig. 7-16). Closets should be placed on interior walls to act as a buffer for noise.

The minimum width of a coat closet is 2′ × 2′, but a more efficient size is 2′ × 3′. The coat closet should be located near the front door, and if the house has a foyer it should be next to it (see Fig. 7-17).

At least one linen closet that is a minimum of 1′6″ deep and 3′ wide should be built in all houses. As a general rule of thumb there

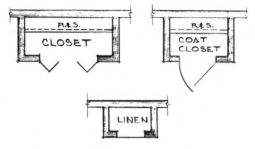

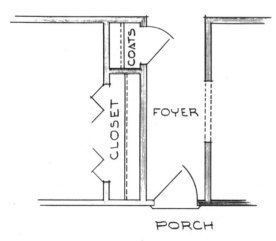

FIGURE 7-15 (above)    Basic types of closets
FIGURE 7-16 (below)    Bi-fold door

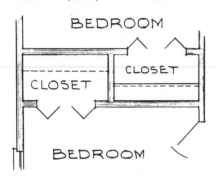

FIGURE 7-17 (above)    Coat closet
FIGURE 7-18 (below)    Utility room

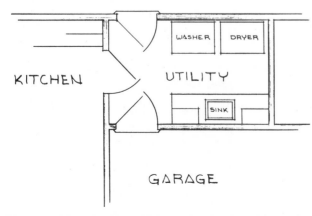

should be 10 square feet of linen space for a two-bedroom home and 15 square feet for a three-bedroom home.

## The Utility Room

The utility room is used to house the washer and dryer and is usually located near the kitchen and back door (see Fig. 7-18). The washer and dryer should be located side by side; for venting purposes, the dryer is usually located on an outside wall. A counter-top and sink should also be included in the utility room. The sink is used for hand-washable items and the counter-top is used for folding clothes.

The minimum floor area for a utility room is 60 square feet.

## The Garage or Carport

A garage is enclosed on three sides and can be completely enclosed with a door (see Fig. 7-19), while a carport has one or more open sides (see Fig. 7-20). The garage or carport is usually attached to the house and has an entrance near the kitchen. The floor of a garage or carport should be constructed of concrete, 4 inches above grade and sloped toward the entrance.

A garage can have one large door or two small doors, but the minimum width for a garage opening is 8 feet. Regardless of the size, the door(s) should be simple in design.

The wall between the garage and house should be fire-resistant; usually ⅝″ gypsum or plaster is used.

The minimum size of a one-car garage or carport is $10' \times 18'$, and of a two-car, $18' \times 18'$.

## Doors

Doors are used for gaining entrance to a room and provide a certain amount of privacy. There are three basic types of interior doors that are used in homes: sliding doors, swinging doors, and folding doors (see Fig. 7-21). The sliding door operates on an overhead track and is used primarily in closets. Swinging doors operate on two or more hinges and in most cases provide an entrance to a room. Folding doors also operate on overhead tracks; they are popular closet doors and sometimes serve as room dividers.

Three other types of doors that are sometimes used are accordion, double-acting, and pocket doors (see Fig. 7-22). The accordion door has many narrow leaves of wood or plastic and operates on a track in the head jamb. It can also double as a movable wall. A double-acting door swings in either direction and can be paneled, flush, or louvered. This type of door is often used between the kitchen and dining room, or in an area that has a great deal of traffic. A pocket door is usually a flush door and requires no space along a wall when it is open. The door units are purchased pre-assembled and are not suitable as exterior doors.

## Windows

Window units are a source of light and, in some cases, provide ventilation. There are many different types of window units; some of the more popular units are double-hung, casement, horizontal sliding, awning, hopper, and fixed units (see Fig. 7-23). Double-hung windows are equipped with two operating sashes, each of which moves vertically and provides 50 percent ventilation. Horizontal sliding windows have a minimum of two sashes and operate horizontally. Casement windows are hinged on one side and swing in or out. Windows of this nature are usually operated by a crank or lever.

Hopper windows have the sash hinged at the bottom and are a variation of the awning window. They provide draft-free ventilation, because the incoming air is deflected up. This particular type of window is sometimes used in basements.

The awning window is hinged at the top and swings out horizontally. Most awning windows have one or more sashes and are operated by a crank.

A fixed window is sometimes called a picture window; it provides no ventilation, is usually large, and is made of ¼″ plate glass or insulating glass.

FIGURE 7-19 (top right)     Garage
FIGURE 7-20 (upper right)     Carport
FIGURE 7-21 (center right)     Three basic types of doors:
          (a) sliding; (b) swinging; and (c) folding
FIGURE 7-22 (lower right)     Three door types:
     (a) accordion; (b) double-acting; and (c) pocket
     FIGURE 7-23 (bottom right)     Window units:
     (a) double-hung; (b) casement; (c) horizontal sliding;
          (d) awning; (e) hopper; and (f) fixed

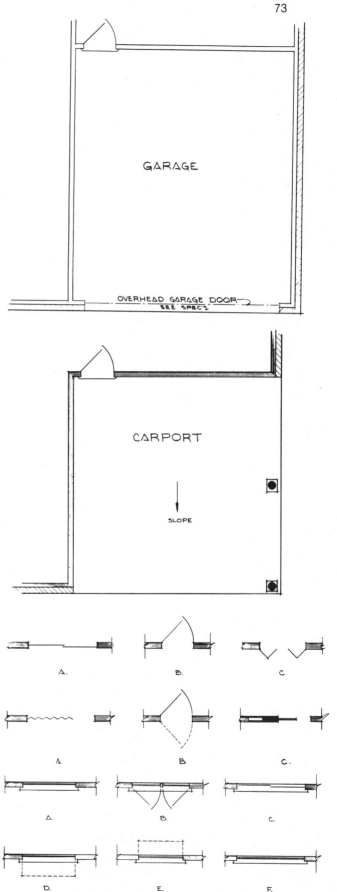

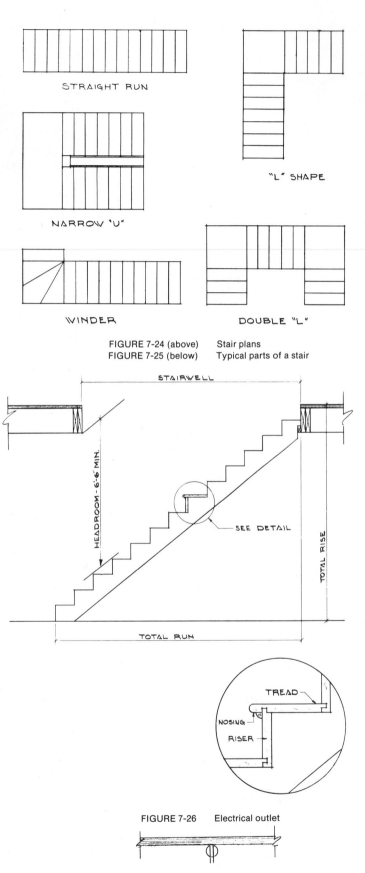

STRAIGHT RUN

"L" SHAPE

NARROW 'U'

WINDER

DOUBLE "L"

FIGURE 7-24 (above)    Stair plans
FIGURE 7-25 (below)    Typical parts of a stair

STAIRWELL

HEADROOM - 6'-6" MIN.

SEE DETAIL

TOTAL RISE

TOTAL RUN

TREAD

NOSING

RISER

FIGURE 7-26    Electrical outlet

## Stairs

There are five basic plans that can be used for stairs: the straight run, the L-shaped, the narrow U, the winder, and the double L or U (see Fig. 7-24).

The straight-run stair leads from one level to another without a turn and is the most popular of the five designs. The L-shaped stair has one landing and makes a 90-degree turn at the landing. The narrow U stair has two flights of stairs in reversed directions; the two flights run parallel to each other, and make a 180-degree turn at the landing. The winder is the most difficult stair to construct and is also the most dangerous. The double L or U has two landings and makes two 90-degree turns. This particular type of stair is not often used.

The width of a main stair should be 2'8" clear of the handrail. A basement stair, however, requires only a 2'6" handrail clearance. The typical parts of a stair include the tread, the riser, the total run, the total rise, headroom, and nosing (see Fig. 7-25). The tread is the horizontal member of the stair that is stepped on and is usually 10 to 11" in width. The riser is the vertical face of the stair, directly below the tread. The height of a riser is usually 6 to 7". The total run is the horizontal length of the stairs, and the stairwell is the opening in which a set of stairs is placed. The total rise is the vertical distance from one floor to another. To find the number of treads required for the floor plan, divide the total rise by 7 and subtract 1. (The 7 is the average height of a riser, and there is always one less tread than the total number of risers.) Headroom is the vertical distance from the edge of the nosing to the ceiling above. The nosing is the projection of the tread beyond the riser.

## Electrical Outlets

In the living areas of a home, electrical outlets should be spaced 8' apart. Other areas, such as halls, carports, foyers, and storage rooms, should be provided with at least one electrical outlet. A circle $\frac{3}{16}$" in diameter with two short lines perpendicular to the stud wall is the symbol used for convenience outlets (see Fig. 7-26). If a 220-volt outlet is needed, a third line is added to the circle. For outdoor use, outlets are sometimes placed on patios, porches, and in carports. These outlets usually have a cover over them and are designated on the floor plan by a WP by the outlet symbol.

## Electrical Fixtures

Every room or area of a house should be properly lighted with at least one fixture, and if the area is larger than 150 square feet there should be two (see Fig. 7-27). The kitchen usually has two fixtures—one overhead and one over the sink (see Fig. 7-28). A hall should have ceiling fixtures 15′ apart and the stairway should have adequate lighting controlled at the head and foot of the stairs (see Fig. 7-29). Each closet should have a light fixture that can be operated by a pull-cord or switch (see Fig. 7-30). Entrances should have one or more light fixtures and the garage should have a ceiling fixture for every two cars (see Fig. 7-31).

Most of the fixtures are controlled by a wall switch located 4′ above the floor. The symbol for the wall switch is the letter S. The symbol for an incandescent ceiling fixture is a circle with four short lines protruding from it, and the symbol for a fluorescent fixture is two parallel lines terminated by a short arc. To connect the switch and fixture on the drawing, a curved center line is used. The switch should be located on the doorknob side of the door. If a room has two entrances, a three-way switch (see Fig. 7-32) should be used so the fixture can be turned on at one location and turned off at another.

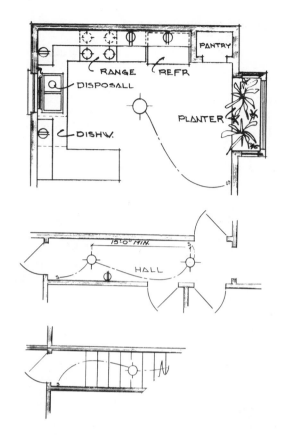

FIGURE 7-28 (top)   Electrical features in a kitchen
FIGURE 7-29 (above)   Stairway lighting

FIGURE 7-30 (below)   Closet lighting
FIGURE 7-31 (bottom)   Garage lighting

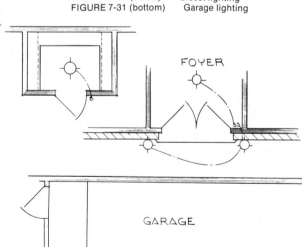

FIGURE 7-27   Position of electrical features

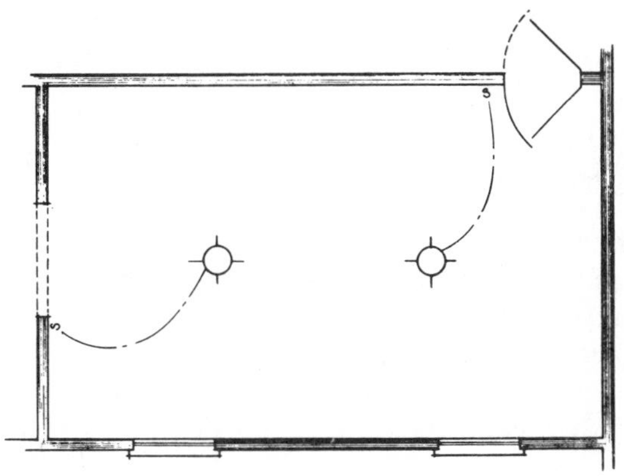

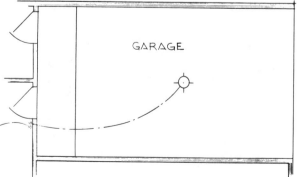

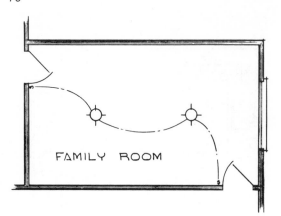

FAMILY ROOM

FIGURE 7-32 (left)      Three-way switch

## DRAFTING PROCEDURES FOR THE FLOOR PLAN

A floor plan is usually started by a light drawing-in of the perimeter of the building. Other lines are then drawn parallel to the perimeter line. The number and placement of the lines will vary with the type of construction used.

There are three basic types of walls used in light construction. They are veneered walls, solid masonry walls, and cavity walls (see Fig. 7-33). Brick veneer is typically placed over and anchored to wood-frame construction with corrosion-resistant metal ties. Two techniques are used to secure the veneer to the wall frame. The one that is most widely used is the placement of a corrosion-resistant wall tie for each 2 square feet of wall area. The wall ties should be corrugated and at least $\frac{3}{4}''$ wide and $6\frac{5}{8}''$ long.

It is also possible to attach veneer to the frame wall by grouting it to paper-backed, welded wire mesh. The wire mesh is attached directly to the frame wall, eliminating the need for wall sheathing. This technique is sometimes called reinforced masonry veneer.

Regardless of the technique used, there should be at least a 1″ space between the brick and the wall frame. In the case of the reinforced masonry veneer, the space is fitted with mortar or grout. Satisfactory perfor-

mance from a brick veneer wall requires an adequate foundation, strong and well-braced frame wall, sound anchorage system, and the use of good materials and craftsmanship.

A cavity wall consists of two wythes of masonry separated by a continuous air space not less than 2″ wide. The individual wythes can be constructed of clay tile, brick, concrete masonry, or a combination of two of the materials. To connect the two wythes, metal ties are firmly anchored in the mortar. The ties should be $\frac{3}{16}''$ diameter steel rods, or the metal ties should have equivalent stiffness. One wall tie should be placed for each $4\frac{1}{2}$ square feet of wall area, with the wall ties staggered on alternate courses. The exterior wythe is always a nominal 4″ in thickness, while the interior may be 4, 6, or 8″ in width. To assure quality construction, the cavity should be free of mortar droppings and bridgings. A cavity wall should also be built with weep holes, so the cavity can drain.

The two most common types of solid masonry walls used in light construction are concrete masonry walls and single-wythe clay masonry walls. Concrete masonry walls are usually constructed from nominal 8″ × 8″ × 16″ units laid in a full bed of portland cement mortar. To increase the strength of the wall, the masonry units are laid in a lap bond and reinforcement is added to the wall (see Fig. 7-34). The reinforcement can include continuous reinforced concrete bond beam, reinforced concrete studs tied to the footing, reinforced concrete footings, and reinforcement placed in the horizontal mortar joints.

Single-wythe clay masonry walls are usually constructed from 6″ clay masonry

FIGURE 7-33      Basic types of walls

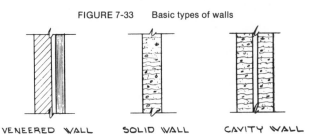

VENEERED WALL          SOLID WALL          CAVITY WALL

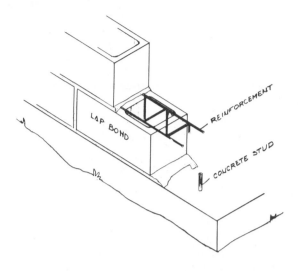

FIGURE 7-34     Lap bond

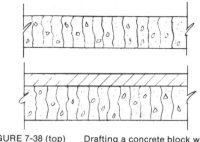

FIGURE 7-38 (top)     Drafting a concrete block wall
FIGURE 7-39 (above)     Placement of brick adjacent to
a block wall

units. These units allow for a maximum wall height of 9′ at the eave line and 15′ to the peak of the gable. The units are laid in common (half) bond with full head and bed joints. Single-wythe clay masonry walls are designed for use with furring strips, which provide a barrier to moisture penetration, permit the installation of plumbing lines and electrical fixtures, and permit the use of blanket insulation.

If the exterior wall has wood or metal siding, or if it is covered with stucco, two parallel lines placed 4″ apart are used (see Fig. 7-35). When brick veneer is used in combination with a wood frame, there are two techniques that can be used to represent the wall in the plan view. The first uses three parallel lines (see Fig. 7-36). The wall is a total of 10″ thick—6″ for the brick and 4″ for the wood frame. The brick portion of the wall is cross-hatched, and the wood frame can be symbolized by a series of light, straight lines.

The second technique uses four parallel lines (see Fig. 7-37). The wall is still 10″ thick, but a 2″ air space separates the brick and frame wall. The brick is 4″ thick and the wood frame is 4″ thick.

If the exterior wall is constructed of concrete blocks, it is indicated by two parallel lines 8″ apart (see Fig. 7-38). Light, wavy lines perpendicular to the two parallel lines and lead specks symbolize concrete blocks. If brick veneer is placed over the block, the wall thickness can be either 12 or 14″ (see Fig. 7-39). The wall thickness is 12″ when brick and block are placed back to back. When there is a 2″ air space between block and brick, the total wall thickness is 14″.

Once all exterior walls have been drawn in, the lines for the interior walls can be added to divide the plan into component parts. These walls are usually represented by two parallel lines 4″ apart.

## Doors, Windows, and Other Elements

After the interior walls have been drawn in, the doors, windows, cabinets, stairs, and other details are added. Each door or window opening has a letter or number placed adjacent to it to indicate size (see Fig. 7-40). Numbers are usually used for doors, and letters for windows.

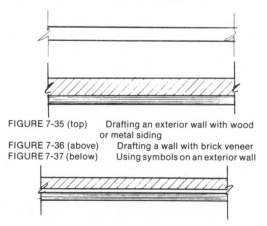

FIGURE 7-35 (top)     Drafting an exterior wall with wood
or metal siding
FIGURE 7-36 (above)     Drafting a wall with brick veneer
FIGURE 7-37 (below)     Using symbols on an exterior wall

FIGURE 7-40     Indicating door and window size

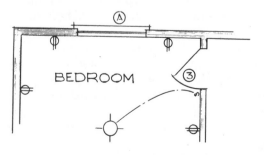

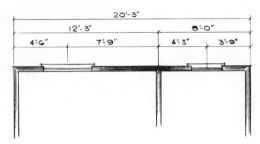

FIGURE 7-42      Placement of dimension lines

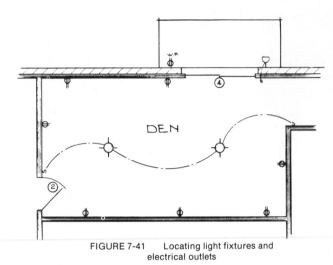

FIGURE 7-41      Locating light fixtures and
electrical outlets

The letters and numbers are then placed in a schedule that will give the size and type of windows and doors.

Appropriate symbols to indicate location of lighting fixtures and convenience outlets are usually placed on the floor plan (see Fig. 7-41). In some cases the electrical features are instead placed on the electrical plan.

## Darkening the Drawing

Once the plan has been drawn to scale with a 6H or 4H pencil, an H or 2H pencil is used to darken in the drawing, starting from the top and proceeding downward, darkening in all horizontal lines. Vertical lines can then be darkened, starting from the left-hand side and proceeding to the right-hand side. This technique will eliminate some of the smudging that is caused by repeated rubbing of the instruments over the darkened lines.

## Labeling and Adding Notes and Dimension Lines

When the drawing has been darkened, the rooms should be separately labeled and notes added. If there are two or more rooms that carry the same label, they should be identified by a number below the room label. This will eliminate confusing the rooms on the room finish schedule. Notes are sometimes added to show the direction of trusses, appliance location, cabinets, shelving, and any other special features.

To complete the floor plan, dimensions are added. There are several methods that may be used to dimension a wood-frame building; most often, three sets of dimension lines are drawn on the outside of the building (see Fig. 7-42). The first measures from the outside surface of the stud wall to the center line of windows, doors, and partitions. The second measures from the outside stud wall to the center of partitions. The third is an overall dimension line, measuring from outside stud wall to outside stud wall. Sometimes it may be necessary to place dimension lines on the inside of the building; in this case, care must be exercised so they do not interfere with other lines.

A brick veneer is also dimensioned by measuring from the outside of the stud wall, (see Fig. 7-43). However, some people prefer to dimension from the outside of the brick veneer.

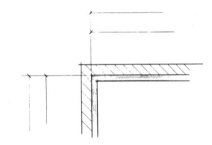

FIGURE 7-43 (above)      Dimensioning brick veneer
FIGURE 7-44 (below)      Dimensioning for a concrete
block building

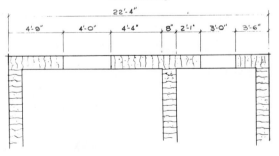

This technique is easier for the draftsperson, but can be confusing for the carpenter who lays out the frame wall.

Dimensions for a concrete block building are started from the outside corner and extend to an opening or intersecting partitions. The opening or wall is dimensioned and the dimension line is continued. A second dimension line, placed ⅜″ from the first, is used to give an overall dimension (see Fig. 7-44).

## Assignment:

1. Using an 18″ × 24″ or 24″ × 36″ sheet of tracing paper, draw a floor plan that has:
   a. Three bedrooms
   b. Two baths
   c. Double garage
   d. Living room
   e. Dining room
   f. Kitchen with U-shaped cabinets
   g. Breakfast area
   h. Den
   i. Utility room
   j. Storage room
   k. 2,000 square feet of heated area
   l. Brick veneer
   m. Patio
2. Using an 18″ × 24″ or 24″ × 36″ sheet of tracing paper, design a bachelor's home that has 1½ baths, 2 bedrooms, a study, living area, kitchen, utility room, storage room, and carport.

The foundation plan is a plan-view drawing used in the construction of the foundation (see Fig. 8-1). It usually includes the size and shape of the foundation; size and location of footings; beams and pilasters; dimensions and notes; and the scale to which the foundation plan is drawn.

## FOUNDATION SYSTEMS

There are two basic types of foundation systems—spread foundations and pile foundations (see Fig. 8-2). Spread foundations distribute the weight of the building over a large area by means of individual footings, while pile foundations direct the weight of the structure through weak soil to a bearing surface that can withstand the weight of the superstructure. The spread foundation system is the most popular of the two, and can be divided into three general classifications: slab-on-grade, crawl space, and basement (see Fig. 8-3). All of these are being used in most areas, but the success of a particular classification is usually dependent upon geographic and climatic conditions and public acceptance.

### Slab-on-grade

In both warm and cold climates there has been a successful trend that involves placing a concrete slab on the ground, thus eliminating the need for floor joists, and wooden subfloor. The slab is supported by only the soil; or it can be supported by a foundation wall; or the slab and footing can be combined to form an integral unit (see Fig. 8.4). Regardless of how the slab is supported, it should rest on a well-formed bed that consists of a base course, fill vapor barrier, and reinforcement (see Fig. 8-5).

Fill dirt is used to create a near-level surface for the slab and should not contain any vegetation or foreign matter that might cause uneven settling. Once the fill has been placed and screeded to the proper elevation, it should be compacted so that settling and water penetration will be reduced and load-bearing characteristics will be increased.

The base course—usually sand, crushed

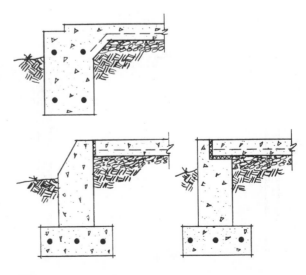

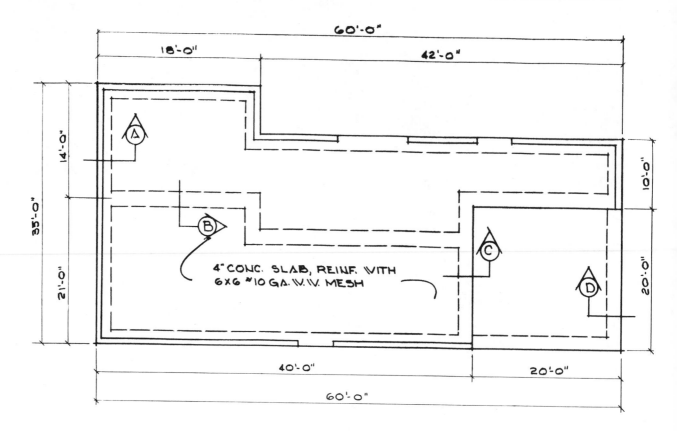

# FOUNDATION PLAN
### SCALE ¼"=1'-0"

FIGURE 8-1 (above)        Foundation plan

FIGURE 8-2 (below left) and 8-3 (below right)        Spread foundation and pile foundation; slab-on-grade, crawl space, and basement

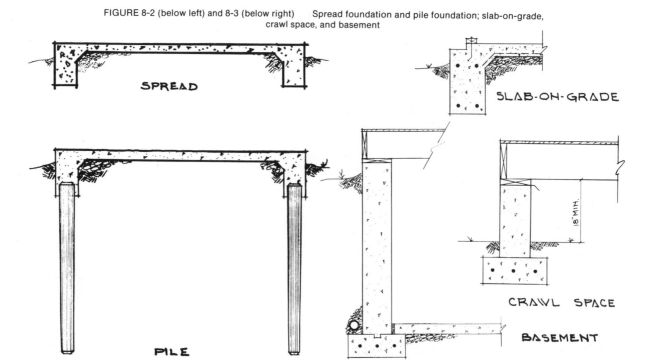

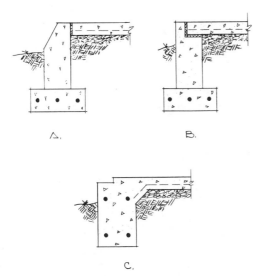

FIGURE 8-4     Techniques used to support the slab

FIGURE 8-6     Frost line

stone, or gravel—acts as a stop for moisture rising through the soil by capillary action. To be an effective barrier, the base course should be a minimum of 4″ thick and of limited capillarity. Once the base course has been properly laid, a polyethylene film is placed. The polyethylene acts as a vapor barrier, stopping any water vapor that might rise from the soil and through the base course. Without this, the slab could become damp. To strengthen the concrete slab, 6″ × 6″ No. 10-gauge welded wire mesh is usually placed over the vapor barrier. The wire is supported by metal chairs that elevate it to a point just below the center of the slab. If chairs are not used, the wire mesh has a tendency to settle to the bottom of the concrete, thus defeating the entire purpose of reinforcement. Concrete slabs have great compressive strength but little shear resistance; the reinforcement in the slab increases their strength.

The elevation of the top of the slab should be a minimum of 8″ above grade, and the footing should extend 6″ into undisturbed soil that provides adequate bearing. When the

bearing capacity of the soil is questionable, soil analysis or bearing tests should be conducted. The bottom of the footing or grade beam should also extend below the frostline established for the area of construction (see Fig. 8-6).

Perimeter insulation helps to keep a slab warmer, but it is often overlooked and not included in the construction process. Perimeter insulation of slabs can be installed either vertically or horizontally (see Fig. 8-7). When it is installed vertically, it should extend from the top of the slab to a point below the frostline. Placed horizontally, it should be over a vapor barrier, then covered with a polyethylene sheet.

Heating ducts, pipes, and coils are often embedded in the concrete slabs (see Fig. 8-8).

FIGURE 8-7 (below)     Perimeter insulation
FIGURE 8-8 (bottom)     Slab with heating duct
imbedded in it

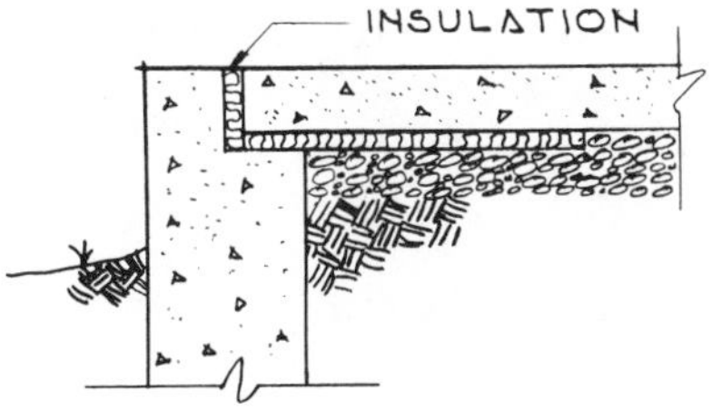

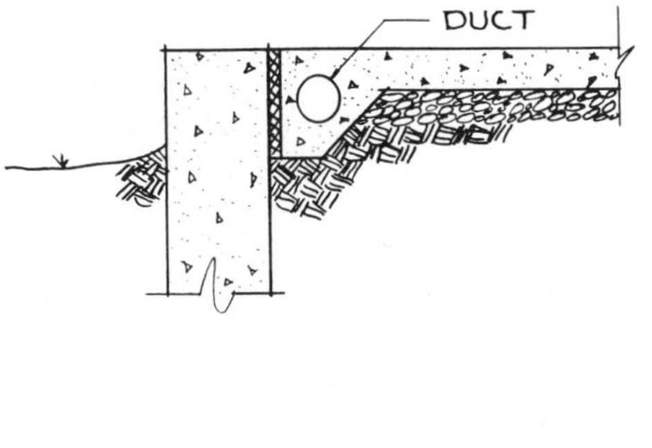

FIGURE 8-5     Slab bed

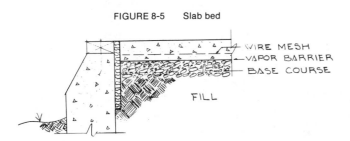

The heating ducts are usually constructed from metal, mineral fiber, wax-impregnated paper, ceramic tile, or concrete pipe. They should be completely enclosed in a minimum of 2″ of concrete; if they are placed at or below grade level, they should be of ceramic tile or concrete pipe with watertight joints. If the ducts are placed well above grade, metal or paper ducts with taped joints can be used. If the building is heated by the circulation of heated liquids through copper pipes, the pipes should be placed 3″ below the top of the slab.

## BASEMENT AND CRAWL-SPACE CONSTRUCTION

A basement or crawl space is constructed of load-transmitting elements such as foundation walls, pilasters, columns, and piers. The loads are transmitted to the footings, and are spread out over a large area. The footing is usually a concrete pad that spreads the weight of the superstructure and the weight of the load-transmitting elements. Concrete is usually used as a footing material because of its ability to maintain relatively high-strength qualities, its resistance to decay, and its dependability.

There are several methods used to construct footings; most are stepped at the base of the foundation wall, with the projection equal to one-half the width of the footing (see Fig. 8-9).

In light construction, very little calculation needs to be done in establishing load limits for the size of the footing. But if there is a need to calculate the footing size, both the dead and live load should be considered. The dead load is the load that is superimposed on the foundation system; it includes all stationary structural materials such as exterior walls, floor systems, cabinets, fireplaces, roof systems, and interior partitions. The live load includes the weight of objects or forces that are not stationary such as snow, wind, rain, people, and furniture.

The footing should extend 6″ into undisturbed soil and should be placed below the frostline. This is because some soils do not drain as readily as others—and any moisture that is retained in the soil may freeze. If the ground is saturated with moisture and the water freezes, the soil expands and begins to move. This reaction is called frost heave. If the footing is not below the frostline and water in the soil freezes, the foundation could possibly be tilted. The frostline varies considerably in the United States; in some areas it may be at 5′ and in some there is no frostline at all. In geographical locations where severe winters are experienced, it is usually recommended that the footings be placed 1½′ below the frostline to avoid the possibility of frost heave.

Reinforcement bars are added to plain footings to alleviate some of their shear and tensile weaknesses. The steel combined with the concrete furnishes the tensile strength needed to balance the compressive strength. When the footings are spread over a wide area, the reinforcement is placed perpendicular to the foundation wall, but in most cases the reinforcement rods are parallel to the foundation wall.

### Stepped Footings

When a structure is located on a steep grade it is often more feasible and economical to use stepped footings rather than other types (see Fig. 8-10). In the construction of the footing the vertical step should not exceed more than three-fourths the distance of the horizontal step; to obtain the optimum amount of structural value from the footings, the horizontal steps should be as long as possible. The

FIGURE 8-9    Sizing a footing

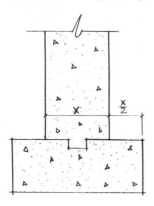

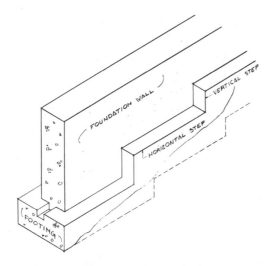

FIGURE 8-10     Stepped footing

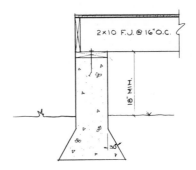

FIGURE 8-12     Flared footing

reinforcement for the stepped footings should act as an integral unit with the concrete and should be shaped to extend a minimum of 18″ into the horizontal step. For a structurally sound footing, the horizontal and vertical steps should be placed as an integral unit on undisturbed soil and well below the frostline.

## Column Footings

A column footing is an isolated or independent footing that supports a single column or post and carries a concentrated load (see Fig. 8-11). The footings should be at least 12″ thick and measure 2′ × 2′. If a column footing supports a light load, it could consist of nothing more than a concrete mat. However, for a heavy load, reinforcement bars should be placed longitudinally and transversely on the footing.

## Flared Footings

In some cases a footing is constructed by flaring the base of the poured concrete founda-

tion wall (see Fig. 8-12). The footing and the foundation wall are usually formed together, with the base projecting 30 degrees from the foundation wall. If this technique is used, the concrete for both the footing and the foundation wall should be placed at the same time. This particular system is popular in crawl-space construction, but has not gained wide acceptance in basement construction.

## Foundation Walls

The function of a foundation wall is to receive the load of the superstructure, transmit the load to the footings, and retard any moisture that might seep into the basement or crawl space. The three most popular materials used in the construction of foundation walls are concrete, concrete block, and wood.

For a foundation wall constructed of concrete and placed separately from the footing, a key should be used to help the wall resist any lateral pressures (see Fig. 8-13). If the height of a foundation wall is more than ten times its thickness, the wall should be reinforced with vertical reinforcement bars; if the length of the wall exceeds 20′, reinforcement with pilasters is necessary. The minimum thickness of a foundation wall should not be

FIGURE 8-11     Column footing

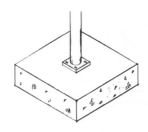

FIGURE 8-13     Placement of a keg in a foundation wall

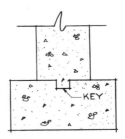

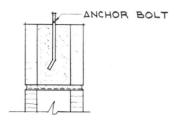

FIGURE 8-14    Placement of anchor bolts

less than the width of the wall it is supporting, but exterior walls of masonry veneer over frame construction may be corbeled 1″.

If concrete blocks are used to construct the foundation wall, they should be laid in a lap bond and with no two corresponding vertical joints. The joints should be completely filled with mortar and metal reinforcing placed on alternate courses. The metal reinforcing helps keep lateral forces from dislodging the foundation wall. To aid in the support of the foundation wall, pilasters are used every 25′ and the cores of the masonry units can be filled with concrete. Concrete blocks are available in a variety of shapes and sizes, but those used for foundation walls are usually 8″ × 8″ × 16″ or 8″ × 12″ × 16″. The actual size of an 8″ × 8″ × 16″ unit is 7⅝″ × 7⅝″ × 15⅝″. The ⅜″ variance allows for the mortar joint, thus making the distance from the center line of one mortar joint to another center line 8 or 16″.

To act as a termite barrier and distribute the load from the floor beams, the foundation wall should be capped with solid units called "half-solids." There are three basic techniques used to top a foundation wall: stretcher blocks with cores full of mortar; solid blocks; and 4″ thick units. If a stretcher block is used, a piece of metal lath is placed under the top course and the cores are filled with mortar. A solid-top block is the same size as a regular unit, but it has a 4″ solid top.

To tie the frame structure to the foundation system, anchor bolts are placed in the cores of the masonry units and the cores are filled with mortar (see Fig. 8-14). If the foundation wall is constructed of concrete, anchor bolts are embedded in the freshly placed concrete. The bolts should be placed on 8′ centers, and each sill member should have a minimum of two anchor bolts securing it to the foundation wall.

The foundation wall can also be constructed of wood; this is a relatively new concept in the construction industry (see Fig. 8-15). A typical foundation wall is constructed of 2 × 4 studs spaced on 16″ centers and sheathed with pressure-treated plywood. (The structural requirements for vertical framing plates and footings are shown in Table 8-1). If the studs are spaced 16″ on center, the frame can be covered with ½″ plywood, but if they are spaced 24″ on center, ⅝″ plywood should be used. (The structural requirements for plywood are shown in Table 8-2.)

When the plywood panels are placed, there should be a ⅛″ space between them to allow for possible expansion. The space will later be filled with a sealant. Once the panels are in place, a 6-mil polyethylene film is put below the grade portion of the treated plywood wall. A treated strip is then nailed over the intersection of the plywood and polyethylene and the joint between the strips and plywood panel are caulked with a suitable construction adhesive. Once the panels are constructed, they are nailed to a wood footing. The footings for a wood frame are 2 × 6s or 2 × 8s, and for brick veneer 2 × 10s or 2 × 12s.

If the foundation wall is constructed of concrete or concrete blocks, it should be damp-proofed to prevent the entry of any moisture into the basement (see Fig. 8-16). There are several techniques that can be used to do this, but the three used most often are:

□ Covering the foundation wall with polyethylene

FIGURE 8-15    All-weather wood foundation system

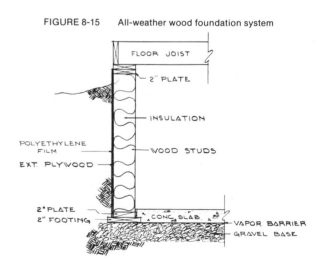

**TABLE 8-1 MINIMUM STRUCTURAL REQUIREMENTS FOR EXTERIOR FOUNDATION WALL FRAMING**
2,000 lbs per sq ft allowable soil bearing pressure, 30 lbs per cu ft soil equivalent fluid density

| House Width (Feet) | Number of Stories | Height of Fill (Inches) | *Roof—40 PSF Live, Ceiling—10 PSF Live / 1st Floor—50 PSF Live and Dead / 2nd Floor—50 PSF Live and Dead* | | | | *Roof—30 PSF Live, Ceiling—10 PSF Live / 1st Floor—50 PSF Live and Dead / 2nd Floor-50 PSF Live and Dead* | | | |
|---|---|---|---|---|---|---|---|---|---|---|
| | | | Lumber Species and Grade | Stud and Plate Size (Nominal) | Stud Spacing (Inches) | Size of Footing (Nominal) | Lumber Species and Grade | Stud and Plate Size (Nominal) | Stud Spacing (Inches) | Size of Footing (Nominal) |
| | | | *Basement Construction* | | | | | | | |
| 24 to 28 | 1 | 24 | C / B | 2×4 / 2×4 | 12 / 16 | 2×8 / 2×8 | C | 2×4 | 16 | 2×6 |
| | | 48 | C | 2×6 | 16 | 2×8 | B / C | 2×4 / 2×6 | 12 / 16 | 2×6 / 2×8 |
| | | 72 | B / A | 2×6 / 2×6 | 12 / 16 | 2×8 / 2×8 | B / A | 2×6 / 2×6 | 12 / 16 | 2×8 / 2×8 |
| | | 86 | A | 2×6 | 12 | 2×8 | A | 2×6 | 12 | 2×8 |
| 29 to 32 | 1 | 24 | C / B | 2×4 / 2×4 | 12 / 16 | 2×8 / 2×8 | C / B | 2×4 / 2×4 | 12 / 16 | 2×8 / 2×8 |
| | | 48 | C | 2×6 | 16 | 2×8 | C | 2×6 | 16 | 2×8 |
| | | 72 | B / A | 2×6 / 2×6 | 12 / 16 | 2×8 / 2×8 | B / A | 2×6 / 2×6 | 12 / 16 | 2×8 / 2×8 |
| | | 86 | A | 2×6 | 12 | 2×8 | A | 2×6 | 12 | 2×8 |
| 24 to 32 | 2 | 24 | C | 2×6 | 16 | 2×10 | C | 2×6 | 16 | 2×10 |
| | | 48 | C | 2×6 | 16 | 2×10 | C | 2×6 | 16 | 2×10 |
| | | 72 | B / A | 2×6 / 2×6 | 12 / 16 | 2×10 / 2×10 | B / A | 2×6 / 2×6 | 12 / 16 | 2×10 / 2×10 |
| | | 86 | A | 2×6 | 12 | 2×10 | A | 2×6 | 12 | 2×10 |
| | | | *Crawl-Space Construction* | | | | | | | |
| 24 to 28 | 1 | Max. 2-ft difference in outside and inside fill height | B / C | 2×4 / 2×6 | 16 / 16 | 2×8 / 2×8 | B / C | 2×4 / 2×6 | 16 / 16 | 2×6 / 2×6 |
| 29 to 32 | 1 | | B / C / B | 2×4 / 2×6 / 2×6 | 12 / 12 / 16 | 2×8 / 2×8 / 2×8 | B / C | 2×4 / 2×6 | 16 / 16 | 2×8 / 2×8 |
| 24 | 2 | | B / C | 2×6 / 2×6 | 16 / 12 | 2×8 / 2×8 | B / C | 2×6 / 2×6 | 16 / 12 | 2×8 / 2×8 |
| 25 to 32 | 2 | | B / C | 2×6 / 2×6 | 16 / 12 | 2×10 / 2×10 | B / C | 2×6 / 2×6 | 16 / 12 | 2×10 / 2×10 |

*Uniform Load Conditions*

TABLE 8-2    MINIMUM PLYWOOD GRADE AND THICKNESS FOR BASEMENT CONSTRUCTION
(30 cu ft equivalent fluid density)

| Height of fill (Inches) | Stud Spacing (Inches) | Face grain across studs[1] | | | Face grain parallel to studs | | |
|---|---|---|---|---|---|---|---|
| | | Grade[2] | Minimum Thickness (Inches) | Identification Index | Grade[2] | Minimum Thickness[3] (Inches) | Identification Index |
| 24 | 12 | B | ½ | 32/16 | B | ½ (3,4,5 ply) | 32/16 |
| | 16 | B | ½ | 32/16 | B | ½ (4,5 ply) | 32/16 |
| 48 | 12 | B | ½ | 32/16 | B / A | ½[4] (4,5 ply) / ½ | 32/16 / 32/16 |
| | 16 | B | ½ | 32/16 | A / B | ⅝ / ¾ | 42/20 / 48/24 |
| 72 | 12 | B | ½ | 32/16 | A / B | ½[4] / ⅝[4] | 32/16 / 42/20 |
| | 16 | A | ½ | 32/16 | B | ¾[4] | 48/24 |
| 86 | 12 | B | ½ | 32/16 | A / B | ⅝ / ¾ | 42/20 / 48/24 |

[1]Blocking between studs required at all horizontal panel joints more than 4 feet below adjacent ground level.

[2]Minimum grade: A—STRUCTURAL I C–D: B—C–D (exterior glue). If a major portion of the wall is exposed above ground, a better appearance may be desired. In this case, the following Exterior grades would be suitable: A—STRUCTURAL I A–C, B–C, or C–C (Plugged); B—Exterior Group 1 A–C, B–C, C–C (Plugged), or MDO.

[3]Where face grain is parallel to studs, all panels 5 ply except as noted.

[4]For this combination of fill height and minimum panel thickness, panels that are continuous over less than three spans (across less than three stud spacings) require blocking 2 feet above bottom plate. Offset adjacent blocks and fasten through studs with two 16d corrosion-resistant nails at each end.

NOTE: Plywood recommendations are based on APA grade-trademarked plywood.

□ Parging the wall with two applications of cement grout
□ Hotmopping the foundation wall with asphalt or tar

FIGURE 8-16    Dampproofing a foundation wall

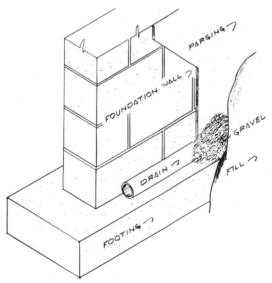

These three procedures utilize the same principle or technique as the vapor barrier in a slab-on-grade.

Other precautionary methods used to eliminate a damp basement include sloping grades around the perimeter of the building, and building a drainage system. Surface water often presents a problem to basements; the water should be directed away from the building by sloping grades, a minimum of 5 percent for a grassed perimeter and 1 percent when the area adjacent to the building is concrete. The grade provides a natural drain and helps in dispersing surface water from the area of the foundation wall.

Ground water is a result of water rising by capillary action and by variation in rainfall. One of the better methods of controlling ground water is to build some type of drainage system. A system constructed with 4″ tile laid in a base of wash gravel or crushed stone is most often used. The tile, or pipe, should have perforated openings along its length. It should have a slight fall so the water can be carried

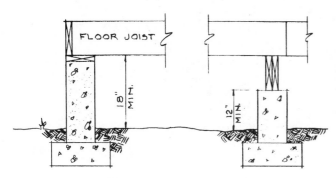

FIGURE 8-17    Crawl-space construction

from the foundation and into a storm sewer. To enable the water to flow freely into the drain tile, a backfill of wash gravel should be placed over the drain tile.

In crawl-space construction, the ground level should be a minimum of 18″ below the bottom of the floor joist and 12″ below the bottom of any girders, unless pressure-treated wood is used (see Fig. 8-17). All sod, stumps, and organic materials should be removed from the crawl space to deter termites.

## Pilasters

Pilasters are an integral part of most foundations walls and are used to support the ends of beams and to increase the rigidity of the wall (see Fig. 8-18). They are also used to transmit

FIGURE 8-18    Pilaster construction

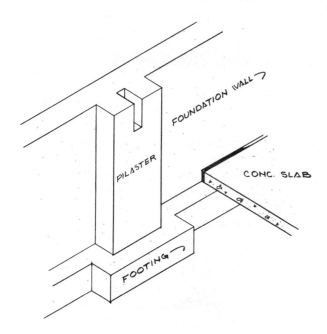

the load of the superstructure to the footings. A pilaster should be a minimum of 2′ in width and as thick as the foundation wall. Pilasters are placed on the inside of the foundation wall; they should be placed on 25′ centers, and provided under girders that are framed into the wall.

## Columns

A column, usually made of wood or steel, helps support the superstructure. The majority of columns are steel, although solid timber or laminated timber columns can also be used.

To help prevent decay, wood columns should be placed so that they will not come into direct contact with any moisture. One of the basic elevating techniques is to place a solid masonry base under the column. When a masonry base is used, it should not be less than 3″ above the finish floor.

Columns should be firmly anchored to the floor so they won't become dislodged. They can be anchored by a dowel, a metal boot, a metal strap that has been attached to the floor, or by steel columns embedded in a minimum of 2″ of concrete (see Fig. 8-19).

## Piers

Piers are used to support girders and can be divided into two classes: exterior and interior. Exterior piers are subjected to compressive loads as well as forces produced by the wind. Interior piers are located within foundation walls and receive only compressive loads. Piers may be constructed of concrete, solid masonry, or hollow masonry filled with concrete (see Fig. 8-20). Unless reinforcement is added in the construction of the exterior pier, it should not be built over three times its least dimension. An exterior pier built of concrete or solid masonry may be built to a

FIGURE 8-19    Column anchorage

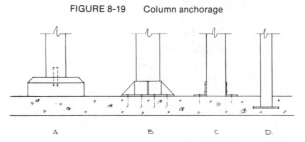

A                    B                    C            D

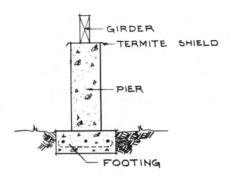

FIGURE 8-20    Pier construction

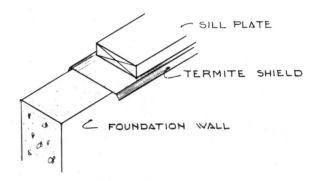

FIGURE 8-21    Termite shield placement

height of ten times its least dimension. However, if it is constructed of hollow masonry its height should not exceed four times its least dimension. In light construction piers should be spaced 6 to 8' on center and project a minimum of 18" above grade.

## Decay and Termite Protection

In the design and construction of a foundation system, attention should be given to the protection of wood structural units against decay and termites. These can be prevented by proper site drainage, segregation of the structural timbers from the ground, adequate ventilation, and termite barriers.

To allow a building site to drain properly, a sloped grade should be placed around the perimeter of the building. If there is any danger from surface or ground water, a drainage tile should be installed and the foundation wall damp-proofed. To properly segregate the structural timbers from the ground, a minimum of 18" should exist between the floor joist and ground, and a 12" minimum from the ground to timber girders or beams. These clearances allow visual inspection, provide a safe distance from possible moisture contact, and act as a termite barrier—a shield—visible or invisible—that cannot be penetrated by termites. Such a barrier drives the insects into the open where they can be detected and eliminated. They are usually metal shields, chemically treated soil, or chemically treated lumber.

A metal termite shield is usually made of copper or another noncorrosive material. It should not be less than 26-gauge and should be placed between the foundation wall,

column, or pier, and the sill plate or girder (see Fig. 8-21). It should be bent at a 45-degree angle, protrude a minimum of 2" from the edge of the wall, and set in a full bed of mortar.

If the foundation wall is constructed of hollow concrete blocks, termites can infest the sills by crawling through the openings. To prevent this, the blocks should be capped with solid masonry caps, or a termite shield should be placed along the top of the foundation wall.

One of the most effective methods of repelling termites is to treat the soil chemically. A chemical such as aldrin, benzene hexachloride, gamma, or chlordane is sprayed on the soil before the slab is placed or after the superstructure has been raised.

Wood is protected from decay and insects by water-borne preservatives, creosote, and oil-borne preservatives. Their effectiveness is dependent upon the type of chemicals used, the amount of penetration, the amount of retention, and the uniform distribution of the preservative.

## Pile Foundations

Piles are not used extensively in light construction, but in low-lying coastal area, and in some other areas, they are used to minimize settlement. Piles are vertical members that can be made from wood, concrete, steel, or a combination of wood and concrete. A point-bearing pile is a vertical member that transmits loads through soil that has a poor bearing capacity to a soil that can support the load (see Fig. 8-22). Such piles may rest on soil that is compacted by the driving of the piles.

A pile supported by only the friction between soil and pile is called a friction pile (see Fig. 8-23). In utilizing what is called skin

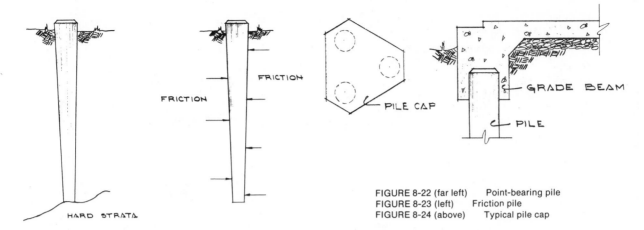

FIGURE 8-22 (far left)    Point-bearing pile
FIGURE 8-23 (left)       Friction pile
FIGURE 8-24 (above)      Typical pile cap

friction, the pile incorporates the use of the total bearing surface. A friction pile is usually used in cohesive soils, and a point-bearing pile is usually used in granular soils.

The load of the structure is transmitted to the piles by means of pile caps or grade beams (see Fig. 8-24). These are constructed of reinforced concrete and rest on a minimum of three piles, which should be a minimum of 10″ in diameter and spaced on at least 8′ centers.

## DRAFTING PROCEDURES FOR THE FOUNDATION PLAN

A foundation plan is usually drawn by placing a sheet of clean tracing paper over the floor plan and tracing the general shape of the structure. This procedure eliminates the necessity of scaling the foundation plan on a sheet of tracing paper. While the tracing paper is covering the floor plan, all load-bearing partitions should be located by means of light construction lines. These will be used to help locate interior footings, piers, and columns. The two sheets of tracing paper can now be removed from the drawing board. The sheet of tracing paper used for the foundation plan should then be aligned and retaped to the drawing board.

If a thickened edge slab is used for the foundation, hidden lines are usually placed

12″ from the outside edge of the foundation. These represent the footing. If the building is bricked, a solid line representing the brick ledge should be drawn 5½″ from the outside edge (see Fig. 8-25). The brick ledge extends around the outside perimeter of the building and is terminated in locations where there will be no brick, such as doors. With light construction lines that locate load-bearing partitions used as a guide, interior footings are then represented with dashed lines. If there are no load-bearing wall partitions, these footings are usually omitted. However, in areas that have problem soil, footings are placed on 15′ centers (see Fig. 8-26). This is sometimes called a Type III foundation.

If the design includes foundation wall and footing, two dark parallel lines are used to represent the foundation wall. These two lines are usually centered between the two hidden lines that represent the footing. Interior piers, columns, and footings are then located, with the previously placed construction lines used as a guide.

Two dimension lines on each side of the foundation are usually required to dimension the overall shape of the foundation plan (see Fig. 8-27). The first is used to locate any offsets in the foundation plan, while the

FIGURE 8-25    Drafting procedure for a thicker edge slab

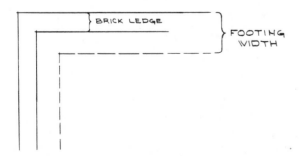

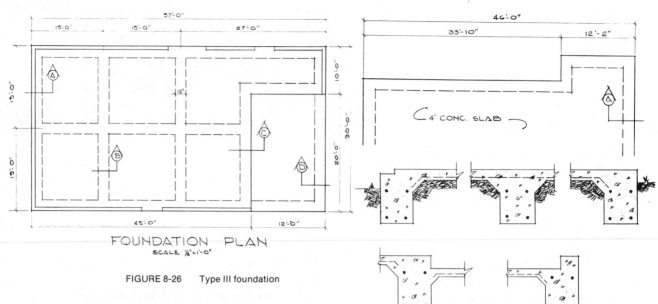

FOUNDATION PLAN
SCALE ¼"=1'-0"

FIGURE 8-26      Type III foundation

second gives the overall measurement. Other features such as footing size and location also need to be dimensioned. Notes are added to the drawing to call attention to any particular feature, and all the lettering should be done with the aid of guidelines.

Cutting-plane lines are placed on the foundation plan to indicate the location of details. These need to be placed in locations that show special features. Each time there is a variation in the construction of the foundation, a detail should be drawn (see Fig. 8-28).

FIGURE 8-27 (top)      Dimensioning the foundation
FIGURE 8-28 (above)    Footing details
FIGURE 8-29 (below)    Lettering a title

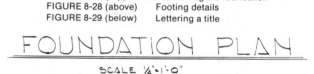

FOUNDATION PLAN
SCALE ¼"=1'-0"

Last, the foundation plan is darkened in with an H lead. A title should accompany the drawing—this is usually about ½" high and has the scale directly below it (see Fig. 8-29).

## Assignment:

1. Using an 18″ × 24″ or 24″ × 36″ sheet of tracing paper, draw a foundation plan for the detached garage in Fig. 8-30.
2. Using an 18″ × 24″ or 24″ × 36″ sheet of tracing paper, draw a foundation plan for the building in Fig. 8-31.

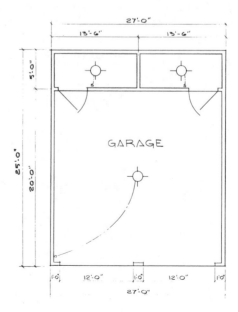

GARAGE

FIGURE 8-30 (right)      Garage plan

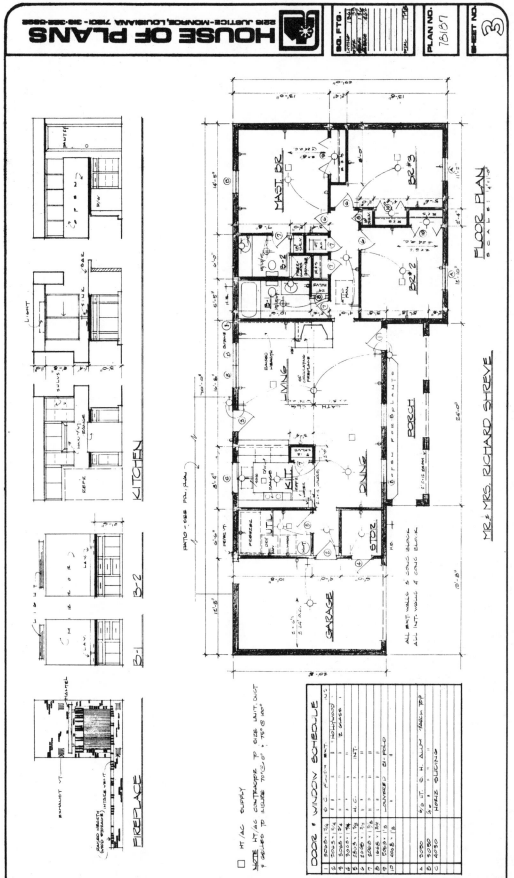

FIGURE 8-31    typical floor plan

A "detail" is used to better describe a particular feature (see Fig. 9-1). For an adequate description, the detail should be drawn to a scale larger than ¼″ to 1′0″; it should be fully dimensioned, have sufficient notes, and contain the correct symbols. Some of the features that are usually detailed are windows, doors, cornices, fireplaces, stairs, kitchen cabinets, and most connections.

## TYPICAL WALL SECTION _____

A typical wall section includes the footing detail, sill detail, cornice detail, and in some cases window detail (see Fig. 9-2). If all the exterior walls are the same, only one wall section is needed, but if there are construction variations, there should be more than one wall section.

A longitudinal section is a full section of a building (see Fig. 9-3). The cutting-plane line is imagined to pass completely through the building, revealing the interior details. Longitudinal sections can be taken in one or more locations, but usually only one is required. The section provides an excellent means of showing the various levels and vertical distances of a structure. It is especially helpful when a split-level, two-story, or story-and-a-half house is drawn. By using the section as a reference, headroom can be established, room widths can be determined, and stair calculations can be made.

### Footing Details

The first part of the wall section that is usually drawn is the footing detail (see Fig. 9-4). In some cases, the footing is only blocked in and detail references are referred to the foundation plan (see Fig. 9-5). The references should call out the sheet and detail numbers; this procedure eliminates the need of duplicating notes and dimensions that have previously been placed on the foundation plan.

The different types of footings and foundations were discussed in Chapter 8.

## SILL DETAILS _____

A sill detail is drawn between the wall frame and the foundation system. This detail is used

# 9
# Details

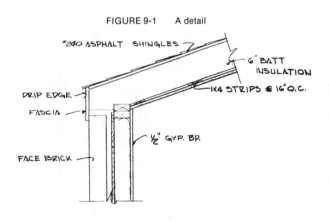

FIGURE 9-1    A detail

SECTION A-A
SCALE 1″=1′-0″

to show the relationship and sizes of joist, sill plate, header, and subflooring (see Fig. 9-6).

## Sills

Sills are constructed of nominal 2″ lumber and should be firmly anchored to the foundation wall with ½″ anchor bolts that are usually spaced on 8′ centers (see Fig. 9-7), although in some states they are required to be placed on much closer centers. If the foundation wall is constructed of concrete blocks, the anchor bolts should be embedded in 15″ of mortar, but if the foundation wall is concrete, they are embedded in only 10″.

9-2 If sills are placed on free standing masonry

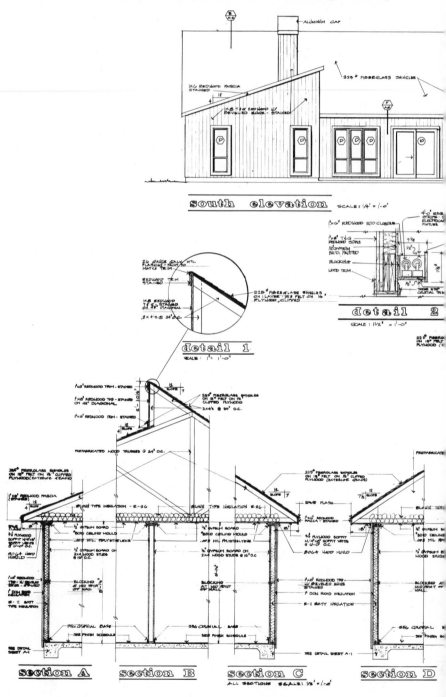

piers, they should be anchored with ½″ bolts embedded in the piers (see Fig. 9-8). The sill can be either solid or built-up, and should be designed to carry the load of the superstructure.

## Floor Joists

Floor joists are used to support the subfloor,

partitions, and other dead and live loads (see Fig. 9-9). They are usually made of nominal 2″ lumber placed on edge. However, aluminum and steel joists can be used and are finding a more acceptable market than ever before. To allow conventional sheets of plywood to be used as subflooring, the joists are usually spaced on 12, 16, or 24″ centers. Their spacing

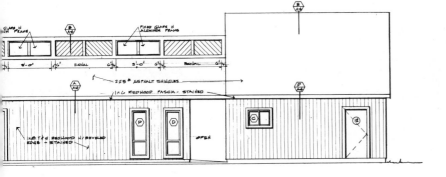

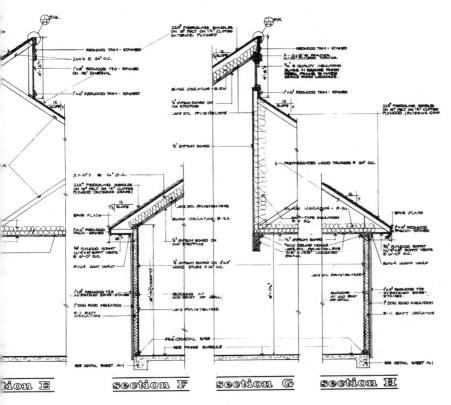

FIGURE 9-2 (opposite page and left)    Wall details

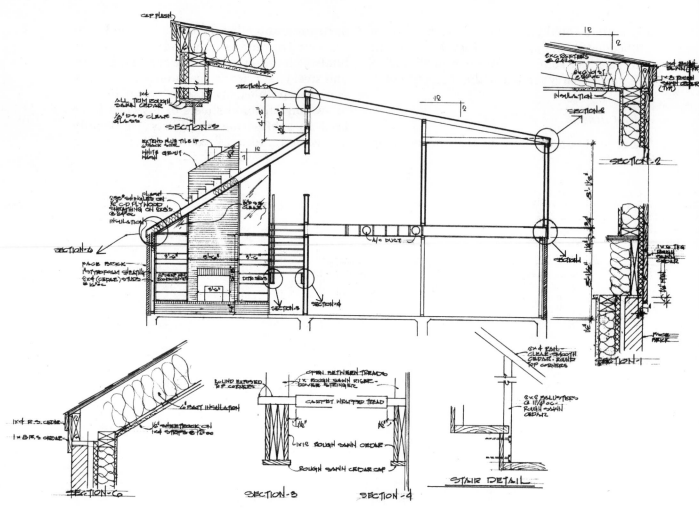

FIGURE 9-3 (above)     Longitudinal section

FIGURE 9-4 (below)     Footing details

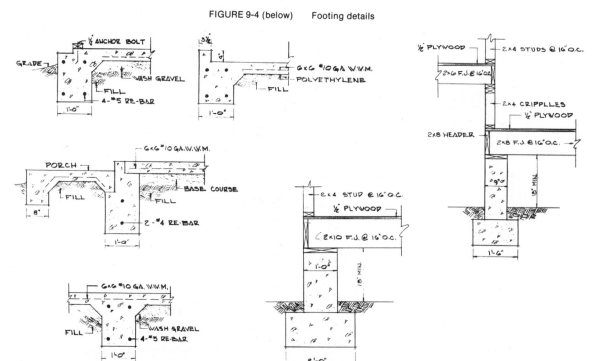

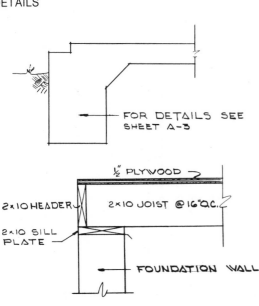

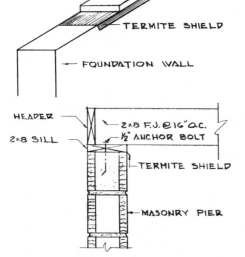

FIGURE 9-5 (top)        Blocked-in flooring detail
FIGURE 9-6 (above)      Sill detail
FIGURE 9-7 (below)      Sill anchorage

FIGURE 9-8 (above)      Sills on free-standing piers
FIGURE 9-9 (below)      Floor joist

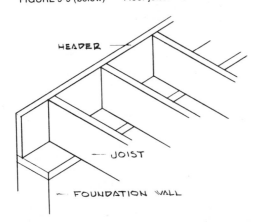

depends on the species of wood, grade of wood, size of the joist, and whether the subfloor is glued or nailed. Once the joists have been placed, a header joist is nailed to their ends. This is of nominal 2″ stock, and its width is equal to the width of the floor joists (see Fig. 9-10).

## Subflooring

To complete the floor frame, a subfloor is placed over the joists (see Fig. 9-11). The subfloor is usually of tongue-and-groove boards or plywood placed diagonally to the joists to increase the lateral bracing and to allow the finish floor to be laid either parallel or perpendicular to the joists. If plywood subflooring is used, it should be installed with the grain of the outer plies perpendicular to the floor joists. When the panels are placed, they should be staggered so that end joints in adjacent panels occur over different joists.

To increase the stiffness of the floor and reduce squeaks and nail pops, the subfloor can be glued. When it is bonded in this manner, the floor stiffness is increased up to 70 percent.

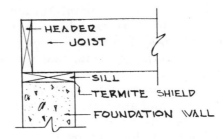

FIGURE 9-10 (above)        Header joist

FIGURE 9-11 (below)        Sub-floor application

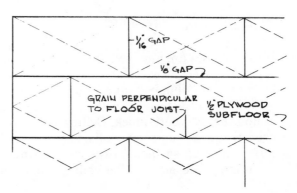

## WALL FRAME

A wall frame is constructed of three basic components: studs, bottom and top plates, and wall sheathing (see Fig. 9-12). Each of these pieces help to make a strong and durable wall frame.

### Studs

Studs are the most numerous framing members in a wall and are usually 2 × 4s or 2 × 6s placed on 16 or 24″ centers. In the past, studs were almost always 2 × 4s placed on 16″ centers, but recently there has been a trend to use 2 × 4s or 2 × 6s on 24″ centers.

### Plates

The studs are sandwiched between a top and bottom plate, which increase the stiffness of the wall frame and add additional height. If a bottom plate is placed on a slab, it should be pressure-treated so it will not decay.

### Wall Sheathing

Wall sheathing is used to increase the strength of the wall frame, prevent air infiltration, and provide a nailing base for siding. There are four basic types of wall sheathing: wood board, fiberboard, gypsum, and plywood sheathing.

Wood boards are usually tongue-and-groove or shiplapped and are covered by sheathing paper. The boards can be placed either diagonally or horizontally, and are nailed to the studs with 8d nails.

Fiberboard wall sheathing is made from wood pulp, sugarcane fibers, or cornstalks, and is one of the most popular types of wall

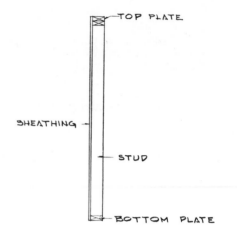

FIGURE 9-12    Wall frame

sheathing. Standard-size fiberboard panels are ½″ in thickness and 4′ × 8′ in width and length. They can be placed either vertically or horizontally, and are attached to the frame wall with roofing nails.

Gypsum sheathing is fireproof and is highly resistant to water absorption. It is available in 8′ and 9′ lengths and 2′ and 4′ widths. The panels are ½″ in thickness and have either "V" tongue and groove or square edges.

Plywood wall sheathing adds strength and rigidity to the wall frame. The panels can be applied either horizontally or vertically, although horizontal application is recommended when shingles are to be nailed directly to the sheathing. Horizontal application increases the stiffness of the wall-frame loads perpendicular to the surface. Vertical application increases the racking resistance of the wall frame. The panel thicknesses are ⁵⁄₁₆, ⅜, ½, and ⅝″ and can be selected from Table 9-1.

## THE CEILING FRAME

If roof trusses are not used, the ceiling frame is placed after the walls and partitions have been erected, plumbed, and braced (see Fig. 9-13). The ceiling frame is usually constructed of nominal 2″-width stock. Ceiling joists are used to tie the exterior walls together and form a nailing surface for the ceiling finish materials. The size of the ceiling joists is

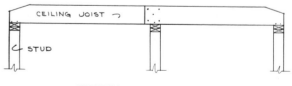

FIGURE 9-13    Ceiling frame

TABLE 9-1.  PLYWOOD SIDING DIRECT TO STUDS (APA SINGLE WALL)
Recommendations apply to all species groups.

| Plywood Siding | | Max. Stud Spacing (inches) | | Nail Size (Use nonstaining box, siding or casing nails) | Nail Spacing (inches) | |
|---|---|---|---|---|---|---|
| Description | Nominal Thickness (inches) | Face Grain Vertical | Face Grain Horizontal | | Panel Edges | Intermediate |
| **PANEL SIDING** | | | | | | |
| A-C EXT-DFPA B-C EXT-DFPA C-C Plugged EXT-DFPA MDO EXT-DFPA | ⅜ | 16 | 24 | 6d for panels ½″ thick or less; 8d for thicker panels | 6 | 12 |
| | ½ & thicker | 24 | 24 | | | |
| T 1-11 EXT-DFPA | ⅝ | 16 | 24 | | | |
| 303-16 o.c. Siding EXT-DFPA | 5⁄16 & thicker | 16 | 24 | | | |
| 303-24 o.c. Siding EXT-DFPA | 7⁄16 & thicker | 24 | 24 | | | |
| **LAP SIDING** | | | | | | |
| A-C EXT-DFPA B-C EXT-DFPA C-C Plugged EXT-DFPA MDO EXT-DFPA HDO EXT-DFPA | ⅜ | — | 16 | 6d for siding ⅜″ or less; 8d for thicker siding | 4″ @ vertical butt joints; one nail per stud along bottom edge. | 8″ @ each stud, if siding wider than 12″ |
| | ½ & thicker | — | 24 | | | |
| 303-16 o.c. Siding EXT-DFPA | 5⁄16 or ⅜ | — | 16 | | | |
| 303-16 o.c. Siding EXT-DFPA 303-24 o.c. Siding EXT-DFPA | 7⁄16 & thicker | — | 24 | | | |

NOTE: With sanded panels, only APA Qualified Coatings are recommended for a quality finish.

Reprinted by permission of the American Plywood Association.

determined by the span, species of wood, and the spacing of the joists (see Table 9-2). In most cases the joists are placed on 16 or 24″ centers.

TABLE 9-2.  PLYWOOD ROOF DECKING
Maximum allowable uniform live loads[1][2][3] (5 psf dead load assumed. Live load is applied load, like snow. Dead load is weight of plywood and roofing.)

| Panel Identification Index | Plywood Thickness (inch) | Max. Span (inches) | Unsupported Edge—Max. Length (inches)[4] | Allowable Roof Loads (psf)[5] Spacing of Supports (inches center to center) | | | | | | | | | | |
|---|---|---|---|---|---|---|---|---|---|---|---|---|---|---|
| | | | | 12 | 16 | 20 | 24 | 30 | 32 | 36 | 42 | 48 | 60 | 72 |
| 12/0 | 5⁄16 | 12 | 12 | 135 | | | | | | | | | | |
| 16/0 | 5⁄16, ⅜ | 16 | 16 | 165 | 80 | | | | | | | | | |
| 20/0 | 5⁄16, ⅜ | 20 | 20 | 210 | 115 | 65 | | | | | | | | |

TABLE 9-2. Continued

| Panel Identification Index | Plywood Thickness (inch) | Max. Span (inches) | Unsupported Edge—Max. Length (inches)[4] | Allowable Roof Loads (psf)[5] Spacing of Supports (inches center to center) | | | | | | | | | | |
|---|---|---|---|---|---|---|---|---|---|---|---|---|---|---|
| | | | | 12 | 16 | 20 | 24 | 30 | 32 | 36 | 42 | 48 | 60 | 72 |
| 24/0 | ⅜, ½ | 24 | 24 | 275 | 155 | 105 | 60 | | | | | | | |
| 30/12 | ⅝ | 30 | 26 | 450 | 250 | 175 | 100 | 50 | | | | | | |
| 32/16 | ½, ⅝ | 32 | 28 | 420 | 235 | 160 | 100 | 55 | 45 | | | | | |
| 36/16 | ¾ | 36 | 30 | | 320 | 220 | 140 | 75 | 60 | 45 | | | | |
| 42/20 | ⅝, ¾ ⅞ | 42 | 32 | | 360 | 250 | 155 | 95 | 75 | 55 | 35 | | | |
| 48/24 | ¾, ⅞ | 48 | 36 | | | 320 | 200 | 130 | 110 | 85 | 50 | 35 | | |
| 2·4·1 | 1⅛ | 72 | 48 | | | | 390 | 250 | 215 | 170 | 100 | 75 | 45 | 30 |
| 1-1/8 G1&2 | 1⅛ | 72 | 48 | | | | 315 | 200 | 175 | 140 | 80 | 60 | 35 | 25 |
| 1-1/4 G3&4 | 1¼ | 72 | 48 | | | | 340 | 215 | 190 | 150 | 85 | 65 | 40 | 25 |

[1]These values apply for STANDARD C-D INT-DFPA: C-C EXT-DFPA: STRUCTURAL I C-D INT-DFPA, and STRUCTURAL I C-C EXT-DFPA grades only. Plywood continuous over 2 or more spans; grain of face plies across supports.

[2]Use 6d common, smooth, ring-shank, or spiral-thread nails for ½ inch thick or less and 8d common, smooth, ring-shank, or spiral-thread for plywood 1 inch thick or less. Use 8d ring-shank or spiral-thread or 10d common, smooth-shank nails for 2·4·1, 1⅛ inch and 1¼ inch panels. Space nails 6 inches at panel edges and 12 inches at intermediate supports, except that where spans are 48 inches or more, nails shall be 6 inches at all supports. Space panel ends $\frac{1}{16}$ inch, and panel edges ⅛ inch. Where wet or humid conditions prevail, double these spacings.

[3]Special conditions, such as heavy concentrated loads, may require constructions in excess of these minimums.

[4]Provide adequate blocking, tongue and groove edges or other suitable edge support such as Plyclips when spans exceed indicated value. Use two Plyclips for 48-inch or greater spans and one for lesser spans.

[5]Uniform load deflection limit: $\frac{1}{180}$ th span under live load plus dead load, $\frac{1}{240}$ th under live load only.

Reprinted by permission of the American Plywood Association.

## ROOF FRAME

To better understand the construction of the roof frame, it is first necessary to discuss some basic related terminology.

Slope is a ratio of the vertical rise to the horizontal run (see Fig. 9-14). The ratio is expressed as *X* distance in 12′. If the slope is 4 in 12, the roof will rise 4″ for every horizontal foot. If the slope is not used to indicate the vertical rise of a rafter, the pitch is usually given. The pitch of a roof is the ratio between the vertical rise and the span. If a roof has a rise of 5′ and a total span of 20′, the pitch would be ¼.

FIGURE 9-14 Slope is a ratio of the vertical rise to the horizontal run

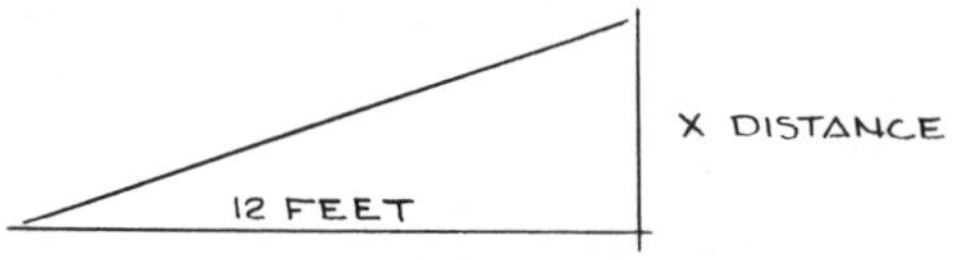


The span is the horizontal distance between the two outside walls and is considered to be the width of the building (see Fig. 9-15). The run is half the distance of the span. It is the horizontal distance covered by one common rafter.

The rise is a vertical distance measured

FIGURE 9-15 The span is the horizontal distance between two outside walls

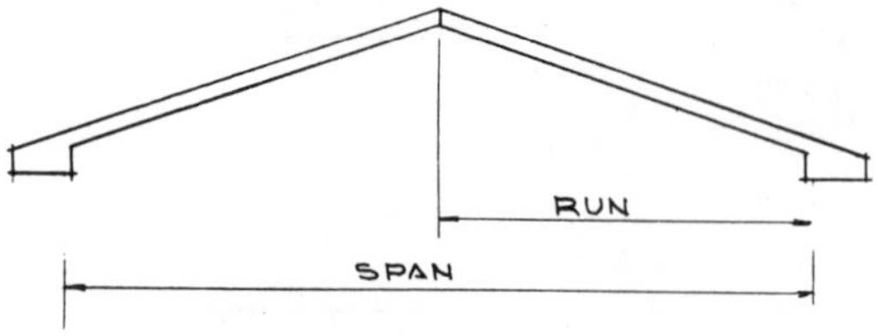

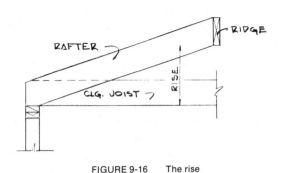

FIGURE 9-16    The rise

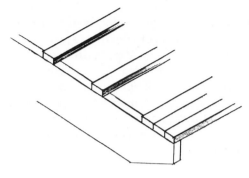

FIGURE 9-18    Spaced sheathing

from a point on the ridge that intersects a line on the common rafter (see Fig. 9-16). The unit run is always considered to be 1'. The unit rise is a vertical distance measured from the end of the unit run. In light construction the unit rise is usually 3, 4, 5, or 6".

## Rafters

Rafters are usually constructed from nominal 2" stock and serve as a nailing base for roof sheathing and roofing (see Fig. 9-17). Roof sheathing is used to provide a covering or skin over the roof frame. It also increases the structural rigidity of the roof frame, provides a nailing base for roofing materials, distributes live loads to the framing members, and provides insulation. There are three basic types of roof sheathing used in light construction: spaced sheathing, plywood sheathing, and nominal 1"-thick boards.

## Sheathing

Spaced sheathing is primarily used when wood shakes are used as a roof covering (see

Fig. 9-18). The sheathing consists of 1 × 4s spaced on centers equal to the weather exposure of the wood shakes. However, the sheathing should not be placed on centers greater than 10".

Plywood sheathing is used extensively in light construction, because the large panels go down fast and cover a large area. The thickness of the plywood and the spacing of the framing members should conform to Table 9-2. As the panels are placed, the joints should be staggered, with a $\frac{1}{16}$" space left at all end joints and a $\frac{1}{8}$" space at all edge joints.

Nominal 1"-thick boards are usually 6 to 8" in width and should be placed perpendicular to the framing members. To provide adequate support for the roofing they should be laid close together and are usually shiplapped or tongue-and-grooved.

## Underlayment

In new construction, if the roof is pitched more than 3" per foot, 15-pound asphalt-saturated felt should be placed directly over the roof sheathing (see Fig. 9-19). The felt is

FIGURE 9-17    Rafter

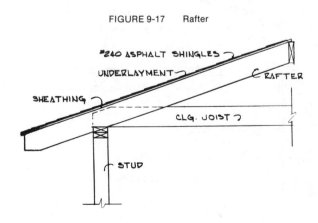

FIGURE 9-19    Underlayment application

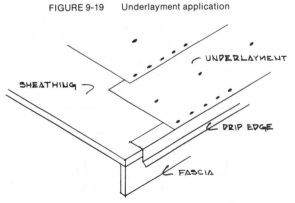

available in 36″-wide rolls, weighs approximately 15 pounds per 108 square feet, and will cover approximately 400 square feet per roll. A heavier felt than No. 15 or a covering of some other material should not be used. Felt that is too heavy acts as a vapor barrier, allows accumulation of moisture between roof sheathing and underlayment, and could lead to the decay of the roof sheathing and could result in structural damage to the framing members.

Underlayment serves a threefold purpose: it acts as a primary barrier against moisture penetration until the shingles can be placed; it acts as a secondary barrier against moisture penetration once the shingles have been placed; and it acts as a buffer between the resinous areas on the roof sheathing and the asphalt shingles.

### Roof Covering

There are several different types of roof coverings that can be used in residential construction; the two most common are asphalt shingles and wood shakes or shingles. Because of their fire-resistant quality, color, and style, asphalt shingles are often preferred over wood shakes.

Although wood shakes and shingles are not as popular as asphalt shingles, they have been successfully used for many years and are strong, provide good insulation, are wind-resistant, and have a pleasing appearance.

## CORNICE DETAILS

Cornice detail is used to show the construction details at the intersection of the wall, wall frame, and roof (see Fig. 9-20). The cornice is a part of the exterior trim that is used to complement a particular architectural style, insulate the eave line, and in some cases, to protect the sidewall from the elements.

The cornice may be either open or closed, but in most cases a closed cornice is preferred. The closed cornice is subdivided into two basic classifications: the horizontal soffit and the sloping soffit (see Fig. 9-21). A horizontal soffit is nailed to framing members that are placed perpendicular to the frame wall; a sloping soffit is nailed directly to the sloping rafter tails. The soffit is usually constructed of hardboard, plywood, or aluminum, but gypsumboard or plaster can be used. Most soffits are constructed with ventilation openings.

In addition to the soffit, the cornice includes the fascia, drip edge or shingle strip, rough fascia, lookouts, ledger, deadwood, frieze, and molding. The fascia is usually a $1 \times 6$ and is used to close the ends of the rafter tails. It may be either plain or slotted to receive the soffit. The slotted fascia is more desirable, for it

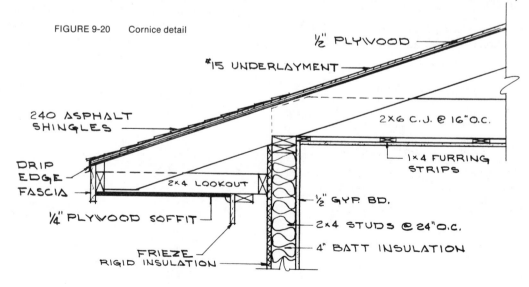

FIGURE 9-20    Cornice detail

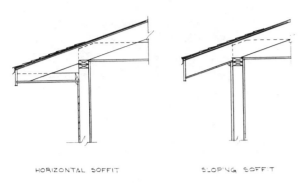

HORIZONTAL SOFFIT          SLOPING SOFFIT

FIGURE 9-21     Closed cornice

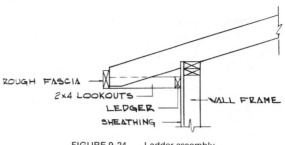

ROUGH FASCIA
2x4 LOOKOUTS
LEDGER
SHEATHING
WALL FRAME

FIGURE 9-24     Ladder assembly

often eliminates the necessity of scribing and cutting the soffit. Because the fascia is exposed to an excessive amount of moisture, a material that is highly resistant to decay should be used—usually cedar, cypress, or redwood is recommended.

A drip edge is placed under the underlayment and over the fascia; its purpose is to help shed water at the roof's edge (see Fig. 9-22). There are several different styles of drip edges, but most are formed from 26-gauge galvanized sheet metal. They extend over the roof sheathing approximately 3″ and are bent over the fascia to allow the water to drip free of the fascia. A shingle strip is used for the same purpose as a drip edge, but it is nailed to the finished fascia with 6d hot-dipped galvanized nails, aluminum nails, or stainless steel nails (see Fig. 9-23).

A rough, or false, fascia is sometimes nailed to the rafter tails to provide a straight and level nailing base for the finish fascia. To complete a ladder assembly, a 2 × 4 ledger is nailed directly over the wall frame. Lookouts are usually constructed of 2 × 4s and are used to support the soffit (see Fig. 9-24). They are placed perpendicular to the wall frame and are usually placed on 16 to 48″ centers.

Deadwood serves no structural purpose

other than to be used as a nailing base for the frieze and molding (see Fig. 9-25). It is usually constructed of 2 × 4s and is only needed for brick veneer buildings, because if plywood is used as siding, the frieze can be nailed directly to it.

Moldings are thin strips of trim that are used to cover the intersection of two surfaces (see Fig. 9-26). They are also used to enhance and complement a particular architectural style. Three basic types of moldings are used in cornice construction: cove, crown/bed, and quarter-round (see Fig. 9-27). Cove molding has a concave profile and is probably the most widely used of the three. Crowns/beds are used to cover large angles and are considered to be more decorative than cove or quarter-round. The basic difference between crown molding and bed molding is that crown molding is always sprung, while bed molding may be sprung or plain. A sprung piece of molding has its backside beveled to allow for a close fit. Quarter-round is a versatile piece of molding that is less decorative, but it is often used to cover the intersection of the frieze and soffit.

## Open Cornices

The open cornice has exposed rafter tails and exposed roof sheathing (see Fig. 9-28). The

FIGURE 9-25     Deadwood

FIGURE 9-22 (left)     Drip edge
FIGURE 9-23 (right)     Shingle strip

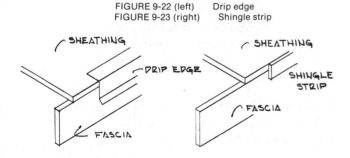

SHEATHING
DRIP EDGE
FASCIA

SHEATHING
SHINGLE STRIP
FASCIA

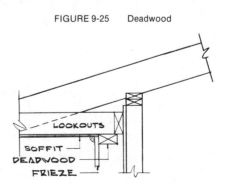

LOOKOUTS
SOFFIT
DEADWOOD
FRIEZE

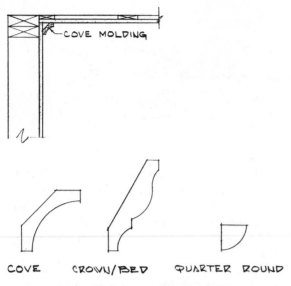

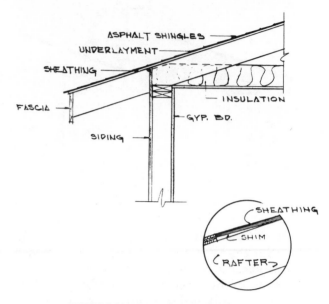

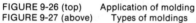

COVE          CROWN/BED          QUARTER ROUND

FIGURE 9-26 (top)      Application of molding
FIGURE 9-27 (above)    Types of moldings

FIGURE 9-28 (top)      Open cornice
FIGURE 9-29 (above) Shimed sheathing

sheathing should be thick enough to prevent the protrusion of roofing nails or staples on the exposed underside. If the sheathing over the open cornice is thicker than the roof sheathing, the intersection should be shimmed at each rafter to provide a flush joint at the

change of the plywood thickness (see Fig. 9-29). The open cornice may or may not have a fascia, but there must be a trim board placed between the rafters at the wall line. The trim board reduces the possibility of air infiltration, and it is used to close or finish the siding.

## DOORS

There are several different types of doors used in light construction; the most popular types are wood flush doors, panel doors, folding

doors, and sliding doors. Wood flush doors are popular as both interior and exterior doors, while panel doors are primarily used inside. Folding doors and sliding doors have gained wide acceptance in light construction and are often used as closet doors or room dividers.

FIGURE 9-30 (left)     Wood flush door
FIGURE 9-31 (right)    Panel door

### Wood Flush Doors

Wood flush doors are available in a wide variety of solid and hollow-core construction, and in wood, hardboard, and plastic-veneered faces (see Fig. 9-30). The core construction and veneered materials vary, but some of the more popular doors have glued block cores, mat-formed composition cores, hollow ladder cores, and hollow mesh or cellular cores.

### Panel Doors

A panel door is constructed of rails and stiles with panels of plywood, hardboard, or solid stock inserted between them (see Fig. 9-31).

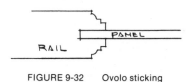

FIGURE 9-32    Ovolo sticking

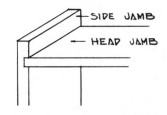

FIGURE 9-34    Connection of head and side jambs

Most rails and stiles of panel doors have ovolo sticking (see Fig. 9-32). If glass inserts are used, the glass bead should be ovolo to match the sticking. Glazing is accomplished by running a bead of glazing or adhesive compound ⅛″ in diameter around the perimeter of the glass rabbet. Wood glass beads are then placed to hold the glass in the proper position.

### Jamb Units

Door jambs are used to close the interior of rough openings and are also used to receive the hinges and strike plate for the door. Door jambs vary in design and do not lend themselves to rigid standardization in the methods of construction, but adjustable jamb units (split jambs) and nonadjustable jamb units are two common types (see Fig. 9-33).

The adjustable jamb unit has two jamb members that are fitted together with an accurately machined rabbet along the two adjoining edges. A doorstop is fastened at the intersection of the two jambs to hold the door. In some cases the jamb members are fitted together with metal pins extending into the adjoining edges. The pins are usually spaced on 12″ centers and should not be more than 8″ from each end. The jamb sections are accurately bored for proper alignment of the jamb

faces. The pins should be approximately 3/16″ in diameter, with a drive fit into one jamb section and a movable snug fit into the adjacent jamb.

A nonadjustable jamb unit has a single jamb member the full width of the rough opening. The casing may be fastened to one side of the jamb only, and furnished with the other side loose, or the casing can be furnished loose for both sides.

The side jamb and the head jamb are connected by a dado joint at least 3/16″ deep (see Fig. 9-34). The width of the dado should not be more than 1/32″ wider than the receiving member. The head and side jambs are fastened together by means of box nails placed in each end of the head jamb.

### Casing

To cover the joint between the jamb and the rough opening, a casing is placed around the head and side jambs (see Fig. 9-35). The casing should be a minimum of ¼″ thick where it is fastened to the jamb and 9/16″ at its thickest part. To connect the side casing to the head casing, the two pieces of trim should be mitered accurately so that the finished joint will be true and tight, with faces in alignment. The casing should be set in 3/16″ for the face of the jamb, and secured with finishing nails.

FIGURE 9-33    Jamb units: (left) split jamb;
(right) non-adjustable jamb

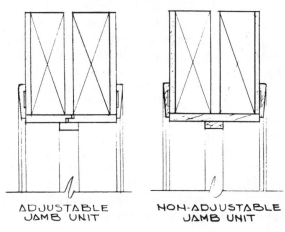

ADJUSTABLE
JAMB UNIT            NON-ADJUSTABLE
JAMB UNIT

FIGURE 9-35    Placement of a casing

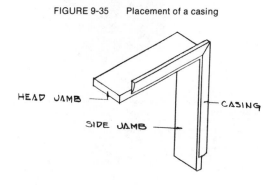

## WINDOWS

There are many window styles; in most cases they fall into one of three basic classifications: swinging, sliding, and fixed (see Fig. 9-36). Swinging windows can be hinged vertically or horizontally. If they are hinged on a vertical side they are called casement windows, but if they are hinged on the top or bottom they are called awning or hopper windows. Sliding windows usually include single-hung and double-hung windows.

### Window Parts

A window is made up of several different parts (see Fig. 9-37). The sash holds the glass. Other parts include jamb liners, anchoring flanges, glass, and weatherstripping.

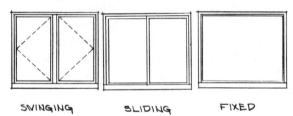

SWINGING        SLIDING        FIXED

FIGURE 9-36 (above)       Window styles

FIGURE 9-37 (below)       Typical window parts

**FEATURES**

1. **FRAME** / Exposed exterior wood members are rigid vinyl covered; color — off-white.

2. **SASH** / Wood core, completely covered and sealed with rigid vinyl; color—off-white.

3. **WEATHERSTRIPPING** / Spring tension rigid vinyl; factory applied.

4. **GLASS STOP** / Rigid vinyl; snap-in feature completely seals where flexible vinyl tip meets glass. Easily removed and replaced for reglazing sash.

5. **GLAZING** / Select quality welded insulating glass; Twindow® or Thermopane®, eliminates need of storm panel; two less glass surfaces to clean.

6. **FLASHING** / Continuation of the rigid vinyl covering on frame forms perimeter flashing and anchoring fin.

7. **INSIDE STOP** / Ponderosa Pine; can be finished to match interior.

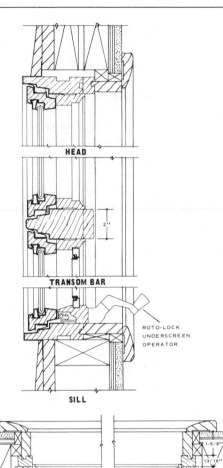

HEAD

TRANSOM BAR

ROTO-LOCK
UNDERSCREEN
OPERATOR

SILL

JAMB                    JAMB

FIGURE 9-38 (top)       Window head and sill details
FIGURE 9-39 (above)     Plan section

The window details on architectural drawings indicate how the individual parts fit together. The head and sill detail is a full section taken longitudinally through the window (see Fig. 9-38). In addition, a plan section is often drawn to show the relationship of sash to the side jambs (see Fig. 9-39). Mullion details are also used to show how multiple units are joined (see Fig. 9-40).

Most detail catalogs also show the basic sizes of the individual windows in elevation (see Fig. 9-41). Included in the elevation size is the unit dimension, rough opening, sash opening, and the unobstructed glass sizes.

## TYPICAL MULTIPLE UNIT COMBINATIONS

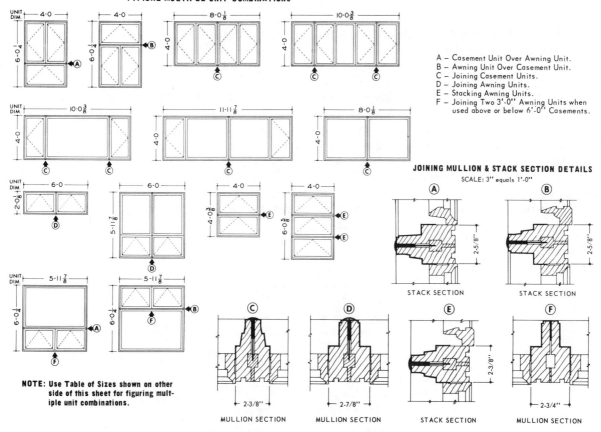

A – Casement Unit Over Awning Unit.
B – Awning Unit Over Casement Unit.
C – Joining Casement Units.
D – Joining Awning Units.
E – Stacking Awning Units.
F – Joining Two 3'-0" Awning Units when used above or below 6'-0" Casements.

### JOINING MULLION & STACK SECTION DETAILS
SCALE: 3" equals 1'-0"

**NOTE:** Use Table of Sizes shown on other side of this sheet for figuring multiple unit combinations.

FIGURE 9-40 (above)    Mullion detail

FIGURE 9-41 (below)    Individual window sizes

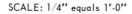
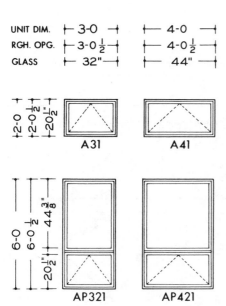
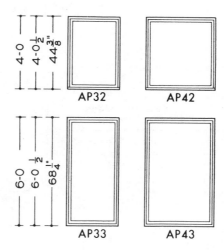

SCALE: 1/4" equals 1'-0"

| | | |
|---|---|---|
| UNIT DIM. | 3-0 | 4-0 |
| RGH. OPG. | 3-0½ | 4-0½ |
| GLASS | 32" | 44" |

A31    A41

AP321    AP421

AP32    AP42

AP33    AP43

**NOTE:** Do not use unit dimensions shown here for figuring multiple unit combinations. Use table of sizes on sheet P-7A, which are exact unit dimensions.

## CABINET DETAILS

The cabinet details may include a section and an elevation of the cabinets (see Fig. 9-42). A section is drawn only if there is a cabinet perpendicular to the cabinet that is in elevation; it gives only the basic outline of the cabinet and the vertical dimensions. The elevations are used to show location of appliances, direction of door swing, number and location of drawers and, doors, and in some cases a manufacturer's number may be indicated on the elevation.

Cabinets are considered to be one of the most important built-in features of a building, so to assure flexibility and maximum usage they should be carefully designed and properly constructed.

The base unit is usually built to a height of 36″ and a width of 24″. Although these dimensions may vary, they are the ones that have been generally adopted by most cabinet builders.

Wall units are usually 12″ wide and 30″ high, and are built much like base units. When the wall-hung unit is placed, there

FIGURE 9-42    Kitchen cabinet details

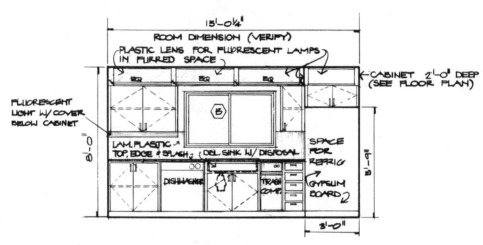

**ELEVATION   C**

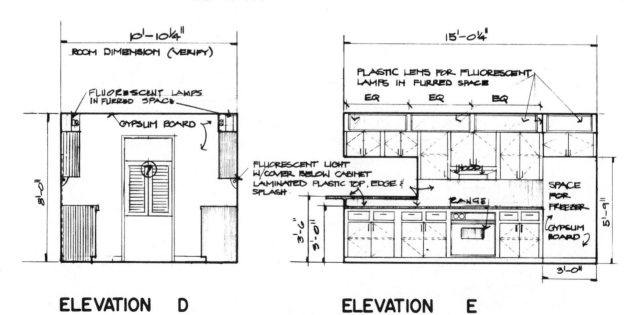

**ELEVATION   D**

**ELEVATION   E**

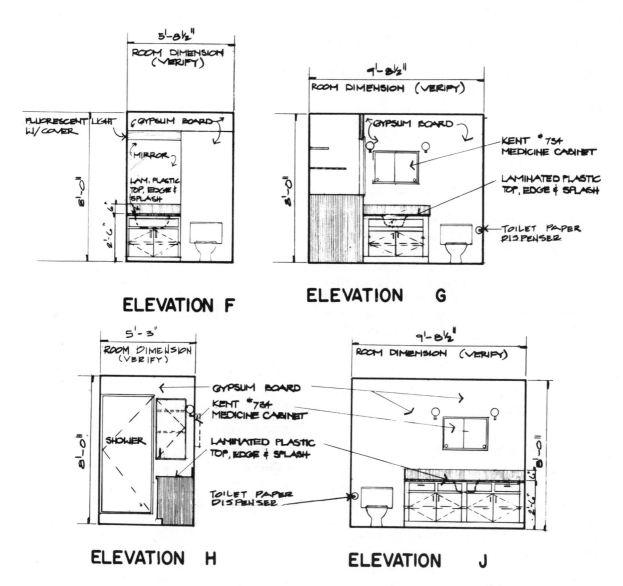

FIGURE 9-43    Bathroom cabinet details

should be a minimum of 18″ between its bottom and the top of the base unit. The space between the ceiling and the top of the wall-hung varies depending on the height of the wall, but in most cases the distance is 12″. The open area directly above the wall unit can be left open, but in most cases the ceiling is furred down to close the open area.

Bathroom cabinet details are drawn like kitchen cabinets, (see Fig. 9-43). The one exception is that the base cabinet is usually 30″ rather than 36″ high. The elevation should include a description of the vanity and the location of the mirror or medicine cabinet lighting, and a note describing the vanity top

covering. The bathroom cabinets are usually drawn to a scale of ⅜″ to 1′0″, but other scales can be used.

Doors and drawers used in cabinet construction are of two general classifications: flush and lipped (see Fig. 9-44). Flush doors are the most difficult to place, because they must be accurately fitted into an opening with only about ¹⁄₁₆″ clearance on each side. The lip door has a ⅜″ rabbet cut around the edges that allows for a slight tolerance in the fit. Because of the ease of fitting the lip door, it is usually the most popular. Cabinet doors are also designed in various styles, ranging from the simplest routed edge to an elaborate overlay.

To surface the cabinet, a high-pressure decorative plastic laminate is usually used. This is generally $\frac{1}{16}''$ thick and is highly resistant to stains, wear, and ordinary household chemicals.

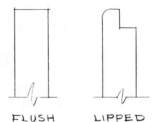

FIGURE 9-44 (right)    Types of cabinet doors

FLUSH        LIPPED

## STAIRS

The main stairway design can vary considerably; the most commonly used types are the straight-run, the winder and straight-run, or the flat landing-split run (see Fig. 9-45). A straight-run stair is a continuous stair that stretches from one level to another without landings or turns. A winder and straight-run stair is constructed with a maximum of two risers across the turn and a straight run of ten treads. The flat-landing-split-run type is commonly referred to as double L and U stairs and are constructed with a landing where the stair run is changed.

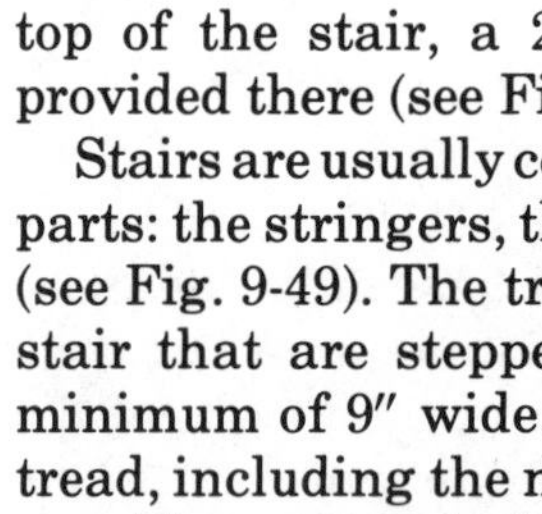

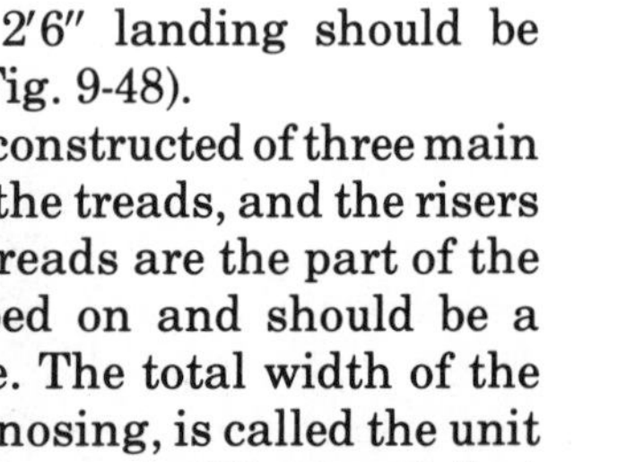

### Stair Terms and Minimum Dimensions

To avoid and eliminate possible dangers, stairways require careful planning. The main stair should be provided with a minimum headroom of 6'8", and for basement stairs, 6'4" or 6'6" (see Fig. 9-46). The headroom is the vertical distance from a line along the front edges of the tread to a parallel line that intersects the bottom of the header.

The main stair should be at least 2'8", clear of the handrail (see Fig. 9-47). The minimum clearance for basement stairs is 2'6". If a door that swings toward the stair is located at the

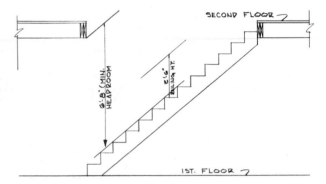

FIGURE 9-46 (above)         Minimum headroom
FIGURE 9-47 (below left)     Minimum width of main stair
FIGURE 9-48 (below right)    Minimum landing width

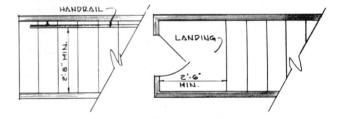

top of the stair, a 2'6" landing should be provided there (see Fig. 9-48).

Stairs are usually constructed of three main parts: the stringers, the treads, and the risers (see Fig. 9-49). The treads are the part of the stair that are stepped on and should be a minimum of 9" wide. The total width of the tread, including the nosing, is called the unit run. The nosing is the part of the tread that extends past the riser. The nosing can project $1\frac{1}{8}''$ to $1\frac{1}{2}''$ past the riser, but seldom should it project more than $1\frac{3}{4}''$. To complement or enhance a particular architectural style, the nosing can be finished in several different ways (see Fig. 9-50).

The riser is the vertical board that is placed directly behind the tread and should not exceed $8\frac{1}{4}''$. The height of the riser is called

FIGURE 9-45    Main stairway designs: (a) straight-run; (b) winder and straight-run; (c) flat-landing–split-run

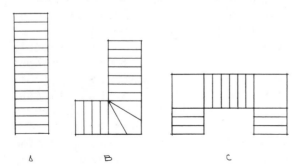

A                B                C

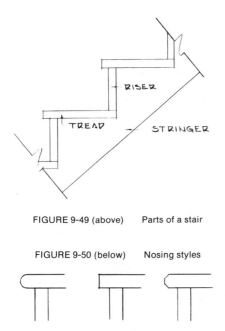

FIGURE 9-49 (above)     Parts of a stair

FIGURE 9-50 (below)     Nosing styles

the unit rise. The sum of all the risers is called the total rise, and the sum of all the treads is called the total run.

A stringer is the inclined piece of a stairway to which the risers and treads are fitted. The stringers are usually cut from two-by-stock sizes (e.g., 2′ × 4′, 2′ × 6′, 2′ × 8′, and so forth) and stretch from one level to another. The opening in which the stringers are placed is called the stairwell; it should consist of well-braced framing members.

To protect the occupants from falls, the stairs should have a continuous handrail on at least one side and railings at open portions of sides where the change of level exceeds 2′.

## Tread and Riser Design

One of the most important safety features of a set of stairs is achieved by assuring a proper relationship between the tread and the riser. To be sure the treads and risers are designed properly, there are three accepted rules that can be followed for calculating the riser-tread ratio:

□ The sum of a tread and a riser should equal 17 to 18″. For example, a riser of 7″ would require a tread run of 10″.
□ The sum of one tread and two risers should equal 25″. For example, a riser 7½″ would require a tread of 10″, because 7½″ + 7½″ + 10 inches = 25″.

□ When the tread width is multiplied by the riser height, the product should equal approximately 75″. For example, 10″ × 7½″ = 75″.

To calculate the number and size of treads and risers, the total rise is first divided by 7. The quotient is the number of risers required in the stair. If the quotient is a fraction it should be rounded off, because there must be a whole number of risers. To find the height of each riser, the total rise is divided by the number of risers. For example, if the total rise is 8′10″, the number of risers and height of the risers would be:

8′10″ (106 inches) ÷ 7 = 15.14 (15 risers)
106 (total rise) ÷ 15 (no. of risers) = 7.06
inches
(this is the riser height)

There will always be one less tread than the total number of risers. Therefore, if there are fifteen risers in a stair there will be fourteen treads. If the riser height is 7″ and the first rule is followed, the tread width should equal 10″.

To find the stairwall length, the tread width should be multiplied by the number of risers.

## Types of Stringer

The stringer is the supporting member of the stair and can be classified as housed, semi-housed, mitered, open, or plain.

A housed stringer has grooves cut into it so that it may receive the treads, risers, and wedges (see Fig. 9-51). The groove is cut wider at the back so that after each riser and tread is positioned a wedge can be inserted and glued in place. Once the treads and risers have been

FIGURE 9-51     Housed stringer

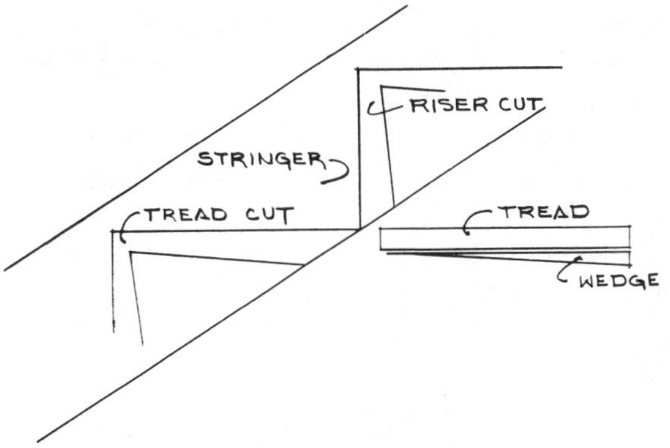

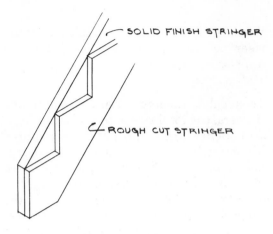

FIGURE 9-52    Semihoused stringer

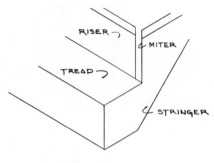

FIGURE 9-53    Mitred stringer

properly placed, glue blocks are usually placed on the underside of the stairway in each of the 90-degree turns created by the treads and risers. To further eliminate squeaks, the treads and risers can be rabbeted and glued into each other. An already cut housed stringer can be purchased or cut at the job site.

A semihoused stringer consists of a rough-cut stringer attached to a solid finish stringer (see Fig. 9-52). The treads and risers are nailed to the rough riser and tread cuts and are butted to the finish stringer. The finish stringer is usually built from 2″ stock and is wide enough to cover the intersection of the tread and riser and project at least 2″ past the tread nosing.

In a mitered stringer, seldom used, each riser is mitered into the stringer so that no end grain shows (see Fig. 9-53). The treads are nailed to the level cut and are allowed to project past the stringer a distance equal to the nosing.

An open stringer is used on open stairways and is constructed by allowing the risers and treads to project beyond the stringer. This particular type of stair construction is usually not recommended unless the stairway is in an inconspicuous place.

A plain stringer is cut only at the top and bottom ends. The treads are fastened to the stringer with cleats that are nailed to the stringer. The cleats should be a minimum of ¾″ thick, 3″ wide, and as long as the tread is wide. This particular type of stair is commonly found in basements and may be built with or without riser boards.

## CHIMNEYS AND FIREPLACES

There are two basic types of fireplaces—the single-faced and multifaced. The former has only one face that is open, while the latter may have two open faces that are adjacent, two open faces that are opposite, or three open faces—two long and one short. The sizes of faces are shown in Table 9-3.

A typical fireplace is constructed of several component parts—ash pit, hearth, firebox, damper, smoke shelf, smoke dome, and flue (see Fig. 9-54).

The inner hearth is the area where the fire is built; the outer hearth extends into the room and protects the floor from flying sparks. Because of the intense heat the inner hearth is usually constructed of firebrick.

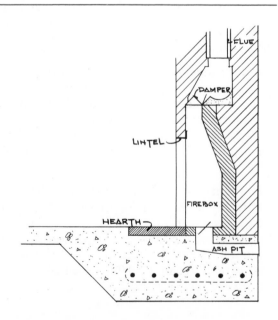

FIGURE 9-54 (right)    Typical fireplace

TABLE 9-3.    FIREPLACE AND CHIMNEY DIMENSIONS

| Area (sq. in.) | A | T | Length |
|---|---|---|---|
| ROUND FLUE LININGS | | | |
| 26 | 6″ | ⅝″ | 2′-0″ |
| 47 | 8″ | ¾″ | 2′-0″ |
| 74.5 | 10″ | ⅞″ | 2′-0″ |
| 108 | 12″ | 1″ | 2′-0″ |
| 171 | 15″ | 1⅛″ | 2′-0″ |
| 240 | 18″ | 1¼″ | 2′-0″ |
| 298 | 20″ | 1⅜″ | 2′-0″ |
| 433 | 24″ | 1⅝″ | 2′-0″ |
| 551 | 27″* | 2″ | 2′-6″ |
| 683 | 30″* | 2⅛″ | 2′-6″ |
| 829 | 33″* | 2¼″ | 2′-6″ |
| 989.5 | 36″* | 2½″ | 2′-6″ |

*Not available in some localities

Areas shown are net inside areas.

Wall thicknesses shown are minimum required.

Nominal flue sizes for round flues is interior diameter, outside dimensions for non-modular rectangular flues. Nominal dimensions for modular flue linings are actual dimensions plus ½″.

Verify with local manufacturers for available types and sizes of flue linings.

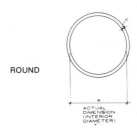

ROUND

| Area (sq. in.) | A | B | T |
|---|---|---|---|
| RECTANGULAR FLUE LININGS | | | |
| Standard | | | |
| 22 | 4½″ | 8½″ | ⅝″ |
| 36 | 4½″ | 13″ | ⅝″ |

| Area (sq. in.) | A | B | T |
|---|---|---|---|
| 51 | 8½″ | 8½″ | ⅝″ |
| 79 | 8½″ | 13″ | ¾″ |
| 108 | 8½″ | 18″ | ⅞″ |
| 125 | 13″ | 13″ | ⅞″ |
| 168 | 13″ | 18″ | ⅞″ |
| 232 | 18″ | 18″ | 1⅛″ |
| 279 | 20″ | 20″ | 1⅜″ |
| 338 | 20″ | 24″ | 1½″ |
| 420 | 24″ | 24″ | 1½″ |

All flue linings listed above are 2′0″ long.

Fireplace flue sizes: ¹⁄₁₀ area of fireplace opening recommended. ¹⁄₁₂ area is minimum.

Flue area should never be less than 70 sq in for fireplace of 840 sq in opening or smaller.

Flues for stoves and ranges and room heaters: 39 sq in minimum using rectangular flue, or 6″ dia. (inside) using round flue.

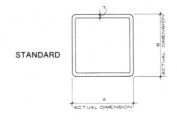

STANDARD

| Area (sq. in.) | A | B | T |
|---|---|---|---|
| RECTANGULAR FLUE LININGS | | | |
| Modular | | | |
| 15 | 4″ | 8″ | ½″ |
| 20 | 4″ | 12″ | ⅝″ |
| 27 | 4″ | 16″ | ¾″ |
| 35 | 8″ | 8″ | ⅝″ |
| 57 | 8″ | 12″ | ¾″ |
| 74 | 8″ | 16″ | ⅞″ |
| 87 | 12″ | 12″ | ⅞″ |
| 120 | 12″ | 16″ | 1″ |
| 162 | 16″ | 16″ | 1⅛″ |

| Area (sq. in.) | A | B | T |
|---|---|---|---|
| 208 | 16″ | 20″ | 1¼″ |
| 262 | 20″ | 20″ | 1⅜″ |
| 320 | 20″ | 24″ | 1½″ |
| 385 | 24″ | 24″ | 1⅝″ |

All flue linings listed above are 2′0″ long, also available, on request, in 12″ lengths.

Cross-section of flue lining shall fit within rectangle of dimension corresponding to nominal size.

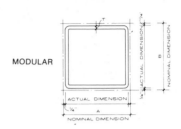

MODULAR

The ash pit is used to collect the ashes on the hearth. They are swept from the hearth through a pivoted metal trap door and into the ash pit. To remove the ashes from the ash pit a cleanout door is provided in the basement, or on the backside of the chimney.

The firebox or combustion chamber is the area where the fire is actually built. It should be lined with firebrick laid with thin joints of fire-clay mortar.

The damper is a device that is placed in the throat of the fireplace to control the flow of air. Its primary purpose is to close off the flue when the fireplace is not in use, thus reducing the possibility of air infiltration. A damper should be large enough to allow an unrestricted flow of air and a proper draft on all sides of the firebox, and it should be properly located to prevent the deflection of smoke into the room.

The smoke shelf is sometimes called the downdraft shelf; it is used to deflect any downdraft that might occur in the chimney. This is usually designed as a flat shelf, but it can also be built in a bowl shape—usually considered the superior design, because it is more effective in deflecting the air in the flue. The smoke shelf should be located directly under the bottom of the flue.

The flue is the open area in the chimney that allows for the passage of air and gases. A clay flue liner of the proper size is recommended for the proper function of a residential chimney. Flue sizes are shown in Table 9-3.

The chimney should be supported on a reinforced concrete footing and should project a minimum of 3′ above the ridge line, or be at least 2′ higher than any portion of the roof within 10′. The thickness of the chimney

should not be less than 8″; if the wall is less than 8″ thick the flue should be separated from the chimney wall. The flue liner should be of approved fire-clay and have a minimum thickness of ⅝″. If two flues are used in the same chimney, the joints in the adjacent flues should be staggered a minimum of 7″.

At the top of the chimney the flue should be allowed to project 4″ above the chimney. To provide drainage and to direct air currents, the top of the chimney should be flat or concave. It is preferable practice to form a cap at the top of the chimney—this forms a drip, allowing the walls to remain dry and clean.

Fig. 9-55 illustrates the specifications needed for a typical fireplace.

FIGURE 9-55    Fireplace specifications

FRONT ELEVATION

SECTION X-X

PLAN

HEARTH

**Construction Details of a Typical Fireplace**
See Notes and Table of Dimensions Below

## TABLE 1
### FIREPLACE DIMENSIONS, INCHES①
### TABLE 1 Continued

| Finished Fireplace Opening | | | | | | | Rough Brick Work and Flue Sizes | | | | | | | | | Steel Angle② |
|---|---|---|---|---|---|---|---|---|---|---|---|---|---|---|---|---|
| | | | | | | | New Sizes③ | | | | | | Old Sizes | | | |
| A | B | C | D | E | F | G | H | I | J | K | L | M | R④ | K | L | M | O |
| 24 | 24 | 16 | 11 | 14 | 18 | 8¾ | 32 | 20 | 19 | 10 | 8x12 | 8 | | 11¾ | 8½x 8½ | | A-36 |
| 26 | 24 | 16 | 13 | 14 | 18 | 8¾ | 34 | 20 | 21 | 11 | 8x12 | 8 | | 12¾ | 8½x 8½ | | A-36 |
| 28 | 24 | 16 | 15 | 14 | 18 | 8¾ | 36 | 20 | 21 | 12 | 8x12 | 10 | | 11½ | 8½x13 | | A-36 |
| 30 | 29 | 16 | 17 | 14 | 23 | 8¾ | 38 | 20 | 24 | 13 | 12x12 | 10 | | 12½ | 8½x13 | | A-36 |
| 32 | 29 | 16 | 19 | 14 | 23 | 8¾ | 40 | 20 | 24 | 14 | 12x12 | 10 | | 13½ | 8½x13 | | A-42 |
| 36 | 29 | 16 | 23 | 14 | 23 | 8¾ | 44 | 20 | 27 | 16 | 12x12 | 12 | | 15½ | 13 x13 | | A-42 |
| 40 | 29 | 16 | 27 | 14 | 23 | 8¾ | 48 | 20 | 29 | 16 | 12x16 | 12 | | 17½ | 13 x13 | | A-48 |
| 42 | 32 | 16 | 29 | 14 | 26 | 8¾ | 50 | 20 | 32 | 17 | 16x16 | 12 | | 18½ | 13 x13 | | A-48 |
| 48 | 32 | 18 | 33 | 14 | 26 | 8¾ | 56 | 22 | 37 | 20 | 16x16 | 15 | | 21½ | 13 x13 | | B-54 |
| 54 | 37 | 20 | 37 | 16 | 29 | 13 | 68 | 24 | 45 | 26 | 16x16 | 15 | | 25 | 13 x18 | | B-60 |
| 60 | 37 | 22 | 42 | 16 | 29 | 13 | 72 | 27 | 45 | 26 | 16x20 | 15 | | 27 | 13 x18 | | B-66 |
| 60 | 40 | 22 | 42 | 16 | 31 | 13 | 72 | 27 | 45 | 26 | 16x20 | 18 | | 27 | 18 x18 | | B-66 |
| 72 | 40 | 22 | 54 | 16 | 31 | 13 | 84 | 27 | 56 | 32 | 20x20 | 18 | | 33 | 18 x18 | | C-84 |
| 84 | 40 | 24 | 64 | 20 | 28 | 13 | 96 | 29 | 61 | 36 | 20x24 | 20 | | 36 | 20 x20 | | C-96 |
| 96 | 40 | 24 | 76 | 20 | 28 | 13 | 108 | 29 | 75 | 42 | 20x24 | 22 | | 42 | 24 x24 | | C-108 |

① See. Fig. A
② Angle Sizes: A-3 by 3 by 3/16 in., B-3 1/2 by 3 by 1/4 in., C-5 by 3 1/2 by 5 1/6 in.
③ New Flue Sizes: Conform to modular dimensional system. Sizes shown are nominal. Actual size is 1/2 in. less each dimension.
④ Round Flues.

## DRAFTING PROCEDURES FOR DETAILS

Details are used to show how individual structural members are fitted together; in most cases, they are drawn to ¾″ or 1″ scale so they can better describe a particular feature. Usually the first drawing of details is extremely light, with a 4H or 6H lead. Then, to complete the detail, light lines are darkened in and dimensioned, and notes are added.

In some cases details are drawn in isometrics so that they may be more readily interpreted. This is not a common practice, but it is becoming more prevalent with some architects (see Fig. 9-56).

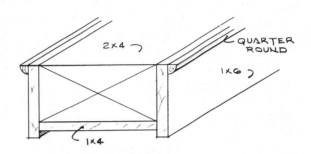

EXPOSED BEAM DETAIL

FIGURE 9-56    Isometric detail

## Assignment:

1. Draw a detail of a closed cornice with a horizontal soffit.
2. Draw the jamb details for a flush door.
3. Draw a typical wall section.
4. Draw the details for a typical set of kitchen cabinets.

# 10
# Elevations

An elevation is a modified orthographic drawing that shows one side of an object (see Fig. 10-1). Most buildings require four elevations, one of each side. Interior elevations of a building can be shown, but in most cases they are considered to be details.

The surface materials used on elevations are indicated by symbol or notes. These materials can include brick, asphalt shingles, stone, plywood, shingle siding, and a variety of other exterior finishing materials. Grade lines, floor and ceiling level, and other important dimensions are also included on the elevations.

Some of the most prominent features of an elevation are roofs, surface materials, windows and doors.

## ROOFS

There are several different types of roofs that can be used in light construction; some of the more common styles are gable roofs, hip roofs, flat roofs, shed roofs, mansard roofs, gambrel roofs, and butterfly roofs (see Fig. 10-2).

### Gable Roof

A gable roof is one of the most popular roof styles, and it has been used for years. This roof consists of two sloping sides that terminate at the ridge line, with a "gable end" at the end of the house.

### Hip Roof

A hip roof is also a popular roof style, and is constructed with four sloping sides. This type is more difficult to build than a gable roof and is not as easily ventilated.

### Flat Roof

A flat roof is not a popular roof design; it is economical to construct, but prone to leak much more readily than other styles. If a flat roof is used, a "built-up" roof covering is usually placed over the roof decking.

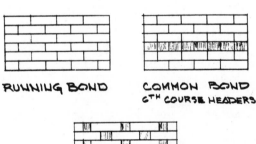

RUNNING BOND

COMMON BOND
6TH COURSE HEADERS

FLEMISH BOND

ENGLISH BOND

STACK BOND

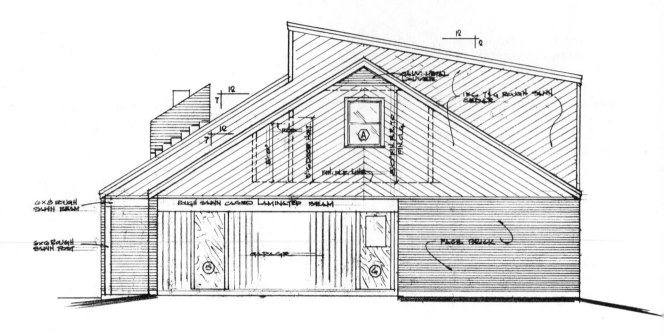

FIGURE 10-1    Typical elevation

## Shed Roof

A shed roof is similar to a flat roof, but it has a slope greater than 3:12. In most cases a roof of this type is used for storage or auxiliary buildings that are separated from the main building. It is also sometimes used for additions to existing buildings.

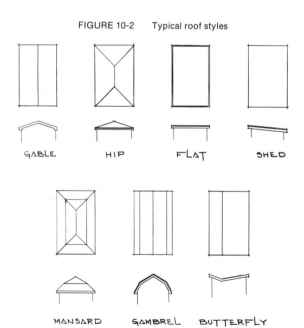

FIGURE 10-2    Typical roof styles

## Mansard Roof

A mansard roof is sloped on four sides, with each sloped side broken into two planes. This particular roof style is a French design and is gaining in popularity in the U.S.

## Gambrel Roof

A gambrel roof is sloped on two sides, with each sloped side broken into planes. This type is sometimes called a barn roof because it has been used on barns for years. It provides added room when the Dutch colonial style of architecture is used.

## Butterfly Roof

A butterfly roof, because of the drainage problem it can present, is not used much in residential construction. In this type of construction the roof is sloped in such a manner that a valley is formed by the intersection of two sloping roofs.

## Roof Pitch

Roof pitch is largely determined by architectural style and the type of roof covering used. In simple terms, roof pitch refers to the

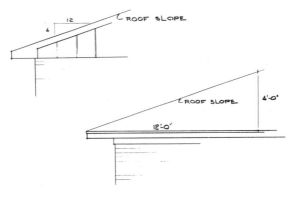

angle at which the rafters are placed. In most cases, the roof is drawn by using a slope-ratio triangle, which has its hypotenuse parallel to the roof slope. The other two sides represent the rise and run slope ratio. The rise is the vertical distance from the cap plate to the bottom of the ridge board, while the run is a horizontal measurement that is taken from the outside of the cap plate to the center of the ridge. In most cases the ratio of the rise of the roof to its run is stated as $3:12, 4:12, 5:12$, etc.

A roof can also be drawn by using a fractional pitch derived from the following formula:

$$\text{Pitch} = \frac{\text{Rise}}{\text{Span}}$$

This particular method is not often used, although many carpenters use fractional pitches for their rafter layout.

To draw a typical gable roof, the general shape of the house must first be blocked in. With the top corners of the wall as a starting point, the roof slope is drawn. It can be determined in two ways: either by using an architectural template that has a roof-pitch indicator or by laying out the slope with an architect's scale.

To use the roof-pitch indicator method, the template must be properly positioned over a top corner of the drawing of the blocked-in house. The desired slope is then selected and marked. A triangle is positioned over the

FIGURE 10-3 (upper left)     Roof slope
FIGURE 10-4 (upper right)    4:12 slope

corner and the previously placed mark, and a line is then drawn to connect the two points. This line represents the roof slope (see Fig. 10-3).

To use the architect's scale method to find the roof slope, the scale should be placed along the top of the blocked-in building. Starting from the top corner of the building 12' is measured along this line. At the end of the 12' a vertical distance is measured that equals the ratio of the desired slope. For example, if a $4:12$ slope is desired, the vertical distance is 4' (see Fig. 10-4). The top of the vertical line is then connected with the corner of the building. This represents the roof slope.

At this point, using either the template or scale, the other side of the roof is drawn. The cornice can now be blocked in, and other features of the elevation added (see Fig. 10-5).

FIGURE 10-5     Completed roof and elevation

FRONT ELEV.

SCALE: 1/4"=1'-0"

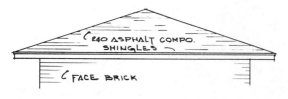

FIGURE 10-6      Complete hip roof

To draw a hip roof, the building must first be blocked in. Then the fascia is drawn, projecting from the building to the desired overhang. From the end of the fascia, the slope is laid out. Then, measuring from the end of the fascia, the total span must be marked using the same slope, and a line drawn from the end of the span until it intersects the other sloping line. The intersection of the two lines is the height of the ridge. To complete the elevation, the lines are then darkened (see Fig. 10-6).

## ROOF COVERING

There are several type of roof covering used in residential construction; the most common are asphalt shingles, wood shakes and shingles, and built-up roofing.

Asphalt shingles can be represented on the elevation by either drawing individual shingles or by using a series of parallel lines to indicate the shingles (see Fig. 10-7). A note should accompany the graphic representation to denote the type of shingle used.

Wood shakes and wood shingles are usually represented by a drawing of a series of individual shingles with a note to indicate which type are to be used (see Fig. 10-8).

A built-up roof is relatively flat and cannot usually be seen; it is represented by two parallel lines (see Fig. 10-9).

FIGURE 10-7      Drawing asphalt shingles on a roof

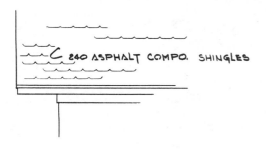

Most of the other roof styles are similar to the hip and gable roof and can be drawn in a similar manner.

### Gable-End Construction

The gable end can be treated in several different ways; in most cases it is treated the same as the cornice. For example, if a 2′ closed horizontal cornice is used, then a 2′ closed rake cornice will be used.

The cornice is usually terminated at the rake edge to form a "bird box." From the "bird box" a fascia is extended along the barge rafter to the ridge board. Once the fascia has been placed, a shingle strip or drip edge is usually secured to the fascia.

To provide adequate ventilation in the attic, gable louvered ventilators are usually used. The total area of the ventilator openings should be at least $\frac{1}{300}$ of the total ceiling area.

## Asphalt Shingles

Asphalt shingles are among the most popular types of roof covering used, accounting for more than 80 percent of the roof covering in U.S. homes. They are economical, durable, and attractive. They are also fire-resistant, wind-resistant, and are available in a wide

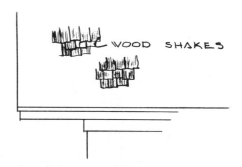

FIGURE 10-8 (above)      Drawing wood shakes and shingles on a roof
FIGURE 10-9 (below)      Elevation of a built-up roof

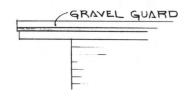

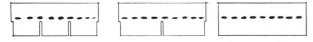

FIGURE 10-10     Asphalt strip shingle

variety of colors and styles. The most popular style are square butt strip shingles. These are rectangular in shape and are available with three tabs, two tabs, or one tab (see Fig. 10-10). The less popular asphalt shingles are the hexagon and the individual types.

Asphalt shingles are made of a base mat of either organic (cellulose fiber) or inorganic (glass or asbestos fiber) material. The base mat is saturated with asphalt and surfaced with opaque mineral granules. The asphalt is used as a waterproofing agent and the granules are used to protect the shingles from the sun's rays.

Shingles are sold by the square and approximate weight per square. A square of shingles will cover 100 square feet of roof surface. The approximate weight per square ranges from 205 to 380 pounds, with the most popular weight being 240 pounds.

To provide adequate drainage, the roof must be properly sloped. If "free tab" square butt strip shingles are used, the degree of slope, or pitch, should be not less than 4″ per foot. However, a self-sealing type square butt strip shingle can be placed on a roof with a slope as small as 2″ per foot. The "free tab" shingle can also be placed on a slope of 2″ per foot if the tabs are cemented down.

## Wood Shakes and Wood Shingles

Wood shakes and wood shingles have successfully been used as a roof covering material for many years. They are strong, provide good insulation, are resistant to winds, and have a pleasing appearance.

Their popularity waned for a while, owing largely to increased cost and fire hazard. However, in recent years a wood shake and shingle has been developed that carries a UL class "B" or "C" rating. To obtain a UL class "C" rating, the cell structure of the shingles is impregnated with fire-retardant chemicals. This reduces the chance of fire starting and/or spreading. A class "B" fire rating is obtained when the wood shakes and shingles are placed over an underlayment of plastic-coated steel foil. The underlayment must be placed over ½″-minimum plywood deck or 2″-minimum tongue-and-groove lumber.

The three most popular species of wood used for wood shakes and shingles are western red cedar, redwood, and cypress. Cypress shingles carry the grades of No. 1, best, prime, and economy. Redwood shingles are graded as No. 1 and No. 2. Red cedar shingles are graded No. 1 (blue label), No. 2 (red label), and No. 3 (black label), as shown in Fig. 10-11. Red cedar shakes are graded as No. 1 straight-split.

Wood shakes and shingles are manufactured in three lengths—16, 18, and 24″. They vary in width from 3 to 14″; if a shingle is wider than 9″ it should be split before it is placed.

Wood shakes and shingles are packaged in bundles. It usually takes four or five bundles to cover a square, but the actual area covered is determined by the weather exposure and the length of the shingle.

To provide adequate drainage, the roof must be properly sloped so that the wood shakes and shingles have the proper exposure. To increase the efficiency of the roof, the exposure is reduced as the slope of the roof decreases. If the roof has a 5-in-12 or steeper slope, a 16″ shingle should have a 5″ exposure, an 18″ shingle should have a 5½″ exposure, and a 24″ shingle should have a 7½″ exposure. If the roof has less than a 5-in-12 but is not under a 3-in-12 slope, a 16″ shingle should have a 3¾″ exposure, a 24″ shingle should have a 4¼″ exposure, and a 24″ shingle should have a 5¾″ exposure.

## Flashing

During the application of the roof covering, the roof must be properly flashed in areas such as chimneys, soil stacks, intersections of other roofs, and projections through the deck. Proper application techniques should be followed for adequate flashing.

A valley is the intersection of two sloping roofs and must be flashed to provide runoff along the joint. The intersection can be flashed by means of an open valley or a closed valley (see Fig. 10-12). An open valley is lined

## CERTIGRADE RED CEDAR SHINGLES

| GRADE | Length | Thickness (at Butt) | No. of Courses Per Bundle | Bdls/Cartons Per Square | | Description |
|---|---|---|---|---|---|---|
| No. 1 BLUE LABEL | 16″ (Fivex) 18″ (Perfections) 24″ (Royals) | .40″ .45″ .50″ | 20/20 18/18 13/14 | 4 bdls. 4 bdls. 4 bdls. | 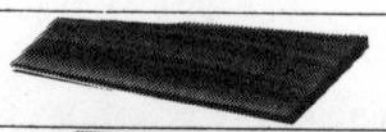 | The premium grade of shingles for roofs and sidewalls. These top-grade shingles are 100% heartwood . . . 100% clear and 100% edge-grain. |
| No. 2 RED LABEL | 16″ (Fivex) 18″ (Perfections) 24″ (Royals) | .40″ .45″ .50″ | 20/20 18/18 13/14 | 4 bdls. 4 bdls. 4 bdls. |  | A proper grade for some applications. Not less than 10″ clear on 16″ shingles, 11″ clear on 18″ shingles and 16″ clear on 24″ shingles. Flat grain and limited sapwood are permitted in this grade. |
| No. 3 BLACK LABEL | 16″ (Fivex) 18″ (Perfections) 24″ (Royals) | .40″ .45″ .50″ | 20/20 18/18 13/14 | 4 bdls. 4 bdls. 4 bdls. |  | A utility grade for economy applications and secondary buildings. Not less than 6″ clear on 16″ and 18″ shingles, 10″ clear on 24″ shingles. |
| No. 4 UNDER-COURSING | 16″ (Fivex) 18″ (Perfections) | .40″ .45″ | 14/14 or 20/20 14/14 or 18/18 | 2 bdls. 2 bdls. |  | A utility grade for undercoursing on double-coursed sidewall applications or for interior accent walls. |
| No. 1 or No. 2 REBUTTED-REJOINTED | 16″ (Fivex) 18″ (Perfections) 24″ (Royals) | .40″ .45″ .50″ | 33/33 28/28 13/14 | 1 carton 1 carton 4 bdls. |  | Same specifications as above for No. 1 and No. 2 grades but machine trimmed for exactly parallel edges with butts sawn at precise right angles. For sidewall application where tightly fitting joints are desired. Also available with smooth sanded face. |

| PITCH | Maximum exposure recommended for roofs: | | | | | | | | |
|---|---|---|---|---|---|---|---|---|---|
| | NO. 1 BLUE LABEL | | | NO. 2 RED LABEL | | | NO. 3 BLACK LABEL | | |
| | 16″ | 18″ | 24″ | 16″ | 18″ | 24″ | 16″ | 18″ | 24″ |
| 3 IN 12 TO 4 IN 12 | 3¾″ | 4¼″ | 5¾″ | 3½″ | 4″ | 5½″ | 3″ | 3½″ | 5″ |
| 4 IN 12 AND STEEPER | 5″ | 5½″ | 7½″ | 4″ | 4½″ | 6½″ | 3½″ | 4″ | 5½″ |

| LENGTH AND THICKNESS | Approximate coverage of one square (4 bundles) of shingles based on following weather exposures | | | | | | | | | | | | | | | | | | | | | | | | | |
|---|---|---|---|---|---|---|---|---|---|---|---|---|---|---|---|---|---|---|---|---|---|---|---|---|---|---|
| | 3½″ | 4″ | 4½″ | 5″ | 5½″ | 6″ | 6½″ | 7″ | 7½″ | 8″ | 8½″ | 9″ | 9½″ | 10″ | 10½″ | 11″ | 11½″ | 12″ | 12½″ | 13″ | 13½″ | 14″ | 14½″ | 15″ | 15½″ | 16″ |
| 16″ x 5/2″ | 70 | 80 | 90 | 100* | 110 | 120 | 130 | 140 | 150‡ | 160 | 170 | 180 | 190 | 200 | 210 | 220 | 230 | 240† | .... | .... | .... | .... | | | | |
| 18″ x 5/2¼″ | .... | 72½ | 81½ | 90½ | 100* | 109 | 118 | 127 | 136 | 145½ | 154½‡ | 163½ | 172½ | 181½ | 191 | 200 | 209 | 218 | 227 | 236 | 245½ | 254½† | .... | .... | .... | .... |
| 24″ x 4 2″ | .... | .... | .... | .... | .... | 80 | 86½ | 93 | 100* | 106½ | 113 | 120 | 126½ | 133 | 140 | 146½ | 153‡ | 160 | 166½ | 173 | 180 | 186½ | 193 | 200 | 206½ | 213† |

NOTES: *Maximum exposure recommended for roofs.  ‡Maximum exposure recommended for single-coursing No. 1 grades on sidewalls. Reduce exposure for No. 2 grades. †Maximum exposure recommended for double-coursing No. 1 grades on sidewalls.

FIGURE 10-11  Wood shingle grades

with sheet metal or roll roofing. The two types of metal valleys are classified as roll valley and formed valleys. The roll valley is formed by rolling 28 or 30-gauge sheet metal in the center of the valley. The galvanized sheet metal is 12 to 20″ wide and is nailed along both sides. The preferred metal valley is a formed valley, which is 18″ wide and 8 to 10′ long and is formed in a metal brake.

A woven valley, created by weaving adjacent courses of shingles over a valley can be used with asphalt strip shingles. This type of valley construction is sometimes preferred because of its double coverage.

Wall flashing is placed at the intersection of a sloping roof and a vertical wall (see Fig. 10-13). Its primary objective is to keep water from penetrating the roof. There are two basic types of wall flashing. Steep flashing is made from sheet metal and is installed after each shingle is cut and placed. The flashing shingle is rectangular in shape—usually 6″ long and 7″ wide. It is bent so that it extends up the vertical wall at least 4″, and extends a minimum of 2″ out over the roof deck.

FIGURE 10-12  Open and closed valley

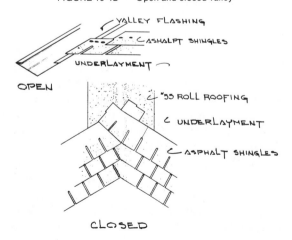

FIGURE 10-13  Wall flashing

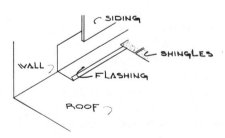

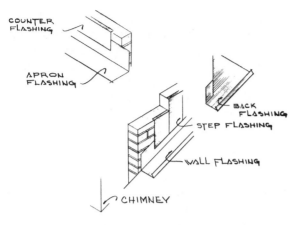

FIGURE 10-14    Chimney flashing

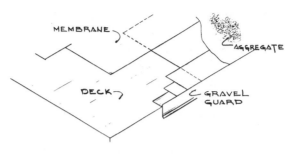

FIGURE 10-15    Built-up roof

The other type of flashing, a *solid-water guide,* is a solid piece of metal flashing 8 to 10′ long and 4″ wide. It is bent down the center, with a ½″ lip turned up on one edge. It is nailed directly to the studs before the finish siding is placed.

Chimney flashing is one of the most complicated and expensive types of flashing. It consists of wall flashing, apron flashing, counterflashing, step flashing, and backflashing (see Fig. 10-14).

Apron flashing is the first piece of flashing placed. It lays 4″ over the previously placed shingles and turns 4″ up the chimney. Its ends are allowed to extend 4″ past the corner of the chimney and are then bent around that corner. When this is done, vertical wall flashing is placed on both sides of the chimney, extending to the bottom of the apron flashing and 4 to 6″ behind the back of the chimney. Once this is done, shingles are placed up the roof to a point at which the corner of the shingle is even with the back of the chimney.

Backflashing is then placed behind the chimney. It extends 18″ up the roof and 4″ up the chimney. When this is finished, straight counterflashing is placed over the apron flashing and allowed to turn the corners of the chimney 2″. The top of all counterflashing is placed and nailed into a raked mortar joint. Then mortar is applied over the junction of the flashing and chimney and counter step flashing is placed on the sides. The width of the chimney determines the number of pieces of step flashing, but in most cases three or four pieces are required. The last piece of flashing is a straight piece of counterflashing

placed over the backflashing. It should project around the corner 2″. Once the flashing is complete, shingles may be placed over the backflashing and the remainder of the roof.

Flashing is placed over and around any protruding stacks. Stack flashing has two basic parts—the flange and the barrel. The flange rests on the roof deck, and the barrel is that portion that fits around the stack. In some cases a third piece called the cap is used; this fits on top of the barrel.

## Built-Up Roof

A built-up roof consists of alternate moppings of bitumen and layers of felt over decking, and is used over roofs that have relatively low slopes (see Fig. 10-15). The decking over which the membrane is placed falls into one of two basic categories—nailable and non-nailable. These two categories can be further subdivided into steel decks, concrete decks, wood decks, gypsum decks, and structural wood-fiber decks. The primary purpose of the roof deck is to support the roofing membrane; to prevent, to a certain degree, heat gain or heat loss; to control sound; and in some cases to provide a desirable inside appearance.

One of the most important qualities of a roof deck is its ability to shed water. Decks, however, are all too often constructed at dead level, which usually develops a depression. Water can collect in this, and its freeze-thaw action will eventually deteriorate the roofing membrane. Standing water invariably finds its way through small openings in the membrane to penetrate the exposed organic felts by capillary action or absorption. Consequently, a roof deck should be designed to provide a minimum of ¼″ slope per foot so that it may drain freely.

The success of the roof is largely dependent upon the deck, so before the roofing membrane is placed, the deck should be properly inspected. A wood deck that is not correctly nailed off could result in warping and cracking boards; nails improperly placed might work loose and come through the membrane.

To prevent the migration of moisture, vulnerable locations should be properly flashed. Some of the common areas that need flashing are the intersection of the roof and a vertical wall; collars for large stacks and flagpoles, vent-pipe connections, and at the eave lines.

## SURFACE MATERIALS

Some of the more common types of material that can be used on the exterior walls of a building include hardboard siding, aluminum and vinyl siding, plywood siding, bevel siding, mineral-fiber siding, wood shakes and shingles, and masonry.

### Hardboard Siding

Hardboard siding is made from clear selected wood fibers pressed under heat. Natural and synthetic binders are used to bind the fibers together. The formation of the fibers accounts for varying characteristics in density, appearance, thickness, and finishing properties.

Hardboard siding is available in a wide variety of patterns and finishes made possible by two basic coating systems: *Flat stock printing* is a process in which liquid coating, simulating woodgrain, mosaic, or marble patterns is applied directly to the hardboard. *Laminating* involves the application of a plastic film such as vinyl or acrylic over the hardboard.

Some of the major advantages of hardboard siding are economy, resistance to moisture, sound control quality, and workability. The siding can be readily worked with ordinary carpenter's tools and will not split, chip, or check. Because of its high density and sound control, quality hardboard siding makes an excellent sidewall covering. Hard-

board also resists all the extremes of the weather, heat, cold, and moisture.

Hardboard siding may be placed over sheathed or unsheathed walls with studs not more than 16″ on center. To prevent air infiltration, building paper should be applied directly to studs or over wood sheathing. If the walls are uninsulated, a vapor barrier should be used to prevent damaging condensation from within the walls.

Hardboard siding can be applied by using the techniques illustrated in Fig. 10-16.

### Aluminum and Vinyl Siding

Aluminum and vinyl siding provide a virtually maintenance-free exterior sidewall covering. Solid vinyl siding is made from polyvinyl chloride, a rigid material that is easily adapted for building applications. In addition to being durable, the material is self-extinguishing and will not conduct electricity. Most vinyl siding is approximately 0.045″ thick and has a ⅜″-thick insulation-board backing. The most popular siding is extruded or molded in two basic patterns: beveled siding with 8″ to the weather and siding molded in such a way as to give the look of 4″ to the weather.

Aluminum siding also simulates 4 or 8″ beveled siding, and is available in a smooth or textured finish. Most aluminum horizontal siding has interlocking horizontal edges, a butt or shadow leg, and a drip bead in the butt (see Fig. 10-17). (The drip bead is used to direct the flow of water from the surface of the panel.) Most such siding also has breather holes in the shadow log of every panel, permitting the wall to breathe and allowing condensation and water vapor within the wall to escape. Elongated nail holes are in the

FIGURE 10-16    Illustrating hardboard siding

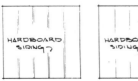

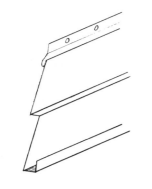

FIGURE 10-17    Aluminum siding

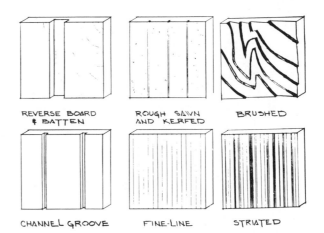

FIGURE 10-19    Plywood siding

nailing hem of the siding to allow for possible expansion and contraction.

Aluminum and vinyl siding can be applied by using one of the techniques shown in Fig. 10-18.

## Plywood Siding

Plywood siding is available in many grades and textures, each designed to meet a specific need and structural requirement. Some of the more popular types of plywood siding are reverse board and batten, rough-sawn and kerfed, channel groove, brushed, fine-line, and striated, (see Fig. 10-19).

Reverse board and batten plywood siding has deep, wide grooves in its surface. The grooves are cut to an approximate depth of ¼″ and to a width of 1 to 1½″. To join individual panels and to provide a continuous pattern, the edges are shiplapped. Rough-sawn and kerfed plywood siding has a rough-textured surface with narrow grooves placed 4″ on center. So that these will be a continuous pattern, the long edges are also shiplapped. Channel groove siding is like reverse board and batten, except for the size of the grooves—usually ¹⁄₁₆″ deep, ⅜″ wide, and placed on 2 or 4″ centers. Brushed siding is often referred to as relief-grain surface and is used to accent

the natural grain pattern. Fine-line siding has fine grooves cut into the surface which are placed on ¼″ centers and are about ¹⁄₃₂″ wide. In striated siding, closely spaced grooves and fine striations produce a vertical pattern. The striations cover joints, nail-heads, and surface defects.

## Bevel Siding

Bevel siding is produced by resawing kiln-dried surfaced lumber. It is cut to produce two pieces thicker on one edge than on the other (see Fig. 10-20). There are several different types of wood that are used for bevel siding; western red cedar is often preferred because it is highly resistant to weather checks and lacks the tendencies to cup and pull loose from the fastenings. The heartwood of western red cedar varies in color from deep reddish-brown to light brown. The texture is fine with even, straight, narrow summer ridges, and it is completely free of pitch.

There are five basic grades of bevel siding. With the exception of siding intended for rough side use, bevel siding is graded form the surfaced side. *Clear VG all-heart bevel siding*

FIGURE 10-18    Illustrating aluminum siding

FIGURE 10-20    Bevel siding

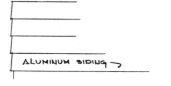

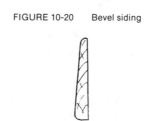

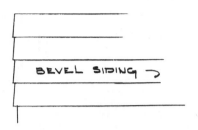

FIGURE 10-21    Illustrating bevel siding

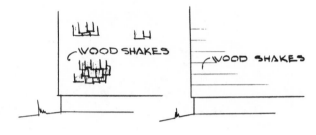

FIGURE 10-22    Illustrating wood shakes and shingles

is used where the highest quality of siding is needed. It is manufactured from 100 percent heartwood and is free of any imperfection.

*Grade A bevel siding* usually has a mixed grain and is intended for use where good appearance is desired. In some cases the siding might have some minor growth characteristic.

*Grade B bevel siding* may contain minor imperfections and occasionally cuts, but when it is painted it makes an economical and quality sidewall covering.

*Rustic bevel siding* may also be mixed grain, but it is usable full length and adds a rustic charm and appearance. It is graded from the resawn side and may be surfaced or rough.

*Grade C bevel siding* is an economical siding suitable for temporary construction, buildings having minimum shelter requirements, and various industrial uses.

The size of bevel siding varies from widths of 3½ to 11½″, top thicknesses of ³/₁₆″, and bottom thicknesses from ¹⁵/₃₂ to ¾″. In addition to the varying sizes, the butt edge of the siding can be plain or rabbeted.

Bevel siding can be applied by using the techniques illustrated in Fig. 10-21.

## Wood Shakes and Shingles

Wood shakes and shingles provide a durable and decorative material that blends a structure into the environment. They can be constructed from several different species of wood, but western red cedar is highly favored because of its natural perservative oils and multiple grooves, which act as channels to shed water from the exposed wall. It is a fine-grained wood that is completely void or pitch or resin and is resistant to decay under most conditions.

Wood shakes and shingles are available in three different lengths: 16, 18, and 24″, with respective butt thicknesses of .40, .45, and .50″. The individual units are packaged in bundles and sold by the square. The number of bundles per square depends on the size of the shake and the weather exposure.

Wood shakes and shingles can be applied with one of the techniques illustrated in Fig. 10-22.

# CLAY AND CONCRETE MASONRY CONSTRUCTION _____

Clay and concrete masonry construction has been used successfully in light construction for decades. The units are permanent, provide good insulation, offer design flexibility, and in most cases, require very little maintenance.

For many years bricks were manufactured in three basic sizes, but in recent years manufactures have developed new styles, characteristics, and sizes of brick units. The three standard sizes are called "standard," "Roman," and "Norman."

Concrete masonry units are manufactured

from heavyweight or lightweight aggregates mixed with water and portland cement. The aggregates in the heavyweight units can be sand, gravel, crushed stone, or air-cooled slag; while the aggregates in the lightweight units are coal cinders, expanded shale, slag, pumice, or volcanic cinders. A concrete masonry unit 8″ × 8″ × 16″ that is constructed from heavyweight aggregate weighs from 40 to 50 pounds, while a unit of the same size, but made with lightweight aggregates weighs from 25 to 35 pounds.

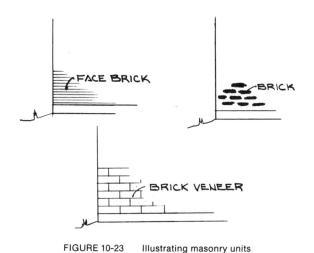

FIGURE 10-23    Illustrating masonry units

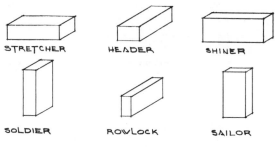

FIGURE 10-24    Various brick positions alter the names of the individual units

The various sizes and shapes of concrete masonry units are each designed for a specific job. Some of the more common units are called stretchers, corners, jambs, full-cut headers, and solid tops. The individual units are usually referred to by their nominal dimensions; a typical stretcher has nominal dimensions of 8″ × 8″ × 16″, but the actual units of measurement are 7⅝″ × 7⅝″ × 15⅝″. When the unit is laid in a ⅜″ mortar bed and when it has a ⅜″ head joint, the jointed assembly will measure 8″ × 8″ × 16″.

Individual masonry units are represented on the architectural elevations by either a series of parallel lines—broad pencil strokes made by a soft lead—or by drawings of the units as they would actually appear (see Fig. 10-23).

## Bonds

The term *bond*, when used in reference to masonry, can have three different meanings:

□ *Mortar bond:* The ability of the mortar to adhere to the masonry units, or to reinforcing steel.
□ *Structural bond:* The technique by which individual masonry units are interlocked or tied together to form an integral unit.
□ *Pattern bond:* The development of a particular pattern through the placement of individual masonry units.

Structural bonding of masonry walls can be accomplished by overlapping the units; by the use of metal ties embedded in the mortar joints of the two adjacent wythes; or by the grouting of adjacent wythes of masonry. The units can be placed in different positions to accomplish a particular pattern or bond. When they are turned or placed in a certain position, they take on a different name (see Fig. 10-24).

The overlapping of masonry units is based on variations of two traditional techniques of bonding (see Fig. 10-25). The *English bond* consists of alternating courses of headers and stretchers, while the *Flemish bond* consists of alternating headers and stretchers in every course. To bond the wall transversely, the headers must be placed with their long axis across the wall. The headers should not be spaced further apart than 24″ and should comprise a minimum of 4 percent of the total wall area.

If metal ties are used to bond the wall, one metal tie should be used for each 4½ square feet of wall area. The ties should be placed on equal centers not to exceed 24″, and should be staggered in alternate courses. The flexibility of metal ties, relieves stress, thus preventing the possibility of cracking.

A pattern bond is the arrangement of masonry units to produce a particular pattern. There are five basic pattern bonds that are used: running bond, common or American bond, Flemish bond, English bond, and block or stack bond (see Fig. 10-26).

The simplest of the five bonds is the running bond. This type utilizes all stretchers

FIGURE 10-25    Traditional bonding

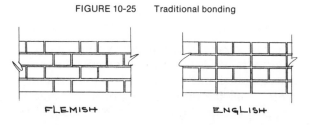

FLEMISH          ENGLISH

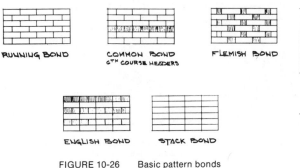

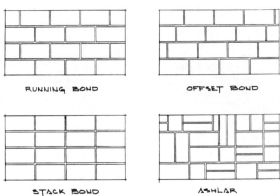

FIGURE 10-26    Basic pattern bonds

FIGURE 10-27    Concrete masonry unit pattern bonds

and is used primarily in cavity-wall construction and veneered walls. The common or American bond is constructed with a course of full-length headers placed at regular intervals. The header course provides structural bonding, and is usually placed every fifth or sixth course. The courses other than the header course are usually placed in a running bond.

The Flemish bond consists of alternating headers and stretchers in every course. Full-length headers can be used to provide a structural bond, or the header units can be broken into to provide a pattern bond.

The English bond consist of alternating courses of headers and stretchers. The bond is also created by centering the headers on the stretchers and by aligning all the vertical joints of the stretchers.

A block or stack bond is strictly a pattern bond, because there is no overlapping of the individual units. For a block or stack bond, the individual units are placed on top of each other, with all the vertical joints aligned.

Several different pattern bonds can be achieved with concrete masonry units. Some of the most popular patterns are running bonds, offset bonds, stack bonds, and several ashlar patterns (see Fig. 10-27). The type of pattern used is dependent upon the desired effects, the availability of the different-sized units, and the relative economy that is associated with the construction of the wall.

## Mortar Joints

Mortar serves three primary functions: it bonds the units together, it compensates for the dimensional variations in the masonry units, and it produces certain architectural effects. The mortar joints can be classified as either troweled or tooled. A troweled joint is created by cutting the extruded mortar flush with the masonry units. A tooled joint is made by compressing the mortar in to the joint with a special forming tool. A tooled joint can also be made by raking a portion of the mortar from the joint.

Three of the most popular types of tooled joints are concave, V-shaped, and raked joints (see Fig. 10-28). Concave and V-shaped mortar joints are effective because the mortar has been compacted in the joint, making them very effective in resisting rain penetration; these are recommended in areas that experience heavy rains and high winds.

The raked joint is made by removing the face of the mortar while it is soft with a special square-shaped tool. The mortar, however, is not tightly compacted in the joint and offers little resistance against water penetration.

## Flashing

Flashing prevents moisture from penetrating a wall, or directs moisture that might penetrate the wall to the outside of the wall. Depending on the function and location of flashing, it can be classified as either external or internal (see Feb. 10-29). External flashing is shown on the elevation and is used to direct

FIGURE 10-28    Tooled joints

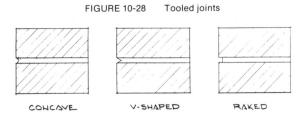

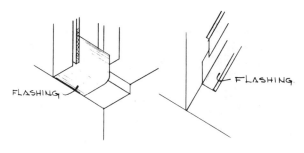

INTERNAL FLASHING     EXTERNAL FLASHING

FIGURE 10-29    Flashing

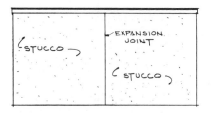

FIGURE 10-31    Illustrating an expansion joint

water away from the intersection of a relatively flat surface and a vertical masonry wall. This type usually consists of two parts (see Fig. 10-30). *Base flashing* covers the flat surface and turns up the vertical masonry wall. *Cap flashing* is built into the masonry wall and is turned down over the base flashing.

Internal flashing is usually built into and concealed by masonry walls and is also used to collect and divert moisture to the outside. To allow moisture to be drained through the masonry walls, weep holes must be constructed by one of several methods: placing sash cords in the mortar joints; using plastic soda straws or copper tubing in the bed joint; or omitting a vertical head joint of mortar. Weep holes are usually placed on 16 or 24″ centers.

Some of the more common materials used for flashing are copper, zinc, aluminum, lead, plastics, and bituminous material.

Copper is durable and an excellent moisture barrier; it is not affected by the caustic alkalis in mortars, but it may stain adjacent masonry and it is one of the most expensive flashing materials. One of the biggest disadvantages of zinc as a flashing material is its tendency to corrode when placed in fresh mortar. However, the corrosion forms a film around the flashing and readily bonds with

the mortar. Aluminum and lead should not be used as flashing in a masonry wall, because the unhardened mortar will attack and destroy the metal. Plastic is one of the most widely used flashing materials; it is relatively inexpensive and highly resistant to corrosion. Bituminous flashing material consists of fabrics saturated with bitumen. If they can be placed without breaking the coating they are effective, but in most cases they are not considered to be as permanent as a good metal flashing.

## Expansion and Control Joint

All building materials will expand and contract owing to changes in temperature, and some materials will make dimensional changes with changes in moisture content. Because these changes can cause stresses that might lead to cracks, expansion joints and control joints are sometimes placed in the masonry wall. These are represented on the elevation as a single vertical line. A note is then used to call attention to the joint (see Fig. 10-31).

To locate and position control joints, the entire wall assembly should be analyzed to determine potential movement locations. In most cases, however, control joints are located at offsets and at junctions of walls in L-, T-, or U-shaped buildings. In cavity walls and solid walls, expansion joints are sometimes placed at or near an exterior corner.

In clay masonry, expansion joints are constructed in a number of ways. Some of the materials that are successfully used as expansion joint fillers are copper, premolded foam rubber or plastic, neoprene, and extruded plastic. Fiberboard and similar materials should not be used because they are not highly compressible, and once they have been compressed they do not return to their original shape and size.

FIGURE 10-30    External flashing

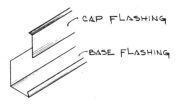

Some of the acceptable techniques for constructing control joints in concrete masonry walls include using a full- and a half-length block to form a continuous joint; and using offset jamb blocks with a noncorroding wall tie. To provide lateral support, some control-joint blocks are provided with tongue-and-grooved ends. A control joint can also be constructed by inserting building paper in the end core of the block and filling the core with mortar. The building paper prevents the mortar from bonding the two units together and the mortar adds lateral strength to the wall; it must be carefully lowered into place.

### Lintels and Sills

One-piece lintels, split lintels, one-piece lintels with stirrups, lintel blocks, and steel angle lintels are the various devices used to span the openings over windows and doors. The distances that these lintels can span are shown in Table Three, Table Four and Table Five.

Regardless of the type used, all lintels should be placed on a noncorroding metal plate. The plate allows the lintel to move and the control joints to function properly. The lintel is placed in a full bed of mortar, which is allowed to stiffen slightly and is then raked from the joint to a depth of ¾". Caulking compound is then forced into the joint.

Precast concrete sills are often used in concrete masonry construction. The sills are sloped to shed water and are constructed with a drip ledge to prevent water from running down the face of the masonry units. The sills should be placed in a full bed of mortar. The joints at the ends of the sill should be filled with mortar or caulking compound.

# STUCCO

Stucco is a popular exterior facing material in some geographic areas, and has been successfully used in all areas of the country.

Used in residential construction, stucco offers an attractive, durable surface with minimum maintenance. For nonresidential construction, it also provides a good facing material that is easily adapted to any architectural treatment. Stucco is a mixture of portland cement or masonry cement, lime, sand, and water; it is extremely durable, fire-resistant, and weather-resistant. In effect, stucco is a thin concrete slab built up with tools and techniques that are associated with plastering. The material can also be formed to complex shapes, planes, and surfaces without any appreciable deteriorating effects.

### Supporting Construction

Stucco can be placed over clay and concrete masonry, cast-in-place concrete, old stucco or plaster, and properly prepared wood and steel frames. The bond between the supporting construction and the stucco is provided by mechanical keying or by suction. Mechanical keying results from the interlocking of the stucco mix with the lath; suction is developed by drawing the cement paste of the mix into the small opening of the base. Suction bonding is associated with concrete and masonry, while mechanical keying is associated with metal reinforcement.

To allow the stucco to form a good bond to metal reinforcement, the reinforcement should be placed a minimum of ¼" away from the supporting construction, and the openings in the lath should not exceed 4 square inches in area. The reinforcement should form a continuous net over the supporting construction. The ends and sides of the lath should be lapped a minimum of 2" and wired securely. The laps should occur at intermediate framing members and should be staggered.

### Stucco Application

Stucco is usually applied in three coats: the scratch coat (first), the brown coat (second), and the finish coat (third). However, if it is placed over clay or concrete masonry, only two coats are required (see Fig. 10-32). Under no circumstances should the stucco be applied in freezing temperatures or to surfaces covered with frost. There should be a temperature of 50°F or higher during application and 48 hours after the finish coat has been applied.

Stucco can be applied by hand or machine;

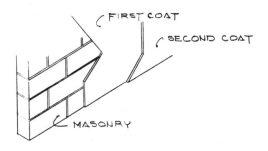

FIGURE 10-32    Stucco placed over a masonry base

each affords certain advantages and disadvantages. Hand application of stucco has been used successfully for centuries, and involves only the use of traditional tools. Machine application of stucco involves the use of expensive equipment, but the process is faster and results in a more uniform texture.

The first, or scratch coat, of stucco should be applied with sufficient pressure to completely embed it in the lath. This coat should be approximately ½″ thick and cover at least 90 percent of the metal reinforcement. Once this coat has been placed, it must be scored horizontally or scratched so that it will allow a good bond with the brown coat.

After the scratch coat has had time to sit, usually four or five hours, the second, or brown, coat is applied. However, if open-frame construction is used, the scratch coat should be allowed to set for 48 hours. This allows the scratch coat to increase in strength, thus providing a rigid base for the application of the brown coat. If the scratch coat dries out, it should be evenly dampened before the brown coat is applied. When the brown coat is applied it should be struck to a thickness of ⅜″. To maintain an even thickness of stucco, stucco screeds are often placed over the scratch coat.

Stucco is usually illustrated on an architectural drawing by a series of dots on the elevation (see Fig. 10-33).

## DOORS

There are several different types of exterior doors used in light construction (see Fig. 10-34).

Wood flush doors, used as exterior doors, are found extensively in storerooms, utility rooms, and rear entrances. Doors of this type are relatively light and inexpensive compared to panel doors. They usually have a

FIGURE 10-33    Stucco illustrated on an elevation

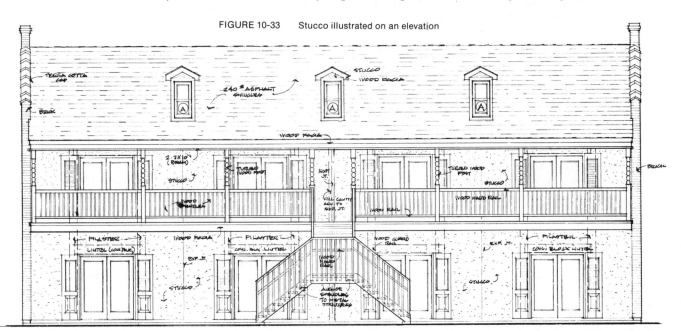

FRONT ELEVATION _____ SCALE: ¼″=1′-0″ _____

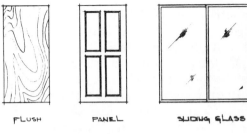

FIGURE 10-34     Exterior doors

glued back core, a hollow ladder core, or a hollow mesh cellular core. There are certain advantages and disadvantages in the different types of cores, but in most cases a solid core is recommended for an exterior door; this provides better insulating qualities, does not warp as easily, and it gives better protection.

A panel door is quite popular as an exterior door. In most cases, it is used as a front entrance, although it can also be used in other areas. The distinguishing characteristic of a panel door is that it is constructed with rails and stiles with insert panels of plywood, hardboard, or solid stock.

Sliding glass doors are popular as patio doors. They usually lead from the den or family room onto a patio or porch. Usually 6' wide, they have large glass panels inserted between aluminum or wood frames.

The standard stock sizes of wood flush doors are considered to be standard for panel doors, also. The recommended thickness for exterior doors is 1¾" and their width is 2'8" to 3'0". According to *minimum property standards,* the main entrance should have a doorway width of 3'0"; other exterior entrances, a minimum doorway width of 2'8". Most doors have standard heights of 6'8".

## WINDOWS

Most windows fall under one of three basic classifications: swinging, sliding, or fixed (see Fig. 10-35).

Swinging windows can be hinged vertically or horizontally. If they are hinged on a vertical side they are called casement windows, but if they are hinged on top or bottom they are called awning or hopper windows.

Casement windows have a sash hinged on one side that allows the windows to swing outward by means of a crank. When the window is opened fully it allows for 100 percent top-to-bottom ventilation. Because of their unrestricted surface, they are very attractive in contemporary construction.

Fixed windows are usually large sheets of glass that are placed in a fixed sash. The window can be used alone, or a movable unit can be used in combination with it.

Double-hung windows consist of two sashes that operate up and down in channels in the frame. The sash is held in place by a friction fit or by various balancing devices placed in the sash or casement. Both sashes are operable and allow for up to 50 percent ventilation. Double-hung windows are the most popular type because they lend themselves well to almost any type of architecture.

The single-hung window is similar to the double-hung window, but it has only one movable sash. The operable sash is usually the lower sash, and allows for possible 50 percent ventilation when the window is fully open.

Sliding windows consist of two sashes that operate horizontally in a comon frame, allowing for 50 percent ventilation. These are available in a variety of sizes and can be combined with other sliding windows to provide a large panoramic view.

Awning windows can be placed so they swing up and out, or in and down; they can also be placed on their sides and be used as casements. They can be opened fully or at any angle for air control. They are often placed at the bottom of fixed windows to allow for ventilation without obstruction of the view.

FIGURE 10-35     Windows

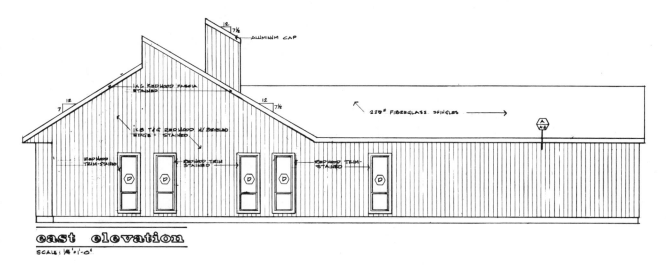

east elevation
SCALE: 1/4"=1'-0"

FIGURE 10-36    Dimensional elevation

## DRAFTING PROCEDURES FOR THE ELEVATIONS

Elevations can be drawn by first taping the completed floor plan directly above a clean sheet of tracing paper. Then distinguishing features and dimensions can be projected to the elevation. This particular technique eliminates unnecessary use of the scale, thus speeding up the drafting procedure. However, many architects and draftspersons prefer to "scale" their elevations.

Once the major features have been located, the general shape of the elevation can be lightly drawn in. A roof pitch indicator can be used to determine the correct slope. After the elevation has been blocked in, the windows and doors can be added. The elevation can now be darkened in and the necessary notes and dimensions added.

### Notes and Dimensions

Once the details have been placed on the elevation, notes and dimensions are added (see Fig. 10-36). In most cases, the dimensions, if they are shown, are vertical, showing the distance from finished floor to finished ceiling, the thickness of the footing, and the distance of the footing to grade line. The only horizontal dimension that is usually given is the roof overhang.

Notes that are usually placed on an elevation include the type of roof covering, the material used as exterior siding, the location of flashing, and any other special features.

## ASSIGNMENT:

1. Complete the elevation in Fig. 10-37. Scale the drawing for the necessary dimensions.
2. Design a front elevation for a fast-food restaurant.

FIGURE 10-37 (right)    Assignment

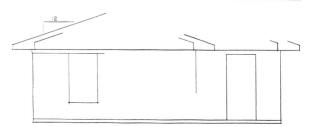

A framing plan is used to describe the shape of the building, show the location of the individual framing members, and indicate where the members are joined.

The roof framing plan and the floor framing plan should always be included in a set of plans, because if there are any questions pertaining to how either the roof or floor is framed, they can be used as a reference.

## FLOOR FRAMING PLAN

The floor framing plan is used when a home is constructed with a basement or crawl space. Its parts include girders, beams, floor joist, bridging, and subfloor (see Fig. 11-1).

### Beams and Girders

Beams and girders are used to support the floor frame as well as the dead and live loads. They are usually constructed of solid timbers, built-up members, laminated timbers, or steel girders. To provide for visual inspections and act as a termite barrier, the top of girders should be placed at least 18″ above grade. When girders are framed into a foundation wall, a ½″ air space should be provided at ends and sides.

To determine the size of a girder, it is first necessary to determine the span, which is considered to be the distance between girder supports. The girder load width must also be calculated; this is the combined distance from the girder to a midpoint of a joist that rests upon it.

The last step in sizing a girder is to determine the total floor load, which includes both dead and live loads. The dead load is a stationary load such as flooring, gypsumboard, joist, and shingles. The live load is a flexible load—a load that can move, such as people, furniture, wind, and snow.

Posts, columns, or piers are used to support the girders. The columns should be anchored to the girders and doweled or anchored to a base. The top of the base should be at least 3″ above the finish floor.

### Floor Joists

Floor joists span the distance between foundation wall, girders, and beams. They are used

# 11
# Framing
# Plans

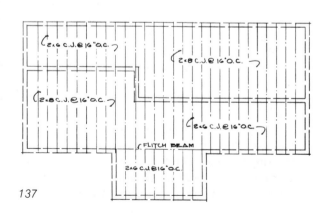

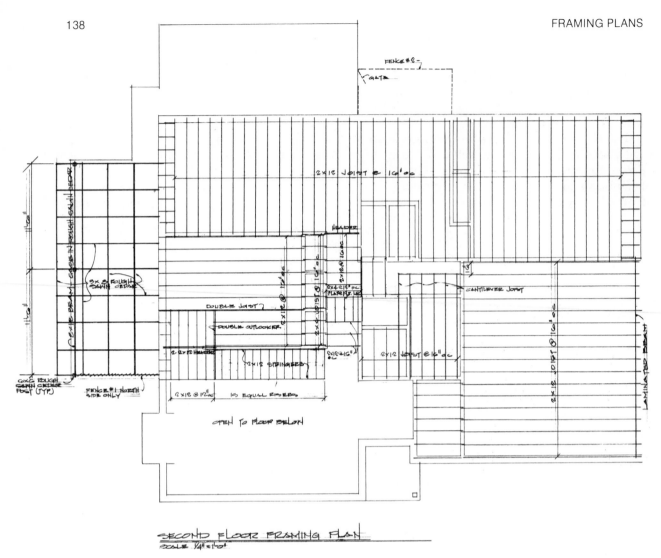

SECOND FLOOR FRAMING PLAN
SCALE 1/4"=1'-0"

FIGURE 11-1    Floor framing plan

to support the subfloor, partitions, and other dead and live loads. A joist is usually made of nominal 2″ lumber and placed on its edge. Because conventional sheets of plywood are usually used as a subfloor, the joists are usually spaced on 12, 16, or 24″ centers.

The end of the joist opposite the sill is supported by a girder. The joist can be placed on top of girder or supported by a framing anchor (see Fig. 11-2).

The size of a joist is dependent upon joist spacing, species of wood, grade of wood, dead load, probable live load, and whether the subfloor is glued or nailed.

If a partition runs parallel to the joist, a double joist (called *trimmer* and *header*) should be used. Double joists are also used around openings in the floor frame. The trimmers and headers should be nailed together

with 16d nails, staggered and clinched to increase their holding power. The joists are doubled if the span of the header exceeds 4′. If the header is longer than 6′ it should be supported by framing anchors or a beam or wall partition. If the tail joists are over 12′ in length, they should also be supported by framing anchors. If the opening is around a

FIGURE 11-2    Joist support

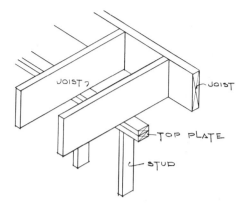

FIGURE 11-3    Cantilevered joist

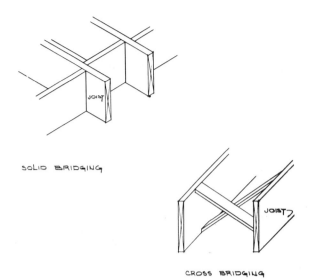

FIGURE 11-4    Bridging: (a) solid; (b) cross

fireplace, the header and trimmer should be placed a minimum of 2″ from the outside face of the masonry.

When a second-floor joist overhangs or projects beyond the first floor and the overhanging wall is at right angles to it, the joist may be cantilevered over the supporting wall (see Fig. 11-3). However, if the overhanging wall is parallel to the supporting joist, a double joist may be used to support the lookout joist. The lookout joists are supported by framing anchors or a ledger strip. The double joist should be placed back from the supporting wall twice the distance of the overhang.

To increase the ridigity of the floor joist, solid bridging or cross-bridging is used (see Fig. 11-4). Solid bridging is cut from joist stock and is placed between the joists. Cross-

bridging is usually made from 1 × 4 stock or metal straps placed at an angle to the joists. If cross-bridging is used, the lower end of the bridging should not be nailed until the subflooring is placed. In most cases bridging is placed on 8′ centers, and if the span is larger than 16′, two rows of bridging are required.

Although the primary purpose of bridging is to increase the rigidity of the joist and to evenly distribute the dead and live loads, some studies indicate that bridging serves no structural purpose. Even so, many building codes still require bridging to be placed on 8′ centers.

## ROOF FRAMING PLAN

A typical roof framing plan is used to show the various framing members in a roof (see Fig. 11-5). The common parts of the roof frame are jack rafters, common rafters, valley rafters, ridges, hip rafters, purlins, purlin studs, and collar beams.

There are three different types of jack rafters. The *hip jack* extends from the cap plate to the hip rafter. The *valley jack* extends from a valley to a ridge; and the *cripple jack* extends from valley rafter to hip rafter.

A common rafter is placed at a right angle to the exterior wall frame and extends from the cap plate to the ridge. The hip is placed at

a 45-degree angle to the exterior wall frame and extends from a corner of the wall frame to the end of the ridge. The valley is the lowest part of two intersecting roofs and extends from an inside corner to a ridge.

The purlin, purlin studs, and collar beams are part of the roof frame, but they are usually considered to be a detail (see Fig. 11-6).

The ridge is the uppermost portion of a roof, and is a framing member that the rafters are nailed to. On a gable roof, the ridge extends the length of the building. For a hip roof, the length of the ridge is equal to the length minus the width of the building. Once the

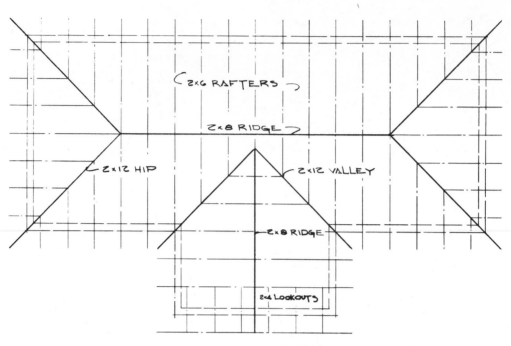

FIGURE 11-5    Roof framing plan

ridge has been cut to proper length, the location of the rafters is marked on it. In most cases the rafters are spaced 16 or 24″ apart. The spacing depends on the span, size of rafter, and species of wood.

## Roof Trusses

In light construction, roof trusses have virtually replaced the traditional joist and rafter system (see Fig. 11-7). They are easier to erect,

FIGURE 11–6.    Roof-bracing detail

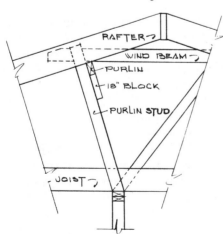

and they are actually stronger than a joist and rafter system. Recent studies indicate that trusses spaced 24″ on center are usually twice as strong as conventional framing that is placed 16″ on center. In addition to the added strength, trusses save time and material. Greater room flexibility is also gained because they require no bearing partitions.

The most popular truss is the standard fink or W truss. Its component parts are top chord, bottom chord, and webs. The webs are used to tie the top and bottom chord together. The webs and chords can be joined by one of several techniques, but the most popular fasteners are either metal plates or plywood gusset plates.

Trusses can be fabricated in a shop and delivered to the job site, or they can be built in the field. In either case, it is important that they be accurately cut to length and angle,

FIGURE 11-7    Roof truss

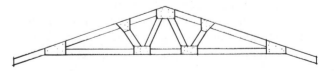

and built in special jigs with the members held tightly in place until the connector plates or rings have been properly located and placed.

After the trusses have been fabricated, they should be stored in a vertical position, resting on temporary bearing supports. During the erection process they should be carefully handled and properly braced so they will stay true and plumb. Truss hangers can be used to secure the truss to the cap plate; these eliminate the need to toenail the truss to the cap plate. When trusses are toenailed, the joint is not as strong.

The end truss, the first truss placed, should be plumbed and braced. Additional trusses are then placed in the truss hangers and equally spaced at the top by means of a notched purlin.

In addition to the regular trusses, gable end trusses can be fabricated that are fully studded, or studded to accommodate a triangular louver.

The plumb-cut overhang is the most popular type of roof overhang, but a square-cut can also be used; or a soffit return can be attached; an overhanging return for brick veneer can be added; or a cantilevered truss with a full return can be constructed. In addition to using the unique construction of overhangs, half-truss, hip louver, and jack truss systems can also be fabricated.

## CEILING FRAMING PLAN

Sometimes a ceiling framing plan is used to indicate the placement and size of ceiling joists (see Fig. 11-8). The ceiling joists are usually constructed of nominal 2"-wide stock. These individual framing members are used to tie the exterior walls together and form a nailing surface for the ceiling finish materials. The size of ceiling joists is determined by the span, species of wood, and the spacing of the joists. In most cases they are placed on 16 or 24" centers.

The joists usually span the narrowest dimension and all are placed in the same direction.

They can also be placed in opposite directions. If a hip roof is used, the first ceiling joist is omitted and stub ceiling joists are placed perpendicular to the first ceiling joist. Regular ceiling joists cannot be used because the sloping rafters would hit them.

The ends of ceiling joists rest on exterior and interior partitions and are nailed to the cap plate. When the distance between exterior and interior partitions is too great, one end of the joists can be supported by a beam; in this case, the ends of the joists should rest on ledger strips or joist hangers.

## DRAFTING PROCEDURES FOR THE FRAMING PLAN

The framing plan is usually started by placing a sheet of tracing paper over the floor plan and lightly tracing it in with a hard-leaded pencil such as a 6H; in this way the framing members take visual precedence over the walls.

Once the floor plan has been traced, individual framing members can be drawn in. They are usually represented by a single dark line; a beam or girder is usually denoted by a heavier line. As the framing members are being drawn in, they are usually placed 16 or 24" on center.

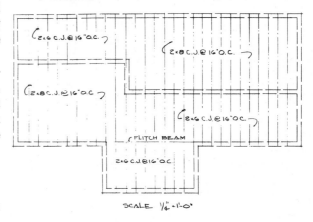

FIGURE 11-8 (right)    Ceiling framing plan

After all the framing members have been drawn in, any necessary notes and dimensions are added. Notes are used to indicate the size of the individual framing members, beam size, spacing of the framing members, and to denote special features. Dimensions are used to locate structural items such as columns, girders, beams, and double joists.

## Assignment:

1. Draw a roof framing plan for the efficiency apartment shown in Fig. 11-9.
2. Using the same plan, draw a roof framing plan for a gable roof.
3. Develop a floor framing plan for the efficiency apartment.

FIGURE 11-9 (below and right)    Apartment floor plan

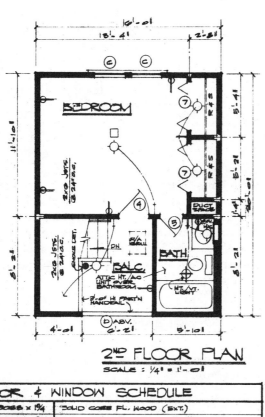

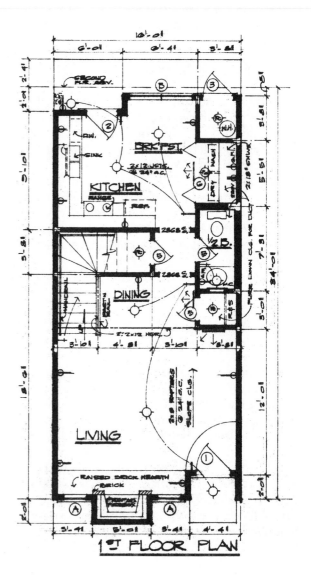

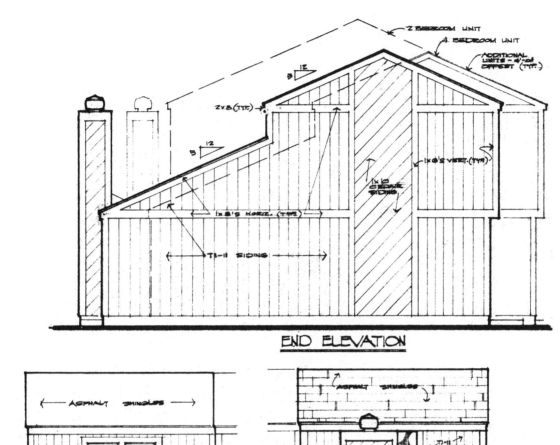

2 BEDROOM UNIT

1 BEDROOM UNIT

ADDITIONAL UNITS - 4'-0" OFFSET (TYP.)

2 X 8 (TYP.)

8 / 12

8 / 12

1 X 6'S VERT. (TYP.)

1 X 10 CEDAR SIDING

1 X 8'S HORIZ. (TYP.)

T1-11 SIDING

 END ELEVATION

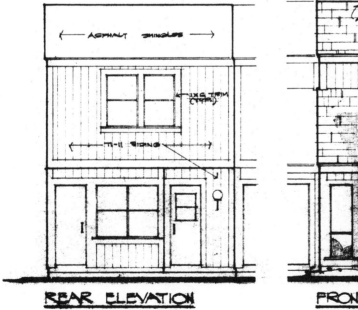

ASPHALT SHINGLES

1 X 6 TRIM (TYP.)

T1-11 SIDING

REAR ELEVATION

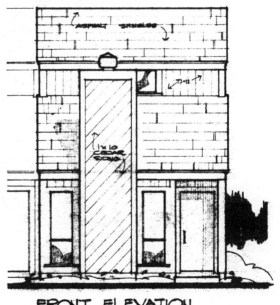

ASPHALT SHINGLES

T1-11

1 X 10 CEDAR SIDING

FRONT ELEVATION

SCALE : 1/4" = 1'-0"

A plot plan is a view looking directly down on a lot and building (see Fig. 12-1). It should locate the building on the lot; show any natural features that exist; indicate the lot size and shape; show necessary elevations and contours; show roads and setbacks; include dimensions of front, rear, and side yards; show the location of walks, driveways, steps, patios, and porches; indicate the elevation of the first floor and the finish grade at each primary corner; show any trees that need to be saved, as well as any that need to be removed; and it should show the location and identification of utility service lines.

## Scale

The scale to which a plot plan is drawn varies with the size of the building and the property on which the building will be placed. In most cases, the plot plan is drawn to a scale in which 1″ = 20′0″. Regardless of the scale used, the property lines should fall well within the borderlines of a standard-size drafting sheet. Since this is so, the size of the drafting sheet also dictates the scale. To provide ease of handling, the drafting sheet should be the same size as other sheets.

## Property Lines

Property lines are drawn as a series of heavy long and short dashes and are used to locate the outline of a particular parcel of land. Dimensions are placed on the property line to indicate the length of each line and in some cases the bearing angles are also recorded. If not, the angle between the two intersecting property lines should be given (see Fig. 12-2). When a bearing angle is given it is usually recorded in degrees, and if necessary, in minutes and seconds.

## Contour Lines

A contour line is an imaginary line that represents a particular elevation, and indicates the amount of slope in a certain area. The dimensions of contour lines are provided either by means of their elevations above sea level or by a reference datum plane. Contour lines are usually spaced on intervals of 2, 4, or

145

## 12
## The Plot Plan

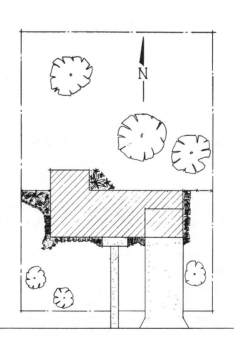

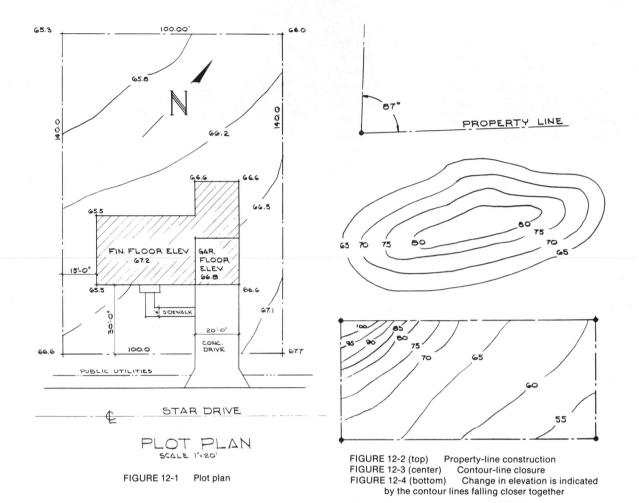

PLOT PLAN
SCALE 1"=20'

FIGURE 12-1     Plot plan

FIGURE 12-2 (top)     Property-line construction
FIGURE 12-3 (center)     Contour-line closure
FIGURE 12-4 (bottom)     Change in elevation is indicated
by the contour lines falling closer together

6', but other intervals can also be used. A contour interval is the vertical distance between adjacent contour lines.

Listed below are some natural characteristics of contour lines:

□ A contour line on the ground will close on itself (see Fig. 12-3).
□ Contour lines that are close together indicate there is a steep rise in elevation (see Fig. 12-4).
□ Adjacent contour lines usually have similar characteristics (see Fig. 12-5).
□ When contour lines are spaced relatively far apart, this usually indicates that the land is flat.
□ Contour lines will not cross each other unless there is an unusual occurrence such as an overhanging cliff.
□ If a contour line crosses a stream, the lines will point upstream (see Fig. 12-6).

□ A depression is indicated by a series of lines projecting from the last contour line (see Fig. 12-7).

## Building Location and Arrangement

In most cases an individual does not have a choice of direction in which a building will face, but may have a choice in positioning the building on the lot. In the decision concerning how to place the building, the following characteristics should be considered: natural contour, trees, utilities, view, surrounding houses, code restrictions, and style of house to be built.

To achieve the optimum value from the topography and the existing climatic conditions, the building arrangement should adhere to the following conditions:

□ The building should be placed so that it relates to the natural topography—avoid deep cuts, fills, excessive foundation-wall depth, unnecessary steps, and steep accesses.

□ The building should be placed so that it may receive optimum benefits from climatic conditions, assuring maximum benefit from/protection against sun, wind, temperature, and precipitation.
□ The building should be placed so that it has attractrive on-site and off-site views.
□ The building should be placed so that adverse noises are minimized.
□ The building should be located to assure adequate open space for an adequate outdoor living area.

Once the position of the building has been decided, the structure is drawn on the plot plan. There are two basic ways in which it can be represented. One method that is often used is to show a roof plan to indicate the location

FIGURE 12-5 (top)      Adjacent contour lines
FIGURE 12-6 (center)   Contour lines crossing a stream
FIGURE 12-7 (bottom)   Depression

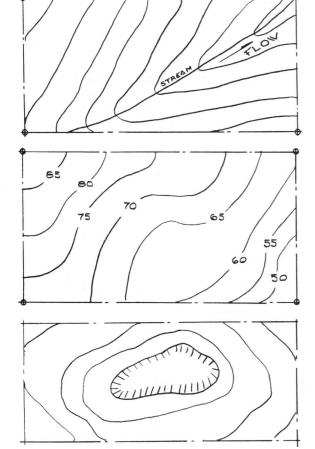

and the position of the structure; the other technique is simply to show the foundation outline.

## Lots, Yards, and Building Setback Distance

In most cases the yard depth and width is arranged to assure adequate distance between buildings. The U.S. Department of Housing and Urban Development minimum guidelines related to adequate distance between building wall and lot line are as follows:

□ The distance from a primary wall to a lot line is 6′ plus 2′ for each story in height plus 1′ for each 10′ of length.

$$(D = 6 + 2S \times L/10)$$

A primary wall is defined as a wall that contains the principal window(s) in a habitable room, except bedrooms and kitchen, and/or the main entrance to the dwelling when it directly faces a primary wall of another dwelling.

□ The distance from a secondary wall to a lot line is a minimum of 5′. A secondary wall is defined as a wall that contains window(s) of rooms for other than a primary wall as defined above.
□ The minimum distance from a windowless wall to the lot line is 5′. A windowless wall is defined as a wall that has no windows.

The setback distance of buildings from the street should conform to the following stipulations:

□ The setback should be sufficient to assure reasonable visual privacy for indoor and outdoor living areas.
□ The setback should provide ample space for drives, walks, parking space, and plant materials.
□ The setback should be consistent with particular topographic features and other site conditions.

## Utilities

Utilities such as water, gas, sewer, electricity, septic tank, and field lines should be properly located and drawn with the correct symbols.

TABLE 12-1    MINIMUM DISTANCES IN FEET

| Source of Pollution | Minimum Distance (feet) |
|---|---|
| Septic tank | 50 |
| Absorption field | 100 |
| Seepage pit | 100 |
| Absorption bed | 100 |
| Sewer lines | 50 |
| Drywell | 50 |

TABLE 12-2    MINIMUM DISTANCES

| From | To | | | |
|---|---|---|---|---|
| | Septic Tank | Absorption Field | Seepage Pit | Absorption Bed |
| Well | 50 | 100 | 100 | 100 |
| Property line | 10 | 5 | 10 | 10 |
| Foundation wall | 5 | 5 | 20 | 5 |
| Water lines | 10 | 10 | 10 | 10 |
| Seepage pit | 6 | 6 | | |
| Drywell | 6 | 20 | 20 | 20 |

When the utilities are placed, they should extend from the utility service to the building and their locations should be dimensioned.

If a well is used to supply potable water to a building, it should be located at least the distances from sources of pollution shown in Table 12-1.

If a septic tank and subsurface absorption field is used as a sewage disposal system, the minimum distances shown in Table 12-2 should be followed.

## Driveway and Parking Space

A driveway and parking space should provide safe and adequate on-site parking space where a garage or carport is not provided; safe, convenient, all-weather vehicular access to

garage, carport, or parking space; and construction having reasonable durability and economy of maintenance.

A driveway should extend from street to carport, garage, or parking space, have a minimum width of 8′, have a flare or radii adequate for safe and convenient ingress and egress, and a minimum ⅛″ per foot crown or cross-slope (see Fig. 12-8). If a parking space is used, it should be a minimum of 22′ in length and 10′ in width.

## Walks

Walks should be provided for safe, convenient, all-weather pedestrian access to the building and should be constructed to assure reasonable durability and economy of maintenance. A walk should extend from the front entrance of the building to the street, public walk, or driveway (see Fig. 12-9). It should have a minimum width of 3′ and a minimum cross-slope of ⅛″ per foot.

FIGURE 12-8    Dimensioning a drive

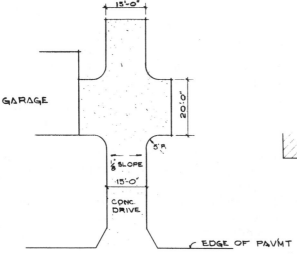

FIGURE 12-9    Locating a sidewalk

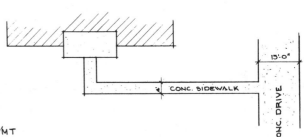

## DRAFTING PROCEDURES FOR THE PLOT PLAN
### Notes and Dimensions

To complete the plot plan, necessary notes and dimensions are added. The sides of the

property and the setbacks should be dimensioned. Notes can include such items as lot number, subdivision, city, location of utilities, name of any streets or roads, title, and scale (see Fig. 12-10).

## North Point Indicator

Each plot plan should have an indicator that establishes the true direction of North (see Fig. 12-11). The indicator is usually in the shape of an arrow and should be functional rather than artistic.

## Landscape Plot Plans

Landscape plot plans are not always used in a typical set of plans, but they are sometimes used to show the location of shrubs, trees, gardens, and pools (see Fig. 12-12). In addition, they often indicate the species of the plantings. To indicate the shrubs and trees, appropriate symbols are used.

In most cases the plan is drawn by a landscape architect and can be used for competitive bids on the plantings and their installation.

PLOT PLAN
SCALE 1"-20'-0"
LOT 133 OAK FOREST SUBDIVISION
EXTENSION 63 & 64
MONROE, LA.

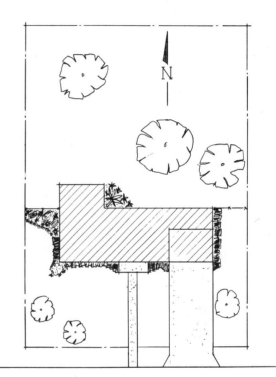

FIGURE 12-10 (above)    Placing title and notes on a plot plan
FIGURE 12-11 (upper right)    North-point indicator
FIGURE 12-12 (lower right)    Landscape plot plan

## Assignment:
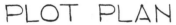

1. Complete the plot plan shown in Fig. 12-13
2. Develop a plot plan using the following criteria:
   a. Lot size 100' × 150'
   b. Rectangular building
   c. Building 30' × 60'
   d. 30' setback
   e. Uniform slope from front of lot to back
   f. Front of the lot has an elevation of 98' and the back an elevation of 95'
   g. Public utilities

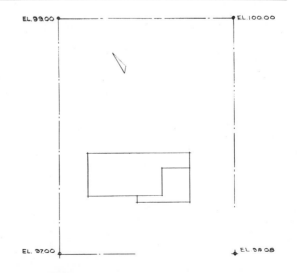

FIGURE 12-13 (right)    Dimensioning the plot plan

An adequate plumbing system is necessary to maintain minimum health standards and is required in homes built today. A typical plumbing system consists of a water supply and a waste disposal system, which entail a network of pipes, connectors, and valves. The most common materials used in a plumbing system are cast iron, copper, plastic, vitrified clay pipe, and galvanized steel pipe.

## 13

# The Plumbing Plan

### Cast Iron Pipe

Cast iron pipes are usually used for sanitary drainage and stacks in waste disposal systems. Such pipe is typically sold in 5' lengths and can have a large-diameter "hub" at one end and a slight ridge "spigot" at the other. To join the different lengths of pipe, the spigot is placed inside the hub, and oakum and lead are packed into the space between them (see Fig. 13-1). The oakum is packed with a "yarning iron" to within ¾ or 1" of the top of the hub. Molten lead is then poured over the oakum and allowed to cool. As soon as the lead hardens, it is "caulked"—that is, caulking irons are tapped against the lead surface, spreading the lead against the hub surface.

Another means of connecting cast iron pipe that has a bell and spigot, is to join the individual pieces with a neoprene gasket (see Fig. 13-2). The gasket is inserted in the bell and mopped with a lubricant; then the spigot end of the connecting pipe is force-fitted into the gasket. This particular technique is faster than using oakum and lead, and according to recent research is very effective.

Hubless cast iron soil pipe and fittings are also finding a market in the plumbing industry (see Fig. 13-3). Cast iron pipe of this nature is joined by a neoprene sealing gasket designed to be compressed around a butted pipe joint with a special stainless steel retaining clamp. The piping is available in 2, 3, and 4" diameters and 5 and 10' lengths. The system is easy to install, requires no heat or flame during installation, and a standard 3" pipe can fit into a 2" × 4" stud wall.

### Vitrified Clay Pipe

Vitrified clay pipe is frequently used for public sewers, house sewers, and drains. It is made

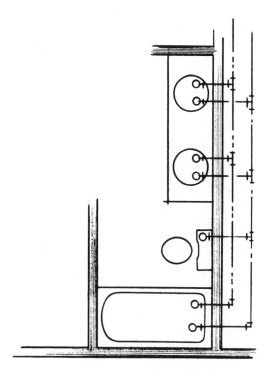

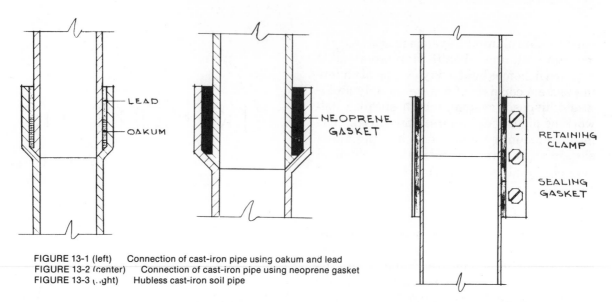

FIGURE 13-1 (left)      Connection of cast-iron pipe using oakum and lead
FIGURE 13-2 (center)    Connection of cast-iron pipe using neoprene gasket
FIGURE 13-3 (right)     Hubless cast-iron soil pipe

of fired clay and water and is available in varying lengths. To join the different lengths of pipe, the spigot is placed inside the hub and oakum is packed between the inside of the hub and the outside of the connecting pipe. A mixture of portland cement, sand, and water is then packed over the oakum.

When the pipe is laid it should be placed on stable soil or on a stone or concrete foundation. If it is laid on an unstable foundation, the pipe may sag, causing the joint to crack.

Individual pipe lengths can also be joined by a mechanical compression joint made of polyvinyl chlorides. The compression joint is first inserted into the hub; it is then mopped with a lubricant, and the spigot end of the connecting pipe is force-fitted into the gasket.

## Plastic Pipe

Plastic pipe is presently being used in all areas of construction, but many local building codes have still not adopted the relatively new material. The plastic is readily cut with a sharp knife or any fine-toothed saw and can be joined with threaded fittings or a special plastic cement. The ends of the pipe must first be coated with cement and then inserted into the fittings. As the pipe is being slid into position, it is slightly twisted so the cement will spread evenly.

## Galvanized Steel Pipe

To join galvanized steel pipe it is only necessary to dope the ends with pipe-joint com-pound and screw the fittings in place. However, if it is necessary, the pipe can be cut, reamed, and threaded with a ratchet die.

## Copper Tubing

Copper tubing is available in three types—K, L, and M. Each type represents a series of sizes with different wall thicknesses. All three types can be purchased in hard-tempered straight lengths, but only types K and L are available in a soft or annealed temper straight length or coil. Type M is only available in hard temper. Hard tempered tubes can be joined by soldering, brazing, or by the use of capillary fittings, while soft-tempered tubes can be joined by soldering, brazing, or by means of flare-type compression fittings.

For a soldered joint, the tube must first be cut to the correct length with a hacksaw or a tube cutter. Then the small burrs should be removed by the reamer on the cutter or by a half-round file. The surfaces to be joined should then be cleaned of any surface dirt or oil. One of the best ways to clean copper tubing is to lightly sand the ends of the tubes with a strip of emery cloth. Cleaning pads and special wire brushes, however, can also be used.

Once the surfaces have been cleaned, they should be covered with a thin film of flux, which is applied with a brush and is used to remove residual traces of oxides and to protect the surfaces to be soldered from further oxidation. The most widely recommended flux is mildly corrosive; it contains zinc and

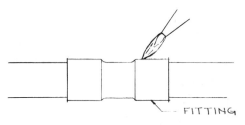

FIGURE 13-4    Connecting copper

ammonium chlorides in a petrolatum base. Once the flux has been spread, the tube can be placed into the fitting and adjacent to the stop in the fitting. As it is being fitted, it should be slightly turned so the flux will spread evenly over the adjoining surfaces. Excess flux is then removed with a rag and the joint is ready for soldering.

To properly solder the joint, an even distribution of heat should be played on the fitting; but the flame should not be pointed into the socket (see Fig. 13-4). When the surface has been heated, the solder should be touched to the joint; if the area has been correctly prepared, the solder will be drawn into the joint by the natural force of capillary action. Under no circumstance should the flame be placed directly on the solder, nor should the fitting be overheated. Overheating may burn the flux from the joint, or it might cause the fitting to crack. Once the joint has been soldered, it should be allowed to cool at room temperature.

To make a flared joint, the copper tube must be cut to the correct length and the burrs removed. The tube is then clamped in a flaring block so that the end projects about ⅛" past the face of the block. The yoke of the flaring tool should be placed so that the beveled end of the compressor cone falls directly over the end of the tube. Pressure is applied to the compressor screw and a flare is formed on the end of the tube. The fitting is placed against the flare and the flange nut engaged with the fitting's threads to assemble the joint (see Fig. 13-5). Once the

FIGURE 13-5    Flared copper joint

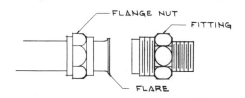

threads have engaged, two wrenches are used to tighten the joint.

If it is necessary, copper tubing can be bent by various methods. One technique is to use a lever-type hand bender.

## Building Drain and Building Sewer

The building drain and building sewer are the lowest horizontal portion of the drainage system and are used to carry waste to the main sewer (see Fig. 13-6). The building drain receives the discharge of all soil and waste stacks; it is a horizontal part of the system located under the building and extending to a point 3' from the outside edge of the building. The building sewer receives the discharge from the building drain and carries the waste to the sewer.

To determine the correct size for the building drain and building sewer, the peak volume of discharge of water and waste must be calculated, which means the total individual fixture-unit values must first be assessed. A fixture unit corresponds to 7½ gallons of water that an ordinary lavatory, with a nominal 1¼" trap, can discharge into a stack. Other fixtures have been tested for maximum flow and fixture-unit value has been assigned to each fixture (see Table 13-1). To determine the size of the building drain or a building sewer, the number of fixture units must be totaled. The size of the building drain or sewer can be determined by following Table 13-2.

For example, if a building has two water closets, two lavatories, a slop sink, a kitchen sink, a pair of laundry tubs, two floor drains, and a shower, there will be a total fixture value of 27. With the 27 fixture units and

FIGURE 13-6    Building drain and sewer

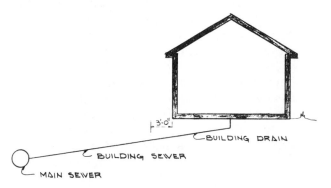

TABLE 13-1    FIXTURE UNITS PER FIXTURE OR GROUP

| Fixture type | Fixture-unit value as load factors | | Minimum size of trap (inches) |
|---|---|---|---|
| 1 bathroom group consisting of water closet, lavatory, and bathtub or shower stall. | Tank water closet | 6 | |
| | Flush-valve water closet | 8 | |
| Bathtub[1] (with or without overhead shower) .................... | | 2 | 1½ |
| Bathtub[1] ................................................... | | 3 | 2 |
| Bidet ...................................................... | | 3 | Nominal ........ 1½ |
| Combination sink-and-tray ................................... | | 3 | 1½ |
| Combination sink-and-tray with food-disposal unit ............ | | 4 | Separate traps .. 1½ |
| Dental unit or cuspidor ...................................... | | ½ | 1¼ |
| Dental lavatory ............................................. | | 1 | 1¼ |
| Drinking fountain .......................................... | | ½ | 1 |
| Dishwasher, domestic ....................................... | | 2 | 1½ |
| Floor drains[2] .............................................. | | 1 | 2 |
| Kitchen sink, domestic ...................................... | | 2 | 1½ |
| Kitchen sink, domestic, with food-disposal unit ............... | | 3 | 1½ |
| Lavatory .................................................. | | 1 | Small P.O ....... 1¼ |
|    Do ...................................................... | | 2 | Large P. O ...... 1½ |
| Lavatory, barber, beauty parlor .............................. | | 2 | 1½ |
| Lavatory, surgeon's ........................................ | | 2 | 1½ |
| Laundry tray (1 or 2 compartments) .......................... | | 2 | 1½ |
| Shower stall, domestic ...................................... | | 2 | 2 |
| Showers (group) per head ................................... | | 3 | |
| Sinks: | | | |
|    Surgeon's ............................................. | | 3 | 1½ |
|    Flushing rim (with valve) ............................... | | 8 | 3 |
|    Service (Trap standard) ................................ | | 3 | 3 |
|    Service (P trap) ........................................ | | 2 | 2 |
|    Pot, scullery, etc. ...................................... | | 4 | 1½ |
| Urinal, pedestal, syphon jet, blowout ........................ | | 8 | Nominal ........ 3 |
| Urinal, wall lip ............................................. | | 4 | 1½ |
| Urinal stall, washout ....................................... | | 4 | 2 |
| Urinal trough (each 2-foot section) ........................... | | 2 | 1½ |
| Wash sink (circular or multiple), each set of faucets ........... | | 2 | Nominal ........ 1½ |
| Water closet: | | | |
|    Tank-operated ........................................ | | 4 | Nominal ........ 3 |
|    Valve-operated ........................................ | | 8 | 3 |

[1]A shower head over a bathtub does not increase the fixture value.
[2]Size of floor drain shall be determined by the area of surface water to be drained.
[3]Lavatories with 1¼- or 1½-inch traps have the same load value; larger P.O. plugs have greater flow rate.

Reprinted from the National Plumber's Code, by permission.

assuming a fall of ¼″ per foot, Table 13-2 indicates that a 3″ building drain is needed. It should be noted that the building drain should have a graduated fall. In most cases the fall is ⅛ or ¼″ per foot, but in some cases there can be a fall of ½″ per foot.

If it is necessary to change direction of the house drain, the change should be made with fittings of long radius. Fittings of this nature decrease the possibility of stoppage, which frequently occurs. To deal with stoppage if and when it does occur, the house drain should be equipped with a cleanout (see Fig.

13-7). A cleanout allows the building drain to be cleaned and should be placed at the base of all soil and waste stacks and at 75′ intervals.

## Soil and Waste Pipes

A soil stack is a vertical portion of the plumbing system that receives the discharge

FIGURE 13-7    Cleanout

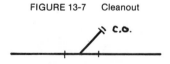

TABLE 13-2    BUILDING DRAINS AND SEWERS

| Diameter of pipe (inches) | Maximum number of fixture units that may be connected to any portion[1] of the building drain or the building sewer at a fall per foot of | | | |
|---|---|---|---|---|
| | $\frac{1}{16}$-inch | $\frac{1}{8}$-inch | $\frac{1}{4}$-inch | $\frac{1}{2}$-inch |
| 2 | ............ | ............ | 21 | 26 |
| 2½ | ............ | ............ | 24 | 31 |
| 3 | ............ | [2]20 | [2]27 | [2]36 |
| 4 | ............ | 180 | 216 | 250 |
| 5 | ............ | 390 | 480 | 575 |
| 6 | ............ | 700 | 840 | 1,000 |
| 8 | 1,400 | 1,600 | 1,920 | 2,300 |
| 10 | 2,500 | 2,900 | 3,500 | 4,200 |
| 12 | 3,900 | 4,600 | 5,600 | 6,700 |

[1]Includes branches of the building drain.
[2]Not over 2 water closets.

Reprinted from the National Plumber's Code, by permission.

of water closets, urinals, or fixtures having similar functions (see Fig. 13-8). A waste pipe is similar to a soil pipe, except that it carries only liquid waste that is free of fecal matter.

Determining the size of a soil or waste stack is done in much the same way as for a building drain. The maximum discharge in terms of fixture units is first calculated, then the pipe diameter is determined (see Table 13-3). The minimum size of a soil stack is 3″

in diameter; however, a pipe 4″ in diameter is preferred.

## Soil Branch

A soil branch is a horizontal portion of the plumbing system that receives the direct discharge of water closets, with or without additional plumbing fixtures (see Fig. 13-9). The

TABLE 13-3    HORIZONTAL FIXTURE BRANCHES AND STACKS

| Diameter of pipe (inches) | Maximum number of fixture units that may be connected to— | | | |
|---|---|---|---|---|
| | Any horizontal[1] fixture branch | 1 stack of 3 stories in height or 3 intervals | More than 3 stories in height | |
| | | | Total for stack | Total at 1 story or branch interval |
| 1¼ | 1 | 2 | 2 | 1 |
| 1½ | 3 | 4 | 8 | 2 |
| 2 | 6 | 10 | 24 | 6 |
| 2½ | 12 | 20 | 42 | 9 |
| 3 | [2]20 | [3]30 | [3]60 | [2]16 |
| 4 | 160 | 240 | 500 | 90 |
| 5 | 360 | 540 | 1,100 | 200 |
| 6 | 620 | 960 | 1,900 | 350 |
| 8 | 1,400 | 2,200 | 3,600 | 600 |
| 10 | 2,500 | 3,800 | 5,600 | 1,000 |
| 12 | 3,900 | 6,000 | 8,400 | 1,500 |

[1]Does not include branches of the building drain.
[2]Not over 2 water closets.
[3]Not over 6 water closets.

Reprinted from the National Plumber's Code, by permission.

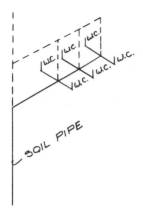

FIGURE 13-8     Soil pipe

soil branch should be equipped with an adequate number of cleanouts. They should be installed whenever the soil branch changes direction, and they should be placed at the end of the branch that is farthest away from the soil stack. To assure the proper waste velocity flow, the soil branch should be placed on a ⅛ or ¼" grade per foot.

The soil branch should be adequately supported through its length so it will not sag. In most cases it is recommended that cast iron pipe be supported at not less than 5' intervals.

## Traps

Traps are used in the plumbing system to prevent the passage of sewer gases (see Fig. 13-10). In its simplest form, a trap is a bend in the plumbing that is filled with water. The water completes a seal and makes it impossible for gases to pass. Various types of

mechanical devices have been tried as traps, but most have proved ineffective. The common seal trap has been used for years; it is inexpensive and has proven to be effective. The trap seal, however, can be lost by direct siphoning, evaporation, and capillary action.

Direct siphoning occurs when there is a pressure drop on the discharge side of a trap; when this happens the atmospheric pressure on the fixture side pushes the water seal through the trap. This usually occurs when the trap is not vented.

When a water seal is lost because of evaporation, it is because the trap has not been used for a considerable length of time. The rate of evaporation depends upon the room temperature and the humidity.

When a water seal is lost because of capillary action, it is usually because some object has become lodged in the trap; the object acts as a wick and drains the water from the trap.

## Vents

There are several approved methods for venting a plumbing system to keep direct siphoning from occurring. The particular method used is determined by the layout and number of the fixtures and the design of the building. There are several common types of vents. A *branch vent* connects one or more individual vents with a vent stack or a stack vent (see Fig. 13-11). A *circuit vent* serves two or more

FIGURE 13-9     Soil branch

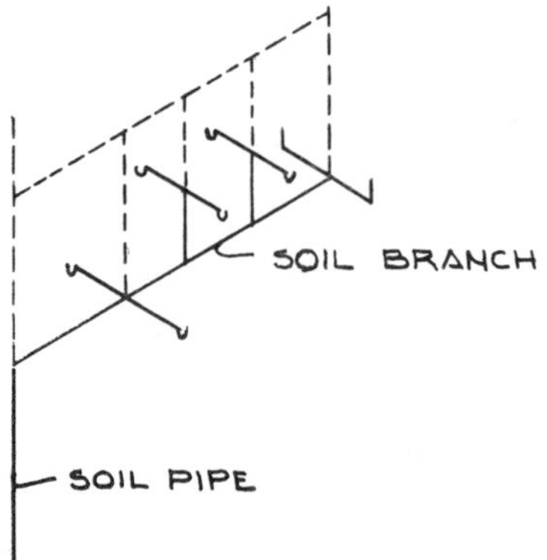

FIGURE 13-10 (left)     Plumbing trap
FIGURE 13-11 (right)     Branch vent

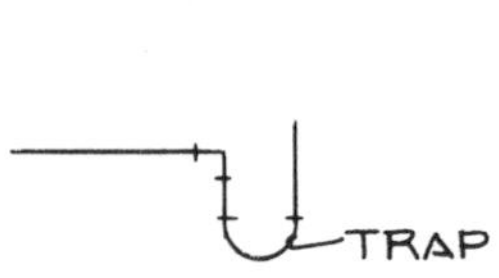

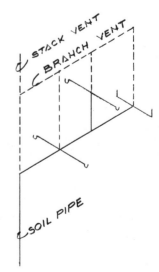

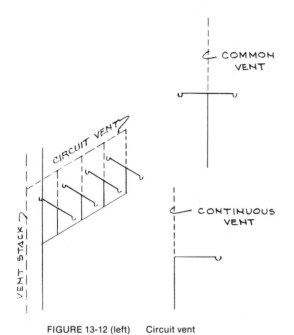

FIGURE 13-12 (left)        Circuit vent
FIGURE 13-13 (upper right)        Common vent
FIGURE 13-14 (lower right)        Continuous vent

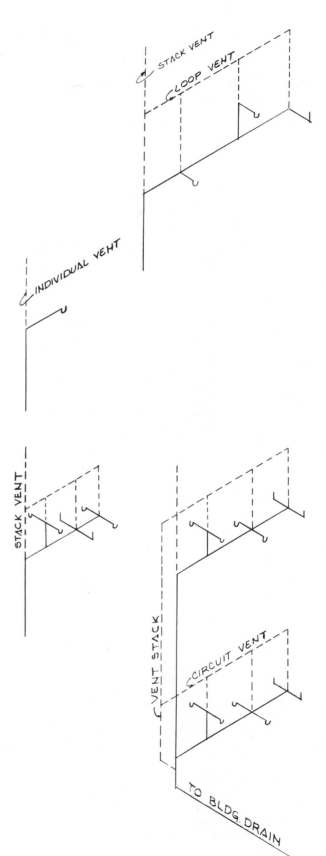

traps and extends from in front of the last fixture connection of a horizontal branch to the vent stack (see Fig. 13-12). A *common vent* serves two fixture drains that are placed back to back or side by side (see Fig. 13-13). A *continuous vent* is the continuation of a vertical drain (see Fig. 13-14). An *individual vent* is a vertical pipe that is placed to vent a particular fixture trap and connects with the vent system above the fixture served (see Fig. 13-15). A *loop vent* serves two or more traps and extends from in front of the last fixture connection of a horizontal branch to the stack vent (see Fig. 13-16). A *stack vent* is the extension of the soil or waste stack (see Fig. 13-17). A *vent stack* is a vertical vent pipe that is placed for the purpose of providing free circulation of air (see Fig. 13-18).

The size of continuous, circuit, and loop vents can be determined from Table 13-4 and the minimum diameters and maximum lengths of vent stacks and stack vents can be determined from Table 13-5.

FIGURE 13-15 (upper near right)        Individual vent
FIGURE 13-16 (upper far right)        Loop vent
FIGURE 13-17 (lower near right)        Stack vent
FIGURE 13-18 (lower far right)        Vent stack

**TABLE 13-4    HORIZONTAL CIRCUIT AND LOOP VENT SIZING TABLE**

| Line No. | Soil or waste pipe diameter (inches) | Fixture units: Number not exceeding | Diameter of circuit or loop vent | | | | | |
|---|---|---|---|---|---|---|---|---|
| | | | 1½" | 2" | 2½" | 3" | 4" | 5" |
| | | | Horizontal length, not exceeding (feet) | | | | | |
| 1 | 1½ | 10 | 20 | | | | | |
| 2 | 2 | 12 | 15 | 40 | | | | |
| 3 | 2 | 20 | 10 | 35 | | | | |
| 4 | 3 | 10 | | 30 | 40 | 100 | | |
| 5 | 3 | 30 | | | 40 | 100 | | |
| 6 | 3 | 60 | | | 30 | 80 | | |
| 7 | 4 | 100 | | 25 | 25 | 52 | 200 | |
| 8 | 4 | 200 | | 10 | 20 | 50 | 180 | |
| 9 | 4 | 500 | | | 14 | 36 | 140 | |
| 10 | 5 | 200 | | | | 16 | 70 | 200 |
| 11 | 5 | 1100 | | | | 10 | 40 | 140 |

**TABLE 13-5    MINIMUM DIAMETERS AND MAXIMUM LENGTHS OF VENT STACKS AND STACK VENTS***

| Diameter of Soil or Waste Stack (in.) | Total Fixture Units Connected to Stack (dfu) | 1¼ | 1½ | 2 | 2½ | 3 | 4 | 5 | 6 | 8 | 10 |
|---|---|---|---|---|---|---|---|---|---|---|---|
| | | (Maximum developed length of vent, in feet, given below) | | | | | | | | | |
| 1¼ | 2 | 30 | | | | | | | | | |
| 1½ | 8 | 50 | 150 | | | | | | | | |
| 1½ | 10 | 30 | 100 | | | | | | | | |
| 2 | 12 | 30 | 75 | 200 | | | | | | | |
| 2 | 20 | 26 | 50 | 150 | | | | | | | |
| 2½ | 42 | | 30 | 100 | 300 | | | | | | |
| 3 | 7 | | 42 | 150 | 360 | 1040 | | | | | |
| 3 | 21 | | 32 | 110 | 270 | 810 | | | | | |
| 3 | 53 | | 27 | 94 | 230 | 680 | | | | | |
| 3 | 102 | | 25 | 86 | 210 | 620 | | | | | |
| 4 | 43 | | | 35 | 85 | 250 | 980 | | | | |
| 4 | 140 | | | 27 | 65 | 200 | 750 | | | | |
| 4 | 320 | | | 23 | 55 | 170 | 640 | | | | |
| 4 | 530 | | | 21 | 50 | 150 | 580 | | | | |
| 5 | 190 | | | | 28 | 82 | 320 | 990 | | | |
| 5 | 490 | | | | 21 | 63 | 250 | 760 | | | |
| 5 | 940 | | | | 18 | 53 | 210 | 640 | | | |
| 5 | 1400 | | | | 16 | 49 | 190 | 590 | | | |
| 6 | 500 | | | | | 33 | 130 | 400 | 1000 | | |
| 6 | 1100 | | | | | 26 | 100 | 310 | 780 | | |
| 6 | 2000 | | | | | 22 | 84 | 260 | 660 | | |
| 6 | 2900 | | | | | 20 | 77 | 240 | 600 | | |
| 8 | 1800 | | | | | | 31 | 95 | 240 | 940 | |
| 8 | 3400 | | | | | | 24 | 73 | 190 | 720 | |
| 8 | 5600 | | | | | | 20 | 62 | 160 | 610 | |
| 8 | 7600 | | | | | | 18 | 56 | 140 | 560 | |
| 10 | 4000 | | | | | | | 31 | 78 | 310 | 960 |
| 10 | 7200 | | | | | | | 24 | 60 | 240 | 740 |
| 10 | 11,000 | | | | | | | 20 | 51 | 200 | 630 |
| 10 | 15,000 | | | | | | | 18 | 46 | 180 | 570 |

*Does not apply to circuit, loop, or sump vents.

## SEWAGE DISPOSAL FOR INDIVIDUAL HOMES _____

In some cases a home may not connect to a sewer, but must use a septic tank and a subsurface disposal field to rid itself of waste and effluent (see Fig. 13-19). A septic tank is a watertight tank, usually made of steel or concrete, in which the solid parts of sewage settle out and are largely changed into liquids or gases by bacteria.

Once the bacteria has worked on the solid waste a heavy black semiliquid sludge remains and must be removed from the tank every few years. Septic tank size varies; in most cases minimum size for a one-bedroom home is a 500-gallon tank; for a two-bedroom home a 750 gallon tank; for a three-bedroom home a 900-gallon tank; and for a four-bedroom home a 1,150-gallon tank.

The septic tank effluent is disposed of in soil-absorption trenches or small oxidation ponds. Before the effluent can be placed in a "subsurface irrigation" field, three general conditions must be met:

☐ The soil percolation rate should be within the acceptable range.
☐ The maximum elevation of the ground water table should be below the bottom of the "subsurface irrigation" field.

FIGURE 13-19   Septic tank and subsurface disposal field

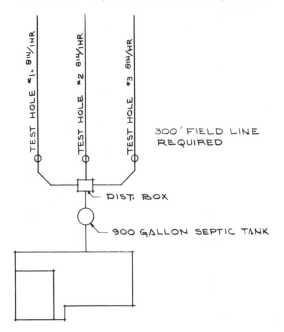

☐ If an impervious strata or a clay formation is located under the irrigation field, it should be at a depth greater than 4' below the trenches.

To determine the absorption trench length, a "percolation test" must be made. To conduct this test, the following steps should be followed:

☐ Three separate test holes should be dug in varying locations on the proposed absorption field. The holes should be 4 to 12" in depth and should have their sides carefully scratched with a knifeblade.
☐ The hole should then be filled with clear water, which is allowed to stand overnight. This is done to insure that the soil is given ample opportunity to swell and to approach the typical operating condition of the wet season of the year.
☐ After the water has been allowed to stand overnight, water is added until the liquid depth is at least 6" but not more than 12". From a reference point, the water-level drop is measured over a 60-minute period.
☐ The water-level drop is measured and recorded for each of the three holes. The average for the three holes is then used to determine the total length of the absorption trench. (The absorption length can be determined from the information in Table 13-6.)

For maximum efficiency, the absorption trench system should comply with the following standards:

☐ The field line should be at least 160 linear feet long. The trench should be 12 to 18" wide and 24 to 36" deep (see Fig. 13-20). An individual field line should not be over 100' in length and the individual lines should be placed 6' apart.
☐ The subsurface absorption trenches should be located a minimum of 100' from any well and 10' from any dwelling or property line.
☐ A minimum of two field lines must be used.
☐ To promote even distribution of the effluent, the trench should not have any slope.
☐ The field lines should be a minimum of 4"

TABLE 13-6    SUBSURFACE ABSORPTION FIELDS
            (MINIMUM REQUIRED TRENCH
            BOTTOM AREA PER BEDROOM)

| Time in minutes for water to fall 1 inch during final test period | Minimum required area, sq ft |
|---|---|
| 2 or less | 85 |
| 3 | 100 |
| 4 | 115 |
| 5 | 125 |
| 10 | 165 |
| 15 | 190 |
| 30 | 250 |
| 45 | 300 |
| 60 | 330 |

Over 60 minutes unsuitable for absorption field.

NOTE: The areas in Table 13-6 provide for plumbing fixtures and appliances common in residential use. Automatic sequence washer, mechanical garbage grinder, and dishwasher included.

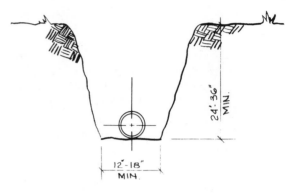

FIGURE 13-20    Absorbtion trench

in diameter, laid on a slope of 2 to 3″ per 100 feet, and consist of either perforated nonmetallic pipe, agricultural drain tile, or vitrified clay bell-and-spigot sewer pipe laid with open joints.

☐ The field line should be surrounded by wash gravel or crushed stone. The bed material should be placed at least 2″ above the top of the pipe to at least 6″ below the bottom of the pipe.

## WATER SUPPLY SYSTEMS

According to most building codes, every occupied building should be provided with an ample water supply that is maintained in satisfactory working condition. If the building is classified as a dwelling unit, it is also required to have at least one kitchen sink equipped with hot and cold running water and a waste connection.

A water supply system is composed of a system of water lines, valves, and fixtures. The water lines, in most cases, are either copper or plastic and are connected using conventional techniques. The sizes of the lines vary, however, and can be computed by using Tables 13-7 and 13-8. Each fixture must first be assigned a fixture value (see Table 13-7); the fixture units can then be totaled. Then the minimum size of the individual fixture supply pipes can be determined (Table 13-8).

### Valves

Valves, in a water supply system, are used to control the flow of water. A *gate valve* has a retractable leaf that is machined to fit tightly

TABLE 13-7    FIXTURE-UNIT RATINGS FOR WATER-
            SUPPLIED FIXTURES

| Fixture | Fixture Units |
|---|---|
| Water closet | 5 |
| Lavatory, 1¼″ waste | 1 |
| Lavatory, 1½″ waste | 2 |
| Bathtub, 1½″ waste | 2 |
| Bathtub, 2″ waste | 4 |
| Shower | 2 |
| Kitchen sink | 2 |
| Kitchen sink with disposer | 3 |
| Dishwasher | 3 |
| Laundry tray | 3 |
| Clothes washer | 2 |

TABLE 13-8    FIXTURE SUPPLY PIPE SIZE

| Water Supply Fixture Units | Pipe size (in inches) |
|---|---|
| 2 | ½ |
| 4 | ¾ |
| 32 | 1 |
| 40 | 1¼ |
| 120 | 1½ |
| 240 | 2 |
| 450 | 2½ |
| 800 | 3 |
| 2,000 | 4 |

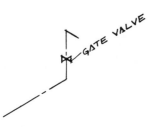

FIGURE 13-21    Gate valve

FIGURE 13-22    Capped-air chamber

against two sloping surfaces. A valve of this type is usually placed in a location where is it left open most of the time (see Fig. 13-21). A *globe valve* is similar to a gate valve and is used for the same purposes. Faucets and hose connections are an example of globe valves.

A *check valve* is used to prevent flow in a direction opposite to that which is planned. The valve is designed with a hinged leaf that swings in the direction of flow but closes against attempted flow in the other direction.

## Pipe Support

Because of the weight of the pipe and water, it is often necessary to support pipe with individual supports, otherwise the pipes might fracture, allowing water leakage. Copper and plastic water supply pipes 1½″ or larger should be placed in a *vertical* position or supported at each story; pipes smaller than 1½″ should be supported at 4′ intervals. Screwed galvanized steel pipes should be supported at not less than every other story height.

Copper and plastic pipes 1½″ and smaller, placed in a *horizontal* position, should be supported at 6′ intervals; piping 2″ and larger should be supported at 10′ intervals. If screwed pipe is used, it should be supported on 12′ centers.

Regardless of the spacing of the hangers, they should be strong enough to support the weight imposed on them.

## Shock and Water Expansion

Water supply systems are often noisy; when valves are abruptly shut off, pipes may rattle and cause excessive noise. One way to eliminate the "water hammer" effect is to extend the fixture branch approximately 18″ (see Fig. 13-22). The added pipe length traps air,

which absorbs the impact of the water. There are commercial devices that can be used, but a capped air chamber is usually sufficient.

## Hot-Water Systems

A hot-water system consists of a hot-water tank and a series of lines to feed the various fixtures. In many buildings the network of pipes is installed so there is instant hot water.

The two systems that are used to provide continuous hot-water circulation are the upfeed gravity return and the pump circuit system. The upfeed gravity return system operates on the principle that water expands and becomes lighter when it is heated above 39.2°F. The piping of a hot-water system using this technique is arranged so that hot water is carried to the farthest fixture and is returned back to the heater with a continuation of the water line (see Fig. 13-23). Perhaps the most successful technique for circulating hot water, however, is through the use

FIGURE 13-23    Gravity-return system

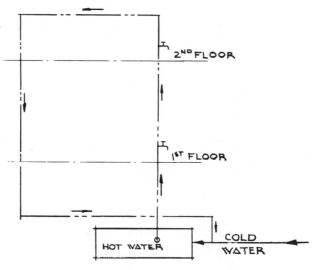

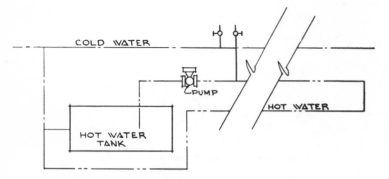

FIGURE 13-24    Circulating hot water with a pump

of a circulating pump. In this system a centrifugal type of pump is placed on the circulating main as close to the heating unit as possible (see Fig. 13-24).

### Fixtures

There are many different types of plumbing fixtures—such as lavatories, water closets, bathtubs, and sinks.

Lavatory bowls may be circular, square, or oval, and are usually made of vitreous china, but may also be made of stainless steel or fiberglass. They usually hold 1 or 2 gallons of water and are equipped with a trap to prevent the escape of sewer gases.

There are five basic types of lavatory styles that are popular today. The *flush mount* type is installed with a metal ring or frame to hold it in place. This type is inexpensive, but presents a small cleaning problem at the junction of the rim and the countertop.

A *self-rimming lavatory* requires no metal frame, but is so designed that its rim supports the entire assembly. When properly installed and sealed, a lavatory of this type does not present a maintenance problem.

An *under-the-counter type of lavatory* is mounted below the counter-top, which is usually marble or a synthetic material that resembles marble. The style of the lavatory is striking but it can present a maintenance problem.

The *integral lavatory and counter* have become increasingly popular with the development of "synthetic marble" counter-tops. These are attractive and are easy to clean.

A popular lavatory is the *conventional wall-hung type*, which is often rectangular in shape. This type is used where space is scarce, or where storage space is not required.

Bathtubs are usually manufactured from one of three materials: molded cast iron with a porcelain enamel surface, formed steel with a porcelain enamel surface, or molded gel-coated glass fiber-reinforced polyester resin (fiberglass).

A cast iron tub with a porcelain enamel surface is available in 4, 4½, 5, 5½, and 6′ lengths. The widths range from 30 to 48″ and the depth from 12 to 16″. A tub of this type can weigh as much as 500 pounds.

A formed-steel tub with a porcelain finish is less expensive and weighs less than a cast iron tub. This type is available in lengths of 4½ and 5′. Widths range from 30 to 31″, and the depth is usually 15 to 15½″.

The fiberglass bathtub has only recently been accepted as a reliable plumbing fixture. There are various styles available, but most are only manufactured in 5′ lengths.

Water closets may be either floor-mounted or wall-mounted, and are constructed so that flushing will siphon out the contents. The water closet usually has a water tank or a flush valve for flushing purposes. There are also several different types of water-closet bowls. The four basic kinds of residential water closets are washdown, reverse trap, siphon jet, and low profile. Regardless of the type, they are all installed in basically the same manner. The bowl is usually set with a wax-ring gasket and bolted to the floor or wall. As it is being lowered into position it is twisted slightly; this helps to settle the wax ring and bowl in the proper position. Once the bowl has been placed, the closet water tank can be hung.

## DRAFTING PROCEDURES FOR THE PLUMBING PLAN

The plumbing plan is usually drawn by placing a clean sheet of tracing paper over the floor plan. Then the floor plan is traced with a 2H or 3H lead. As it is traced, most details are

omitted—there is no need to show electrical features, and it isn't necessary to dimension the drawing.

When the floor plan has been traced, all the

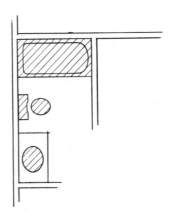

plumbing fixtures are drawn to scale. Some draftspersons crosshatch them to emphasize their location (see Fig. 13-25). The cold-water supply line is then located and drawn in. The plumbing lines are usually drawn with an H lead, in a much darker line than the outline of the building. All other cold-water lines are then drawn in complete with valves, fittings, and pipe size (see Fig. 13-26).

The hot-water lines are drawn in next (see Fig. 13-27). A supply line is first run from the cold-water line to the water heater. Then, with the correct hot-water pipe symbol, the hot-water pipes are drawn in. They should be shown a minimum of 6″ from the cold-water lines. It is also necessary to size and place fittings and valves on the hot-water lines.

The house drain is indicated by a heavy dark line. Any necessary branches can be connected to the house drain. The branches should be made as short and direct as possible. All cleanout symbols and vents are shown in their proper location (see Fig. 13-28).

For clarity, an isometric detail is usually drawn of each cluster of plumbing fixtures. A single-line isometric drawing is used without standard symbols and fixtures. The isometric is not usually drawn to scale and the fixtures are not shown. To complete the detail, it should be properly sized, with notes added for clarity.

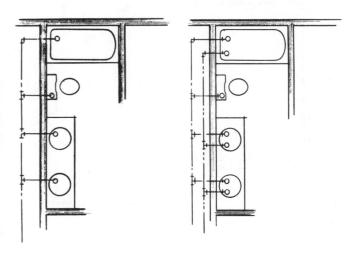

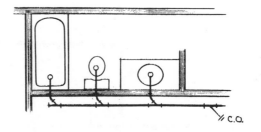

FIGURE 13-25 (upper right)    Crosshatched plumbing fixtures
FIGURE 13-26 (center near right)    Addition of cold-water lines
FIGURE 13-27 (center far right)    Addition of hot-water lines
FIGURE 13-28 (lower right)    Drafting the house drain

## Assignment:

1. Correctly size the detail in Fig. 13-29.
2. On an 18″ × 24″ or 24″ × 36″ sheet of tracing paper, draw the plumbing plan for the house shown in Fig. 13-30.
3. Using an 18″ × 24″ or 24″ × 36″ sheet of tracing paper, draw a plumbing plan for the house in Fig. 13-31. Connect the building sewer to septic tank and field lines for sewage disposal.

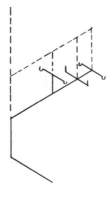

FIGURE 13-29 (right)    Assignment: Size the plumbing detail

FIGURE 13-30    Assignment: Draw the plumbing plan

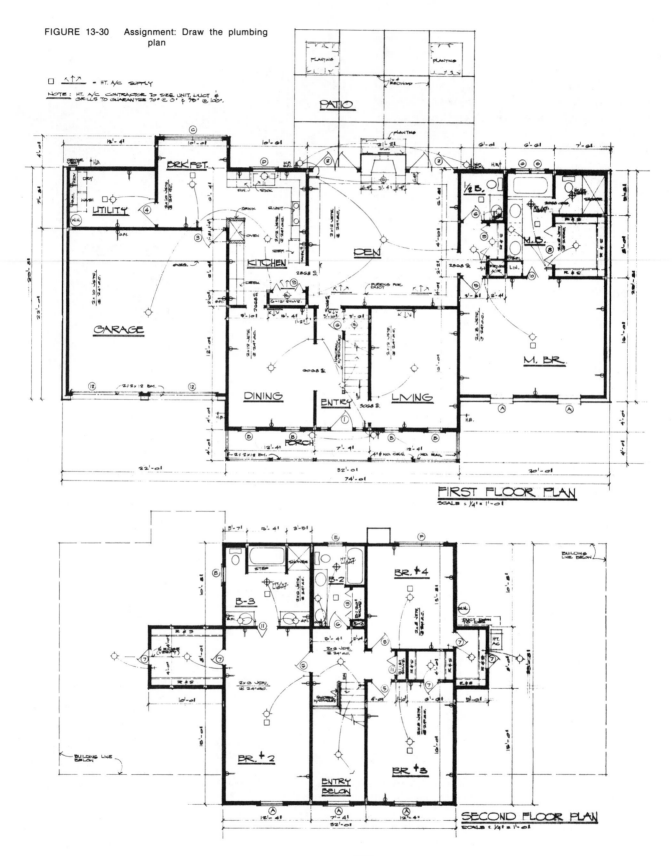

FIRST FLOOR PLAN
SCALE: 1/4" = 1'-0"

SECOND FLOOR PLAN
SCALE: 1/4" = 1'-0"

164

FIGURE 13-31    Assignment: Draw the plumbing
and sewage-disposal plan

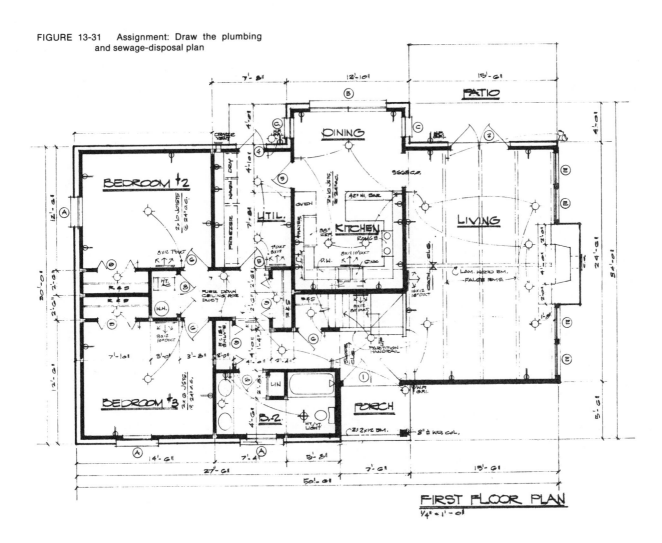

FIRST FLOOR PLAN
1/4" = 1'-0"

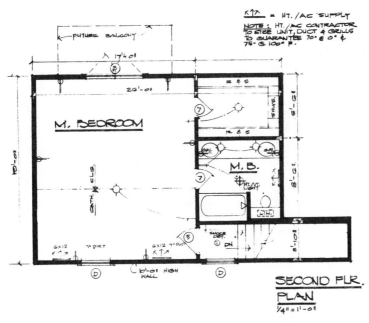

SECOND FLR.
PLAN
1/4" = 1'-0"

The heating and air conditioning plan is basically a floor plan showing piping, heating ducts, furnaces, and other climate control equipment (see Fig. 14-1). The plan shows the location and size of the ducts and the location of thermostat, plenum, and registers.

There are several different methods used to vary and control the temperature in a dwelling, among them forced warm air, hot-water heating, electric heating, window units, and central systems.

## FORCED WARM AIR

A forced-air system operates by heating air in a furnace and forcing it through ducts with a blower. For efficient operation, cool air is brought into the furnace through a return air grill and is heated. Once the air has been heated, the furnace blower drives the warm air through a series of ducts (see Fig. 14-2). To distribute the warm air, registers are placed at the end of the ducts. The registers can be placed in varying locations, but the heating systems operate more efficiently if they are placed low and near windows.

To achieve a proper balance in a forced-air system it is usually recommended that the furnace be located as near the center of the building as possible.

Typical components of a forced warm-air system include furnace, ducts, registers, and controls.

### The Furnace

The furnace is equipped with a fan, blower, motor, filters, heat-transfer surface, and a gas or oil burner. The burner in the furnace operates, in most cases, on fuel gas or fuel oil. If fuel gas is used as an energy source, it is fed to the burner under constant low pressure and is controlled by a pressure regulator. A room thermostat controls the operation of the burner and a pilot light or an electric spark ignites the burner when the thermostat registers a predetermined temperature. A fuel-oil burner operates much like a gas burner except that the oil is pumped from a storage tank and a gun-type oil burner is used as a source of heat.

# 14

# The Heating & Air Conditioning Plan

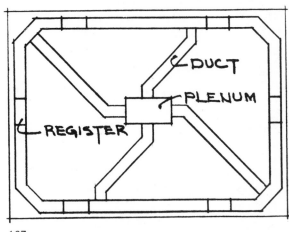

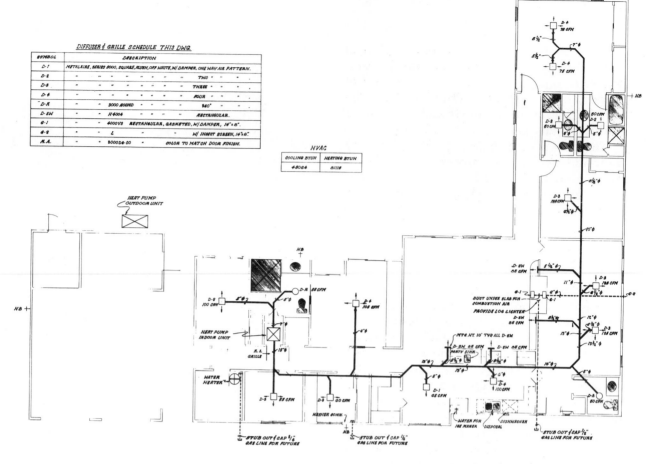

FIGURE 14-1    The heating and air-conditioning plan

The furnace size is based on the total heat loss calculated for a particular building and the total amount of BTUs the unit can produce in an hour.

## Ducts

Ducts are used to deliver the warm air and are constructed of a noncombustible material. At one time ducts were made primarily from galvanized sheet metal, but in recent years asbestos and fiberboard have been used. Ducts can be round, square, or rectangular, but the round ducts are more efficient based on volume of air handled per perimeter distance.

To join sheet-metal ducts, several different types of joints have been developed, among them drive cleats, double "S" slips, reinforced "S" cleats, and button-punch snaplocks.

The three basic types of duct systems are the perimeter system, the radial system, and the extended plenum system (see Fig. 14-3). The perimeter system has a duct that runs around the building and is supplied by interconnecting ducts. The radial system has ducts extending from the plenum. The extended plenum system has a long horizontal plenum with ducts branching off from it.

When a duct is placed in an unconditioned space, heat is often lost that cannot be regained. To prevent excessive heat loss, the ducts should be insulated with an approved material. Regarding duct insulation, the following rules should be followed:

FIGURE 14-2    Forced warm-air system

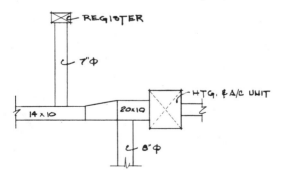

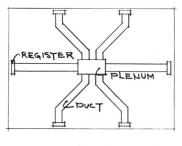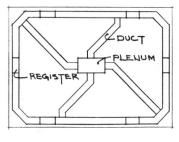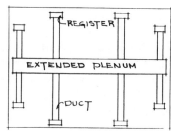

RADIAL SYSTEM    PERIMETER SYSTEM    EXTENDE PLENUM

FIGURE 14-3    Duct system: (a) radial; (b) perimeter; (c) extended plenum

☐ If a supply duct is over 12′ long, it should be insulated.

☐ All warm-air ducts that are placed in garages, attics, and unexcavated subfloor spaces should be insulated.

☐ All cold-air ducts that are placed in attics, basements, and crawl spaces should be insulated.

The size of a duct is usually determined by the total cubic feet of air per minute (CFM) necessary for cooling a given area. The CFM that circulates through a system is usually recommended by the manufacturer, and is usually between 300 and 420 CFM per ton. Once the CFM has been calculated, a table can be used to determine the duct size.

## *Dampers*

A damper is used in a forced-air system to maintain an even distribution of air. It can be located in the diffuser, grill, or duct and is classified as being a butterfly, a multiple blade, or a split damper. For maximum efficiency the dampers should be fitted snugly and operate with minimum leakage.

## *Registers*

A supply register is used to disperse air in a given direction. It should be equipped with dampers and should be able to disperse the air in several directions; in most cases it is equipped with vanes that make this possible.

# *ELECTRIC HEATING SYSTEMS*

Electric heating systems are available in a variety of styles and voltages, such as baseboard units, wall units, cable systems, ceiling units, floor units, central furnaces, infrared heaters, and heat pumps.

## *Baseboard Units*

Baseboard heating units are available in many styles and models. Most, however, are compact in design and can easily be installed in areas of large heat loss. They can be controlled by a centrally located thermostat or individually controlled.

## *Wall Units*

A wall unit often has resistance coils and fans, or it has wires embedded in glass or

ceramic. It can be controlled by an individual thermostat, but most are manufactured without any means of controlling the temperature.

## *Cable Systems*

An electric heating system can also be constructed by embedding wires in the ceiling or floor. Such a system operates by reflecting heat rays from the different surfaces of the room. A thermostat is placed in each room to control the temperature.

When the cables are placed, there should be a minimum distance of 2½″ between the cables; they should be placed 6″ from the wall and 8″ from any ceiling outlet. If the ceiling joists are placed 16″ on center, only ten cables may be placed between them.

### Ceiling Units

Ceiling units are similar to wall units, for they can also be constructed with resistance coils and fans. Units of this type are usually found in bathrooms, but they can also be used in other areas.

### Central Furnaces

In a central electric furnace, air is heated in a furnace and forced through ducts with a blower. Cool air is brought back into the furnace through a return air grill; the cool air is heated and the cycle is repeated.

### Heat Pumps

A heat pump can also be listed as a form of electric heating. It operates by switching the conventional refrigeration cycle. Once the cycle has been switched, the evaporation coils cool the air outside and the condenser coils warm the air inside. If a cooling unit is desired, a reversal of the evaporator and condenser can switch the unit over.

## HYDRONIC SYSTEMS

A hydronic system in its simplest form is nothing more than a forced hot-water system (see Fig. 14-4). The water is first heated in a boiler and then circulated by means of a pump through pipes and into the convectors. Once the water has passed through the pipes it is returned to the boiler and the process is repeated.

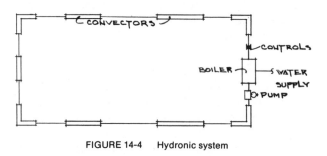

FIGURE 14-4    Hydronic system

mostat is needed to turn the central heating unit on and off.

### The Series Loop

The series loop, in which the supply lines are directly connected to the radiators, is one of the simplest hydronic systems. Hot water is forced through the supply lines and radiators. The biggest disadvantage of the system is that the radiators are connected in series, so each radiator is dependent on all the others. Because of this particular arrangement, all the radiators heat up and cool off at the same time. To regulate the radiators only one ther-

### The One-Pipe System

A one-pipe system is similar to a series loop, except that at each radiator location a branch pipe carries hot water to the radiator and another carries the return water back to the circulating main. With this system, individual room heat is possible.

## SPACE HEATERS

Space heaters are often used to heat individual rooms or buildings, but are often considered to be hazardous. Some building codes even ban their use because unvented, they can consume the oxygen in the air and discharge combustion products into the room. A typical space heater usually operates on electricity, oil, gas, or coal, and though some consider it

undesirable it is a popular means of heating.

### Electric Space Heaters

An electric space heater does not consume the oxygen, nor does it discharge any combustion products, but in most cases it is not capable of heating a large area.

The most popular units have coils and fans, or wires embedded in glass or ceramic. Such a heater is limited in capacity to around 1250 watts and operates on 120 volts. However, some permanent electric space heaters are of higher wattage and require 240 volts.

To determine the necessary watts, a rough rule of thumb to follow is to have about 900 watts for each 10′ of outside wall. This figure is only a rough estimate, and there are other variables that can influence heating efficiency.

### Oil and Gas Heaters

An oil or gas heater can be used to heat a building, but should only be used in conjunction with a flue or vent. (An oil heater uses a flue and a gas heater requires a vent.) A typical oil or gas heater can produce around 50,000 BTUs per hour, although as much as 90,000 or more BTUs can be produced. To heat a full-sized house usually requires three or more heaters producing a minimum of 50,000 BTUs per hour.

## AIR CONDITIONING SYSTEMS

Air conditioning systems are classified as central or unit systems. A central system can be an integral part of the heating system, using the same blower, filters, ducts, and registers, or it can be a separate system with its own distribution method. Unit systems are usually built into the exterior wall, or they are placed in a window opening. Room-sized units are an effective means of cooling a building, especially one with naturally defined zones.

### Electric Cooling Units

Electric cooling units are quite popular. In most cases, they operate simply by changing a liquid to a gas. The gas that is most often used is freon. For a cooling unit to operate efficiently, air is first forced through coils; a blower then forces air around the coils. As the freon is being pumped through the cooling coils it changes into a gas, and when a liquid is changed into a gas it absorbs heat—thus

the air around the coils is cooled. At this point a blower forces the cool air through the ducts and into the house. After the freon has passed through the coils it is pumped through an outside air unit called a condenser. In the condenser the freon is returned to its liquid state; then it is forced back to the cooling coil, where the cycle is repeated.

### Cold-Water Air-Cooling Systems

A water chiller can be designed to work in combination with a forced hot-water heating system, or as a separate cooling system. It usually consists of a compressor, condenser, and evaporator tank and is used to chill water and circulate it to the same units that emitted heat from hot circulated water.

In the chilled-water type of system, an absorptive type of water chiller is charged with lithium bromide and water. Cooled air is then produced by the absorptive principle.

## HEAT-LOSS CALCULATIONS

The amount of heat loss from a particular building must be determined before the size of a heating or cooling unit can be determined.

Before any calculations are made, it is well to understand some basic terms:

- □ *British thermal unit (BTU):* The quantity of heat needed to increase the temperature of 1 pound of water 1 degree F.

- □ *Heat loss:* The amount of heat that passes through exterior building materials of a structure for average temperature.
- □ *Conductance:* The ability of heat to be transferred from one location to another. Tables are available that give the conductance or resistance of a square foot of building material.
- □ *Inside design temperature:* The desired room temperature level.

□ *Outside design temperature:* The average outdoor temperature of the coldest months.

□ *Design temperature difference:* The difference between the outside design temperature and the inside design temperature.

□ *U factor:* The number of BTUs that can be transmitted through 1 square foot of building material in 1 hour for each degree of temperature difference.

□ *Resistivity:* The ability of building material to resist the transfer of heat or cold.

□ *Infiltration:* The ability of heat or cold air to gain entrance to a building from open spaces around doors and windows.

## Heat-Loss Calculations

Before the size of heating and cooling units can be determined it is necessary to figure out the heat loss for floors, walls, and ceilings. To do this, the gross wall area must first be calculated. This is done by multiplying the length of the wall by its height. The net wall area is then determined by subtracting the door and window area from the gross wall area. Once the net wall area has been found, the U factor for the net wall area must be determined. This procedure is accomplished by adding the resistivity of each building material used in the construction of each wall. The design temperature is then calculated by subtracting the outside design temperature from the inside design temperature. The BTU loss per hour (BTU/H) for the net wall area is then figured by multiplying the net wall area by the net wall U factor by the design temperature difference. To complete the heat-loss calculations, the BTU/H is determined for the windows and doors by multiplying the window and door area by the window and door U factor by the design temperature.

To calculate the heat loss of the floor, the total floor area must first be determined by multiplying the length of the floor by the width. The U factor is then found by adding the resistivity of each building material used in the construction of the floor. Next the BTU/H is calculated by multiplying the floor area by the total floor U factor by the design temperature.

To find the heat loss of the ceiling, the length of the ceiling is multiplied by the width. The U factor is then calculated by adding the resistivity of each building material used in the construction of the ceiling. Next the BTU/H is calculated by multiplying the ceiling area by the total ceiling U factor by the design temperature.

The volume of air infiltration is calculated by multiplying the length of a room by the width by the height. This calculation gives the air infiltration per hour. The air infiltration BTU/H heat loss is then calculated by multiplying the volume of air infiltration by the U factor .018 by the design temperature difference.

Once the BTU/H has been found for the

FIGURE 14-5    Office complex

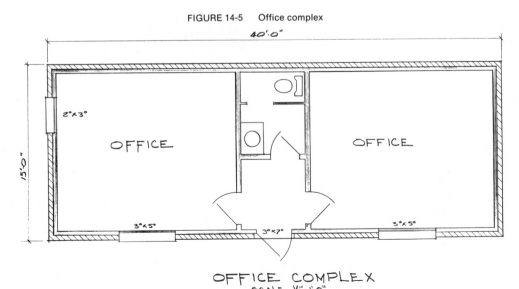

OFFICE COMPLEX
SCALE ¼"=1'-0"

floors, walls, ceilings, and air infiltration, they are all added together to find the total heat loss in BTUs per hour. At this point the size of the heating unit can be determined.

Fig. 14-5 illustrates heat-loss calculation in a small office building.

## Walls

gross wall area:

$$40 \times 8 = 320 \text{ sq ft}$$
$$40 \times 8 = 320 \text{ sq ft}$$
$$15 \times 8 = 120 \text{ sq ft}$$
$$15 \times 8 = 120 \text{ sq ft}$$

total gross area = 880 sq ft

door and window area:

$$3 \times 5 = 15 \text{ sq ft}$$
$$3 \times 5 = 15 \text{ sq ft}$$
$$2 \times 3 = 6 \text{ sq ft}$$
$$3 \times 7 = 21 \text{ sq ft}$$

total door & window area = 57 sq ft

net wall area = 880 sq ft
− 57 sq ft
= 823 sq ft

### RESISTIVITY OF BUILDING MATERIAL

| | |
|---|---|
| 4″ common brick | .82 |
| ½″ fiberboard sheathing | 1.45 |
| 4″ mineral batt insulation | 14.00 |
| ⅜″ gypsumboard | .33 |
| total resistivity | = 16.60 |
| 1.00 ÷ 16.60 | = .06 |
| U factor for net wall | = .06 |

### RESISTIVITY OF DOORS AND WINDOWS

doors 1.92
windows 2.60

### DESIGN TEMPERATURE DIFFERENCE

inside design temperature = 72°
outside design temperature = 5°
design temperature difference = 77°

### BTU/H FOR THE NET WALL AREA

Net wall area × U factor × design temperature difference

$$8.23 \times .06 \times 77 = 3,168$$
BTU/H for the net wall area = 3,802

### BTU/H FOR THE WINDOWS

Window area × window U factor × design temperature difference

$$36 \times 2.60 \times 77 = 7,207$$
BTU/H for the windows = 7,207

### BTU/H FOR THE DOORS

Door area × door U factor × design temperature difference

$$21 \times 1.52 \times 77 = 2,458$$
BTU/H for the doors = 2,458

## Ceilings

Ceiling length × ceiling width

$$15 \text{ ft} \times 40 \text{ ft} = 600 \text{ sq ft}$$

### U FACTOR FOR CEILING

⅜″ gypsumboard .33
4″ insulation 14.00
Resistivity 14.33
$$1.00 \div 14.33 = .069$$
U factor for ceiling = .069

### BTU/H FOR CEILING

Ceiling area × U factor × temperature difference

$$6000 \times .069 \times 77° = 3,187$$
BTU/H for ceiling = 3,187

## Floors

Floor length × floor width

$$15 \text{ ft} \times 40 \text{ ft} = 600 \text{ sq ft}$$

### U FACTOR FOR FLOOR

½″ plywood .65
15 lb asphalt sat. felt .06
flooring .08
Resistivity .79
$$1.00 \div .79 = 1.26$$
U factor for floor = 1.26

### BTU/H FOR FLOOR

Floor area × U factor × temperature difference

$$600 \times 1.26 \times 77° = 58,212$$
BTU/H for floor = 58,212

## Air Infiltration

Volume of air infiltration = length of room × width of room × height of room

$$40 \times 15 \times 8 = 4{,}800 \text{ cu ft}$$
$$\text{volume of air infiltration} = 4{,}800$$

### BTU/H FOR AIR INFILTRATION

Volume of air infiltration × .018 × temperature difference

$$4{,}800 \times .018 \times 77° = 6{,}652$$
$$\text{BTU/H for air infiltration} = 6{,}652$$

## Total BTU/H

| | |
|---|---|
| BTU/H for net walls | 3,802 |
| BTU/H for net windows | 7,207 |
| BTU/H for net doors | 3,104 |
| BTU/H for net ceilings | 3,187 |
| BTU/H for net floors | 58,212 |
| BTU/H for net air infiltration | 6,652 |
| Total BTU/H = | 82,164 |

To summarize the findings, the small office complex has a total heat loss of 82,164 BTU/H. Once this factor has been established, a heating unit capable of producing at least 82,164 BTU/H can be specified.

# DRAFTING PROCEDURES FOR THE HEATING AND AIR CONDITIONING PLAN

Heating and air conditioning plan is started by first tracing the general outline of the floor plan. This is usually done with a 2H lead, but slightly lighter than the outline of object line for the floor plan.

Once the floor plan has been drawn, the heating and air conditioning units, ducts or pipes, and registers can be located on the plan. These distinguished features are usually drawn with a 2H lead, but much darker than the outline of the floor plan. The necessary dimensions and notes complete the drawing.

# Assignment:

1. Calculate the heat loss for house in Fig. 14-6.

FIGURE 14-6 (below and right)    Assignment: Calculate the heat loss for the house

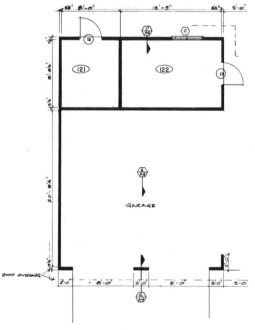

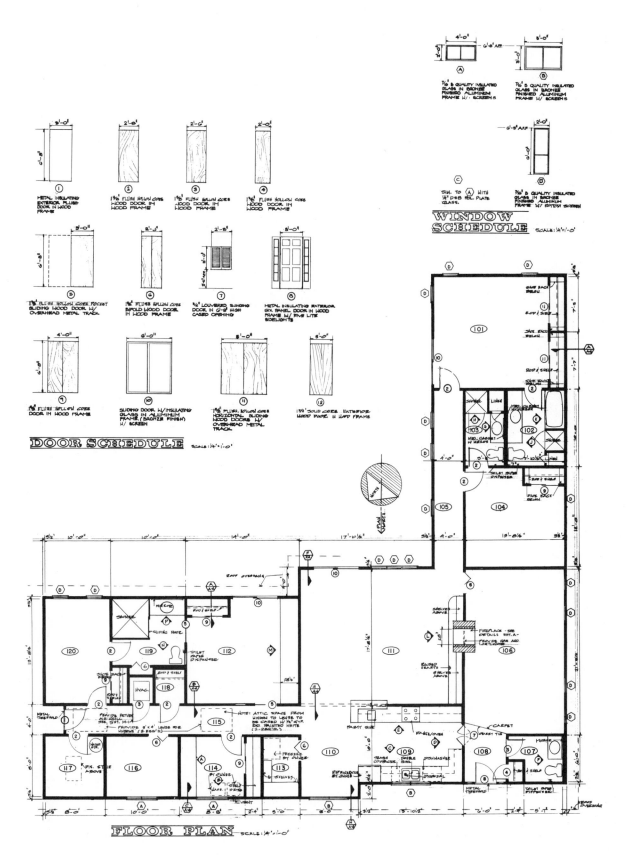

**WINDOW SCHEDULE** SCALE: 1/4"=1'-0"

**DOOR SCHEDULE** SCALE: 1/4"=1'-0"

**FLOOR PLAN** SCALE: 1/4"=1'-0"

175

The schedule is a collection of organized notes and is placed in a convenient location on a set of plans. It is enclosed by a heavy border and has a title strip to identify it. There are three types of schedules usually found in a set of plans: the room finish schedule, the window schedule, and the door schedule.

## THE ROOM FINISH SCHEDULE

A room finish schedule is drawn by the architect to give important information about the type of materials that are used on the interior walls, floor, and ceilings of a room (see Fig. 15-1). For example, the interior walls may be covered with gypsumboard, paneling, plastics, or ceramic tile; the floor can be covered with hardwood flooring, resilient flooring, carpet, or ceramic tile. The materials used to finish the ceiling include acoustical materials and gypsumboard. In addition to listing the wall, ceiling, and flooring material on the schedule, the floor, ceiling trim, and other trim should also be listed.

### Interior Wall Finish Materials

There are several different types of finish materials that can be used for an interior wall. Some, however, are more popular than others. But each material has certain advantages and unique functions.

Some of the most popular materials used to finish interior walls are paneling, gypsumboard, plaster, and ceramic tile.

#### PANELING

Paneling is one of the most popular means of finishing an interior wall. Paneling can be solid lumber, hardboard, or plywood.

Solid lumber is an excellent paneling material; not only is it decorative, but it adds structural strength to the wall frame. Paneling is available with a rough-sawn, textured look or a smooth planed surface. Rough-sawn boards are usually square-edged, tongue-and-grooved, or have a shiplapped edge (see Fig. 15-2). Planed boards usually have machine-molded patterns, but can be purchased without a molded edge.

Hardboard paneling is made from clean

## ROOM FINISH SCHEDULE

| ROOM NUMBER | ROOM NAME | FLOOR | BASE | WALLS | | | | WAINSCOT | WAINSCOT CAP | WAINSCOT HEIGHT | CEILING MOULD | CEILING | CEILING HEIGHT | REMARKS |
|---|---|---|---|---|---|---|---|---|---|---|---|---|---|---|
| | | | | NORTH | EAST | SOUTH | WEST | | | | | | | |
| 101 | MASTER BEDROOM | CAR. | B711 | GBP | GBP | GBP | GBP | | | | 356 | GBP | 8'-1½' | BLOWN ACOUSTICAL CEILING - LIGHT TEXTURE - TYPICAL. |
| 102 | MASTER BATH | 10C | " | WP | WP | WP | WP | CTG | CTG | 4'-0" | " | " | " | WAINSCOT IN TUB AREA ONLY. USE WATER PROOF GYP. BD. |
| 103 | BATH 2 | 10C | " | " | " | " | " | | | | " | " | " | USE WATER PROOF GYP. BD |
| 104 | BEDROOM 2 | CAR. | " | GBP | GBP | GBP | GBP | | | | " | " | " | |
| 105 | HALL | " | " | " | " | " | " | | | | " | " | " | |
| 106 | LIVING/DINING ROOM | " | " | " | " | " | " | | | | " | " | " | |
| 107 | POWDER ROOM | " | " | WP | WP | WP | WP | | | | " | " | " | |
| 108 | ENTRY | Q.T. | " | GBP | GBP | GBP | GBP | | | | " | " | " | |
| 109 | KITCHEN | VIN | " | " | " | " | " | | | | " | " | " | USE 5/8" FIRECODE GYP. BD IN THIS AREA- WALLS & CEILING. |
| 110 | BREAKFAST ROOM | " | " | " | " | " | " | | | | " | " | " | USE 5/8" GYP. BD. IN THIS AREA - CEILING ONLY |
| 111 | FAMILY ROOM | " | " | " | " | " | " | | | | " | " | VARIES | |
| 112 | BEDROOM 3 | " | " | " | " | " | " | | | | " | " | 8'-1½' | |
| 113 | PANTRY | " | " | " | " | " | " | | | | " | " | " | |
| 114 | UTILITY | " | " | " | " | " | " | | | | " | " | " | |
| 115 | HALL | " | " | " | " | " | " | | | | " | " | " | USE 5/8" GYP. BD. IN THIS AREA CEILING ONLY. |
| 116 | STUDY | " | " | " | " | " | " | | | | " | " | " | |
| 117 | STORAGE | " | " | " | " | " | " | | | | " | " | " | |
| 118 | CEDAR CLOSET | " | " | CED. | CED. | CED. | CED. | | | | " | " | " | |
| 119 | BATH 3 | " | " | WP. | WP. | WP. | WP. | | | | " | " | " | |
| 120 | BEDROOM 4 | CAR | " | GBP. | GBP. | GBP. | GBP. | | | | " | " | " | |
| 121 | STORAGE | CON. | - | " | " | " | " | | | | - | " | " | |
| 122 | SHOP | CON. | - | " | " | " | " | | | | - | " | " | |

### FINISH MATERIALS

| FLOORS | | WALLS | | WAINSCOT | | CEILING MOULD | |
|---|---|---|---|---|---|---|---|
| CAR. | CARPET | GBP. | GYPSUM BOARD - PAINTED | CTG. | CERAMIC TILE - GLAZED | 8010 | WOOD MOULD 8000 SERIES |
| VIN. | SHEET VINYL | WP. | WALL PAPER | | | | |
| Q.T | QUARRY TILE (BROKEN) | CED | 1x4 CEDAR | | | CEILING | |
| 10C | INDOOR-OUTDOOR CARPET | | | BASE | | GBP. | GYPSUM BOARD PAINTED |
| | | | | 3x6 | COLONIAL WOOD BASE | | |

FIGURE 15-1    Room-finish schedule

selected wood fibers pressed under heat. The panels are actually wood, but they are hard, dense, and grainless. The standard panel is $4' \times 8' \times \frac{1}{4}''$ and is available in a wide variety of colors, grains, and textures.

Plywood is also a popular type of paneling and is available in plain or processed surfaces. Both hardwood and softwood plywood can be used as paneling, but in most cases hardwood plywood is used. The paneling can be pre-finished at the factory, or the panels can be finished after they have been installed.

FIGURE 15-2    Board edges: (a) square; (b) tongue-and-grooved; (c) ship-lapped

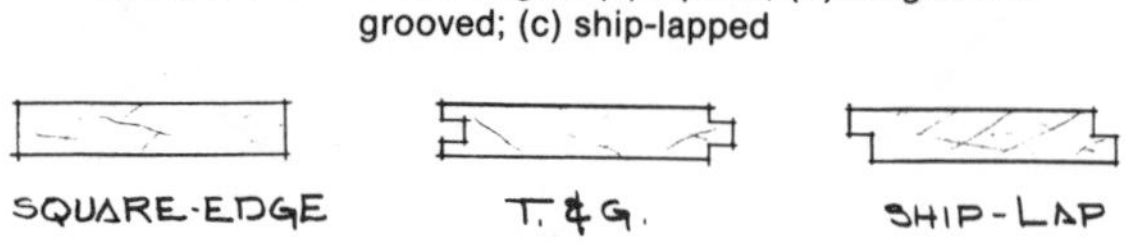

SQUARE-EDGE          T. & G.          SHIP-LAP

## GYPSUMBOARD

Gypsumboard, as an interior wall and ceiling finish material is excellent, fire-resistant, and can control sound transmission between rooms. The large panels have a core of gypsum sandwiched between gray and liner paper on the backside and a special paper covering on the front side. The front covering of paper allows for easy painting and decorating.

Gypsumboard is available in standard thickness, lengths, and widths. The standard thicknesses are $\frac{1}{4}$, $\frac{3}{8}$, $\frac{1}{2}$, and $\frac{5}{8}''$. The $\frac{1}{4}''$ panels should be applied over a solid surface and in most cases are used for the rehabilitation of old walls and ceiling surfaces. The $\frac{3}{8}''$ panels are usually used for the outer layer in multi-layer construction. The ½″ panels are used for direct application to vertical and horizontal framing members. The ⅝″ panels are also used in single-layer construction, but the added thickness insures additional fire resistance and greater control of sound transmission. The standard width of gypsumboard panels is 4′, but they are available in lengths of 8, 10, 12, and 14′. The edges of gypsumboard are also standard. They are rounded, leveled, tapered, or square-edged.

There are several different types of gypsumboard, each performing a unique and specific function.

Insulating gypsumboard has a sheet of aluminum foil bonded to its back. The aluminum foil acts as a vapor barrier and as thermal insulation and is placed next to the framing members, reducing the outward flow of heat in the winter and the inward flow of heat in the summer. This particular type of panel should not be used as a base for ceramic tile.

Predecorated gypsumboard has a sheet of decorative vinyl or paper bonded to it. The decorative covering is available in several different surface patterns and colors. Some of the surface patterns include stippled, linens, woodgrain, textiles, and character woods.

Gypsum backing board is a low-cost product that is used as a base layer in multi-ply construction. The backing board is used for extra fire resistance, reduced sound transmission, and strength.

Water-resistant gypsum backing board has a gypsum core and a specially treated face paper that is water-repellent. Because of its resistance to moisture, it is used as a base for tile in baths and showers.

FASTENERS AND ADHESIVES   Nails, screws, staples, and special adhesives are used to secure gypsumboard to framing members, furring members, or to an under-layer of gypsumboard.

Nails are available in several different sizes and shapes; the two most common types are the cement-coated and the annular ring nail. For greater holding power, the latter is superior, because it has about 20 percent greater holding power than a cement-coated nail of the same length. The shanks of the nails should be long enough to sufficiently penetrate the underlying framing members. If a smooth-shanked nail is used, the shank should penetrate the framing member ⅞″, an annular ring nail, however, must only penetrate the framing members ¾″. The heads of the nails are also important; if they are too small or too large, they might cut into the face paper. In most cases the nail heads are at least ¼″ and not more than 5/16″ in diameter.

Screws are also a popular means of attaching gypsumboard to framing members. The screws have cupped Phillips heads and are designed to be placed with a drywall power screwdriver. There are three basic types of drywall screws—type W for wood, type S for sheet metal, and type G for solid gypsum construction. Type W screws are available in several lengths and are designed to secure gypsum drywall to metal studs or furring. Most type G screws are 1½″ in length and are used in multi-layer adhesively laminated gypsum-to-gypsum partitions. Drywall screws are not recommended for double-layer ⅜″ panels, because they do not provide the desired holding strength.

Staples are used only to attach the base sheet in multi-ply construction. The staples are constructed from 16-gauge galvanized wire. The crown should be 7/16″ wide. The length of the legs vary, depending on the thickness of the gypsumboard. If the gypsumboard is ⅜″ thick the legs should be 1″ long; the legs should be 1⅛″ long for ½″ thick gypsumboard; and for ⅝″ thick gypsumboard they should be 1¼″ long.

Adhesives are used to attach gypsumboard to framing members, furring strips, masonry, concrete, or to underlying gypsum panels. The three adhesives that are most often used are stud adhesive, laminating adhesives, and modified contact adhesives. Adhesives are used to reduce as much as 75 percent of the number of fasteners; they are stronger than conventional nail application, providing up to 100 percent more tensile strength and up to 50 percent more shear strength. Adhesives are not affected by moisture changes, and their use results in fewer loose panels. When adhesive is placed on framing members, it should be applied in a ⅜″ bead and should be 1/16″ thick over the entire support.

## PLASTER

Plaster is a durable wall finish material that is made from gypsum, one of the common minerals of the earth. Gypsum is sold in a powder form; when it is mixed with water and an aggregate, a fire-resistant product is produced. Once the plaster has been mixed to the proper consistency it is applied to a plaster base.

PLASTER BASES   There are two basic classifications of plaster bases: bases that are attached to framing members, and masonry bases. In light construction the plaster base is most often gypsum lath or metal lath. Gypsum lath is either plain or perforated, and in most cases is ⅜″ thick, 16″ wide, and 48″ long (see Fig. 15-1). If the spacing of the framing members exceeds 16″, ½″ lath must be used. The lath is placed with its long dimension perpendicular to the framing members and may be secured with four nails, staples, or screws to the framing members. The heads of the fasteners should be placed slightly below the face paper, but the face paper should not be broken. In addition to holding the lath in place, the fasteners are used to meet necessary fire rating requirements.

Once the lath has been placed, corner beads should be placed on all external corners (see Fig. 15-3). Corner beads are made from 26-gauge galvanized steel and provide plaster protection, true and straight lines at corners, and grounds for plastering. The interior corners are reinforced with cornerite, which is

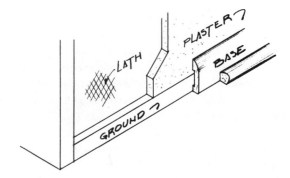

FIGURE 15-4    Plaster grounds

made from a strip of copper alloy, diamond-mesh lath. If clips are used to fasten lath to framing members, cornerite is not recommended.

To provide an even thickness of plaster, grounds are placed around all openings and wherever baseboards and moldings are to be used (see Fig. 15-4). The grounds are usually constructed from 1 × 2s and provide a leveling surface during the application of plaster and later serve as a nailing base. If gypsum lath is used, the grounds should be set to provide a minimum plaster thickness of ½″; and if metal lath is used they should be set to provide a minimum plaster thickness of ⅝″. The size of the grounds allows for the proper basecoat thickness, plus allowing ¹⁄₁₆″ for the thickness of the finish coat.

Metal is a popular lath, because it forms a mechanical bond with the plaster. Gypsum laths provide a suction bond with the plaster. The two most popular types of metal lath are diamond mesh and riblath. Diamond mesh is a general all-purpose lath that can have as many as 11,000 meshes per yard. Riblath has a herringbone mesh pattern with U-shaped ribs running the length of the sheet.

GYPSUM BASECOAT PLASTER   Gypsum basecoat plaster is placed over lath to provide resistance against structural movements and a true and level surface for the finish coat of plaster. There are three basic types of basecoat plasters used in light construction: gypsum neat plaster, gypsum ready-mixed plaster, and gypsum wood-fibered plaster.

Gypsum neat plaster is a mixture of calcined gypsum plaster, sand, perlite or vermiculite aggregate, and water. This particular

FIGURE 15-3    Corner beads

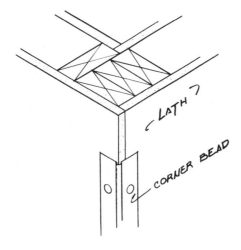

type is often referred to as gypsum cement plaster or hardwall.

Gypsum ready-mixed plaster is mixed at the mill and requires only the addition of clean water. It is a mixture of calcined gypsum plaster and an aggregate, usually sand or perlite.

Gypsum wood-fibered plaster is also mixed at the mill and requires only the addition of clean water. But rather than using sand as an aggregate, wood fibers are used to provide the plaster with more bulk and coverage. This particular type of plaster is used where good plastering sand is not available and where greater base strength is desired.

The basecoat of plaster can be placed over lath by hand or by machine, using either a three-coat or a two-coat application. In three-coat application a scratch coat of plaster is placed over the lath and cross-raked. A brown coat is then troweled over the scratch coat and allowed to partially dry. The brown coat should be brought out to the grounds, darbied, and allowed to partially dry. It is then topped by the finish coat. Three-coat application is required when plaster is placed over a metal lath; when gypsum lath is placed on horizontal framing members that are placed on centers greater than 16″; over ⅜″ perforated gypsum ceiling lath; and when gypsum ceiling lath is supported by clips.

Two-coat application is similar to three-coat application except that the basecoat is not cross-raked, and the brown coat is doubled back over the scratch coat minutes after the application of the scratch coat. Two-coat application is usually used over gypsum lath, although the three-coat is stronger because the scratch coat is allowed to partially dry, thus drawing out the excess water from the brown coat.

FINISH-COAT PLASTERS    After the basecoat of plaster has been placed and allowed to partially dry, a finish coat is applied. There are six different types that can be used: gypsum-lime putty trowel finish, Keene's cement-lime putty trowel finish, prepared gypsum trowel finish, Keene's cement-lime sand-float finish, gypsum-sand finish, and acoustical plaster finish. All are classified according to texture, color, and hardness.

Gypsum-lime putty trowel finish is one of the most popular types, and is sometimes referred to as white-coat finish. It consists of a mixture of lime putty and gypsum-gauging plaster; this type has high plasticity and provides a hard finish at a relatively low cost. However, the finish should be mixed according to manufacturer's specifications; otherwise check-cracking, crazing, bond failure, and lack of hardness will be the result.

Keene's cement-lime putty trowel finish is a mixture of lime putty and Keene's cement. This type can be extremely hard and can be troweled to a smooth monolithic surface. It should only be placed over a strong basecoat, and the surface should be occasionally troweled until complete set has been achieved.

Keene's cement-lime sand-float finish is a mixture of sand, Keene's cement, and dry hydrated lime. It can be placed over all plaster bases, and varying the amount of sand will produce different surface textures. This particular type of finish is also a lot less apt to crack than smooth trowel finishes and can be mixed with a color before its application.

Prepared gypsum trowel finishes and prepared gypsum float finishes are ready-mixed plasters that require only the addition of water. They possess basically the same characteristics as other trowel and float finishes.

Acoustical plasters are also ready-mixed; they are used to absorb sound, and also are fire-resistant, noncombustible, and can follow complex shapes.

Trowel finishes are achieved by being applied onto a dry or nearly dry basecoat. The dry basecoat draws the moisture from the finish coat, resulting in a tight bond between the two layers. A second finish coat is applied once the initial bond is complete. The last finish coat is applied by moistening an area with a wet brush and troweling over the area to produce a smooth, dense surface. A float finish is similar to a trowel finish, except that the first finish coat is applied to the basecoat with a wooden float; immediately following the first floating the area is smoothed over with a rubber float.

Once the plaster has been placed, it should be allowed to dry properly. If it dries too fast before it sets, or if it dries too slowly, its strength may be impaired.

VENEER PLASTER    Veneer plaster is gaining in popularity and acceptance because of the speed with which it can be applied and its quick setting time. Other advantages include durability, variety, versatility, and economy.

Veneer plaster is never mixed with anything except potable water and may be applied by hand or machine. When it is done by hand, a thin coat is applied to an approximate depth of $1/16''$. When the plaster has firmed up, a second coat is doubled back over the first, bringing the total thickness to a minimum of $3/32''$. Before the plaster sets, a trowel is used to smooth the surface. If a textured finish is desired, deep swirls can be accomplished with sponges, wood floats, or brushes.

If the plaster is applied with a machine, it should be sprayed in two even passes and troweled, after which a hard finish coat should be applied. If a textured finish is desired, the troweling operation is omitted and the final coat is sprayed on.

In some cases electric radiant heating cables are embedded in veneer plaster. To properly install the system, the veneer base must be attached to the ceiling and the joints reinforced with glass fiber or paper tape. The heating cables are then attached to the ceiling. They should be installed flat, and in areas that require splicing, a notch should be cut in the veneer base to recess the splices. Once the cables are secured, a full coat of plaster is applied to cover them. If the plaster is applied in one coat, sand is sometimes added to give it sensitivity and increase the bonding properties. After the plaster has been applied, it should be leveled with a darby or a feather edge, but the heating cables should not be used for grounds. Once the fill coat has set, a finish coat can be troweled, floated, or textured as desired.

### CERAMIC TILE

Ceramic tile is a very popular interior wall finish in kitchen and bath areas. It is available in a variety of colors, shapes, and textures which can complement or enhance any decor. The glazed wall-tile units are made from potter's clay and are available in individual units, or they can be purchased in pregrouted sheets of $4\frac{1}{4}'' \times 4\frac{1}{4}''$, $6'' \times 4\frac{1}{4}''$, or $8\frac{1}{2}'' \times 4\frac{1}{4}''$ with thin-set or conventional trim already attached. Because the tile has an impervious glaze it is dent-proof and stain-proof and has less than $\frac{1}{2}$ percent absorption.

The tile units can be bonded to the wall using conventional thick-bed portland cement mortar or thin-bed bonding materials such as dry-set mortars, latex-portland cement mortar, epoxy mortar, epoxy adhesive, furan mortar, and organic adhesive.

## Flooring

Some of the common materials used as finish flooring are wood flooring, resilient flooring, carpet, and ceramic tile. Wood flooring is not as popular as it once was, but many floors are still covered with hardwood and softwood strip flooring, random-width planks, unit blocks, or laminated blocks. Resilient flooring has been popular for many years and is still a leading floor finish material. Some basic types of resilient floors are sheet vinyl, vinyl-asbestos tile, plain linoleum, and asphalt tile. Carpet, as a floor covering, has increased in popularity in recent years, having proved to be outstandingly practical and economical. Ceramic tile is a popular floor finish material that is used in areas that are exposed to intermediate wetting.

### WOOD FLOORS

Wood floors are commonly constructed from hardwoods such as oak, maple, beech, birch, and pecan. Oak, however, is the most popular species and constitutes over 90 percent of the hardwood flooring in the United States. The different species are broadly classified as strip, plank, and block flooring.

Strip flooring, the most popular, is made from thin strips of wood in varying thicknesses and widths (see Fig. 15-5). The most popular pattern size is $25/32''$ thick and $2\frac{1}{4}''$ wide. One edge of the strip flooring has a tongue and the other edge a groove, and they have ends that are sometimes similarly matched.

Plank flooring is constructed from random-width pieces that are usually tongue-and-grooved and can have square or matched ends. In some cases the edges can be beveled to create an early hand-hewn effect. The boards can also have simulated wood plugs glued into them for effect.

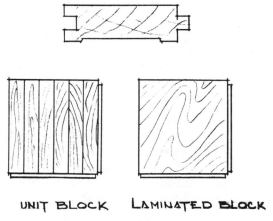

UNIT BLOCK    LAMINATED BLOCK

FIGURE 15-5 (top)    Strip flooring
FIGURE 15-6 (above)  Block flooring

Block flooring is manufactured in two basic types: the unit block and the laminated block (see Fig. 15-6). The unit block is constructed from several short lengths of standard strip flooring joined together edgewise to form a square unit. The laminated block is constructed from three or more plies of veneer bonded together. To increase the strength of the unit, the grain direction of the different plies are placed at right angles to each other. Regardless of whether the block flooring is unit block or laminated block, most of the units are tongued on two adjoining or opposing edges and grooved on the other two.

SUBFLOORS    A subfloor is used to stiffen the floor frame and provide a level base for the finished floor. The two most popular types of subfloor are boards and plywood. If boards are used, they should not be less then 1″ thick nor more than 6″ wide. Boards wider than 6″ are subject to dimensional change due to moisture absorption. Square-edged, ship-lapped, or tongue-and-grooved boards can be used as a subfloor, but squared-edges boards spaced ¼″ apart are usually recommended. The boards should be nailed to each joist with two eightpenny nails. The ends of each board should rest on a joist, and should also be secured to that joist with two eightpenny nails.

If plywood is used as a subfloor it should be installed with the outer plies at right angles to the joist. The plywood is nailed to the joist with eightpenny or tenpenny nails spaced 6″ along the panel edges and 10 and 6″ on

intermediate supports. A 1/16″ space should be left between all panel edge joints. Minimum plywood thicknesses and maximum joist spacing should conform to Table 8-2 (see p. 88).

In no case should green lumber ever be used as a subfloor, because the moisture from the subfloor will be transferred to the finished floor, causing it to cup or buckle and later develop cracks.

Once the subfloor has been placed, it is common practice to place a layer of 15-pound asphalt-saturated felt over it. The felt reduces air infiltration, keeps moisture from rising through the floor, and acts to deaden sound.

CARPETING

There are several different types of carpet, each designed to meet specific needs and requirements. All carpet is classified according to its principal method of manufacture—i.e., tufted, woven, and knitted.

Tufting is one of the newest construction techniques used, and accounts for about 90 percent of the total yardage. This method is used to produce shag, plush, pattern, and sculpture carpet. Thousands of needles are threaded with yarn and forced through the backing to form loops or tufts. Woven carpet is manufactured on looms that interweave pile yarns and backing yarns in one machine operation. Knitted carpets are very similar to woven carpets in that they are manufactured in one operation. They are usually made in solid colors or tweeds. The method of manufacture is to loop the pile and backing together, using several sets of needles.

Regardless of the classification and cost of carpet, it will not perform satisfactorily if it is improperly installed. Before installation, the floors should be cleaned and freed of any loose paint or varnish. If an adhesive is used to attach the carpet, any wax should be removed and a painted or finished floor lightly sanded. Any rough spots should be sanded smooth and joints and cracks should be filled with a good quality patching compound.

Carpet can be installed by means of a tackless strip, or with a direct glue-down installation procedure.

TACKLESS FASTENING    Tackless fastening is the most common installation technique used in the application of carpet. The technique involves the use of wood strips with inserted rows of pins angled toward the wall (see Fig. 15-7). The pins hold the carpet in place.

There are three basic types of tackless strips, and three different pin lengths for the strips. One tackless strip is used for nailing or cementing on wood, concrete, tile, or terrazzo; another is a prenailed strip for concrete floor; and one is a prenailed strip for wood floors. The three pin lengths are classified as Type C, Type D, and Type E. A type C pin is ¼" long and is used with high-pile carpets with double backing; a type C pin is ³⁄₁₆" long and is used with low-profile carpets and/or single back construction; and a type E pin is ⁷⁄₃₂" long and is used with double backing and medium- or high-pile carpets.

The tackless strips are placed a maximum distance of ¼" from the baseboard, but the distance from baseboard to the tackless strip should equal the thickness of the carpet. Temperature of the shield iron should not exceed 240° F, because a higher temperature might possibly damage the carpet. As the iron is passed over the seaming tape, only moderate pressure should be applied—too much pressure can push the adhesive off the tape. When the iron has passed over a section of carpet, the carpet should be adjusted before the melt has had a chance to cool. Localized pressure should be avoided until the seam has cooled, or the carpet may peak along the seam.

Seams can also be sewn with No. 18 waxed linen thread. In this case, there should be a minimum of three stitches per inch, and the stitches should be located at least ⅝" from the cut edge. To reinforce the stitching the raw edges, at seams, should be latexed and seam tape placed beneath the intersection of the two pieces of carpet.

FIGURE 15-7    Tackless fastening

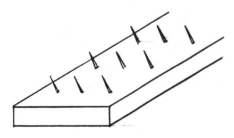

FIGURE 15-8    Gripper bar

To protect the carpet at doorways and island applications, gripper bars are used (see Fig. 15-8). These are available in many different sizes and styles, but most of them are made of aluminum and are folded over to protect the edges of the carpet.

GLUE-DOWN INSTALLATION    Carpet installed by the glue-down installation procedure is applied without a cushion and is placed in areas that are to receive heavy, wheeled traffic.

Before placement of the carpet the floor must be properly cleaned and any faults over ⅛" should be filled. If curing compounds have been used over the concrete slab, the floor should be sanded before adhesive is troweled on.

CERAMIC TILE

Ceramic tile is a popular floor finish, especially in areas that receive intermediate wettings. Ceramic tile is available in many colors, shapes, and textures. The floor units are glazed and are available in individual units, ungrouted sheets, or pregrouted sheets. Because the tile has an impervious glaze it is dent-proof, stain-proof, and has less than ½ percent absorption.

The tile units can be bonded to the floor using conventional thick bed portland cement mortar or thin-bed bonding materials such as dry-set mortars, latex-portland cement mortar, epoxy mortar, epoxy adhesive, furan mortar, and organic adhesive.

RESILIENT FLOORING

Each different type of resilient flooring is designed to meet a specific need. It is usually used in areas that require a dense and non-absorbent surface. Some of the more common types of resilient flooring are sheet vinyl, vinyl-asbestos tile, linoleum, and asphalt tile.

Sheet vinyl is available in varying thicknesses and widths, and is one of the most popular flooring materials. The large sheets are manufactured in many colors, and resist wear, grease, and alkalis. Some sheet vinyl flooring has cushion-backed materials placed on the underside, which reduces the noise level and increases comfort.

Vinyl-asbestos tile is available in tile form and is made from a mixture of vinyl resins and asbestos fillers. This particular type of resilient flooring can be used over suspended subfloors, on-grade slabs, and below-grade concrete. Another popular resilient flooring is asphalt tile—a low-cost material that is a mixture of asphaltic and/or resinous binder, asbestos fibers, pigments, and fillers.

Linoleum is available either plain (sometimes referred to as "battleship linoleum") or embossed. Plain linoleum is composed of oxidized linseed oil, cork, wood flour, color-stable mineral pigments, plasticizers, and stabilizers. This type is primarily used when a solid-color floor of exceptional wearing quality is desired. Embossed linoleum is available in a wide variety of colors and designs. It is well suited for suspended floor, but should not be placed over concrete subfloors or on-or-below-grade slabs.

SUBFLOORS   For resilient flooring to be placed over a concrete subfloor that is on-or below-grade, the concrete should be separated from direct contact with the soil by a suitable vapor barrier. If a vapor barrier is not used the concrete will absorb and retain moisture that will destroy the bond between the adhesive and the subfloor. Other precautionary measures that should be followed when a resilient floor is placed over concrete is to allow the concrete plenty of ventilation for several months so it will dry completely. If concrete curing and parting compounds have been used, they should be removed with a concrete or terrazzo grinder, or by sanding and scraping with a power-driven wire brush. The film must be removed because it keeps the adhesive from making a good bond with the slab. After the curing compound has been removed, a bond test should be conducted to see if an adhesive will bond to the concrete. To do this, panels should be secured to the subfloor with the adhesives that will be used in the actual installation. If they are still properly attached to the subfloor after two weeks, it

can be concluded that the concrete is dry and sufficiently clean for satisfactory installation.

Resilient flooring can also be placed over a combination subfloor underlayment, or a double-layer construction composed of separate subfloor and underlayment. If such an underlayment is used, the plywood should be laid perpendicular to the joists. If square-edge plywood is used, the longitudinal edges should be supported by lumber blocking; however, if ⅝" tongue-and-grooved plywood is used the blocking may be omitted. The thickness, span, and installation of plywood combination subfloor underlayment should conform to the finish flooring manufacturer's instruction, but should not be less than the minimum thickness and maximum joist spacing shown in Table 8-2 (see p. 88). When the subfloor panels are placed, a ⅟₃₂" space should be left for all joints and a ⅛" space should be left between the subfloor and all vertical surfaces. Once the subfloor underlayment has been installed, the floor area should be sanded smooth.

Usually either a mastic-type or board-type underlayment is used in conjunction with a subfloor. The most effective mastic-type underlayments contain a binder of latex, asphalt, or polyvinyl-acetate resins in the mix. A mastic that contains cement, gypsum, and sand can also be used, but this often breaks down under traffic. Mastic-type underlayment can be troweled to a featheredge in leveling a worn or damaged area.

The three basic types of board-type underlayments are hardboard, plywood, and particleboard. In most cases hardboard is used in remodeling projects and either plywood or particleboard is used in new construction. Hardboard, as an underlayment, minimizes the need to build up old subfloors, but in new construction it may be necessary to increase the thickness of the subfloor.

## Acoustical Ceiling Systems

Acoustical ceiling systems are used to decorate and complement a room's decor. They also reduce the noise level, provide protection against fire, cover exposed pipes and ducts, and in some cases are used to lower a ceiling that is too high.

There are two basic types of acoustical ceiling systems—the suspended ceiling and the tile system. Both ceiling panels and ceiling tiles have a wide range of attractive designs, including embossed white, two-tone effects, smooth-surfaced decorator styles, and a type made with small perforations or fissures to enhance the noise-quieting properties.

### ACOUSTICAL TILE CEILINGS

Individual acoustical tiles are usually $12'' \times 12''$ and are also manufactured from cellulose or mineral fibers. They are designed with tongue-and-grooved edges that make them fit together snugly. The tiles are stapled to furring strips or cemented to a level, sound existing ceiling.

When the tiles are stapled to furring strips, the first strip is placed adjacent to the wall; the second is equal to the width of the border; the third and remaining furring strips are placed on $12''$ centers.

When the tiles are cemented to the ceiling, daubs of adhesive should be applied about $\frac{1}{8}''$ thick and spread to an approximate diameter of $2\frac{3}{4}''$. Direct pressure should be applied directly over the adhesive, and the tile should be moved back and forth to make sure of a good bond. When the tile is positioned, all four corners should be level; if they are not, the tile will have a drooping appearance. If it is necessary to reposition the tile, the adhesive should be cleaned from the tile and ceiling, the tile should be rebuttered and then repositioned on the ceiling.

### SUSPENDED ACOUSTICAL CEILINGS

The suspended ceiling consists of a simple metal grid framework suspended on wires from above (see Fig. 15-9). The ceiling panels,

usually $2' \times 2'$ or $2' \times 4'$ and made from cellulose or mineral fibers, are dropped into and supported by the framework.

A suspended acoustical ceiling consists of four different components: wall angle molding, main runners, cross-tees, and $2' \times 4'$ panels. Wall angle molding is an L-shaped strip that is nailed around the perimeter of the room; it is available in $10'$ lengths and is placed at ceiling height. Main runners are available in $12'$ lengths and are used to create the strength and levelness of a suspended ceiling. They are placed perpendicular to the ceiling joist and are supported by 12-gauge wire nailed to the joist at $4'$ intervals. Cross-tees are available in 2 or $4'$ lengths and are locked into the main runners to form the total grid.

The first step in installing a suspended ceiling is to nail or screw the wall angle molding to the wall. This should be placed a minimum of $3''$ below the joist.

## Interior Trim and Wood Moldings

Wood molding is a thin strip of wood that is milled with a plain or curved surface. There are several areas in a building that requires wood molding, such as the floor lines, around windows, and around ceilings. Base molding is used at the floor line to protect the bottom portion of the wall and to cover the raw edge of some flooring materials (see Fig. 15-10). (In many cases a base shoe is also placed at the intersection of the base and the floor. This protects the base molding and conceals any uneven lines.) Windows are usually trimmed to cover the termination of the interior wall finish materials (see Fig. 15-11). Ceiling moldings cover the intersection where the wall and ceilings meet (see Fig. 15-12).

### BASE MOLDING

Base molding is available in various styles, or it can be combined with other types of molding to form various shapes. It can be purchased in lengths from 3 to $20'$. When molding is purchased, the correct length should reflect an added dimension for each miter. To compensate for a miter, the width of the molding should be added to the desired length. For example, if the molding is $3''$ wide and requires three miters, add $9''$ to the total

FIGURE 15-9    Acoustical-ceiling-system framework

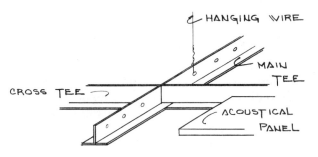

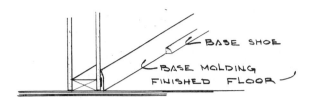

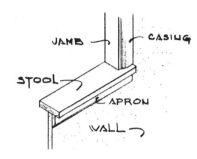

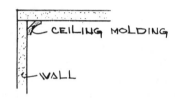

FIGURE 15-10 (top)      Base molding
FIGURE 15-11 (center)   Window trim
FIGURE 15-12 (bottom)   Ceiling molding

length of the molding, then round the length off to the next foot. When molding is purchased, the thickness and the width as well as the length must be specified. The thickness is given first, the width second, and the length last. The thickness is determined by measuring from the top extremity to the bottom extremity. The width is also measured from the widest point.

### WINDOW TRIM

Windows are usually trimmed out by one of two techniques: with casing, stool, and apron, or with the picture-framing technique. In the first case, a stool is first fitted to the unfinished windowsill; it usually projects ¾″ past the side casing and is often placed in a bed of caulking compound or white lead. Once the stool has been placed, three pieces of casing are installed around the window. The bottom of the two side pieces butt the stool, and the intersection of the side and head casing is connected by a miter joint. To complete the job, an apron is placed beneath the stool. The apron is used to conceal the joint made by the

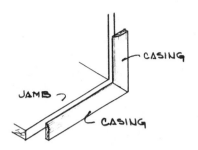

FIGURE 15-13     Picture-frame technique

intersection with the interior wall finish. The length of the apron should equal the distance between the outside edges of the side casing.

For the picture-framing technique, the window opening is framed by the application of four pieces of casing (see Fig. 15-13). Each piece is cut with two 45-degree miters, so that the intersecting pieces can be tightly fitted. When the casing is applied it is not placed flush with the jamb, but back about ¼″.

Regardless of the technique used, the nails should be set and the trim lightly sanded.

### CEILING AND CORNER TRIM

Ceilings are trimmed to close the joint between the wall and the ceiling and to provide an attractive architectural feature. The most popular ceiling trims are cove molding, bed molding, and crown molding (see Fig. 15-14). Several different pieces of molding can be used to form an outstanding architectural feature.

### CHAIR RAILS

Chair rails are thin strips of molding used to protect the wall (see Fig. 15-15). They are usually placed one-third the distance from the floor to the ceiling, or at a level equal to the height of a chair.

FIGURE 15-14 (left and cnter)     Ceiling trim:
(a) cove; (b) bed crown
FIGURE 15-15 (right)     Chair rail

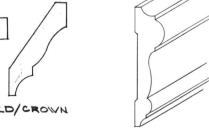

COVE   BED/CROWN

| WINDOW SCHEDULE |||
|---|---|---|
| MARK | SIZE | DESCRIPTION |
| A | 3'-0"x4'-0" | MAYFAIR · SINGLE HUNG BRONZE W/ HALF SCREEN |
| B | 5'-0"x3'-0" | " HORIZONTAL SLIDE " " " " |
| C | 4'-0"x3'-0" | " " " " " |
| D | 1'-4"x6'-0" (VERIFY) | 3/16 CLEAR · FLOAT PLATE GLASS (SAFETY GLASS IN WINDOWS @ DOOR #9) |
| E | 8'-0"x2'-0" (VARIES) | " " " " " |
| F | 8'-0"x7'-4" (VARIES) | " " " " " |
| G | 1'-4"x7'-6" (VERIFY) | " " " " " |
| H | 3'-0"x1'-8" | 1/8" DSB CLEAR |
| I | 1'-4"x6'-3" (VERIFY) | SAFETY GLASS - CLEAR. |

FIGURE 15-16   Window schedule

## THE WINDOW SCHEDULE

The window schedule which the architect draws includes the symbol, size, type of window, manufacturer, material, and remarks (see Fig. 15-16). The symbol used for windows is a letter. The size of a window is given in terms of first its width and then its height. The schedule should indicate the type of window—double-hung, casement, fixed, etc. The manufacturer or the manufacturer's number is given so that an order can be placed with a particular company. The material column indicates the type of material of which the window is made. The remarks column can be used for any further description.

## THE DOOR SCHEDULE

A door schedule is drawn much like a window schedule, but it may be presented in a pictorial or tabular form (see Fig. 15-17). The pictorial form shows the elevation of the door, the type of door, the width, and the height. The symbols used for doors are numbers. Each different number indicates a different type of door. The quantity of doors is not usually given, but rather the schedule indicates how many doors of a certain type are used. The type of door indicates whether the door is a flush hollow core, panel, etc. The size of the door is first indicated by its width, then its height—for example, $3'0'' \times 6'8''$. The manufacturer's number represents a particular firm. The material column indicates the type of material of which the door is made. The finish column is used to indicate the type of finish that will be used on the door—for example, varnish, shellac, enamel paint. The remarks column can be used for any further description.

There are several different types of doors used for interior doors—the more popular types are wood flush doors, folding doors, and sliding doors (see Fig. 15-18).

### Folding Doors

Folding doors operate on overhead tracks and rollers, and are popular units for closets and room dividers. The four most popular patterns are full louvered, louvered with raised bottom panel, flush, and panel. The door units are also available in different widths and varying panel numbers.

### Sliding Doors (Bypass)

Sliding, or bypassing, doors are used extensively in closets, and like the folding doors they operate on overhead tracks and rollers. Most sliding doors are installed by first attaching a track to the head jamb. The track can be designed to cover the rollers, or a piece

| MARK | SIZE | INT'R | EXT'R | TYPE | DESCRIPTION | FINISH |
|------|------|-------|-------|------|-------------|--------|
| DOOR SCHEDULE | | | | | | |
| 1 | 3'-0"x6'-8"x1¾" | | ● | H | FLUSH, SOLID CORE BIRCH W/ FIXED TEMPERED GLASS | STAIN EXT'R · PAINT INT'R |
| 2 | 2'-4"x6'-8"x1⅜" | ● | | A | " HOLLOW " " | PAINT |
| 3 | 2'-4"x6'-8"x1⅜" | ● | | E | WOOD FULL LOUVERED - WHITE PINE | " |
| 4 | 2'-8"x6'-8"x1⅜" | ● | | A | FLUSH, HOLLOW CORE BIRCH | " |
| 5 | 2'-8"x6'-8"x1¾" | | ● | A | " SOLID " " | " |
| 6 | 2'-8"x6'-8"x1¾" | | ● | C | " " " " " W/ 21" x 30" FIXED TEMPERED GLASS W/ WOOD STOPS | " |
| 7 | 4'-0"x6'-8" | ● | | D | MIRROR BI-FOLD - BY GLASS COMPANY | |
| 8 | 2'-0"x6'-8"x1¾" | | ● | B | PANEL - FULL TEMPERED GLASS - WHITE PINE | STAIN EXT'R - PAINT INT'R |
| 9 | 2'-6"x6'-8"x1¾" | | ● | B | " " " " " | " " " " |
| 10 | PR 2'-0"x6'-8"x1⅜" | ● | | A | FLUSH, HOLLOW CORE BIRCH | PAINT |
| 11 | 2'-6"x6'-8"x1⅜" | ● | | A | " " " " POCKET DOOR | " |
| 12 | 2'-0"x6'-8" | ● | | G | GLASS SHOWER DOOR BY GLASS COMPANY | |
| 13 | 5'-0"x6'-8"x1⅜" | ● | | D | FLUSH, HOLLOW CORE BIRCH BI-FOLD | |
| 14 | 2'-8"x6'-8"x1¾" | | ● | H | " SOLID CORE " W/ FIXED TEMPERED GLASS | STAIN EXT'R - PAINT INT'R |
| | | | | | | |
| | | | | | | |
| | | | | | | |
| | | | | | | |
| | | | | | | |

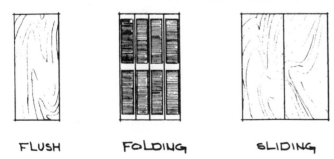

A   B   C   D   E   F   G   H

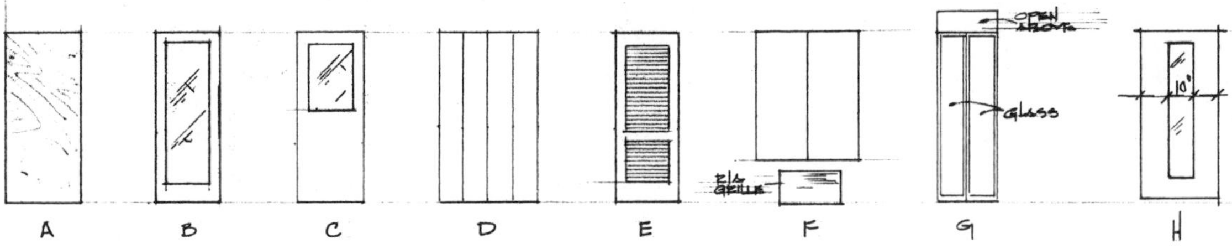

FIGURE 15-17   Door schedule

of trim can be used to cover the track assembly. The standard bypass track can be used with either ¾ or 1⅜" doors.

The size of interior doors varies, but in most cases habitable rooms have a minimum doorway width of 2'0". Regardless of the width of the doors, most doors have a standard height of 6'8" or 7'0".

FIGURE 15-18   Interior doors: (a) flush; (b) folding; (c) sliding

FLUSH          FOLDING          SLIDING

## Assignment:

1. Develop a room finish schedule for the floor plan in Fig. 15-19.
2. Develop a window schedule for the floor plan in Fig. 15-19.
3. Develop a door schedule for the floor plan in Fig. 15-19.

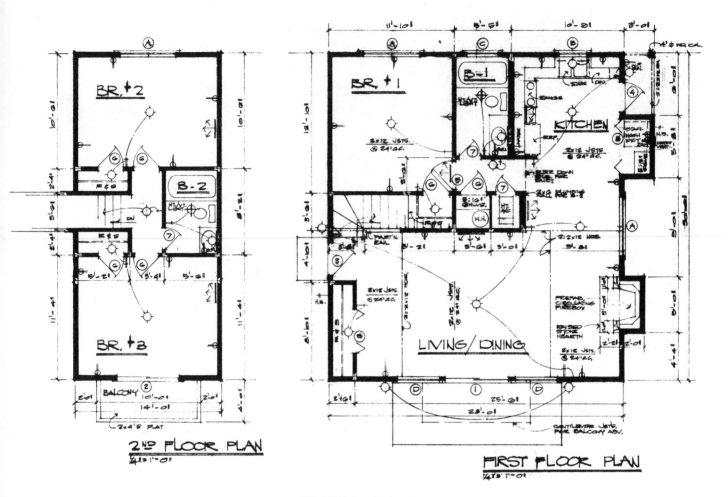

FIGURE 15-19    Typical floor plan

A building is constructed of several different structural members, each playing a significant role in the development of the structure. Structural members fall into two basic categories: those that support dead loads and those that support live loads. A dead load is defined as a stationary load, while a live load is classified as any load that is movable. Roof shingles would be an example of a dead load, and furniture or people could be considered a live load.

Some structural members that are commonly used in construction are floor joists, ceiling joists, columns, rafters, and girders. Each one of these members must be properly designed to carry the imposed dead and live loads. To assist in the design and proper selection of structural members, charts and grafts are often used.

## Floor Joists

A floor joist is a member of the floor frame and is used to support the subfloor, partitions, and other dead and live loads. A typical floor joist is usually nominal 2″ lumber placed on edge and spanning from foundation wall to girder (see Fig. 16-1). The span of a joist is usually considered to be the distance between the interfaces of the two supporting factors. In order that conventional sheets of plywood can be used as a subfloor, the floor joists are usually spaced 12, 16, or 24″ on center. The actual spacing of the joists depends on the species of wood, grade of wood, size of the joist, and whether the subfloor is glued or nailed. Table 16-1 can be used to determine the correct size floor joist for a particular span.

## Ceiling Joists

Ceiling joists are used to "tie" the exterior walls together and to form a nailing surface for the ceiling finish materials (see Fig. 16-2). A ceiling joist is usually constructed of nominal 2″ lumber placed on edge and spanning the distance from an exterior wall to a load-bearing interior partition, or between two interior load-bearing partitions. For 4′ × 8′ sheets of gypsumboard to be used as a ceiling finish material or for standard lengths

191

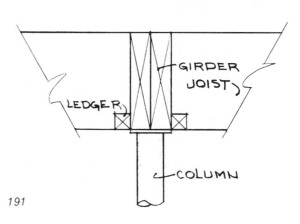

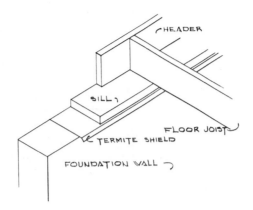

FIGURE 16-1     Typical floor joist

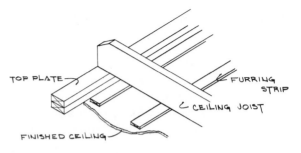

FIGURE 16-2     Typical ceiling joist

of striping to be used, the ceiling joists are usually spaced on 12, 16, or 24″ centers. The actual spacing of ceiling joists depends upon the species of wood, grade of wood, size of the joist, and whether the joists will have any live or dead loads imposed upon them. Table 16-2 can be used to determine the correct size ceiling joists.

## Girders

The correct girder size is determined by calculating first the span and then the load width. The span is considered to be the distance between two girder supports, while the girder load width is considered to be the combined distance from the girder to a midpoint of a joist that rests upon it. The total floor load

that will be imposed on a girder must also be considered. The total floor load includes both live and dead loads. Some recognized loads per square foot are given in Table 16-3. The total load of the girder is then found by multiplying the girder span × girder load × total floor load. The proper size girder can then be selected from Table 16-4.

## Rafters

Most rafters span the distance from the top of the wall frame to the ridge and are used to support the roof sheathing and roof covering (see Fig. 16-3). To determine the correct size of the rafters, the span must first be calculated. The easiest method used in finding the rafter span is to use the conversion diagram. Once the size of the span has been calculated, Table

TABLE 16-1.     FLOOR JOIST: *Forty-Pound Live Load*

| Nominal size | Spacing | S.Y. Pine No. 1 2″ Dim. | S.Y. Pine No. 2 2″ Dim. | Douglas Fir | Redwood |
|---|---|---|---|---|---|
| 2 × 6 | 12 | 10′6″ | 10′6″ | 10′6″ | 9′8″ |
| | 16 | 9′8″ | 9′8″ | 9′8″ | 8′8″ |
| | 24 | 8′4″ | 8′4″ | 8′4″ | 7′8″ |
| 2 × 8 | 12 | 14′4″ | 14′4″ | 14′4″ | 13′0″ |
| | 16 | 13′0″ | 13′0″ | 13′0″ | 11′10″ |
| | 24 | 11′6″ | 11′6″ | 11′6″ | 10′4″ |
| 2 × 10 | 12 | 17′4″ | 17′4″ | 17′4″ | 16′2″ |
| | 16 | 16′2″ | 16′2″ | 16′2″ | 15′0″ |
| | 24 | 14′6″ | 14′6″ | 14′6″ | 13′2″ |
| 2 × 12 | 12 | 20′0″ | 20′0″ | 20′0″ | 18′8″ |
| | 16 | 18′8″ | 18′8″ | 18′8″ | 17′4″ |
| | 24 | 16′10″ | 16′10″ | 16′10″ | 15′8″ |

TABLE 16-2.     CEILING JOISTS

| Nominal size | Spacing | No Attic Storage S.Y. Pine No. 1 2″ Dim. | No Attic Storage S.Y. Pine No. 2 2″ Dim. | Limited Attic Storage S.Y. Pine No. 1 2″ Dim. | Limited Attic Storage S.Y. Pine No. 2 2″ Dim. |
|---|---|---|---|---|---|
| 2 × 6 | 12 | 11′10″ | 11′10″ | 9′6″ | 9′6″ |
| | 16 | 10′10″ | 10′10″ | 8′6″ | 8′6″ |
| | 24 | 9′6″ | 9′6″ | 7′6″ | 7′6″ |
| 2 × 8 | 12 | 17′2″ | 17′2″ | 14′4″ | 14′4″ |
| | 16 | 16′0″ | 16′0″ | 13′0″ | 13′0″ |
| | 24 | 14′4″ | 14′4″ | 11′4″ | 11′4″ |
| 2 × 10 | 12 | 21′8″ | 21′8″ | 18′4″ | 18′4″ |
| | 16 | 20′2″ | 20′2″ | 17′0″ | 17′0″ |
| | 24 | 18′4″ | 18′4″ | 15′4″ | 15′4″ |
| 2 × 12 | 12 | 24′0″ | 24′0″ | 21′10″ | 21′10″ |
| | 16 | 24′0″ | 24′0″ | 20′4″ | 20′4″ |
| | 24 | 21′10″ | 21′10″ | 18′4″ | 18′4″ |

TABLE 16-3.   COMMON DESIGN LOADS FOR LIVE LOADS

| Design Factor | Live Load PSF[1] | Dead Load PSF[1] |
|---|---|---|
| Floors of rooms used for sleeping area | 30 | 10 |
| Floors of rooms other than sleeping | 40 | 10 |
| Floors with ceiling attached below | — | 10 |
| Ceiling joists with limited attic storage | 20 | 10 |

| Design Factor | Live Load PSF[1] | Dead Load PSF[1] |
|---|---|---|
| Ceiling joists with no attic storage | 5 | 10 |
| Ceiling joists if attic rooms are used | 30 | 10 |
| Roof rafters with roof slope less than 3-in-12 | 20 | see roof mat. |
| Roof rafters with roof slope over 3-in-12 | 15 | see roof mat. |

[1]Pounds per square foot

TABLE 16-4   PERMISSIBLE SPANS OF SOLID WOOD GIRDERS
Allowable fiber stress 1,600 pounds per square inch; modulus of elasticity, E-1,600,000
(Allowable uniformly distributed loads for solid wood girders and beams in pounds computed for actual dressed sizes)

| Solid dressed sizes | Span in Feet | | | | | | | | | | | | | | |
|---|---|---|---|---|---|---|---|---|---|---|---|---|---|---|---|
| | 4, 5, 6 | 7 | 8 | 9 | 10 | 11 | 12 | 13 | 14 | 15 | 16 | 17 | 18 | 19 | 20 |
| 3 by 6 | 2,435 | 2,078 | 1,812 | 1,602 | 1,434 | 1,296 | 1,180 | 1,080 | 995 | 921 | 855 | 796 | 744 | 696 | 654 |
| 4 by 6 | 3,366 | 2,875 | 2,505 | 2,213 | 1,981 | 1,791 | 1,630 | 1,493 | 1,375 | 1,272 | 1,183 | 1,101 | 1,030 | 965 | 905 |
| 6 by 6 | 4,885 | 4,165 | 3,633 | 3,211 | 2,873 | 2,596 | 2,363 | 2,166 | 1,995 | 1,845 | 1,714 | 1,595 | 1,492 | 1,396 | 1,310 |
| 2 by 8 | 2,145 | 2,145 | 2,016 | 1,785 | 1,600 | 1,446 | 1,320 | 1,213 | 1,119 | 1,038 | 967 | 902 | 846 | 795 | 749 |
| 3 by 8 | 3,460 | 3,460 | 3,233 | 2,864 | 2,567 | 2,322 | 2,118 | 1,944 | 1,794 | 1,663 | 1,549 | 1,445 | 1,354 | 1,263 | 1,197 |
| 4 by 8 | 4,770 | 4,770 | 4,470 | 3,960 | 3,549 | 3,212 | 2,930 | 2,690 | 2,484 | 2,304 | 2,145 | 2,002 | 1,878 | 1,765 | 1,662 |
| 6 by 8 | 7,260 | 7,260 | 6,783 | 6,008 | 5,386 | 4,875 | 4,446 | 4,082 | 3,768 | 3,495 | 3,255 | 3,039 | 2,850 | 2,678 | 2,522 |
| 8 by 8 | 9,880 | 9,880 | 9,247 | 8,193 | 7,344 | 6,646 | 6,063 | 5,566 | 5,139 | 4,766 | 4,437 | 4,143 | 3,886 | 3,651 | 3,438 |
| 2 by 10 | 2,700 | 2,700 | 2,700 | 2,700 | 2,564 | 2,323 | 2,120 | 1,949 | 1,802 | 1,672 | 1,561 | 1,459 | 1,371 | 1,290 | 1,217 |
| 3 by 10 | 4,370 | 4,370 | 4,370 | 4,370 | 4,139 | 3,749 | 3,424 | 3,146 | 2,908 | 2,699 | 2,517 | 2,353 | 2,210 | 2,079 | 1,961 |
| 4 by 10 | 6,035 | 6,035 | 6,035 | 6,035 | 5,719 | 5,177 | 4,731 | 3,348 | 4,019 | 3,732 | 3,480 | 3,255 | 3,057 | 3,878 | 2,715 |
| 6 by 10 | 9,160 | 9,160 | 9,160 | 9,160 | 8,680 | 7,862 | 7,179 | 6,598 | 6,100 | 5,664 | 5,283 | 4,940 | 4,641 | 4,368 | 4,121 |
| 8 by 10 | 12,500 | 12,500 | 12,500 | 12,500 | 11,835 | 10,720 | 9,790 | 9,000 | 8,318 | 7,724 | 7,205 | 6,738 | 6,329 | 5,957 | 5,620 |
| 10 by 10 | 15,805 | 15,805 | 15,805 | 15,805 | 14,992 | 13,581 | 12,401 | 11,399 | 10,536 | 9,785 | 9,126 | 8,535 | 8,017 | 7,546 | 7,120 |
| 2 by 12 | 3,265 | 3,265 | 3,265 | 3,265 | 3,265 | 3,265 | 3,122 | 2,871 | 2,657 | 2,469 | 2,305 | 2,158 | 2,028 | 1,911 | 1,806 |
| 3 by 12 | 5,260 | 5,260 | 5,260 | 5,260 | 5,260 | 5,260 | 5,037 | 4,633 | 4,285 | 3,982 | 3,716 | 3,478 | 3,270 | 3,081 | 2,909 |
| 4 by 12 | 7,270 | 7,270 | 7,270 | 7,270 | 7,270 | 7,270 | 6,963 | 6,404 | 5,925 | 5,507 | 5,140 | 4,813 | 4,525 | 4,265 | 4,029 |
| 6 by 12 | 11,050 | 11,050 | 11,050 | 11,050 | 11,050 | 11,050 | 10,566 | 9,718 | 8,991 | 8,357 | 7,802 | 7,303 | 6,869 | 6,472 | 6,115 |
| 8 by 12 | 15,050 | 15,050 | 15,050 | 15,050 | 15,050 | 15,050 | 14,408 | 13,252 | 12,260 | 11,396 | 10,638 | 9,959 | 9,366 | 8,826 | 8,337 |
| 10 by 12 | 19,080 | 19,080 | 19,080 | 19,080 | 19,080 | 19,080 | 18,249 | 16,786 | 15,529 | 14,435 | 13,475 | 12,615 | 11,863 | 11,180 | 10,560 |
| 12 by 12 | 23,130 | 23,130 | 23,130 | 23,130 | 23,130 | 23,130 | 22,090 | 20,320 | 18,797 | 17,474 | 16,311 | 15,270 | 14,360 | 13,533 | 12,783 |
| 2 by 14 | 4,115 | 4,115 | 4,115 | 4,115 | 4,115 | 4,115 | 4,115 | 4,115 | 3,669 | 3,412 | 3,186 | 2,885 | 2,808 | 2,587 | 2,502 |
| 3 by 14 | 6,165 | 6,165 | 6,165 | 6,165 | 6,165 | 6,165 | 6,165 | 6,165 | 5,931 | 5,515 | 5,150 | 4,825 | 4,540 | 4,281 | 4,046 |
| 4 by 14 | 8,510 | 8,510 | 8,510 | 8,510 | 8,510 | 8,510 | 8,510 | 8,510 | 8,200 | 7,626 | 7,123 | 6,674 | 6,280 | 5,923 | 5,600 |
| 6 by 14 | 12,930 | 12,930 | 12,930 | 12,930 | 12,930 | 12,930 | 12,930 | 12,930 | 12,440 | 11,571 | 10,810 | 10,125 | 9,530 | 8,987 | 8,498 |
| 8 by 14 | 17,630 | 17,630 | 17,630 | 17,630 | 17,630 | 17,630 | 17,630 | 17,630 | 16,964 | 15,780 | 14,740 | 13,809 | 12,996 | 12,258 | 11,590 |
| 10 by 14 | 22,335 | 22,335 | 22,335 | 22,335 | 22,335 | 22,335 | 22,335 | 22,335 | 21,487 | 19,986 | 18,670 | 17,490 | 16,460 | 15,524 | 14,676 |
| 12 by 14 | 27,040 | 27,040 | 27,040 | 27,040 | 27,040 | 27,040 | 27,040 | 27,040 | 26,010 | 24,194 | 22,600 | 21,171 | 19,925 | 18,192 | 17,766 |
| 14 by 14 | 31,760 | 31,760 | 31,760 | 31,760 | 31,760 | 31,760 | 31,760 | 31,760 | 30,512 | 28,390 | 26,530 | 24,860 | 23,390 | 22,040 | 20,838 |

*Built-up girders:* Multiply above figures by 0.897 when 4-inch girder is made up of two 2-inch pieces.
.887 when 6-inch girder is made of three 2-inch pieces.
.867 when 8-inch girder is made up of four 2-inch pieces.
.856 when 10-inch girder is made up of five 2-inch pieces.
NOTE: Built-up girders of dressed lumber will carry somewhat smaller loads than solid girders; that is, two 2-inch dressed planks will equal only 3¼, whereas dressed 4-inch lumber will equal 3⅝. It is, therefore, necessary to multiply by the above figures in order to compute the loads for built-up girders.

Reprinted with permission from *Light-Frame House Construction,* U.S. Department of Health, Education & Welfare.

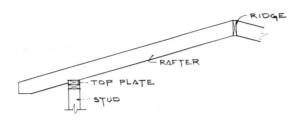

FIGURE 16-3    Rafters span from wall frame to ridge

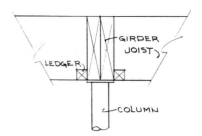

FIGURE 16-4    Columns are used to support girders
and beams

16-5 can be used to determine the appropriate size of the rafter.

## Columns

Girders and beams are sometimes supported by columns that must be properly designed to support the dead and live loads imposed on them (see Fig. 16-4). To determine the correct size of columns, the total load in pounds per square foot for the floor must first be calculated. This procedure can be accomplished by multiplying the total load by the number of square feet of floor space. The spacing of the columns is then determined and the number of square feet supported by the columns is calculated. The load is determined from the column to the midpoint of the span, or it can carry half the load to the nearest foundation wall. The load imposed on the column can be found by multiplying the number of square feet by the load per square foot. The height of

the column is then determined; Table 16-6 can be used to select the correct size column.

TABLE 16-5.    RAFTERS: *Light Roofing*

| Nominal size | Spacing | S.Y. Pine No. 1 Dim. | S.Y. Pine No. 2 Dim. | Redwood | Cypress |
|---|---|---|---|---|---|
| 2 × 4 | 12 | 11'6" | 11'4" | 10'6" | 10'6" |
| | 16 | 10'6" | 9'10" | 9'6" | 9'6" |
| | 24 | 8'10" | 8'10" | 8'4" | 8'4" |
| 2 × 6 | 12 | 16'10" | 16'10" | 15'8" | 15'8" |
| | 16 | 15'8" | 15'0" | 14'6" | 14'6" |
| | 24 | 18'4" | 12'2" | 12'8" | 12'8" |
| 2 × 8 | 12 | 21'2" | 21'2" | 19'10" | 19'10" |
| | 16 | 19'10" | 19'10" | 18'4" | 18'4" |
| | 24 | 17'10" | 16'8" | 16'8" | 16'8" |
| 2 × 10 | 12 | 24'0" | 24'0" | 23'8" | 23'8" |
| | 16 | 23'8" | 23'8" | 22'0" | 22'0" |
| | 24 | 21'4" | 21'0" | 19'0" | 19'10" |

TABLE 16-6.    MAXIMUM LOADS FOR WOOD COLUMNS (in pounds)

| Column Size (Inches) | Compressive Strength (Lbs per sq in) | Height of Column | | | | | | |
|---|---|---|---|---|---|---|---|---|
| | | 6'0" | 7'0" | 8'0" | 9'0" | 10'0" | 11'0" | 12'0" |
| 3⅝ | 1150 to 1400 | 13,460 | 12,170 | 10,280 | 7,700 | 5,670 | 4,340 | |
| X | 1400 to 1750 | 15,370 | 13,060 | | | | | |
| 3⅝ | 1750 | 17,000 | 13,130 | | | | | |
| 5⅝ | 1150 to 1400 | 33,800 | | 32,800 | 31,500 | 27,800 | 23,500 | |
| X | 1400 to 1750 | 40,800 | | 38,700 | 35,300 | 30,000 | | |
| 5⅝ | 1750 | 49,700 | | 45,850 | 39,000 | 30,500 | | |

## Assignment:

1. Determine the size of the floor joists in Fig. 16-5.

2. Determine the size of the ceiling joists in Fig. 16-6.

3. Determine the size of the rafters in Fig. 16-7.

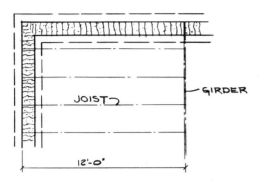

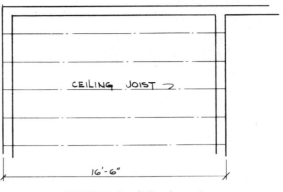

FIGURE 16-6    Ceiling-frame plans

FIGURE 16-5    Floor-framing plan

FIGURE 16-7    Roof-framing plans

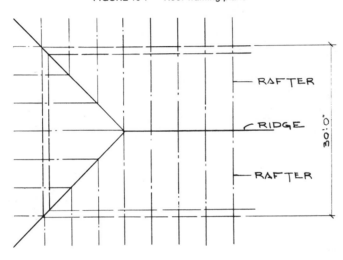

A perspective is a pictorial drawing that is used to illustrate design principles (see Fig. 17-1). It is also used to illustrate the basic architectural design concept to a prospective client and to "sell" the client on a particular design.

In the actual drafting of the perspective there are six basic terms that are used extensively:

□ *Ground plane* (G.P.): Represents the intersection of the picture plane and the ground. It is always drawn parallel to the picture plane and the horizon.

□ *Station point* (S.P.): Usually thought of as the place where an individual is standing to view an object. The station point can be placed in any appropriate location, but in most cases it is placed about twice as far away from the picture plane as the length of the building.

□ *Picture plane* (P.P.): A transparent plane that is placed in a vertical position, with the lower edge of the plane intersecting the ground plane. All horizontal measurements are taken on the picture plane and are projected to the perspective. If any part of an object touches the picture plane, it is projected as true height.

□ *Horizon line* (H.L.): A line that represents the intersection of the ground and the sky. The line is drawn parallel to the ground plane and the picture plane.

□ *Vanishing points* (V.P.): Located on the horizon line, with the sides of the object receding toward them. A two-point perspective has a right and a left vanishing point, while a one-point perspective has only one vanishing point.

□ *True-length line* (T.L.L.): A true-length line is established when a vertical line touches the picture plane; it projects heights to the objects in the drawing. It is always necessary to find at least one true-length line so that the dimension of height can be determined.

There are two basic types of perspectives that are used in architectural drafting: a two-point perspective and a one-point perspective.

# 17
# Perspectives

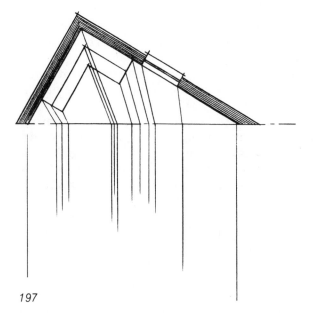

197

RENDERINGS BY RICHARD TOGLIA

FIGURE 17-1    Perspective

## The Two-Point Perspective

Listed below are the necessary steps required to draw a two-point perspective.

☐ Draw the top view in the upper left-hand corner of the drawing paper. Then draw the right-side view in the lower right-hand corner. The top view may be drawn at any convenient angle, but is usually placed at 30 degrees (see Fig. 17-2).

☐ Locate the picture-plane line, the horizon line, and the station point. The horizon line is located at eye level from the ground line. A station point is usually located at least twice the length of the object from the picture plane (see Fig. 17-3).

☐ Then locate the vanishing points by drawing two lines parallel to the top view. The lines should be drawn from the station point, one line parallel to the front view and one line parallel to the side view. Where the two lines intersect the picture plane, a vertical line should be dropped to the horizon.

The vanishing points will be located at the intersection of the vertical lines and the horizon (see Fig. 17-4).

☐ Locate the true height line by projecting a vertical line from the corner of the object that is touching the picture plane. Then project horizontal lines from the profile view. The intersection of the lines indicates true height (see Fig. 17-5).

☐ From the true-height line, draw light construction lines to the vanishing points (see Fig. 17-6).

☐ Draw light construction lines from the station point to the top view. Where the construction lines intersect the picture plane, project vertical lines to locate the corners of the perspective (see Fig. 17-7). Once the features are blocked in, the sight lines can be erased and the features darkened in.

FIGURE 17-2 (top right)       Step 1
FIGURE 17-3 (center right)    Step 2
FIGURE 17-4 (bottom right)    Step 3

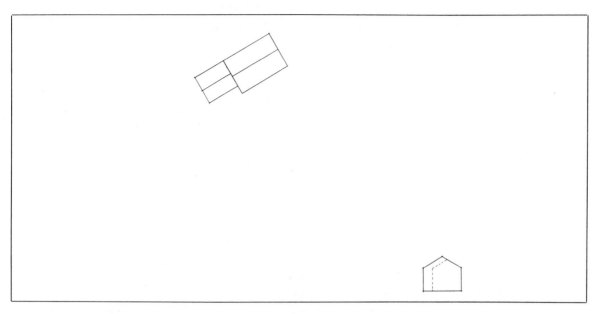

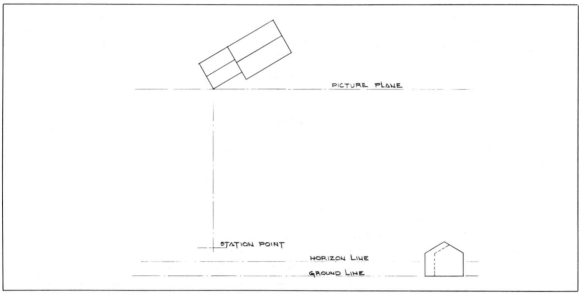

PICTURE PLANE

STATION POINT

HORIZON LINE

GROUND LINE

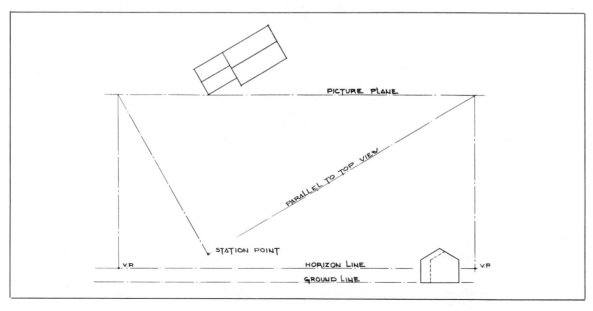

PICTURE PLANE

PARALLEL TO TOP VIEW

STATION POINT

V.P.                                    V.P.

HORIZON LINE

GROUND LINE

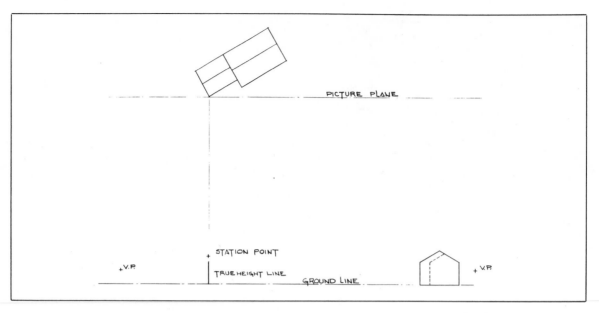

PICTURE PLANE

+ V.P.

STATION POINT

TRUE HEIGHT LINE

GROUND LINE

+ V.P.

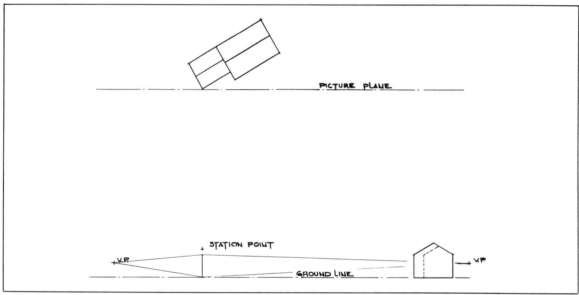

PICTURE PLANE

V.P.

STATION POINT

GROUND LINE

V.P.

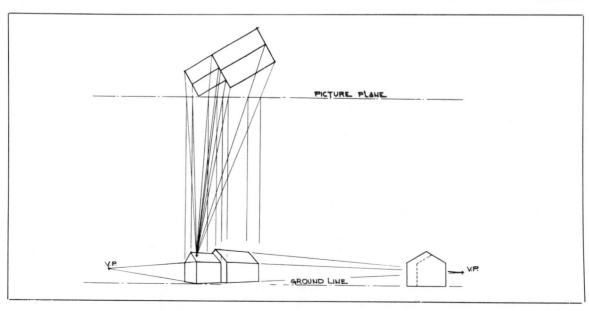

PICTURE PLANE

V.P.

GROUND LINE

V.P.

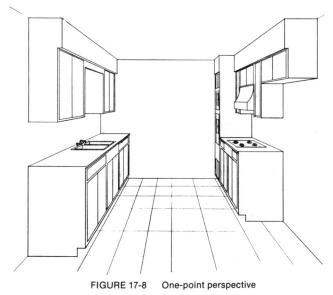

FIGURE 17-8    One-point perspective

## The One-Point Perspective

A one-point perspective is primarily used to show interior features and is achieved when the picture plane is parallel to the face of the object (see Fig. 17-8).

Listed below are the necessary steps for the completion of a one-point perspective:

☐ Draw a rectangle (see Fig. 17-9). The height and width should correspond to the height and width of the room being drawn. Lines AB and CD represent the dimension of width, while lines AC and BD represent height. If the room is 10' in width, then lines AB and CD will also be 10'. (In most cases lines AC and BD will be 8', because this represents ceiling height.)

☐ Locate the vanishing point (V.P.). It is usually placed on a point 5'3" above line AB, or it can be placed at viewing height. The V.P. can be moved horizontally between lines AC and BD; the final location depends on where the observer is standing.

☐ Locate two station points. The station points are located on the same line as the V.P. The distance from SP[1] and SP[2] to the V.P. equals the distance from the observer to the back wall. For example, if the observer is 7' from the back wall, the distance from SP[1] to the V.P. will be 7'.

☐ Draw a light construction line from points A, B, C, and D to the V.P. (see Fig. 17-10). The two bottom lines represent the intersection between wall and floor. The two top lines represent the intersection between ceiling and wall.

☐ Add the dimension of depth to the perspective (see Fig. 17-11). To achieve this, mark off the dimension of depth on line AB. This means if the observer is standing 7' from the back wall, a point 7' from point A should be marked. From this mark a line is projected to SP[1]. At the intersection of this line and the line that represents the intersection of the floor and ceiling, draw a vertical and horizontal line. These two

FIGURE 17-9 (top)        Step 1
FIGURE 17-10 (center)    Step 2
FIGURE 17-11 (bottom)    Step 3

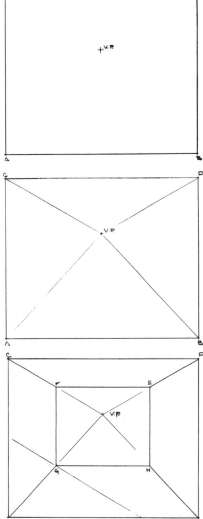

FIGURE 17-5 (top left)       Step 4
FIGURE 17-6 (center left)    Step 5
FIGURE 17-7 (bottom left)    Step 6

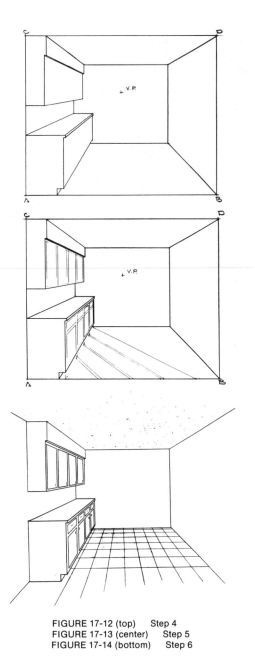

FIGURE 17-12 (top)    Step 4
FIGURE 17-13 (center)    Step 5
FIGURE 17-14 (bottom)    Step 6

lines form GH and GF. Line FE is created by projecting from point F. Line EH is created by projecting from point E. The figure G, H, F, E represents the back wall of the room.

□ If there are any built-in features in the room, draw the profile to its true shape and size on the plane A, B, C, D (see Fig. 17-12). For example, if the base cabinet is 3′ in height, it will be drawn 3′. Once the profile has been drawn, project all points to the V.P.

□ Any dimensions of depth will be measured

along line AB and projected to SP[1] (see Fig. 17-13). For example, if you want to find a point 3′ from the end of the cabinet, measure 3′ from the end of the cabinet along line AB. Then project a line to SP[1]. Where the line intersects, the base of the cabinet is 3′. If the point is on the wall, it needs to be measured from point A.

□ Before you darken in the drawing, lines AB, CD, AC, and BD need to be erased (see Fig. 17-14). Add details to complete the drawing.

## The Two-Point Perspective for Interiors

A two-point perspective can also be used to illustrate the interior. Listed below are the necessary steps required in drawing a two-point perspective:

□ Establish the picture plane and draw or temporarily tape the floor plan to the drawing. It is usually best to place it at a 30-degree angle to the picture plan (see Fig. 17-15).

□ Establish the station point. It is usually located below the picture plane at a distance equal to twice the width of the plan being drawn.

□ From the station point, draw two lines that are parallel to the two walls of the floor plan (see Fig. 17-16).

□ Where the two lines intersect the picture plane, drop two lines down that are perpendicular to the picture plane (see Fig. 17-17).

□ Draw a line parallel to the picture plane. This should be placed at eye level on the elevation. This line will be the horizon. Where the two previously drawn vertical lines intersect, the horizon will be the two vanishing points (see Fig. 17-18). At this point draw an elevation of the room. The horizon line should intersect the elevation at eye level.

□ Project all points on the plan view to the station point. Where the projection lines cross the picture plane, project a series of vertical construction lines (see Fig. 17-19).

□ Then project detail points from the elevation; the point at which the elevation line

FIGURE 17-15 (top right)    Step 1
FIGURE 17-16 (center right)    Step 2
FIGURE 17-17 (bottom right)    Step 3

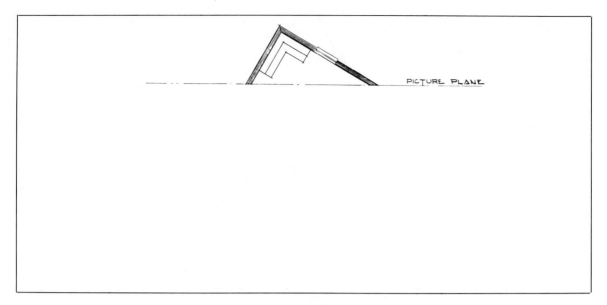

PICTURE PLANE

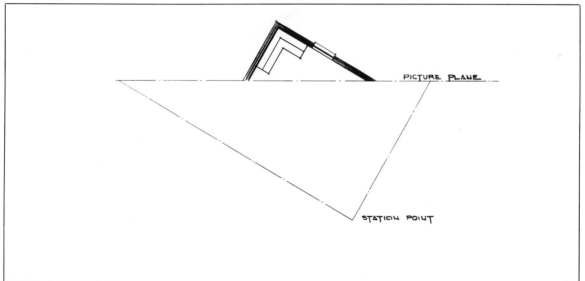

PICTURE PLANE

STATION POINT

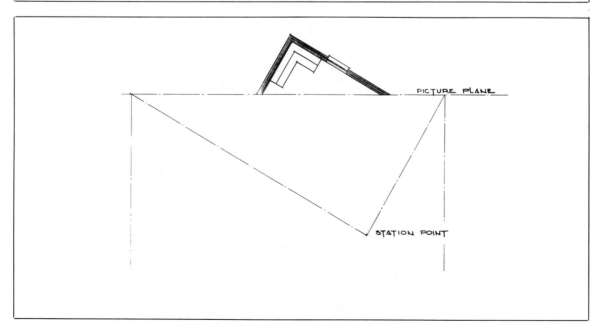

PICTURE PLANE

STATION POINT

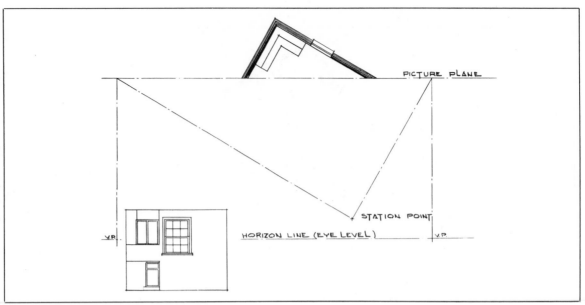

PICTURE PLANE

STATION POINT

V.P.

HORIZON LINE (EYE LEVEL)          V.P.

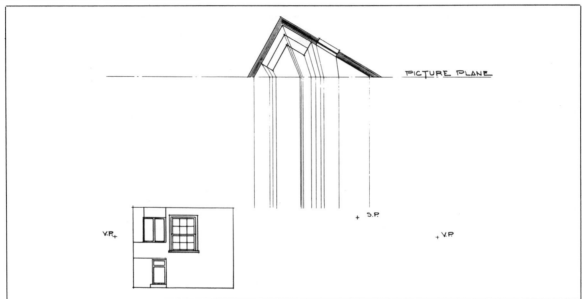

PICTURE PLANE

V.P.+

+ S.P.

+ V.P.

PICTURE PLANE

V.P.+

TRUE HEIGHT LINE

+

V.P.

intersects the vertical line is the true height line. Then take all measurements of height from the true height line (see Fig. 17-20).

□ Once all the features have been clocked in, erase the construction lines and darken in the perspective.

## Assignment:

1. Draw a one-point and two-point perspective of the kitchen in Fig. 17-21.

FIGURE 17-21   Assignment: Draw a one-point and a two-point perspective of the kitchen

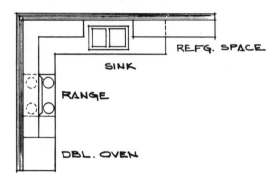

2. Draw a two-point perspective of the sculptured block in Fig. 17-22.

FIGURE 17-22   Draw a two-point perspective of the sculptured block

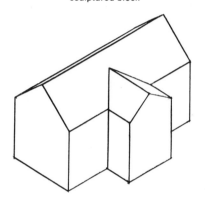

FIGURE 17-18 (top left)     Step 4
FIGURE 17-19 (center left)     Step 5
FIGURE 17-20 (bottom left)     Step 6

A rendering is used to show how a building will look in its natural environment or setting (see Fig. 18-1). A finished three-dimensional rendering is used to show clients what the building will look like when it is finished— many clients are not able to visualize this from a working drawing. The building is drawn in perspective and can be rendered using one of several different mediums. The most common are: pencil, pen and ink, scratchboard, appliqué, water color, tempera, and a combination of all the techniques.

## 18
## Rendering

### Pencil Rendering

Pencil rendering is one of the most popular means of rendering (see Fig. 18-2). The advantage of this technique is that no special equipment is needed and if a mistake is made it can be quickly corrected. The only materials needed are pencil and paper. A soft pencil, such as a B, 2B, 3B, or 4B will produce a dark line or tone. A medium tone is achieved by using an HB, F, or H; and a light tone is achieved with a 4H, 3H, or 2H. There are three basic types of points that can be placed on the leads: conical, blunt, and chisel (see Fig. 18-3). A sharp conical point is usually used for layout and detail work, and chisel or blunt points are best suited for broad strokes.

The pencil should be held in a firm, natural position. To keep the drawing from being smudged, a small piece of paper can be placed under the drawing hand. As the hand is moved, the paper should be repositioned. During the various drawing stages it will be necessary to frequently change pencils for different tones. The rendering should not be a photographic reproduction, but rather a drawing with some exaggerated features, such as the contrast between light and dark.

### Ink Rendering

Ink renderings require more skill than pencil rendering, but can also produce attractive end results (see Fig. 18-4). The paper used for an ink rendering should be smooth. A rough finish produces a drawing with inconsistent line quality. The paper should also be compatible with the ink, so that it won't become fuzzy

B. NATHAN.

FIGURE 18-1    Typical rendering

when the ink is applied. A good-quality tracing paper or cloth, mat board, Bristol board, or Strathmore paper can be used.

A technical fountain pen is usually used to apply the ink. The point sizes for the pens are: 00 (fine), 0 (medium fine), 1 (medium), 2 (medium heavy), and 3 (heavy). Black ink is most often used, but there are other colors

FIGURE 18-2    Pencil rendering

FIGURE 18-3    Lead points

A                          B                          C

FIGURE 18-4    Ink rendering

available. In some cases the ink is even diluted with water to provide varying shades. Pens of different widths should be used for the drawing so it won't look monotonous. Work that appears close to the observer should be done with a broad pen; as the object recedes in the distance, fine-line pens should be used. To keep from smearing the fresh ink, most work should be started at or near the top of the drawing, proceeding down toward the bottom of the page. If there are any large areas that require ink it is usually better to fill them with a brush that has been dipped in ink.

## Scratchboard Rendering

A scratchboard rendering is not often used, but it does produce a striking drawing (see Fig. 18-5). An illustration of this type consists of white lines displayed on a black background. The rendering is started by covering a white surfaced board with black ink. Then, with tools having various shapes and points, portions of the black surface are scratched off, leaving a series of white lines to describe the object. Fine detail work is achieved by using sharp, pointed instruments; broader instruments are used to scrape off large areas of black ink.

Scratchboard rendering makes excellent photographic reproductions, but is time-consuming to prepare.

## Appliqué

An appliqué is a printed figure or shape that has adhesive on its back side (see Fig. 18-6). Appliqués are usually purchased on a large transparent sheet that has various shapes that can be peeled off and applied to the rendering to represent trees, people, automobiles, etc. Appliqués speed up the work on the rendering and can lend a special artistic look.

FIGURE 18-5   Scratchboard rendering

### Water Color and Tempera

Water color is a transparent water-based paint, while tempera is an opaque water-based paint. Water color is applied in a thin mixture called a wash. Tempera is usually applied from the palette. A water-color rendering is attractive, but it is often difficult for a beginning illustrator to achieve the proper results (see Fig. 18-7). Various shades of color can be achieved by controlling the amount of water used to dilute the paint. Before the solution is used it should always be tested for intensity. The colors used should be soft and subdued and restful to the eye, not bright and overpowering.

## Assignment:

1. Do a pencil rendering of a concrete block.
2. Do an ink rendering of a one-point perspective.
3. Use water color or tempera as a medium for rendering. Practice on a previously drawn perspective.

FIGURE 18-6   Applique

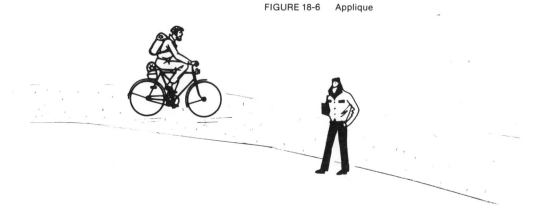

FIGURE 18-7    Watercolor rendering

Specifications consist of a written set of instructions used to convey any information that cannot easily be placed on the working drawings. More specifically, they are a legal document, a basis for bidding, a guide for construction, and they give technical descriptions.

The specifications indicate the quality and kind of materials, workmanship, colors, and finishes.

## FHA and VA Forms

There are many different types of forms used for specifications; two of the most popular used for residential construction are the FHA Form 2005 and the VA Form 26-1852 (see Fig. 19-1). The specifications are divided into sections and are listed in sequence as they occur.

In the writing of the specifications, there are standard rules that should be followed:

- Use simple, direct language
- Avoid repetition
- Use standard items
- Use accepted standards
- Specify number and names
- Give a description of the material used

## The CSI Format

The Construction Specifications Institute has successfully standardized a specification format that is being used by many large and small contracting firms. The advantage in using this format is that it is a standard form and many contractors and material suppliers are familiar with it.

The format of the written specification is based on the "Division-Section" concept. A typical set of specifications is broken down into sixteen basic divisions that carry policy about a particular craft. The different sections of the specifications are used to denote a particular trade section.

The CSI format includes the following divisions:

- Division 1—*General requirements:* Covers topics that are pertinent to the job as a whole.
- Division 2—*Site work:* Deals with the development and preparation of the job site.

# 19
# Specifications

213

FHA Form 2005
VA Form 26-1852
Rev. 4/73

U. S. DEPARTMENT OF HOUSING AND URBAN DEVELOPMENT
FEDERAL HOUSING ADMINISTRATION

For accurate register of carbon copies, form
may be separated along above fold.   Staple
completed sheets together in original order.

Form Approved
OMB No. 63—RO055

☐ Proposed Construction

# DESCRIPTION OF MATERIALS   No. _____

(To be inserted by FHA or VA)

☐ Under Construction

Property address _____  City _____  State _____

Mortgagor or Sponsor _____  _____
                              (Name)                        (Address)

Contractor or Builder _____  _____
                              (Name)                        (Address)

## INSTRUCTIONS

1. For additional information on how this form is to be submitted, number of copies, etc., see the instructions applicable to the FHA Application for Mortgage Insurance or VA Request for Determination of Reasonable Value, as the case may be.
2. Describe all materials and equipment to be used, whether or not shown on the drawings, by marking an X in each appropriate check-box and entering the information called for in each space. If space is inadequate, enter "See misc." and describe under item 27 or on an attached sheet. THE USE OF PAINT CONTAINING MORE THAN ONE PERCENT LEAD BY WEIGHT IS PROHIBITED.
3. Work not specifically described or shown will not be considered unless required, then the minimum acceptable will be assumed. Work exceeding minimum requirements cannot be considered unless specifically described.
4. Include no alternates, "or equal" phrases, or contradictory items. (Consideration of a request for acceptance of substitute materials or equipment is not thereby precluded.)
5. Include signatures required at the end of this form.
6. The construction shall be completed in compliance with the related drawings and specifications, as amended during processing. The specifications include this Description of Materials and the applicable Minimum Property Standards.

**1. EXCAVATION:**
Bearing soil, type _____

**2. FOUNDATIONS:**
Footings: concrete mix _____; strength psi _____   Reinforcing _____
Foundation wall: material _____   Reinforcing _____
Interior foundation wall: material _____   Party foundation wall _____
Columns: material and sizes _____   Piers: material and reinforcing _____
Girders: material and sizes _____   Sills: material _____
Basement entrance areaway _____   Window areaways _____
Waterproofing _____   Footing drains _____
Termite protection _____
Basementless space: ground cover _____; insulation _____; foundation vents _____
Special foundations _____
Additional information: _____

**3. CHIMNEYS:**
Material _____   Prefabricated (make and size) _____
Flue lining: material _____   Heater flue size _____   Fireplace flue size _____
Vents (material and size): gas or oil heater _____; water heater _____
Additional information: _____

**4. FIREPLACES:**
Type: ☐ solid fuel; ☐ gas-burning; ☐ circulator (make and size) _____   Ash dump and clean-out _____
Fireplace: facing _____; lining _____; hearth _____; mantel _____
Additional information: _____

**5. EXTERIOR WALLS:**
Wood frame: wood grade, and species _____   ☐ Corner bracing.  Building paper or felt _____
Sheathing _____; thickness _____; width _____; ☐ solid; ☐ spaced _____" o. c.; ☐ diagonal; _____
Siding _____; grade _____; type _____; size _____; exposure _____"; fastening _____
Shingles _____; grade _____; type _____; size _____; exposure _____"; fastening _____
Stucco _____; thickness _____"; Lath _____; weight _____ lb.
Masonry veneer _____   Sills _____   Lintels _____   Base flashing _____
Masonry: ☐ solid ☐ faced ☐ stuccoed; total wall thickness _____"; facing thickness _____"; facing material _____
Backup material _____; thickness _____"; bonding _____
Door sills _____   Window sills _____   Lintels _____   Base flashing _____
Interior surfaces: dampproofing, _____ coats of _____; furring _____
Additional information: _____
Exterior painting: material _____; number of coats _____
Gable wall construction: ☐ same as main walls; ☐ other construction _____

**6. FLOOR FRAMING:**
Joists: wood, grade, and species _____; other _____; bridging _____; anchors _____
Concrete slab: ☐ basement floor; ☐ first floor; ☐ ground supported; ☐ self-supporting; mix _____, thickness _____";
reinforcing _____; insulation _____; membrane _____
Fill under slab: material _____; thickness _____".  Additional information: _____

**7. SUBFLOORING:** (Describe underflooring for special floors under item 21.)
Material: grade and species _____; size _____; type _____
Laid: ☐ first floor; ☐ second floor; ☐ attic _____ sq. ft.; ☐ diagonal; ☐ right angles.  Additional information: _____

**8. FINISH FLOORING:** (Wood only.  Describe other finish flooring under item 21.)

| LOCATION | ROOMS | GRADE | SPECIES | THICKNESS | WIDTH | BLDG. PAPER | FINISH |
|---|---|---|---|---|---|---|---|
| First floor | | | | | | | |
| Second floor | | | | | | | |
| Attic floor ___ sq. ft. | | | | | | | |
| Additional information: | | | | | | | |

FIGURE 19-1 (pages 214-17)   FHA Form 2005 and VA Form 26-1852

**9. PARTITION FRAMING:**
Studs: wood, grade, and species _____ size and spacing _____ Other _____
Additional information: _____

**10. CEILING FRAMING:**
Joists: wood, grade, and species _____ Other _____ Bridging _____
Additional information: _____

**11. ROOF FRAMING:**
Rafters: wood, grade, and species _____ Roof trusses (see detail): grade and species _____
Additional information: _____

**12. ROOFING:**
Sheathing: wood, grade, and species _____ ; ☐ solid; ☐ spaced _____ " o.c.
Roofing _____ ; grade _____ ; size _____ ; type _____
Underlay _____ ; weight or thickness _____ ; size _____ ; fastening _____
Built-up roofing _____ ; number of plies _____ ; surfacing material _____
Flashing: material _____ ; gage or weight _____ ; ☐ gravel stops; ☐ snow guards
Additional information: _____

**13. GUTTERS AND DOWNSPOUTS:**
Gutters: material _____ ; gage or weight _____ ; size _____ ; shape _____
Downspouts: material _____ ; gage or weight _____ ; size _____ ; shape _____ ; number _____
Downspouts connected to: ☐ Storm sewer; ☐ sanitary sewer; ☐ dry-well. ☐ Splash blocks: material and size _____
Additional information: _____

**14. LATH AND PLASTER**
Lath ☐ walls, ☐ ceilings: material _____ ; weight or thickness _____ Plaster: coats _____ ; finish _____
Dry-wall ☐ walls, ☐ ceilings: material _____ ; thickness _____ ; finish _____ ;
Joint treatment _____

**15. DECORATING:** *(Paint, wallpaper, etc.)*

| Rooms | Wall Finish Material and Application | Ceiling Finish Material and Application |
|---|---|---|
| Kitchen _____ | | |
| Bath _____ | | |
| Other _____ | | |

Additional information: _____

**16. INTERIOR DOORS AND TRIM:**
Doors: type _____ ; material _____ ; thickness _____
Door trim: type _____ ; material _____ Base: type _____ ; material _____ ; size _____
Finish: doors _____ ; trim _____
Other trim *(item, type and location)* _____
Additional information: _____

**17. WINDOWS:**
Windows: type _____ ; make _____ ; material _____ ; sash thickness _____
Glass: grade _____ ; ☐ sash weights; ☐ balances, type _____ ; head flashing _____
Trim: type _____ ; material _____ Paint _____ ; number coats _____
Weatherstripping: type _____ ; material _____ Storm sash, number _____
Screens: ☐ full; ☐ half; type _____ ; number _____ ; screen cloth material _____
Basement windows: type _____ ; material _____ ; screens, number _____ ; Storm sash, number _____
Special windows _____
Additional information: _____

**18. ENTRANCES AND EXTERIOR DETAIL:**
Main entrance door: material _____ ; width _____ ; thickness _____ ". Frame: material _____ , thickness _____ "
Other entrance doors: material _____ ; width _____ ; thickness _____ ". Frame: material _____ , thickness _____ "
Head flashing _____ Weatherstripping: type _____ ; saddles _____
Screen doors: thickness _____ "; number _____ ; screen cloth material _____ Storm doors: thickness _____ "; number _____
Combination storm and screen doors: thickness _____ "; number _____ ; screen cloth material _____
Shutters: ☐ hinged; ☐ fixed. Railings _____ , Attic louvers _____
Exterior millwork: grade and species _____ Paint _____ ; number coats _____
Additional information: _____

**19. CABINETS AND INTERIOR DETAIL:**
Kitchen cabinets, wall units: material _____ ; lineal feet of shelves _____ ; shelf width _____
Base units: material _____ ; counter top _____ ; edging _____
Back and end splash _____ Finish of cabinets _____ ; number coats _____
Medicine cabinets: make _____ ; model _____
Other cabinets and built-in furniture _____
Additional information: _____

**20. STAIRS:**

| Stair | Treads | | Risers | | Strings | | Handrail | | Balusters | |
|---|---|---|---|---|---|---|---|---|---|---|
| | Material | Thickness | Material | Thickness | Material | Size | Material | Size | Material | Size |
| Basement _____ | | | | | | | | | | |
| Main _____ | | | | | | | | | | |
| Attic _____ | | | | | | | | | | |

Disappearing: make and model number _____
Additional information: _____

**21. SPECIAL FLOORS AND WAINSCOT**

| | LOCATION | MATERIAL, COLOR, BORDER, SIZES, GAGE, ETC. | THRESHOLD MATERIAL | WALL BASE MATERIAL | UNDERFLOOR MATERIAL |
|---|---|---|---|---|---|
| FLOORS | Kitchen | | | | |
| | Bath | | | | |
| | | | | | |
| | | | | | |

| | LOCATION | MATERIAL, COLOR, BORDER, CAP. SIZES, GAGE, ETC. | HEIGHT | HEIGHT OVER TUB | HEIGHT IN SHOWERS (FROM FLOOR) |
|---|---|---|---|---|---|
| WAINSCOT | Bath | | | | |
| | | | | | |
| | | | | | |

Bathroom accessories: ☐ Recessed; material _____; number _____; ☐ Attached; material _____; number _____

Additional information: _____

**22. PLUMBING:**

| FIXTURE | NUMBER | LOCATION | MAKE | MFR'S FIXTURE IDENTIFICATION NO. | SIZE | COLOR |
|---|---|---|---|---|---|---|
| Sink | | | | | | |
| Lavatory | | | | | | |
| Water closet | | | | | | |
| Bathtub | | | | | | |
| Shower over tub △ | | | | | | |
| Stall shower △ | | | | | | |
| Laundry trays | | | | | | |
| | | | | | | |
| | | | | | | |
| | | | | | | |
| | | | | | | |

△☐ Curtain rod    △☐ Door    ☐ Shower pan: material _____

Water supply: ☐ public; ☐ community system; ☐ individual (private) system.★

Sewage disposal: ☐ public; ☐ community system; ☐ individual (private) system.★

★Show and describe individual system in complete detail in separate drawings and specifications according to requirements.

House drain (inside): ☐ cast iron; ☐ tile; ☐ other _____    House sewer (outside): ☐ cast iron; ☐ tile; ☐ other _____

Water piping: ☐ galvanized steel; ☐ copper tubing; ☐ other _____    Sill cocks, number _____

Domestic water heater: type _____; make and model _____; heating capacity _____

_____ gph. 100° rise. Storage tank: material _____; capacity _____ gallons.

Gas service: ☐ utility company; ☐ liq. pet. gas; ☐ other _____    Gas piping: ☐ cooking; ☐ house heating.

Footing drains connected to: ☐ storm sewer; ☐ sanitary sewer; ☐ dry well. Sump pump; make and model _____

_____; capacity _____; discharges into _____

**23. HEATING:**

☐ Hot water.  ☐ Steam.  ☐ Vapor.  ☐ One-pipe system.  ☐ Two-pipe system.

   ☐ Radiators.  ☐ Convectors.  ☐ Baseboard radiation.  Make and model _____

   Radiant panel: ☐ floor; ☐ wall; ☐ ceiling.  Panel coil: material _____

   ☐ Circulator.  ☐ Return pump.  Make and model _____; capacity _____ gpm.

   Boiler: make and model _____    Output _____ Btuh.; net rating _____ Btuh.

Additional information: _____

Warm air: ☐ Gravity.  ☐ Forced.  Type of system _____

   Duct material: supply _____; return _____  Insulation _____, thickness _____  ☐ Outside air intake.

   Furnace: make and model _____    Input _____ Btuh.; output _____ Btuh.

   Additional information: _____

☐ Space heater; ☐ floor furnace; ☐ wall heater.  Input _____ Btuh.; output _____ Btuh.; number units _____

   Make, model _____    Additional information: _____

Controls: make and types _____

Additional information: _____

Fuel: ☐ Coal; ☐ oil; ☐ gas; ☐ liq. pet. gas; ☐ electric; ☐ other _____; storage capacity _____

   Additional information: _____

Firing equipment furnished separately: ☐ Gas burner, conversion type.  ☐ Stoker: hopper feed ☐; bin feed ☐

   Oil burner: ☐ pressure atomizing; ☐ vaporizing _____

   Make and model _____    Control _____

   Additional information: _____

Electric heating system: type _____    Input _____ watts; @ _____ volts; output _____ Btuh.

   Additional information: _____

Ventilating equipment: attic fan, make and model _____; capacity _____ cfm.

   kitchen exhaust fan, make and model _____

Other heating, ventilating, or cooling equipment _____

**24. ELECTRIC WIRING:**

Service: ☐ overhead; ☐ underground.  Panel: ☐ fuse box; ☐ circuit-breaker; make _____ AMP's _____ No. circuits _____

Wiring: ☐ conduit; ☐ armored cable; ☐ nonmetallic cable; ☐ knob and tube; ☐ other _____

Special outlets: ☐ range; ☐ water heater; ☐ other _____

☐ Doorbell.  ☐ Chimes.  Push-button locations _____    Additional information: _____

**25. LIGHTING FIXTURES:**

Total number of fixtures _____    Total allowance for fixtures, typical installation, $ _____

Nontypical installation _____

Additional information: _____

**26. INSULATION:**

| LOCATION | THICKNESS | MATERIAL, TYPE, AND METHOD OF INSTALLATION | VAPOR BARRIER |
|---|---|---|---|
| Roof | | | |
| Ceiling | | | |
| Wall | | | |
| Floor | | | |

**HARDWARE:** *(make, material, and finish.)* _____

**SPECIAL EQUIPMENT:** *(State material or make, model and quantity. Include only equipment and appliances which are acceptable by local law, custom and applicable FHA standards. Do not include items which, by established custom, are supplied by occupant and removed when he vacates premises or chattles prohibited by law from becoming realty.)*_____

**27. MISCELLANEOUS:** *(Describe any main dwelling materials, equipment, or construction items not shown elsewhere; or use to provide additional information where the space provided was inadequate. Always reference by item number to correspond to numbering used on this form.)* _____

**PORCHES:**

**TERRACES:**

**GARAGES:**

**WALKS AND DRIVEWAYS:**

Driveway: width _____ ; base material _____ ; thickness _____ "; surfacing material _____ ; thickness _____ "

Front walk: width _____ ; material _____ ; thickness _____ ". Service walk: width _____ ; material _____ ; thickness _____ "

Steps: material _____ ; treads _____ "; risers _____ ". Cheek walls _____

**OTHER ONSITE IMPROVEMENTS:**

*(Specify all exterior onsite improvements not described elsewhere, including items such as unusual grading, drainage structures, retaining walls, fence, railings, and accessory structures.)*

**LANDSCAPING, PLANTING, AND FINISH GRADING:**

Topsoil _____ " thick: ☐ front yard; ☐ side yards; ☐ rear yard to _____ feet behind main building.

Lawns *(seeded, sodded, or sprigged)*: ☐ front yard _____ ; ☐ side yards _____ ; ☐ rear yard _____

Planting: ☐ as specified and shown on drawings; ☐ as follows:

| | | |
|---|---|---|
| _____ Shade trees, deciduous, _____ " caliper. | _____ Evergreen trees. _____ ' to _____ ', B & B. |
| _____ Low flowering trees, deciduous, _____ ' to _____ ' | _____ Evergreen shrubs. _____ ' to _____ ', B & B. |
| _____ High-growing shrubs, deciduous, _____ ' to _____ ' | _____ Vines, 2-year _____ |
| _____ Medium-growing shrubs, deciduous, _____ ' to ____ ' | |
| _____ Low-growing shrubs, deciduous, _____ ' to _____ ' | |

IDENTIFICATION.—This exhibit shall be identified by the signature of the builder, or sponsor, and/or the proposed mortgagor if the latter is known at the time of application.

Date_____     Signature _____

Signature _____

FHA Form 2005
VA Form 26-1852

- Division 3—*Concrete:* Covers all items that are constructed from concrete.
- Division 4—*Masonry:* Defines all materials, labor, and equipment necessary to complete concrete block and brick walls as shown on a set of drawings.
- Division 5—*Metals (structural and miscellaneous):* Includes most structural metals and metals that do not fall under specific provisions.
- Division 6—*Carpentry:* Covers both rough carpentry and millwork.
- Division 7—*Moisture protection:* Includes most items that are used to stop the infiltration of water or water vapor.
- Division 8—*Doors, windows, and glass:* Includes doors, window frames, metal and glass curtain walls, and transparent and translucent glazing.
- Division 9—*Finishes:* Includes those items not normally considered to be the work of the carpenter.

- Division 10—*Specialties:* Covers hardware-related and factory-assembled items.
- Division 11—*Equipment:* Describes any specialized equipment.
- Division 12—*Furnishings:* Includes items that will be placed within the finished building.
- Division 13—*Special construction:* Covers items that could possibly fall under another division, but used primarily for control.
- Division 14—*Conveying systems:* Includes those items that move people or materials.
- Division 15—*Mechanical:* Describes those items that have been traditionally associated with the mechanical trades.
- Division 16—*Electrical:* Describes those items that have been traditionally associated with the electrical trades.

Fig. 19-2 shows a set of specifications that illustrates the CSI format.

FIGURE 19-2 (pages 218–44)    The C.S.I. format

**Specifying: Rough Carpentry**

**CSI Specification Series**

**06100**
October 1978

## This Document

This document provides requirements for lumber framing, plywood sheathing, insulating and gypsum sheathing, light timber construction, wood decking, fire-retardardant and preservative treated wood products, and rough hardware, used in building construction for rough carpentry work.

This document does not cover heavy timber construction, wood trusses, laminated wood decking or pole construction. Interior plywood panelwork, casework, and architectural woodwork are not included in this document.

This document was produced by the Atlanta Chapter, CSI, and was last printed in June 1972.

## Drawings and Specifications

### Drawings:

Indicate framing plans and dimensions; partition locations and sizes; roof and floor areas to be covered with wood decking. Typical framing details; timber connections; typical wall details; locations and sizes of wood blocking, furring, and grounds; and connection details including materials, methods of installation, and spacing of fastenings, should be included on drawings. Sizes and types of fastenings depend on strength requirements, location, and construction requirements. Structural members and their connections should be detailed as to dimensions and sizes.

### Specifications:

Describe lumber and plywood grades, species, group types, fastening devices, and special requirements such as grade marking, fire retardant treatments, and preservative treatments.

### Coordination:

Rough carpentry should be coordinated with finish carpentry. Fastening devices, specified in this section should be coordinated with the requirements of other sections where fasteners are specified with the particular item.

Plywood roof sheathing requirements should be consistent with requirements of roofing, and subflooring and underlayment should be coordinated with requirements for finish flooring.

The installation of roof decking should be coordinated with the installation of roofing materials to avoid decking exposure to weather.

# Guide Specifications

*This Guide Specification is intended to be used as a basis for the development of an office master specification or in the preparation of specifications for a particular project. In either case, this Guide Specification must be edited to fit the conditions of use. Particular attention should be given to the deletion of inapplicable provisions. Include necessary items related to a particular project. Include appropriate requirements where blank spaces have been provided.*

SECTION 06100

ROUGH CARPENTRY

PART 1—GENERAL

1.01 DESCRIPTION

A. Related Work Specified Elsewhere:
1.  Forms: Section 03150.
2.  Finish Carpentry: Section 06200.
3.  Heavy Timber Construction: Section 06130.
4.  Prefabricated Structural Wood: Section 06170.
5.  Architectural Woodwork: Section 06400.
6.  Gypsum Wallboard: Section 09250.
7.  Painting: Section 09900.

B. Work Installed but Furnished by Others:
1.  Steel splice plates in Structural Metal Framing: Section 05100.
2.  Bearing plates in Structural Metal Framing: Section 05100.

1.02 QUALITY ASSURANCE

A. Lumber Grading Rules and Wood Species to be in conformance with PS 20.

B. Grading rules of following associations apply to materials furnished under this section:

> 1.02.B. Check for availability of species in project locality before specifying.

1.  Northeastern Lumber Manufacturer's Association, Inc. (NELMA).

> 1.02.B.1 Includes Red or White Spruce (Eastern Spruce) and Eastern White Pine (Northern White Pine).

2.  Southern Pine Inspection Bureau (SPIB).
3.  West Coast Lumber Inspection Bureau (WCLIB).

> 1.02.B.3 Includes Douglas Fir, Western Cedar, Mountain Hem-Fir, and Sitka Spruce.

4.  Western Wood Products Association (WWPA).

> 1.02.B.4 Includes Douglas Fir, Douglas Fir (South), Hem-Fir, Western Larch, Mountain Hemlock, Idaho White Pine. Lodgepole Pine, Ponderosa Pine, Sugar Pine; Western Red Cedar, Englemann · Spruce, Subalpine Fir, and Incense Cedar, Western Hemlock.

5.  Redwood Inspection Service (RIS).

6.  Northern Hardwood and Pine Manufacturer's Association (NHPMA).

C. Plywood Grading Rules:
1.  Softwood Plywood - Construction and Industrial: PS 1.
2.  Hardwood Plywood: PS 51.

D. Grade Marks:
1.  Identify lumber and plywood by official grade mark.
2.  Lumber:
    a. Grade stamp to contain symbol of grading agency certified by Board of Review, American Lumber Standards Committee, mill number or name, grade of lumber, species or species grouping or combination designation, rules under which graded where applicable, and condition of seasoning at time of manufacture.
    b. S-GRN: Unseasoned.
    c. S-Dry: Maximum 19% moisture content.
    d. MC-15 or KD: Maximum of 15% moisture content.

> 1.02.D.2.d    Abbreviation "KD" applies to Southern Pine.

    e. Dense.

> 1.02.D.2.e Density classification applies to Douglas Fir and Southern Pine, when applicable.

3.  Softwood Plywood:
    a. Conforming to PS 1.
4.  Hardwood Plywood: Appropriate grade mark of qualified inspection, testing, or grading agency.

E. Testing:
1.  ASTM E 84, maximum 25 flame spread rating.

F. Requirements of Regulatory Agencies:
1.  Fire hazard classification: Underwriters' Laboratories, Inc., for treated lumber and plywood.
2.  Preservative treated lumber and plywood: American Wood Preservers Bureau, Quality Mark.
3.  Pressure treated material: American Wood Preservers Bureau Standards.
4.  Span tables: National Forest Products Association.
5.  Working stresses: Softwood Lumber, National Design Specification, National Forest Products Association.

G. Reference Standards:
1.  American Society for Testing and Materials (ASTM):
    a. ASTM A 525-77, Steel Sheet, Zinc Coated (Galvanized) by the Hot-Dip Process, General Requirements.
    b. ASTM C 79-76a, Gypsum Sheathing Board.
    c. ASTM C 208-72, Insulating board (Cellulosic Fiber), Structural and Decorative.
    d. ASTM D 226-77, Asphalt-Saturated Organic Roofing Felt for Use in Membrane Waterproofing and Built-up Roofing.
    e. ASTM D 250-77, Asphalt-Saturated Asbestos Felts for Use in Waterproofing and in Constructing Built-up Roofs.
    f. ASTM D 2277-75, Fiberboard Nail-base Sheathing.
    g. ASTM E 84-77a, Surface Burning Characteristics of Building Materials.
2.  American Wood Preservers Association (AWPA):
    a. C20-74, Structural Lumber, Fire-Retardant Treatment by Pressure Processes.
    b. C27-74, Plywood Fire-Retardant Treatment by Pressure Processes.

3. American Wood Preservers Bureau (AWPB):
   a. AWPB LP-2, Standard for Softwood Lumber, Timber, and Plywood Pressure Treated with Water-borne Preservatives for Above Ground Use.
   b. AWPB LP-3, Standard for Softwood Lumber, Timber, and Plywood Pressure Treated with Light Petroleum Solvent-Penta Solution for Above Ground Use.
   c. AWPB LP-4, Standard for Softwood Lumber, Timber, and Plywood Pressure Treated with Volatile Petroleum Solvent (LPG)-Penta Solution for Above Ground Use.
   d. AWPB LP-5, Standard for Softwood Lumber, Timber, and Plywood Pressure Treated with Creosote or Creosote Coal Tar Solutions for Above Ground Use.
   e. AWPB LP-7, Standard for Softwood Lumber, Timber and Plywood Pressure Treated with Heavy Petroleum Solvent-Penta Solution for Above Ground Use.
   f. AWPB LP-22, Standard for Softwood Lumber, Timber, and Plywood Pressure Treated with Water-borne Preservatives for Ground Contact Use.
   g. AWPB LP-33, Standard for Softwood Lumber, Timber, and Plywood Pressure Treated with Light Petroleum Solvent-Penta Solution for Ground Contact Use.
   h. AWPB LP-44, Standard for Softwood Lumber, Timber, and Plywood Pressure Treated with Volatile Petroleum Solvent (LPG)-Penta Solution for Ground Contact Use.
   i. AWPB LP-55, Standard for Softwood Lumber, Timber, and Plywood Pressure Treated with Creosote or Creosote Coal Tar Solutions for Use in Ground Contact.
   j. AWPB LP-77, Standard for Softwood Lumber, Timber, and Plywood Pressure Treated with Heavy Petroleum Solvent-Penta Solution for Ground Contact Use.
   k. AWPB FDN, Standard for Softwood Lumber, Timber, and Plywood Pressure Treated with Water-Borne Preservatives for Ground Contact Use in Residential and Light Commercial Foundations.
4. Federal Specifications (FS):
   a. FF-B-561C, Bolts, (Screw), Lag.
   b. FF-B-575C, Bolts, Hexagon and Square.
   c. FF-B-584E, Bolts, Finned Neck; Key Head; Machine; Ribbed Neck; Square Neck; Tee Head.
   d. FF-B-588C(1), Bolts, Toggle; and Expansive Sleeve, Screw.
   e. FF-N-105B(3), Nails, Wire, Brads, and Staples.
      INT AMD 4
   f. FF-N-836D(1), Nut, Square, Hexagon, Cap, Slotted, Castellated, Clinch Knurled, and Welding.
   g. FF-S-111D, Screw, Wood.
   h. FF-S-325, Shield Expansion; Nail Expansion; and Nail; Drive-Screw (Devices, INT AMD 3 Anchoring, Masonry).
   i. UU-B-790A, Building Paper, Vegetable Fiber: (Kraft, Waterproofed, Water INT AMD 3 Repellent and Fire-Resistant).
5. National Forest Products Association (NFPA):
   a. National Design Specifications for Wood Construction, 1977.
   b. Span Tables for Joists and Rafters.
   c. Working Stresses for Joists and Rafters.
   d. Wood Structural Design Data.
6. Product Standards (PS)
   a. PS 1-74, Construction and Industrial Plywood.
   b. PS 20-70, American Softwood Lumber Standard.
   c. PS 51-71, Hardwood and Decorative Plywood.
   d. PS 56-73, Structural Glued Laminated Timber.
7. Redwood Inspection Service (RIS):
   a. Standard Specifications for Grades of California Redwood Lumber.
8. Southern Pine Inspection Bureau (SPIB):
   a. Standard Grading Rules for Southern Pine Lumber.

9. Western Wood Products Association (WWPA):
   a. Standard Grading Rules for Western Lumber, 1977.

## 1.03 SUBMITTALS

A. Samples:
   1. Submit samples of wood decking which will be exposed in finished work, to show face texture and color of material.

> 1.03.A.1 Delete if wood deck-
> ing is not required.

B. Shop Drawings:
   1. Submit shop drawings indicating framing connection details, fastener connections, and dimensions.

> 1.03.B.1 Delete when details
> are included on architectural or
> structural drawings.

   2. Indicate pattern of wood decking members.

> 1.03.B.2 Delete if wood deck-
> ing is not required.

C. Certification:
   1. Pressure treated wood: Submit certification by treating plant stating chemicals and process used, net amount of salts retained, and conformance with applicable standards.
   2. Preservation treated wood: Submit certification for water-borne preservative that moisture content was reduced to 19% maximum, after treatment.
   3. Fire-retardant treatment: Submit certification by treating plant that fire-retardant treatment materials comply with governing ordinances and that treatment will not bleed through finished surfaces.

## 1.04 PRODUCT DELIVERY, STORAGE, AND HANDLING

A. Immediately upon delivery to job site, place materials in area protected from weather.

B. Store materials a minimum of 6 in. (150 mm) above ground on framework or blocking and cover with protective waterproof covering providing for adequate air circulation or ventilation.

C. Do not store seasoned materials in wet or damp portions of building.

D. Protect fire-retardant materials against high humidity and moisture during storage and erection.

E. Protect sheet materials from corners breaking and damaging surfaces, while unloading.

## PART 2—PRODUCTS

## 2.01 MATERIALS

A. Lumber:
   1. Dimensions:
      a. Specified lumber dimensions are nominal.
      b. Actual dimensions to conform to PS 20.
   2. Surfacing: Surface four sides (S4S), unless specified otherwise.
   3. End jointed lumber:
      a. Structural purposes interchangeable with solid sawn lumber.
      b. Glued joints of loadbearing lumber: PS 56.

4. Framing lumber, any commercial softwood species:
  a. Light framing:
    (1) General framing: Standard and Better or Stud grade.

> 2.01.A.4.a(1) Suitable for all bearing construction.

    (2) Plates, blocking, bracing, and nailers: Utility grade.
    (3) Bracing, blocking, bulk headings, and general utility purposes: Economy grade.
  b. Studs:
    (1) Loadbearing: Stud, Standard, or No. 3 grade.

> 2.01.A.4.b(1) Stud grade available up to 6 in. wide.

  c. Structural light framing, 2 in. to 4 in. thick, 2 in. to 6 in. wide. Grades _____.

> 2.01.A.4.c Selection of grade and species will be dependent on lumber design values. Refer to Reference Standards. (Select structural); (No. 1); (No. 2); (No. 3)

** OR **

  c. Structural light framing, 2 in. to 4 in. thick, 2 in. to 6 in. wide:

> 2.01.A.4.c Use $F_b$ and E values in place of grade and species. See grading rules for typical values.

    (1) Allowable extreme fiber stress in bending ($F_b$): _____.
    (2) Modulus of elasticity (E): _____.
    (3) Maximum moisture content 15%, MC-15 or KD on grade stamp.

> 2.01.A.4.c(3) Vary moisture content as required.

    (4) Dense Douglas Fir, Dense Southern Yellow Pine, or MG (medium grain) Southern Pine.

> 2.01.A.4.c(4) Include dense grade when density is a factor and delete "any commercial softwood species" from paragraph.

  d. Structural joists and planks, 2 in. to 4 in. thick, 6 in. and wider: Grades: _____.

> 2.01.A.4.d Selection of grade and species will be dependent on lumber design values. Refer to Standards. (Select structural); (No. 1); (No. 2); (No. 3).

** OR **

  d. Structural joists and planks, 2 in. to 4 in. thick, 6 in. and wider:

> 2.01.A.4.d. Use $F_b$ and E values in place of grade and species.

(1) Allowable extreme stress in bending ($F_b$): _____.
(2) Modulus of elasticity (E): _____.
(3) Maximum moisture content 15%, MC-15 or KD on grade stamp.

> 2.01.A.4.d(3)  Vary moisture content as required.

(4) Dense Douglas Fir, Dense Southern Yellow Pine, or MG Southern Yellow Pine.

> 2.01.A.4.d(4)  Include dense grade when density is a factor and delete "any commercial softwood species" from paragraph.

**      **      **

e. Beams and stringers, posts and timbers: 5 in. and thicker.

> 2.01.A.4.e  Usually shipped unseasoned. S-GRN indicated on grade stamp. Selection of grade and species will be dependent on design values. Refer to grading rules.

(1) Allowable extreme stress in bending ($F_b$): _____.
(2) Modulus of elasticity (E): _____.
(3) Grade: _____.

> 2.01.A.4.e(3)  In species other than Southern Pine, grades are available below No. 1 for use where strength is not a factor, such as No. 2 or Standard No. 3 or Utility.

5. Board Sheathing: 1 in to 2 in. thick; any commercial softwood species:
   a. Furring and grounds:
      Minimum grade, _____.

> 2.01.A.5.a (No. 2 S.P.); (Standard); (No. 3. Common other species). No. 4 or Utility may be used as an alternative.

   b. Roof Sheathing:
      (1) Nominal size: _____.

> 2.01.A.5.b(1) (1 in. x 6 in.); (1 in. x 8 in.) Delete if indicated on drawings.

      (2) Minimum grade: _____.

> 2.01.A.5.b(2)  (No. 2 S.P.); (Standard); or (No. 3 Common other species). No. 4 or Utility may be used as an alternative.

      (3) Surfacing: _____.

> 2.01.A.5.b(3)  (Tongue and groove, CM, S2S); (Square edge, S4S).

c. Wall Sheathing:
  (1) Nominal size: _____ .

> 2.01.A.5.c(1) (1 in. x 6 in.); (1 in. x 8 in.) Delete if indicated on drawings.

  (2) Minimum grade: _____ .

> 2.01.A.5.c(2) (No. 2 S.P.); (Standard); or (No. 3 Common other species) (S4S).

  (3) Surfacing: _____ .

> 2.01.A.5.c(3) (Tongue and groove, S2S); (Square edge, S2S); (Shiplap, S2S).

d. Subflooring:
  (1) Nominal size: _____ .

> 2.01.A.5.d(1) (1 in. x 6 in.); (1 in. x 8 in.). Delete if indicated on drawings.

  (2) Minimum grade: _____ .

> 2.01.A.5.d(2) (No. 2 S.P.); (Standard); or (No. 3 Common other species).

  (3) Surfacing: _____ .

> 2.01.A.5.d(3) (Tongue and groove, S2S); (Square edge, S4S).

6. Wood decking: 2 in. to 4 in. thick, 4 in. to 12 in. wide, any commercial softwood species:
  a. Selected Decking grade, 15% maximum moisture content, MC-15 or KD on grade stamp, _____ tongue and groove edges.

> 2.01.A.6.a Selected Decking grade is recommended for exposed areas where appearance is a prime factor. Specify (single) tongue and groove for 2 in. thick decking or (double) tongue and groove for 3 in. and 4 in. thicknesses.

** OR **

  a. Selected Decking grade, 19% maximum moisture content, "DRY" on grade stamp, _____ tongue and groove edges.

** ** **

  b. Commercial Decking grade, 15% maximum moisture content, MC-15 or KD on grade stamp, _____ tongue and groove edges.

> 2.01.A.6.b Commercial Decking grade recommended where appearance and strength are less critical than for selected grade. Specify (single) tongue and groove for 2 in. thick decking and (double) tongue and groove for 3 in. and 4 in. thicknesses.

** OR **

b. Commercial Decking grade, 19% maximum moisture content, "DRY" on grade stamp, _____ tongue and groove edges.

** ** **

B. Plywood:

> 2.01.B Project requirements and local availability should be considered in plywood grade, surfaces, and identification Index or Species Group Selection. Refer to PS 1 for designations.

1. Exterior graded plywood where edge or surface is permanently exposed to weather.

2. Roof sheathing:
   a. Grade: _____.
   b. Identification Index: _____.
3. Wall sheathing:
   a. Grade: _____.
   b. Identification Index: _____.
4. Subflooring:
   a. Grade: _____.
   b. Identification Index: _____.
   c. Edge: Tongue and groove.
5. Combined subfloor-underlayment:
   a. Grade: _____.
   b. Identification Index: _____.
   c. Edge: _____.
   d. Surface: _____.
6. Underlayment:
   a. Grade: _____.
   b. Identification Index: _____.
   c. Surface: _____.

C. Insulating Sheathing:
   1. Type: Nail-base, ASTM D 2277.

** OR **

1. Type: Standard: ASTM C 208, Class E.
Size:

> 2.01.C.2 Sizes vary with type selected. Refer to Reference Standards.

   a. Length: _____.
   b. Width: _____.

3. Thermal conductivity: _____.

> 2.01.C.3 Varies with thickness. Refer to Reference Standards.

4. Edge Finish: _____.

> 2.01.C.4 (Square); ("V" tongue and groove)

D. Gypsum Sheathing:
   1.   ASTM C 79.
   2.   Nominal size: _____ width and length, square edge.

> 2.01.D.2 Nominal width is 24
> in. and 48 in. Nominal lengths
> are 6 ft. and 8 ft.

   3.   Thickness: 1/2 in. (13 mm).

E. Building Paper:

> 2.01.E Delete types not ap-
> plicable.

   1.   Asphalt-saturated felt: ASTM D 226, 15 lb. nonperforated.
   2.   Asphalt-saturated asbestos felt: ASTM D 250, 15 lb. nonperforated.
   3.   Building paper: FS UU-B-790, Type 1, width of _____.

> 2.01.E.3 Refer to Reference
> Standards for width dimen-
> sions.

F. Fire-Retardant Treated Products:
   1.   Lumber: AWPA C20.
   2.   Plywood: AWPA C27.

G. Preservative Treated Wood Products:
   1.   Water-borne salt preservatives for painted, stained, or exposed natural wood product:
      a. AWPB LP-2, above ground application.
      b. AWPB LP-22, ground contact application.
      c. Lumber redried to maximum moisture content of 19%, stamped "DRY."

> 2.01.G.1.c Recommended
> when redrying of lumber is
> necessary.

   2.   Oil-borne preservatives for any construction except when in contact with salt water.
      a. AWPB LP-3, above ground application, light petroleum solvent.
      b. AWPB LP-33, ground contact application, light petroleum solvent.
      c. AWPB LP-4, above ground application, volatile petroleum solvent for interior application and hardwoods to be painted.
      d. AWPB LP-44, ground contact application, volatile petroleum solvent.
      e. AWPB-LP-7, above ground application, heavy petroleum solvent - penta solution for outdoor applications exposed to weather where painting is not required.
      f. AWPB LP-77, ground contact application, heavy petroleum solvent - penta solution.

   3.   Creosote and creosote preservatives for wood placed in ground or in water:

> 2.01.G.3 Not recommended for
> subflooring in contact with
> materials subject to staining, or
> in contact with roofing felts.

      a. AWPB LP-5, above ground application, creosote or creosote coal tar solutions.
      b. AWPB LP-55, ground contact application, creosote or creosote coal tar solution.

4. Untreated Lumber: All heartwood grades.

> 2.01.G.4 In cases where high strength is not a factor heartwood grades of Western Red Cedar or Redwood can be specified in lieu of treated lumber.

5. AWPB FND ground contact use in residential and light commercial foundations.

> 2.01.G.5 Recommended for all weather pressure treated wood foundations.

H. Rough Hardware:
  1. Bolts:
    a. FS FF-B-575.

> 2.01.H.1.a Use for insertion into assembled parts not intended to be tightened or released by torque.

    b. FS-FF-B-584.

> 2.01.H.1.b Use for insertion into assembled parts not intended to be tightened or released by torque.

  2. Nuts: FS FF-N-836.
  3. Expansion shields: FS FF-B-561.
  4. Lag screws and bolts: FS FF-B-561.
  5. Toggle bolts: FS FF-B-588.
  6. Wood screws: FS FF-S-111.
  7. Nails and staples: FS FF-N-105.
  8. Metal nailing discs:
    a. Flat caps, minimum 1 in. (25 mm) diameter.
    b. Minimum 30 ga. sheet metal.
    c. Formed to prevent dishing.
    d. Bell or cup shapes not acceptable.
  9. Joist hangers: 18 ga. zinc-coated steel.
  10. Metal cross bridging, 16 ga. zinc-coated steel:
    a. Nailable type with two holes in each end.
    b. Compression type with prongs at each end.
  11. Bar or strap anchors: ASTM A 525, zinc-coated steel, 18 ga. minimum.

> 2.01.H.11 18 ga. is minimum, 16 ga. and 12 ga. are commonly used depending on structural requirements.

  12. Ply-clips: Extruded 6063-T6 aluminum alloy.

I. Termite Shields: Minimum 26 ga. zinc-coated steel.

** OR **

J. Termite Shields: Minimum 30 ga. terne coated steel, 40 lb. coating.

** ** **

**PART 3—EXECUTION**

**3.01 INSPECTION**

    A. Verify that surfaces to receive rough carpentry materials are prepared to require grades and dimensions.

**3.02 INSTALLATION**

    A. Sills:

> 3.02.A Use treated lumber any commercial softwood species or all heart wood western cedar or redwood.

      1. Set level 1/16 in., (1.6 mm) in 6 ft., (1.8 m), in mortar bed, 1 in. (25 mm) from exterior face of foundation.
      2. Secure sills with 1/2 in. x 8 in. (13 mm x 203 mm) minimum size anchor bolts embedded in the structure minimum of 6 in. (152 mm), spaced maximum of 4 ft. (1.2 m) o.c.
      3. Join solid sill members with halved joints, where not continuous and at corners, minimum of 1 ft. (0.3 m) lapped joint.
      4. Lap built-up sill members minimum distance of 2 ft. (0.6 m).
      5. Termite shields:
        a. Bed termite shield in mortar bed and extend across top of foundation wall, bend down 2 in. (51 mm) at angles of 45 degrees both inside and out.

> 3.02.A.5.a Use full termite shields over masonry foundation wall.

**\*\* OR \*\***

        a. Bed termite shield in mortar bed and extend half distance across top of foundation wall, bend down 2 in. (51 mm) at angle of 45 degrees on outside.

> 3.02.A.5.a Use half termite shield over concrete foundation wall.

**\*\* \*\* \*\***

        b. Fit around anchor bolts and fill joints with asphaltic mastic or solder.

    B. Posts or Columns:
      1. Provide two surfaces on posts at right angles to each other for installation of interior finish materials.
      2. Built-up posts: Arrange and nailed together to accommodate type of construction.
      3. Provide mortise in posts to receive tenon connections of girts.

> 3.02.B.3 Mortise and tenon connections for post construction only. Delete if not required.

      4. Erect posts straight, plumb with straight edge and level, and brace with tack boards at plate and sill.

    C. Girts:
      1. Install continuous girts, running from post to post.

2.  Pin mortise and tenon connection together with hardwood pins 1 in (25 mm) diameter.

> 3.02.C.2 Delete if mortise and
> tenon joints are not required.

3.  Set girts, running parallel to floor joists, with top edge at same elevation as top of joists.
4.  Set girts, perpendicular to joists, with top edge at elevation of joist bottoms.

D. Stud Framing:
  1.  Plates and stud members:
      a.  Provide single bottom plate and double top plates for loadbearing partitions, 2 in. thick by width of studs.
      b.  Provide single bottom plates and single top plates for nonloadbearing partitions, 2 in. thick by width of studs.
      c.  Provide studs in continuous lengths without splices.
      d.  Toenail studs to bottom plate and endnail to lower top plate.
      e.  Overlap double top plates minimum of 6 in. (152 mm) at corners and intersections.
      f.  Face nail upper top plate to lower top plate.
      g.  Nail bottom plate to wood construction.
      h.  Anchor bottom plate to concrete structure with anchor bolts, expansion sleeves and lag bolts, or power driven studs, spaced 4 ft. (1.2 m) o.c.
      i.  Triple studs at corners and partition intersections.
      j.  Anchor studs abutting masonry or concrete with 1/2 in. (13 mm) anchor bolts, maximum spacing of 4 ft. (1.2 m) o.c.
      k.  Partition parallel with joists: Locate joists directly below studs.
      l.  Frame openings:
          (1) Double studs and headers: openings less than 4 ft (1.2 m).
          (2) Triple studs and headers: openings 5 ft. (1.2 m) and greater.
  2.  Headers:

> 3.02.D.2 Specify header where
> required in lieu of top plates.

      a.  Continuous headers, same width as studs, depth required to span widest opening.
      b.  Toenail headers to studs and opening framing.
      c.  Stagger joints in individual header members a minimum of three stud spaces, allowing no joints to occur over openings.
      d.  Lap headers at intersections with bearing partitions or tie with metal straps.
      e.  Maximum span:

> 3.02.D.2.e Specify maximum
> spans only when not indicated
> on Drawings.

          (1) Spans to 3 ft.-6 in. (1.1 m) - Two 2 in. x 4 in.
          (2) Spans to 4 ft.-6 in. (1.4 m) - Two 2 in. x 6 in.
          (3) Spans to 6 ft.-0 in. (1.8 m) - Two 2 in. x 8 in.
          (4) Spans to 8 ft.-0 in. (2.4 m) - Two 2 in x 10 in., braced.
  3.  Blocking:
      a.  Install in continuous horizontal row at mid-height of single story partitions over 8 ft. (2.4 m) high and multi-story partitions.
      b.  Wedge, align, and anchor blocking with countersunk bolts, washers and nuts, or nails.
      c.  Locate blocking to facilitate installation of finishing materials, fixtures, specialty items, and trim.
  4.  Corner bracing:
      a.  Run bracing member diagonally from intersection of post and girt to point on sill approximately 4 ft. (1.2 m) away, or three stud spaces.

3.02.D.4.a Bracing method for
first story construction.

b. Run bracing member diagonally from intersection of post and plate to similar point on girt.

3.02.D.4.b Bracing method for
upper stories.

c. Fit lower ends of braces against blocks spiked to tops of girts and sills.
d. Provide continuous braces with studs cut to fit braces.
e. Plywood sheathing: 4 ft. x 8 ft. sheets, installed with face grain across studs.

3.02.D.4.e Delete if plywood
bracing is not required.

E. Joist Framing
1. Install with crown edges up.
2. Support ends of each member minimum 1 1/2 in. (38 mm) of bearing on _____.

3.02.E.2 (wood); (metal).

3. Support ends of each member minimum 3 in. (76 mm) of bearing on masonry.
4. Support joists alternately at ends with solid blocking, 2 in. thick by depth of joists, between members crossing bearing points.

3.02.E.4 Not necessary when
joists are nailed to headers or
band member.

5. Lap members framing from opposite sides of beams, girders, or partitions, minimum 4 in. (102 mm), or tie opposing members together by toenailing or metal connectors.
6. Anchor joists bearing on masonry using 1/4 in. x 1 1/4 in. (6.4 mm x 31 mm) metal straps or "T" anchors, wall ends bent 4 in. (102 mm) at every second joist, extending anchors minimum 1 ft.-4 in. (0.43 m).
7. Anchor joists parallel to masonry walls at bridging lines using 1/4 in. x 1 1/4 in. (6.4 mm x 31 mm) metal strap anchors, spaced 8 ft. (2.4 m) o.c., extending into masonry a minimum of 4 in. (102 mm) and turn up or down 4 in. (102 mm), extending over three joists.
8. Provide solid blocking between joists under door posts.
9. Notches:
   a. Do not notch in middle third of joists.
   b. Notches in top or bottom of joists: maximum of 1/6 depth of member.
   c. Notched ends: Maximum of 1/3 depth of member.
10. Bored holes: Maximum 1/3 depth of member, 2 in. (51 mm) minimum distance to top or bottom of joists.
11. Bridging:
    a. Nominal depth-to-thickness ratio of joists exceeding 6, install bridging at 8 ft. (2.4 m) intervals.
    b. Metal cross bridging: Install nailable type with two 8d nails in each end, leaving a space between members minimum of 1/8 in. (3.2 mm).

** OR **

b. Metal cross bridging: Install compression type by forcing all prongs on each end full depth into joists.

** OR **

b. Wood cross bridging:
  (1) Install 1 in. x 3 in. wood strips with beveled ends in double cross manner at mid-span of joists with span of 16 ft. (4.9 m) or less.

> 3.02E.11.b.(1) Wood bridging is sometimes furnished in 2 in. x 3 in. pieces.

  (2) Secure cross bridging with two 8d nails in each end.
  (3) Nail bottom end of all cross bridge strips after subfloor is installed.

** OR **

b. Solid bridging:
  (1) Size: 2 in. x depth of joist x length of suit.

** OR **

  (1) Size: 2 in. thickness x 2 in. less in height than joists, length to suit.

** ** **

  (2) Install offset to permit toenailing or end-nailing.
  (3) Space bridging maximum:
     (a) Spans to 10 ft. (3 m) - one row midspan.
     (b) Spans 10 ft. to 20 ft. (3 m to 6 m) - two rows at 1/3 span.
     (c) Spans over 20 ft. (6 m) rows not over 8 ft. (2.4 m) apart.

F. Rafters:
  1. Notch to fit exterior wall plates and toe-nail to plates.
  2. Double rafters at opening in roof framing to provide headers and trimmers, and support with metal hangers.
  3. At ridge, place rafters directly opposite each other and nail to ridge member or support with metal hangers.
  4. At valleys, bevel ends of rafters for bearing against valley rafters.

> 3.02.F.4 Valley rafters sizing: twice as thick as regular rafters and 2 in. (51 mm) deeper.

  5. At hips, bevel ends of rafters for bearing against hip rafters.

> 3.02.F.5 Hip rafters sizing: same thickness as regular rafters and 2 in. (51 mm) deeper.

  6. Collar beams:
     a. Located at every third pair of rafters, one-third distance to ceiling joists.
     b. Cut ends to fit slope, and nail to rafters.

G. Beams and Girders:
  1. Install with crown edge up.
  2. Provide bearing at ends of each member: Minimum 4 in. (102 mm).
  3. Nail built-up beams or girders with two rows of 20d nails spaced maximum of 2 ft. 8 in. (0.8 m) o.c., locating one row near top edge and other near bottom edge of member.
  4. Girders not continuous: Splice together with _____.

> 3.02.G.4 Milled wood splices for girders: (scarfed splice); (Section at wedges); (mortised splice).

5.  Beams not continuous:

3.02.G.5 Metal connection
splices for cantilever beams:
(steel plate splice); (joist
splice).

6.  Beams or girders framed into pockets of exterior concrete or masonry walls: provide minimum of 1 in. (25 mm) air space between sides and ends of wood members and concrete or masonry wall.

H. Miscellaneous Framing:
1.  Firestops:

3.02.H.1 Revise to comply with
local building codes.

a.  Stud walls: 2 in. thick x depth of member blocking at each floor level and top story ceiling level.
b.  Floor and ceiling framing: 2 in. thick x depth of wood member blocking, fitted to fill openings from one space to another to prevent drafts.
c.  Chimneys and fireplaces: Keep wood framing minimum of 2 in. (51 mm) from outside face of masonry and 4 in. (102 mm) from fireplace back wall.
2.  Framing for mechanical work:
a.  Frame members for passage of pipes and ducts to avoid cutting structural members.
b.  Do not cut, notch, or bore framing members for passage of pipes or conduits without concurrence of Architect/Engineer.
c.  Reinforce framing members where damaged by cutting.

I.  Wood Decking:
1.  Install single span pieces with all end joists on supports.

** OR **

1.  Install equal length pieces, except short pieces at ends, cantilevered with end joists at 1/4 points every fourth row of decking, with end joints over supports.

** OR **

1.  Install random length pieces continuous over minimum of three spans, each piece resting on one support with end joints in adjacent rows minimum of 24 in. (0.6 m) apart.

** OR **

1.  Install random length pieces continuous over a minimum of three spans, each piece resting on one support with end joints in adjacent rows separated by one row of decking measured along length of piece 12 in. (0.3 m), or separated by two rows of decking.

** ** **

2.  Drive deck members tight using short block; do not hammer tongue.
3.  Nail each member at support with one 30d common blind and face nail for decking up to 2 1/4 in. thick and 40d common blind and face nail for decking 2 3/4 in. and 3 in. thick.
4.  Nail each member at support with one 7 in. (178 mm) spike for 4 1/2 in. thick decking.

3.02.I.4 Delete if decking
thickness is different than 4 1/2
in.

5.  Toenail groove to tongue at 40 to 50 degree angle starting 1 1/4 in. (31 mm) from groove edge, spaced 12 in. (0.3 m) from each end and a maximum of 30 in. (0.7 m) on centers between end nails using _____.

> 3.02.1.5 (8d common nails for 2 1/4 in. thick decking); (10d common nails for 2 3/4 in. thick); (16d common nails for 3 in. up to 4 1/2 in.).

6.  Provide a minimum of 1/4 in. (6 mm) and maximum of 1/2 in. (12 mm) expansion space where decking covers beam or wall, parallel to decking.

> 3.02.1.6 Delete when decking is not in panel units.

**\*\* OR \*\***

6.  Provide minimum expansion space of 1 1/2 in. (38 mm) along each edge for each 30 ft. (9 m) of decking panel width.

> 3.02.1.6 Delete when decking is not in panel units.

**\*\* \*\* \*\***

J. Roof Sheathing:
1.  Board sheathing:
    a. Lay _____ sheathing _____ to framing members.

> 3.02.J.1.a (square edge); (tongue and groove); (perpendicular); (45° diagonal).

    b. Cut ends parallel to framing members and locate over supports.
    c. Nail at each bearing using two 8d nails, placing one through _____ and one through face.

> 3.02.J.1.c (edge); (tongue).

    d. Drive nails to full penetration.
2.  Plywood sheathing:
    a. Install plywood with face grain perpendicular to supports, using panel with continuous end joints over two or more spans staggered between panels and locate over supports.
    b. Allow minimum space 1/16 in. (1.6 mm) between end joints and 1/8 in. (3.2 mm) at edge joints for expansion and contraction of panels.

> 3.02.J.2.b Include for normal humidity conditions.

**\*\* OR \*\***

    b. Allow minimum space of 1/8 in. (3.2 mm) between end joints and 1/4 in. (6 mm) between edge joints for expansion and contraction of panels.

> 3.02.J.2.b Include for high humidity conditions.

**\*\* \*\* \*\***

    c. Support edge joints by use of _____.

> 3.02.J.2.c (plyclips); (tongue and groove panels); (lumber blocking).

     d. Nail 6 in. (152 mm) o.c. along panel edges and 12 in. (0.3 m) o.c. at intermediate supports.

     e. Nail 6 in. (152 mm) o.c. at all supports, for support spaced 4 ft. (1.2 m) o.c.

     f. Use 6d common, smooth ring-shank, or spiral-thread nails for panels 1/2 in. (13 mm) thick or less and 8d for greater thickness, except that when panels are 1 1/8 in. (28 mm) or 1 1/4 in. (31 mm) use 8d ring-shank or 10d common.

K. Wall Sheathing:
1. Board sheathing:
   a. Install _____ with end joints staggered and terminated on supports.

   > 3.02.K.1.a     (diagonally);
   > (horizontally).

   b. Nail at each bearing two 8d nails driven to full penetration.
   c. Cover wood sheathing with sheathing paper applied horizontally in "shingle" fashion starting at bottom, minimum lap of 4 in. (102 mm).
   d. Secure sheathing paper using roofing nails with metal nailing discs spaced 12 in. (0.3 m) on center vertically and horizontally, starting at each horizontal lap.

2. Plywood sheathing:
   a. Install with face grain horizontal or vertical.
   b. Allow minimum 1/16 in. (1.6 mm) space at end joints and 1/8 in. (3.2 mm) at edge joints, doubling these spacings in wet or humid conditions.
   c. Nail 6 in. (152 mm) o.c. along panel edges and 12 in. (305 mm) o.c. at intermediate supports with 6d common nails for panels 1/2 in. (13 mm) thickness and 8d nails for greater thickness.

L. Subflooring:
1. Board subflooring:
   a. Lay diagonally at 45° angle to joists.
   b. Cut ends parallel to joists and terminate over supports.
   c. Depress for ceramic tile and nail over cleats to side of joists.

   > 3.02.L.1.c Delete when not applicable.

   d. Support edges with wood blocking.

   ** OR **

   d. Tongue and groove material:
      (1) Nail each board at each bearing point using one 8d nail for each 2 in. nominal face width of board.
      (2) Drive one nail through tongue and other nail(s) through face.
      (3) Drive nails to full penetration.

   ** ** **

2. Plywood subflooring:
   a. Install with face grain perpendicular to joists; end joints occurring over the joists.
   b. Allow 1/16 in. (1.2 mm) space at end joists and 1/8 in. (3.2 mm) at edge joists.
   c. Stagger panel end joists.
   d. Nail subflooring 6 in. (152 mm) on center along panel edges and 10 in. (254 mm) on center at intermediate supports with 6d common nails for 1/2 in. (12 mm) plywood and 8d nails for greater thickness.
   e. Nail subflooring with 8d ring-shank or 10d common nails, spaced 6 in. (152 mm) on center at all supports for 1 1/8 in. (28 mm) or 1 1/4 in. (31 mm) thick panels, and supports are 4 ft. (1.2 m) on center.

3.02.L.2.e. Delete if not applicable.

3. Combined subfloor underlayment:
   a. Install with face grain perpendicular to joists, end joint supported on joists.
   b. Install lumber blocking between joists when tongue and groove panels are not used.
   c. Stagger end joints.
   d. Butt ends and edges, allowing 1/16 in. (1.6 mm) space between panels.
   e. Nail plywood 3/4 in. (19 mm) thick or less maximum of 6 in. (152 mm) o.c. at panel edges and 10 in. (254 mm) o.c. at intermediate supports with 6d ring shank or screw-type nails with 1 in. (25 mm) penetration into structural members, except when supports are spaced 45 in. (1.2 m) o.c., space nails maximum of 6 in. (152 mm) o.c. at all supports with 1 in. (25 mm) penetration.
   f. Nail plywood 7/8 in. (22 mm) thick and greater and 2-4-1 plywood with 8d common nails spaced maximum of 6 in. (152 mm) o.c. at panel edges and 10 in. (254 mm) at intermediate supports.
   g. Set nail heads into plywood 1/32 in. (0.8 mm) without dimpling surface or breaking surface fiber.

M. Insulating Sheathing:
   1. Apply sheathing with long dimension perpendicular to supports.
   2. Abut ends of sheathing at centers of supports.
   3. Stagger end joints.

** OR **

   1. Apply sheathing with long dimension parallel with supports.
   2. Abut sides and ends to vertical framing members, top and bottom plates, or headers.
   3. Allow 1/8 in. (3.2 mm) space between sheets.

** ** **

   4. Attach sheathing using staples minimum of 1 3/8 in. (35 mm) long spaced 3 in. (76 mm) on center at ends and 6 in. (152 mm) o.c. at intermediate supports, or 1 1/3 in. (38 mm) long galvanized roofing nails, or 6d common nails spaced 4 in. (102 mm) o.c. at ends and 8 in. (203 mm) o.c. at intermediate supports.

N. Gypsum Sheathing:
   1. Apply tongue and groove sheathing with long dimension horizontal.
   2. Abut ends of sheathing at center of supports.
   3. Stagger end joints.
   4. Attach sheathing using nails spaced at 8 in (203 mm) o.c. on all supports, or staple at 6 in. (152 mm) o.c. at all supports.

** OR **

   1. Apply square edge sheathing with long dimension parallel with supports.
   2. Sides and edges abut vertical framing members, top and bottom plates or headers.
   3. Attach sheathing using nails or staples spaced 4 in. (102 mm) o.c. at all edges of sheet and 8 in. (203 mm) o.c. on intermediate supports.

** ** **

O. Pressure-Treated Wood Products:
   1. Provide pressure-treated wood for all framing, blocking, furring, nailing strips built into exterior masonry walls, wood in contact with concrete and in conjunction with gravel stops and built-up roofing.

3.02.O.1 Add additional locations for pressure-treated wood
if necessary.

2. Re-dry and clean lumber, after treatment, to maximum moisture content of 19%, stamped "DRY."

3.02.O.2 When re-drying of lumber is desired, specify AWPB LP-2 or AWPB LP-22.

3. Apply two brush coats of same preservative used in original treatment to all sawed or cut surfaces of treated lumber.

3.03. PROTECTION

A. Protect wood decking with protective waterproof covering until roofing has been installed.

**\* END OF SECTION \***

# Reference Standards

*This information provided below is intended only as an aid in understanding the reference standards contained in the Guide Specification part of this study. Guidance on the use of reference standards is contained in CSI Manual of Practice*

## American Society for Testing and Materials (ASTM)

ASTM A 525-77, Steel Sheet, Zinc Coated (Galvanized) by the Hot-Dip Process, General Requirements, covers the general requirements for the delivery of steel sheet in coils and cut lengths, zinc-coated (galvanized) on continuous lines by the hot-dip process. Galvanized steel sheet is customarily available in commercial quality, lock-forming quality, drawing quality, drawing quality special killed, and structural (physical) quality, which are fully described in separate standards. Galvanized steel sheet is produced to various zinc-coated designations, designed to give coatings compatible with the service life required. Except for differential-coated sheet, the coating is always expressed as the total coating of both surfaces. Galvanized steel sheet can be produced with the following types of coatings:

Regular spangle.
Minimized spangle.
Iron-zinc alloy.
Wiped, and
Differential.

ASTM C 79-76a, Gypsum Sheathing Board, covers gypsum sheathing board which is designed to be used as a sheathing in buildings.

ASTM C 208-72, Insulating Board (Cellulosic Fiber), Structural and Decorative, covers the principal types, grades, and sizes of insulating board. Requirements are specified for composition, construction, physical properties, tolerances, sampling procedures, and test methods to determine compliance. Reference is provided to an established source for nomenclature and definitions.

ASTM D 226-77, Asphalt-Saturated Organic Roofing Felt for Use in Membrane Waterproofing and Built-up Roofing, covers asphalt-saturated felts, either with or without perforations, 36 in. (914 mm) in width, suitable for use with mopping asphalts conforming to ASTM D 449 in the membrane system of waterproofing, and with mopping asphalts conforming to ASTM D 312 in the construction of built-up roofs.

ASTM D 250-77, Asphalt-Saturated Asbestos Felts for Use in Waterproofing and in Constructing Built-up Roofs, covers asphalt-saturated asbestos felts, with or without perforations, for use with asphalts conforming to the requirements of ASTM D 312 in the construction of built-up roofs, and with asphalts conforming to the requirements of ASTM D 449 in the membrane system of waterproofing.

ASTM D 2277-75, Fiberboard Nail-base Sheathing, covers fiberboard nail-base sheathing, a 1/2 in. (12.5-mm) thick high-density structural insulating fiberboard produced designed for use in frame construction to permit the direct application of exterior siding materials such as wood and asbestos shingles. When this material is properly attached to the frames of walls according to the manufacturer's recommendations, it will also result in a wall that will satisfy the requirements for rigidity from racking forces of certain specifying agencies without auxiliary bracing of the frame.

ASTM E 84-77a, Surface Burning Characteristics of Building Materials, is applicable to any type of building material that, by its own structural quality or the manner in which it is applied, is capable of supporting itself in position or may be supported in the text furnace to a thickness comparable to its recommended use.

The purpose of the test is to determine the comparative burning characteristics of the material under test by evaluating the flame spread over its surface burning characteristics of different materials may be compared without specific considerations of all the end-use parameters that might affect the surface burning characteristics.

Smoke density as well as the flame-spread rate are recorded in this test. However, there is not necessarily a relationship among these measurements.

It is the intent of this method to register performance during the period of exposure, and not to determine suitability for use after the test exposure.

This standard should be used to measure and describe the properties of materials, products, or systems in response to heat and flame under controlled laboratory conditions and should not be used for the description or appraisal of the fire hazard of materials, products, or systems under actual fire conditions.

### American Wood Preservers Association (AWPA)

C20-74 Structural Lumber Fire-Retardant Treatment by Pressure Processes, defines acceptable minimums for lumber that has been fire-retardant pressure treated.

C27-74 Plywood Fire-Retardant Treatment by Pressure Processes, defines acceptable minimums for plywood that has been fire-retardant pressure treated.

### American Wood Preservers Bureau (AWPB)

AWPB LP-2, Standard for Softwood Lumber, Timber, and Plywood Pressure Treated with Water-borne Preservatives for Above Ground Use.

AWPB LP-3, Standard for Softwood Lumber, Timber, and Plywood Pressure Treated with Light Petroleum Solvent-Penta Solution for Above Ground Use.

AWPB LP-4, Standard for Softwood Lumber, Timber, and Plywood Pressure Treated with Volatile Petroleum Solvent (LPG) Penta-Solution for Above Ground Use.

AWPB LP-5, Standard for Softwood Lumber, Timber, and Plywood Pressure Treated with Creosote or Creosote Coal Tar Solutions for Above Ground Use.

AWPB LP-7, Standard for Softwood Lumber, Timber and Plywood Pressure Treated with Heavy Petroleum Solvent-Penta Solution for Above Ground Use.

AWPB LP-22, Standard for Softwood Lumber, Timber, and Plywood Pressure Treated with Water-borne Preservatives for Ground Contact Use.

AWPB LP-33, Standard for Softwood Lumber, Timber, and Plywood Pressure Treated with Light Petroleum Solvent-Penta Solution for Ground Contact Use.

AWPB LP-44, Standard for Softwood Lumber, Timber, and Plywood Pressure Treated with Volatile Petroleum Solvent (LPG)-Penta Solution for Ground Contact Use.

AWPB LP-55, Standard for Softwood Lumber, Timber, and Plywood Pressure Treated with Creosote or Creosote Coal Tar Solutions for Use in Ground Contact.

AWPB LP-77, Standard for Softwood Lumber, Timber, and Plywood Pressure Treated with Heavy Petroleum Solvent-Penta Solution for Ground Contact Use.

AWPB FDN, Standard for Softwood Lumber, Timber, and Plywood Pressure Treated with Water-Borne Preservatives for Ground Contact Use in Residential and Light Commercial Foundations.

### Federal Specifications (FS)

FF-B-561C, Bolts, (Screw), Lag, classifies several types and grades of lag screws and bolts in different styles and includes a variety of material. The type, style, grade, material, and sizes should be considered when this specification is referenced.

FF-B-575C, Bolts, Hexagon and Square, discusses four types of bolts as well as a variety of materials and sizes in both hexagon and square head.

FF-B-58E, Bolts, Finned Neck; Key Head; Machine; Ribbed Neck; Square Neck; Tee Head, defines requirements for several types, classes, styles, materials, and size of bolts.

FF-B-588C(1) Bolts, Toggle; and Expansive Sleeve, Screw, covers self-contained anchoring devices with collapsible or swinging wings that automatically open or swing in place after being pushed through a prepared hole, accessible from one side only.

FF-N-105B(3), Nails, Wire, Brads, and Staples, enumerates minimum requirements for types of INT AMD 1 fasteners, styles, sizes and materials.

FF-N-836D(1), Nut, Square, Hexagon, Cap, Slotted, Castellated, Clinch Knurled, and Welding, covers several types and styles of nuts in a variety of metal and sizes.

FF-S-111D, Screw, Wood, covers types of wood screws, and various styles, materials, and sizes commonly used.

FF-S-325, Shield Expansion; Nail, Expansion; and Nail, Drive-Screw (Devices, Anchoring, INT AMD 3 Masonry), covers several types and styles of masonry anchoring devices in a variety of materials and sizes.

UU-B-790A, Building Paper, Vegetable Fiber: Kraft, Waterproofed Water (Repellent and Fire-INT AMD 10 Resistant), covers vapors barrier paper, concrete curing paper, fire resistant paper, and insulation tape papers.

Type 1 - Barrier papers is intended for use in waterproofing, and as a vapor barrier, flashing, or similar protection. Type 1 is available in widths of 36 in., 40 in., 48 in., 60 in., 72 in., 84 in., and 96 in.

## National Forest Products Association (NFPA)

National Design Specification for Wood Construction, 1977, covers general requirements for design of structural wood members including allowable unit stresses, design loading, and formulas and provisions. Joint design and fastening materials and methods are included in the specifications.

Span Tables for Joist and Rafters, includes span tables which are calculated on the basis of a series of modulus of elasticity (E) and fiber stress ($F_b$) values. The range of values in the tables provide allowable spans for all species and grades of nominal 2 in. framing lumber customarily used in construction. Spans for floor and ceiling joists, used over single span, spans for rafters used over single span, and spans for floor joists continuous over two equal spans are included.

Working Stresses for Joists and Rafters, is recommended for use with span tables for joists.

## Wood Structural Design Data.

## Product Standards (PS)

PS 1-74, Construction and Industrial Plywood, covers requirements and methods of test for the wood species, veneer and packing of plywood intended for construction and industrial uses.

Also included are a glossary of trade terms and a quality certification program. Information regarding generally available sizes, methods of ordering, and reinspecting practices, is provided in an appendix.

PS 20-70, American Softwood Lumber Standard, covers the principal trade classifications and sizes of softwood lumber for yard, structural, and shop use. It provides a common basis of understanding for the classification, measurement, grading, and grade marking of rough and dressed sizes of various items of lumber, including finish, boards, dimensions, and timber.

PS 51-71, Hardwood and Decorative Plywood, covers the principal types, grades, and constructions of plywood made primarily with hardwoods. Included are requirements for wood species and veneer grading lumber-core, particleboard-core and hardboard core, glue bond, panel construction, moisture content and panel dimensions and tolerances.

PS 56-73, Structural Glued Laminated Timber, covers minimum requirements for production of structural glued laminated timber, including plant qualification, quality control systems of the laminator, inspection, and testing, identification, and certification of the production. Quality control by the laminator is essential.

### Redwood Inspection Service (RIS)

Standard Specifications for Grades of California Redwood Lumber, covers standard grading rules for redwood lumber. Characteristics permitted in the General Purpose, Special Purpose, and Structural grades are provided as well as rules for the manufacture, moisture content, and measurement of redwood lumber.

### Southern Pine Inspection Bureau, (SPIB)

Standard Grading Rules for Southern Pine Lumber, 1977, covers standard grading rules for Southern Pine Lumber. Grade markings, manufacture, and measurement are governed by these rules. Grading provisions of these rules, unless otherwise indicated, are based on lumber and allowances made for different dressing and working. Grading variations include stain provisions, bundling of lumber, knot limitations, and slope of grain in stress-graded lumber.

### Western Wood Products Association (WWPA)

Standard Grading Rules for Western Lumber, 1977, covers grading standards for western species for softwood lumber. The grading rules maintain a standard between mills manufacturing the same or similar stocks of lumber. Standard manufacturing sizes and moisture content permissible in a piece of lumber are included. Grade, trade, and species marks identify materials.

# Inspection

### Before Installation

1. Labels or marking: Verify that all lumber and plywood has appropriate grading, quality, and treatment brand, mark, stamp, label, or certificate.
2. Appearance of lumber: Verify that material does not exceed maximums established by appropriate standards for warp, cup, and bow.
3. Moisture content: Verify that moisture content of delivered material does not exceed maximums as specified with appropriate indications on grade stamp. A moisture meter may be essential for additional verification.
4. Protection: Insure that the Contractor has provided protection from elements for materials delivered.

### During Installation:

1. Compliance with specifications: Check that materials and installation methods meet standards required in the specification as detailed.
2. Appearance of lumber: Verify that lower grade materials and nongrademarked lumber are not used in substitution for the specified requirements.
3. Confirm that work in progress is secured. (Nailed, screwed, braced, or bridged).
4. Verify that joists, rafters, and beams have been set with crown edge up.

### After Installation

1. Verify that framing members have been installed accurately to assure placement of finish surface materials.
2. Assure wood decking is covered with moisture protection paper until roofing is completed.

# Glossary

Beams—The structural member, supported at the ends, laid horizontally to bear a load and brace a frame.

Boards—Lumber less than 2 in. thick and 1 or more inches wide.

Bridging—Diagonal braces between the joists, used to stiffen the structure, spread concentrated loads to adjacent joists, and brace joists against lateral deflection.

Crown Edge—A term used to indicate that a timber having a crook or edge warp is placed so that the ends are bearing on a surface and the mid-part of the timber is raised off of the bearing surface forming an arch or crown.

Exterior Grade—Plywood manufactured with 100% waterproof glue, veneers in backs and inner plies are of higher grade than those used in Interior grade.

Firestops—Wood blocking used to fill or close open parts of a structure for preventing the spread of fire or smoke.

Girt—A horizontal member framed into corner posts, or running from column to column or from bent to bent of a building frame to stiffen the framework and to carry siding material.

Hardboard—A generic term for a flat homogeneous panel manufactured primarily from interfelted lignocellulosic fibers consolidated under heat and pressure to a minimum density of 31 lbs. cu. ft.

Hardwood—One of a group of broad-leaf trees (deciduous).

Heavy Framing Lumber—5 in. nominal thickness and thicker.

Interior Grade—Plywood manufactured with "Highly moisture resistant glue." Not recommended for use in areas exposed to weather or high humidity.

Joists and Planks—Horizontal parallel beams which carry floor or ceiling loads placed from wall to wall to which boards or a floor or lath of a ceiling are fastened. 2 in. to 4 in. thick, 6 in. and wider.

Laminated Decking—Decking made up of separate pieces of wood glued together to form one solid unit.

Leger—A narrow strip of lumber nailed to the side of a girder and flush with its bottom edge to help support floor or ceiling joists.

Light Framing Lumber—2 in. to 4 in and less, nominal thickness and width.

Plates—Horizontal wood members which provide bearing and anchorage for wall, floor, ceiling, and roof framing.

Plywood, Hardwood—A panel composed of a cross-banded assembly of layers or plies of veneer (or veneers in combination with lumber core, particleboard core, hardboard core, or of special core material) joined with an adhesive. Except for special constructions, the grain of alternative plies is always approximately at right angles and the face veneer is usually hardwood.

Posts or Columns—Vertical members supporting horizontal plate which carries roof structure.

Rafters—Framing members which support the roof of a structure, similar to floor joists except they are set in an inclined position, 2 in. to 4 in. thick, 6 in. and wider.

Sill—Plate on top of foundation wall which supports floor framing.

Softwood—One of the group of trees which have needle-like or scale-like leaves. The expression has no specific reference to the softness of the wood (Coniferous trees).

Studs—Vertical framing members which support roof and other vertically imposed loads and are sheathed with interior and exterior finish materials.

Note: An extensive list of definitions of terms used in describing "Standard Grades of Lumber" may be found in PS 20-70. Additional definitions are industry recognized abbreviations may be found in American "Standard Definitions, Abbreviations, and References."

## Assignment:

1. **Draft the specifications for the illustrated set of plans in Fig. 19-3.**

FIGURE 19-3 (pages 245–47)    An illustrated set of plans

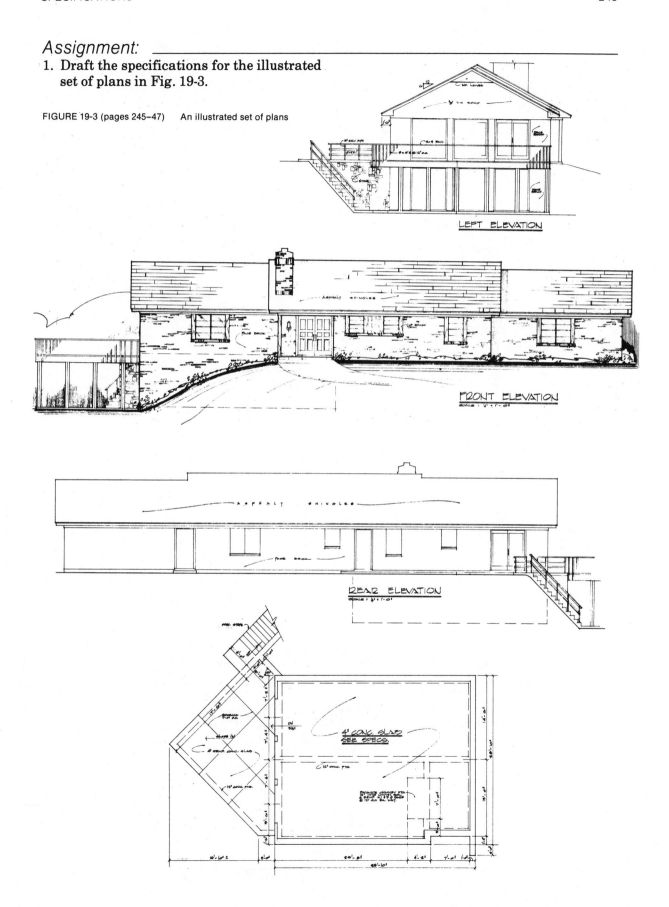

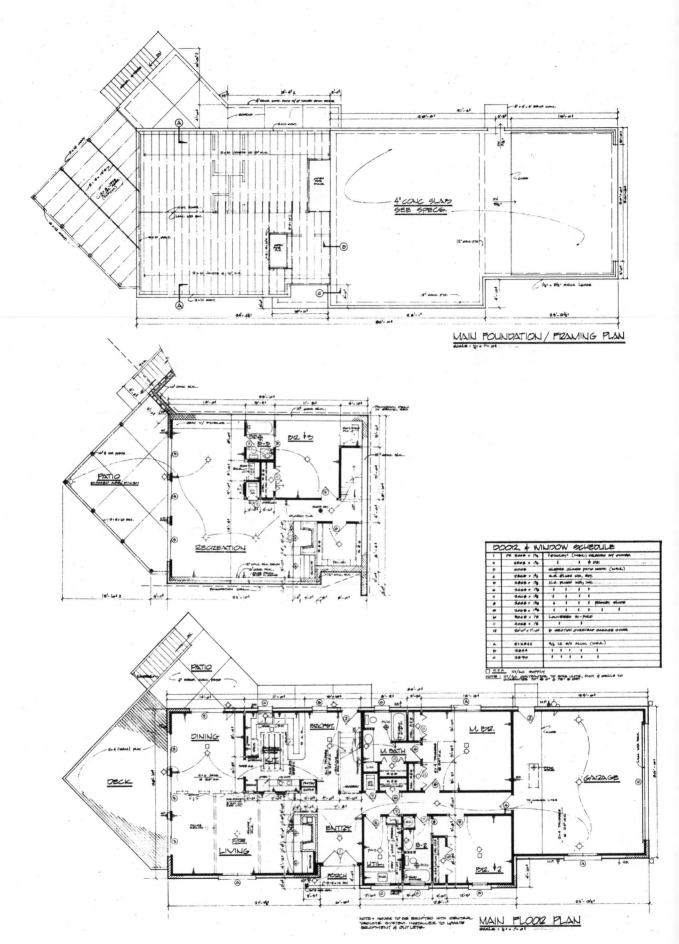

MAIN FOUNDATION / FRAMING PLAN

DOOR & WINDOW SCHEDULE

RECREATION

PATIO

DINING

DECK

LIVING

BR'K'FST.

M. BATH

M. BR.

GARAGE

ENTRY

UTIL.

PORCH

BR. #2

PATIO

MAIN FLOOR PLAN

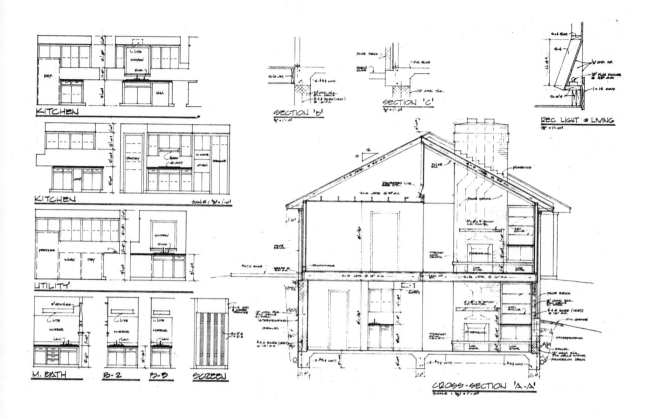

KITCHEN

KITCHEN

UTILITY

M. BATH    B-2    B-3    SCREEN

SECTION 'B'

SECTION 'C'

REC. LIGHT @ LIVING

CROSS-SECTION 'A-A'

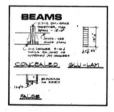

**BEAMS**

CONCEALED    GLU-LAM

FALSE

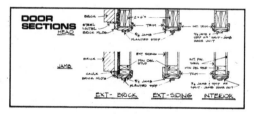

**DOOR SECTIONS** HEAD

JAMB

EXT-BRICK    EXT-SIDING    INTERIOR

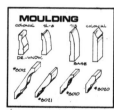

**MOULDING**

DR-WNDW.

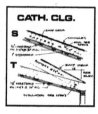

**CATH. CLG.**

S

T

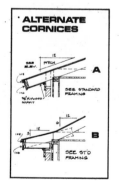

**ALTERNATE CORNICES**

A

B

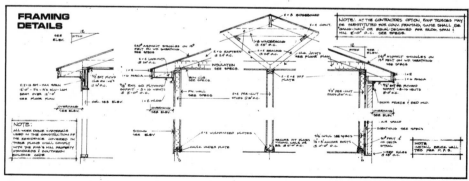

**FRAMING DETAILS**

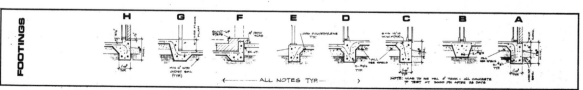

**FOOTINGS**

H    G    F    E    D    C    B    A

← ALL NOTES TYP →

# 20

# Architectural Models

Architectural models are often used to investigate design principles and to show a prospective client what the finished structure might look like (see Fig.20-1). Many people are not able to understand preliminary drawing, or a complete set of working drawings. An architectural model is able to convey a message that might otherwise be lost.

There are two basic types of models. A *structural model* is often used by students so they can learn the relationship of all component parts of a building (see Fig. 20-2). One of the most successful types of structural models is a full section of a typical wall. The model is usually built to a $\frac{3}{4}'' = 1'0''$ scale. In order to show all the parts of the wall, the model needs to be only 10' in width and 5' in depth. Using this technique, materials are kept to a minimum, yet students learn how the structural members of a typical wall fit together. Some structural models are built of the entire building. This however, is costly and time-consuming.

A *presentation model* usually shows only the exterior of a building and the landscaping that accompanies it (see Fig. 20-3). Models of this type are usually built to $\frac{1}{4}'' = 1'0''$ scale. These models show the varying roof lines; the shape of the exterior wall, the location and style of windows and doors, and the contour of the surrounding land. Some presentation models are built so the roof can be removed (see Fig. 20-4). In this case, the individual rooms are shown, sometimes complete with furniture and accessories.

## Materials

Materials used in model making are as varied as an individual's imagination. Many household items such as thread, buttons, mirrors, straight pins, paint, yarn, felt, steel wool, pipe cleaners, paper, and glue can be used in a typical model. Some of the common materials and how they are used are discussed below.

Illustration board or balsa wood are both used to construct exterior walls and roofs. Balsa wood is available in varying shapes and sizes, but in some areas is hard to obtain. It is easy to work with and can be easily

FIGURE 20-1 (right)    Architectural model

shaped with a model-maker's knife or razor knife. Illustration board can be purchased in most art or office supply outlets. Boards of different colors can be used to match particular building materials. This material can also be cut with a razor knife, but with more difficulty than the balsa wood.

A model-maker's knife or single-edge razor blade or razor knife can be used to cut the balsa wood or illustration board. Some model-makers take the precaution of taping the ends of their fingers when they use a single-edge razor blade. To guide the cutting edges, an old triangle or T-square should be used (see Fig. 20-5). Old straightedges should be used because the cutting tools could damage new ones, making them useless for drafting purposes.

Thumbtacks and straight pins are used to hold the various glued parts together until the glue dries. Straight pins are usually better than thumbtacks because they leave smaller holes; they are, however, harder to work with because of the small head and they sometimes bend, especially when used with illustration board. Airplane or model cement is usually used to hold the model parts together.

Scissors are indispensable in model making. They are used to cut paper, trim sponges, cut thread, and many other similar tasks.

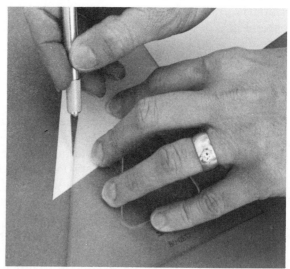

FIGURE 20-2 (top left)      Structural model
FIGURE 20-3 (center left)      Presentation model
FIGURE 20-4 (bottom left)      Model with removable roof
FIGURE 20-5 (above)      Cutting illustration board with a razor knife

## CONSTRUCTION OF A STRUCTURAL MODEL _____

There are many different methods and techniques used to construct structural models; a few of these are discussed below.

### Earth Contour

The shape of the building site can be constructed by using papier-mâché, water putty, or plaster of Paris (see Fig. 20-6). Before these materials are used, it is usually necessary to construct some type of form. Wire mesh can be stretched over a plywood base to conform to the various elevations of the site. To support the mesh, small spacer blocks should be placed in varying locations. The papier-mâché, putty, or plaster of Paris can now be troweled over the mesh. The fillers should be placed in thin layers and allowed to dry; this will prevent cracking.

Illustration board can also be used to show the various contours (see Fig. 20-7). As the elevation of the building site changes, the illustration board is cut so that the various layers are staggered. As each layer is cut, it is glued to the preceding contour interval.

### Plant Forms and Trees

Plants and trees can be formed from several different types of materials (see Fig. 20-8). A sponge can be shredded and painted green to represent bushes. Shredded sponge can also be glued to a small twig to look like a tree. (One important thing to remember when constructing plants and trees, or any other part of a model, is to keep everything in proper scale.) Steel wool can also be pulled apart and glued to small twigs. Dried plants and weeds can also be used for trees. A dried goldenrod makes a realistic scale elm tree.

### Grass

Grass can be made from dyed burlap or green felt. When cloth is used as grass, it is usually glued to a flat surface. Plywood makes an excellent base. Before the cloth is placed, a light coat of glue should be brushed over the surface. The cloth can then be gently pressed into position. Green flock and dyed sawdust,

FIGURE 20-6 (above)    Construction of earth contour using plaster of paris
FIGURE 20-7 (below)    Construction of earth contour using illustration board
FIGURE 20-8 (bottom)    Tree construction

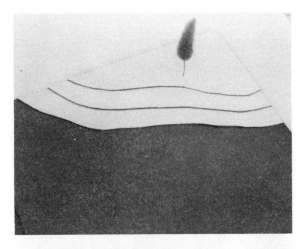

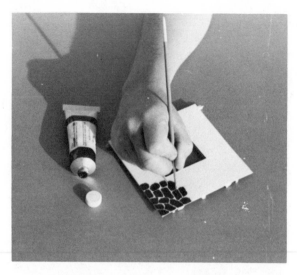

FIGURE 20-9     Brick or stone representation

sprinkled on a base that has been brushed with glue or shellac, can also be used for grass. They make good covering for a sloped terrain.

FIGURE 20-10     Horizontal-siding construction

## Roads and Drives

Roads and drives can be painted on the model, or sandpaper can be glued to the base to represent them. Sandpaper is available in a variety of colors and grit size.

## Water

A mirror can be used to simulate water. To get a wave effect, colored cellophane can be placed on top of the mirror—it should only be glued around the edges of the mirror that will later be covered. Glass or patterned glass can also be used for water. The best effect can be achieved by painting the underside of the glass light blue.

## Brick or Stone

Brick or stone can be painted on the sides of illustration board or balsa wood (see Fig. 20-9). Balsa wood can also be grooved to simulate mortar joints. A blunt instrument, such as a nail, is drawn across the balsa wood, leaving a small impression. White water-color paint can be placed on illustration board with a ruling pen. When this technique is used, only the horizontal courses are lined.

## Vertical or Horizontal Siding

Siding can be made from strips of heavy paper glued to a wall (see Fig. 20-10). If bevel or lap siding is to be represented, each course of paper strips should be overlapped to create the effect of real siding. The interior and exterior corner post that the siding butts can be made from small strips of balsa wood or a heavier grade of paper. If plywood is used, the paper can be lined to represent the grooves found on plywood. If battens are placed over the plywood, small strips of the heavy paper can be glued on 16" centers.

## Stucco

Joint compound is one of the easiest materials to work with when there is a need to simulate stucco (see Fig. 20-11). It is used to cover nail holes and cracks in drywall construction and is available in ready-mixed form. It can be easily troweled over an area to give the appearance of stucco. Plaster of Paris or Keene cement can also be used to simulate stucco. These materials often require mixing. They should be mixed to the consistency of heavy cream and then troweled on the model.

## Roofing

For models, the best roofing material is sandpaper (see Fig. 20-12). There are two techniques used in the application of sandpaper as a roof covering. The first involves gluing a precut sheet to the roof. When this procedure is used no shingle lines or cutouts will show. A roof showing the individual shingles can also be made. Long strips (1'0") of sandpaper should first be cut to scale. After several strips have been cut, they should be stacked and secured together with a rubber band around each end. Small slits, representing the cutouts on the shingles, are then cut on 6" centers.

## Windows

To make windows, openings must be cut out of the illustration board or balsa wood. Acetate can then be glued to the back side of the openings. Small pieces of cloth can be placed over the acetate (see Fig. 20-13) to give the look of drapery and keep anyone from seeing inside the model. Window trim can be made from straws, balsa wood, or heavy paper.

## Doors

Doors can be made from balsa wood or illustration board (see Fig. 20-14). If there are

FIGURE 20-11 (top right)     Joint compound used to represent stucco
FIGURE 20-12 (center right)     Sandpaper used for roofing
FIGURE 20-13 (bottom right)     Small pieces of cloth used to cover insides of windows
FIGURE 20-14 (above)     Doors cut from illustration board

any openings in the doors, they should be cut out and acetate glued to the back side. If a panel door is used, it is usually better to draw in the rail and stile assembly. Door trim can be cut from balsa wood or from heavy posterboard.

*Scale Items*

Hobby shops often have scale items for sale that can be used on a model, such as windows, doors, trees, fireplaces, plumbing fixtures, I-beams, people, and cars.

## *CONSTRUCTION OF A PRESENTATION MODEL*

The first step in the construction of a presentation model is to lay out the walls and any openings on the walls. This is usually done by first taping the illustration or balsa wood to a drafting board. A parallel edge or T-square and triangles are then used to measure out the walls. The lines for the walls and openings should be lightly drawn in. A razor knife and an old triangle can then be used to cut along the layout lines. Once the walls have been cut, their raw edges should be lightly sanded with a piece of fine sandpaper wrapped around a small sanding block.

After the walls have been cut and sanded, the exterior wall finish can be painted or drawn on the walls, and windows and doors placed.

The walls can then be glued together. Wall corners can be made with one of three techniques (see Fig. 20-15). The easiest is to butt the two wall panels and glue them into the correct position. They can also be mitered so that no raw edges will show—however, unless the proper cutting tools are used, it is often difficult to obtain a satisfactory fitting joint. A wrapped corner can also be constructed by cutting a groove through two-thirds of the board, from the back side. The board can then be bent so the two panels intersect to form a 90 degree angle. Most panels are glued together and reinforced with a small block placed at the joint intersection. Straight pins are used to temporarily hold the model together until the glue dries.

Before the roof is cut, the roof plan and elevations should be consulted. The size of the individual roof panels can be scaled from the drawing. Their width can be obtained by measuring the barge rafter along the gable end. The length can be determined by measuring along the fascia on the front elevation. The roof is then laid out and cut (see Fig. 20-16). If the roof is a gable, the shape of the two main roof panels will be rectangular in shape. Even if there are intersecting roofs, the main parts remain solid. In the case of a hip roof, a drafting template can be used to determine the correct slope on the ends of the panel. When this roof is first laid out, the layout lines form a rectangle. With the roof slope indicator, the correct slope should be marked on each end of the panel (see, Fig. 20-17).

Intersecting roofs should be laid out and cut much like the hip roof was done. The width of the rectangle, however, is determined by measuring along the ridge line of the intersecting roof rather than the fascia.

Once all the roof panels have been cut, they can be glued together. A heavy paper tab is one of the easiest ways to secure them (see Fig. 20-18). After the roof assembly has dried,

FIGURE 20-16     Roof construction

FIGURE 20-15     Corner wall treatment: (a) butted corner; (b) mitered corner; (c) wrapped corner

A                    B                    C

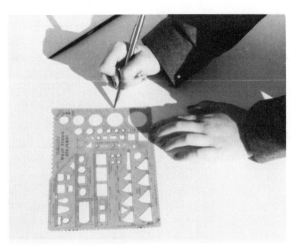

FIGURE 20-17 Using a roof-slope indicator to mark the correct slope

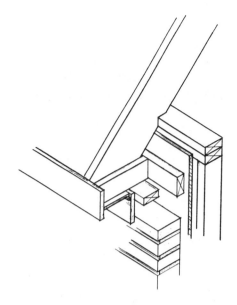

FIGURE 20-19 Cornice construction

the tabs can secure it to the wall panels.

It is not necessary to finish the cornice and the gable end. A strip of balsa wood, representing the fascia, should be glued to a wider piece of balsa wood that represents the soffit (see Fig. 20-19). When the assembly has dried, they are positioned and glued to the roof overhang. If a gutter is used it can now be glued to the fascia. (A split soda straw makes an excellent gutter.)

The roof covering can now be placed over the roof panels. If there are any valleys in the roof, aluminum foil can be used to represent flashing.

FIGURE 20-18 Paper tab used to help secure roofing panels together

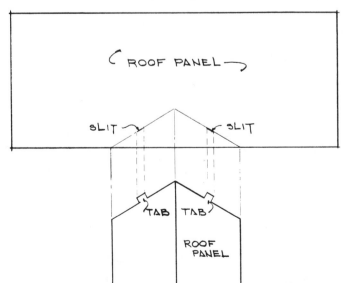

If a base has not already been prepared now is the time to do this step. If the site has contours, they should be formed and allowed to dry. Last, drives and walks, and then grass, shrubs, and trees, should be added.

The model can now be lowered slowly onto the base. Once it is properly positioned, it can be permanently secured with glue.

The base of a model should be constructed in a manner that will allow the foundation to be displayed (see Fig. 20-20). It is, however, sometimes easier to form the foundation first, place it on a suitable flat surface, then form the base around it.

The floor, wall, and roof frame are constructed using conventional framing techniques. The framing members are usually made from balsa wood cut to the proper scale. As the different members are glued, they should be pinned together until the glue dries.

FIGURE 20-20 Structural model showing the foundation

*Assignment:* _____

1. Construct a presentation model, using a previously drawn set of plans.

2. Construct a structural model, using a typical wall section as a guide.

# GLOSSARY OF ARCHITECTURAL TERMS

## A

ACCESS: A passageway; a corridor between rooms.

ACCORDION DOORS: Doors that fold and are supported by rollers inserted in a track.

ACOUSTICAL BOARD: A board that is used to control sound, such as insulating board.

AIR SPACE: A space between walls; or the space between the brick veneer and the wall frame.

ANCHOR BOLT: A bolt that is used to secure the frame of a building against wind and vibration forces.

APRON: A piece of window trim that is placed under the stool and against the wall.

AREAWAY: An open space around a basement window.

ASPHALT SHINGLES: Composition roof shingles that are made from asphalt-impregnated felt covered with mineral granules.

ATTIC: The space or area that is located directly below the roof.

## B

BACKFILL: Earth or other material that is placed in an area that has been excavated.

BALUSTER: A thin column that is used to support a railing.

BANNISTER: A handrail supported by small vertical post on a stair.

BASE COURSE: A layer of aggregate that is used to stop the capillary action of ground water.

BASEMENT: A full-story space that is located below grade.

BASE SHOE: A piece of interior trim that is placed adjacent to the baseboard.

BATT: A type of insulation that is placed between framing members.

BATTEN: A thin strip of wood that is used to cover the intersection of two panels.

BATTER BOARD: A horizontal board that is nailed to posts, used to indicate the proper elevation and serves to hold the building line.

BEAM: A principal horizontal member in a building.

BEARING PLATE: A plate that is used to support structural members.

BEVEL: An angular cut across the edge of a piece of stock.

BIRDSMOUTH: A portion of a structural member that has been cut out so the member may fit over a cross-timber.

## (Column 2)

BOND: A joining or adhering to.

BRICK MOLDING: Molding that is used to trim out exterior window and door frames. It closes the space between the brick and the door or window.

BRICK VENEER: An outer covering of brick tied to a wall frame.

BRIDGING: Framing members placed between the floor joists to brace the joists and spread the load.

BUILDING PAPER: Paper that is placed between sheathing and outside wall covering.

BUILDING SEWER: The lowest portion of a drainage system that extends from the building drain to the street sewer.

BUILT-UP ROOF: A roof that is composed of several layers of rag felt saturated with tar or asphalt.

## C

CANT STRIP: A strip of wood that is placed under shingles or siding.

CAPILLARY ACTION: The ability of water to move through space, regardless of gravity.

CARPORT: Shelter of an automobile that is not fully enclosed.

CARRIAGE: A wooden support for stair treads and risers.

CASED OPENING: An opening that is finished with jambs and casing but has no door.

CASING: Molding used to trim door and window openings.

CHAIR RAIL: A piece of molding that is placed along the wall of a room to keep a chair from marring the wall.

CHORD: The lowest horizontal framing member of a truss.

COLLAR BEAM: A beam that is used to connect two rafters; sometimes called a wind beam or rafter tie.

CONCRETE: A mixture of sand, gravel or stone, and cement.

CONDUIT (electrical): A metal pipe in which electrical wiring is placed.

CONTOUR LINES: Imaginary lines on a plot plan, representing particular elevations.

CONVECTOR: An electric hot-water or steam-heating room unit.

CONVENIENCE OUTLET: An electrical outlet into which may be plugged electrical appliances and equipment.

COPE: To cut the end of a piece of molding so it will fit the contour of an intersecting piece of molding.

CORNICE: A part of the exterior trim that is located where the roof and side walls meet.

COUNTER FLASHING: Flashing placed under cap flashing.

COVE: A piece of concave molding.

CRAWL SPACE: The space between the first floor and the surface ground.

CRICKET: Sometimes called a saddle. It is placed behind a vertical wall on a sloping roof to divert rainwater.

CRIPPLE: A stud that is cut less than full length.

## D

DADO: A rectangular groove cut across the grain of a board.

DAMPER: A regulating device that controls the draft in a duct or flue.

DEAD LOAD: A stationary load imposed on a structure; a constant weight.

DEFORMED BAR: A reinforcing bar that has luglike ridges around it to provide a tight bond with surrounding concrete.

DEGREE: One-360th part of the circumference of a circle.

DIRECT LIGHTING: A lighting system in which the majority of the light is directed downward.

DOOR CASING: The trim that is placed around a door opening.

DOOR JAMB: The vertical and horizontal piece of wood that is placed in rough door openings.

DOORSTOP: A thin strip of wood that is nailed to the door jamb to keep the door from swinging through.

DORMER: A framed window on a sloping roof.

DOUBLE-HUNG: A window that has two operating sashes that operate vertically.

DOWEL: A small wooden pin used to strengthen a joint.

DOWNSPOUT: Sometimes called a leader. It is used to carry rain water from the gutter to the ground or sewer connection.

DRAIN TILE: A pipe that is used to carry ground water to a storm sewer or dry stream bed.

DROP SIDING: Exterior side-wall covering usually ¾″ thick and 6″ wide, with tongue-and-grooved or shiplapped joints.

DRYWALL: A type of interior wall finish that is placed without the use of water.

DUCTS: A round or rectangular pipe used for distributing warm or cool air.

DUPLEX OUTLET: An electrical wall outlet that has two plug receptacles.

## E

EASEMENT: The right of access to a piece of property that belongs to someone else.

EAVE: A part of the roof that projects over the side wall.

EFFLORESCENCE: White stains that form on masonry walls.

ELBOW: A plumbing fitting that is used to make a 90-degree turn.

ELEVATION: A modified orthographic drawing that shows one side of an object.

ENAMEL: A type of paint in which the vehicle is a drying oil or combination of drying oil and resin.

EXCAVATE: To remove earth below grade level.

EXPANSION JOINT: A space between members that allows for possible expansion and contraction.

## F

FASCIA: A board that is placed at the lower end of the rafter tails; can be used by itself or in combination with moldings.

FILL: Soil or loose rock that is used to raise a grade.

FIRE RESISTANCE: The ability of a material to withstand fire or give protection from it.

FLASHING: A particular type of material used to cover open joints to make them waterproof.

FLITCH BEAM: A built-up beam constructed by placing a metal insert between two wooden members.

FLUE: An enclosed area that carries gases and smoke.

FOOTING: An enlarged base upon which the foundation wall rests.

FRIEZE: A horizontal band that is placed at or near the top of a wall.

FROSTLINE: The depth of frost penetration.

FURR DOWN: A drop in ceiling height, usually found over kitchen cabinets.

FURRING: Thin strips of wood that are used to level a surface.

## G

GABLE: The triangular portion of a side wall that is located above the eave line.

GAMBREL ROOF: A roof that has two pitches, the lower one having a steeper slope than the upper.

GIRDER: A main supporting element of the floor frame.

GLAZING: The placing of glass in an opening.

GLUE BLOCK: A small piece of wood that is used to

strengthen and support two pieces of wood that are joined at an angle.

GRADE: The slope, elevation, or face of the ground.

GRADE BEAM: A horizontal foundation member.

GRAVEL STOP: A formed piece of sheet metal used to contain the gravel on a built-up roof.

GROUND: A thin strip of wood that is used in a plastered wall; used to keep the wall straight and serving as a nailing base for interior trim.

GROUT: A fluid mixture of portland cement, sand, and water that is used to fill joints of masonry and tile.

GUSSET: A plywood or metal plate placed over the intersection of two framing members on a truss.

GUTTER: A trough that is used to collect water from the eave line.

GYPSUM: Commonly known as plaster of Paris; a mineral, hydrous sulphate of calcium.

GYPSUM WALLBOARD: A sheet of wallboard that has a core of gypsum sandwiched between covers of paper. Also known as "gypsumboard."

# H

HANGER: A metal device used to support pipes or the ends of joists.

HEADER: A wooden structural member that is placed at right angles to the joist.

HEADLAP: A portion of a shingle that is covered by another shingle.

HIP: The angle that is formed by the intersection of two sloping roofs that have their plates running in opposite directions.

HIP JACK RAFTER: A short rafter that extends from the plate to the hip rafter.

HIP RAFTER: A rafter used to form the hip of a roof.

HIP ROOF: A roof that is inclined from all four sides.

HOSE BIBB: A water faucet that has a threaded end for the attacement of a water hose.

HOUSE DRAIN: The main lower horizontal pipe that receives the discharge of soil and waste stacks.

HOUSE SEWER: The lowest portion of the plumbing system that extends from the house drain to the public sewer.

# I

INSULATION: A material used for the reduction of heat gain and heat loss.

# J

JAMB: The exposed interior lining of an opening.

JOIST: A structural member that is used to support floor and ceiling loads.

# K

KEY: A protruding piece of metal, wood, or concrete that is used to hold one or both parts of a joint together.

# L

LALLY COLUMN: A cylindrically shaped steel member that is used as a girder or beam; sometimes filled with concrete.

LAMINATED BEAM: A large beam constructed by gluing several smaller pieces of wood together.

LANDING: A platform placed between flights of stairs or at the termination of stairs.

LATH: A base for plastering, usually expanded metal.

LEADER: A vertical pipe connected to a gutter; used to carry rainwater from the gutter to the ground or drain.

LEDGER STRIP: A supporting piece of lumber fastened to the lower edge of a beam or girder.

LIGHT: A single piece of glass in a window or door.

LIGHT CONSTRUCTION: Primarily residential in nature, although it can include small commercial buildings.

LINTEL: A horizontal structural member placed over an opening; a header.

LIVE LOAD: A variable load that may be placed upon a structure.

LOOKOUT: The supporting agency for the soffit.

LOOP VENT: A pipe that connects to the stack vent to prevent back siphonage.

LOT LINE: An imaginary legal line that surrounds a piece of property.

LOUVER: An opening used for ventilating a closed area.

# M

MANSARD ROOF: A roof that is sloped twice on each of the four sides.

MASONRY: A type of construction that is composed of shaped or molded units.

METAL WALL TIES: Small pieces of metal used to tie masonry veneer to a wall frame.

MITER: The joint formed by the intersection of two abutting pieces.

MOLDING: Thin strips of wood that are used for esthetic purposes, or to cover various joints.

MONOLITHIC: Usually refers to a concrete slab that has no joints.

MORTAR: A mixture of cement, sand, and lime that is used to bond masonry units together.

MULLION: The thin vertical bars that separate the individual lights in a window.

## N

NEWEL: The supporting post that is found at the foot of a staircase.

NOMINAL SIZE: The size of lumber before it is planed.

NOSING: The projecting part of a windowsill or stair tread.

## O

ON CENTER: The distance from the center of one structural member to the center of another.

OUTLET: A distribution source for electrical current.

OVERHANG: The projection of a roof beyond the supporting wall.

## P

PARGE COAT: A thin coat of cement plaster placed over a masonry wall.

PATIO: A surfaced area that is an extension of the residence; can be partially or entirely enclosed by the residence.

PENNY: A measure of nail length that is abbreviated by the letter "d."

PERSPECTIVE: A pictorial drawing that is used to illustrate design principles.

PIER: A support for beams and girders, usually constructed of concrete or masonry.

PILASTER: A columnar projection that is part of the foundation wall.

PILE: A structural member that is placed into the earth to help support a structure.

PITCH: The degree of inclination of a roof.

PLASTER: A mixture of lime, cement, and sand that is used as an exterior and interior wall finish.

PLATE: A flat horizontal member that is connected to the top and bottom of the studs.

PLENUM: A chamber area forming a part of an air conditioning system.

PLUMB: To place an object in a vertical position.

PORCH: A roofed structure placed at an entrance to a building.

POST AND BEAM CONSTRUCTION: A type of construction in which the roof and floor framing rest directly on a wall post.

PURLING: A horizontal member that is used to brace the rafters.

## Q

QUARTER-ROUND: A small piece of molding that has a quarter-circle profile.

## R

RABBET: A rectangular groove cut in the edge of a board.

RAFTER: A structural member that is used to support roof loads.

RAIL: The horizontal member of the framework of a sash, door, or any paneled assembly.

REGISTER: The end of a duct, usually covered with grille work.

REINFORCED CONCRETE: Concrete that has some form of steel in it to increase its structural strength.

REINFORCEMENT BAR: Metal bars that are embedded in concrete.

RESILIENT: The ability of a material to return to its original shape after temporary deformation.

RIBBON: A narrow board that is let into the studding to help support the joist.

RIDGE: The uppermost horizontal board of a roof.

RISE: The upward slope of a roof.

RISER: The vertical board of a stair that is placed under the nosing.

ROOF SHEATHING: Material that is fastened to the rafters, on which the roof covering is laid.

ROUGH OPENING: An unfinished opening.

RUBBLE: Irregular broken stone.

RUN: In roof construction, the horizontal distance between the ridge and the face of a wall. In stair construction, the horizontal distance covered by the stairs.

## S

SADDLE: A raised area behind the chimney that is used to support flashing and divert moisture away from the chimney.

SASH: The framework that holds glass in a window.

SCHEDULE: A collection of organized notes.

SCRIBING: Marking a piece of construction material to fit an irregular-shaped surface.

SEPTIC TANK: A part of an individual sewage system; used to collect the waste until decomposition can occur.

SETBACK: An imaginary line established by law or deed restriction, fixing the distance from the property line to the face of a building.

SHAKE: Hand-split shingle.

SHEATHING: Exterior wall or roof covering, usually plywood or nominal 1″ × 6″ boards.

SHIM: A thin strip of wood that is used to level framing members.

SHIPLAP: A type of lumber that has rabbeted edges.

SIDING: A type of material that is used to cover the exterior of a frame wall.

SILL: A horizontal structural member that is placed on top of a foundation wall. In a door frame, the sill is a horizontal board that is placed at the bottom of the frame.

SOFFIT: A board attached to the underside of the raftertail.

SOIL STACK: A vertical pipe that receives the discharge of a fixture that receives human excreta.

SOLEPLATE: Sometime called the bottom plate. It is a horizontal framing member placed directly below the studs.

SPECIFICATION: A written document that is used to stipulate the kind, quality, and quantity of materials and workmanship required for a construction project.

SPLINE: A small strip of wood that is used to reinforce a joint.

STILE: A vertical member on a door or panel.

STOOL: A narrow piece of trim that is used to "trim out" a window; placed at the bottom of the window.

STRINGER: An inclined structural member of a stair that supports the treads and risers.

STUCCO: A cement plaster placed and used as an exterior wall finish.

STUD: Vertical framing member in a wall.

SUBFLOOR: A floor that is nailed directly to the floor joists, onto which a finished floor is placed.

SYMBOL: A mark, character, or figure that represents the name of something.

## T

TERMITE SHIELD: A metal barrier used to prevent the entrance of termites into a structure.

THERMOSTAT: An automatic device that is used to regulate the temperature of a room.

THRESHOLD: A member used to close the space beneath the bottom of a door.

TOENAILING: Driving a nail at an angle so that it penetrates two intersecting boards.

TOE SPACE: The recessed space at the bottom of a kitchen cabinet or other built-in unit.

TRAP: A device used to prevent sewer gases from escaping through a plumbing fixture.

TREAD: The horizontal member on a stair that is stepped on.

TRIMMER: A part of the floor frame that is placed around an opening in the floor.

TRUSS: An assemblage of structural members fastened together to form a supporting assembly for the roof sheathing.

## V

VALLEY RAFTER: The diagonal rafter placed at the intersection of two sloping roofs.

VAPOR BARRIER: A material that is used to stop the flow of vapor into a wall or floor.

VEHICLE: The liquid portion of a finishing material; consists of binders and thinners.

VENEERED CONSTRUCTION: A method of construction in which face brick or other facing material is applied to a frame wall.

VENT: A pipe or opening that is used to allow trapped gases to escape.

VENT STACK: A vertical pipe that carries foul gases from a building and prevents back siphonage.

## W

WAINSCOT: To finish the lower portion of an interior wall with a finish that differs from the upper portion.

WALL TIE: A small piece of metal that is used to bind brick veneer to the wall frame.

WATER CLOSET: A toilet that flushes.

WEATHERSTRIP: Narrow strip of material that is installed around the door and windows.

WEEP HOLES: Small openings left in masonry walls to permit drainage and reduce pressures.

WHALER: A horizontal member that is placed across the studding in concrete form construction.

WYTHE: A single vertical-width masonry wall.

# APPENDIX

## LUMBER AND PANELING SIZES AND CLASSIFICATIONS _____

### Lumber Product Classification

| | thickness in. | width in. | | thickness in. | width in. |
|---|---|---|---|---|---|
| board lumber | 1″ | 2″ or more | beams & stringers | 5″ and thicker | more than 2″ greater than thickness |
| light framing | 2″ to 4″ | 2″ to 4″ | posts & timbers | 5″ x 5″ and larger | not more than 2″ greater than thickness |
| studs | 2″ to 4″ | 2″ to 4″ 10′ and shorter | decking | 2″ to 4″ | 4″ to 12″ wide |
| structural light framing | 2″ to 4″ | 2″ to 4″ | siding | thickness expressed by dimension of butt edge | |
| structural joists & planks | 2″ to 4″ | 6″ and wider | mouldings | size at thickest and widest points | |
| Lengths of lumber generally are 6 feet and longer in multiples of 2′ | | | | | |

### Standard Lumber Sizes

## standard lumber sizes / nominal, dressed, based on WWPA rules

| Product | Description | Nominal Size | | Dressed Dimensions | | |
|---|---|---|---|---|---|---|
| | | Thickness In. | Width In. | Thicknesses and Widths In. | | Lengths Ft. |
| | | | | Surfaced Dry | Surfaced Unseasoned | |
| DIMENSION | S4S ......................... | 2 3 4 | 2 3 4 6 8 10 12 Over 12 | 1-1/2 2-1/2 3-1/2 5-1/2 7-1/4 9-1/4 11-1/4 Off 3/4 | 1-9/16 2-9/16 3-9/16 5-5/8 7-1/2 9-1/2 11-1/2 Off 1/2 | 6 ft. and longer in multiples of 1′ |
| SCAFFOLD PLANK | Rough Full Sawn or S4S ........ | 1¼ & Thicker | 8 and Wider | Same | Same | 6 ft. and longer in multiples of 1′ |
| TIMBERS | Rough or S4S ................... | 5 and Larger | | Thickness In. Width In. ½ Off Nominal | | 6 ft. and longer in multiples of 1′ |

| Product | Description | Nominal Size | | Dressed Dimensions | | |
|---|---|---|---|---|---|---|
| | | Thickness In. | Width In. | Thickness In. | Width In. | Lengths Ft. |
| DECKING | 2″ Single T&G ................. | 2 | 6 8 10 12 | 1½ | 5 6¾ 8¾ 10¾ | 6 ft. and longer in multiples of 1′ |
| | 3″ and 4″ Double T&G .......... | 3 4 | 6 | 2½ 3½ | 5¼ | |
| FLOORING | (D & M), (S2S & CM)............ | 3/8 1/2 5/8 1 1¼ 1½ | 2 3 4 5 6 | 5/16 7/16 9/16 3/4 1 1¼ | 1⅛ 2⅛ 3⅛ 4⅛ 5⅛ | 4 ft. and longer in multiples of 1′ |
| CEILING AND PARTITION | (S2S & CM) .................... | 3/8 1/2 5/8 3/4 | 3 4 5 6 | 5/16 7/16 9/16 11/16 | 2⅛ 3⅛ 4⅛ 5⅛ | 4 ft. and longer in multiples of 1′ |
| FACTORY AND SHOP LUMBER | S2S ........................... | 1 (4/4) 1¼ (5/4) 1½ (6/4) 1¾ (7/4) 2 (8/4) 2½ (10/4) 3 (12/4) 4 (16/4) | 5 and wider except (4″ and wider in 4/4 No. 1 Shop and 4/4 No. 2 Shop) | 25/32 (4/4) 1 5/32 (5/4) 1 13/32 (6/4) 1 19/32 (7/4) 1 13/16 (8/4) 2⅜ (10/4) 2¾ (12/4) 3¾ (16/4) | Usually sold random width | 4 ft. and longer in multiples of 1′ |

**ABBREVIATIONS**
Abbreviated descriptions appearing in the size table are explained below.
S1S — Surfaced one side.
S2S — Surfaced two sides.

S4S — Surfaced four sides.
S1S1E — Surfaced one side, one edge.
S1S2E — Surfaced one side, two edges.
CM — Center matched.

D & M — Dressed and matched.
T & G — Tongue and grooved.
EV1S — Edge vee on one side.
S1E — Surfaced one edge.

## *Paneling Coverage Estimator*

The following estimator provides factors for determining the exact amount of material needed for the five basic types of wood paneling. Multiply square footage to be covered by factor (length x width x factor).

| | Nominal Size | Width: Overall | Width: Face | Area Factor* |
|---|---|---|---|---|
| **SHIPLAP** | 1 x 6 | 5½ | 5⅛ | 1.17 |
| | 1 x 8 | 7¼ | 6⅞ | 1.16 |
| | 1 x 10 | 9¼ | 8⅞ | 1.13 |
| | 1 x 12 | 11¼ | 10⅞ | 1.10 |
| **TONGUE AND GROOVE** | 1 x 4 | 3⅜ | 3⅛ | 1.28 |
| | 1 x 6 | 5⅜ | 5⅛ | 1.17 |
| | 1 x 8 | 7⅛ | 6⅞ | 1.16 |
| | 1 x 10 | 9⅛ | 8⅞ | 1.13 |
| | 1 x 12 | 11⅛ | 10⅞ | 1.10 |
| **S4S** | 1 x 4 | 3½ | 3½ | 1.14 |
| | 1 x 6 | 5½ | 5½ | 1.09 |
| | 1 x 8 | 7¼ | 7¼ | 1.10 |
| | 1 x 10 | 9¼ | 9¼ | 1.08 |
| | 1 x 12 | 11¼ | 11¼ | 1.07 |
| **PANELING PATTERNS** | 1 x 6 | 5 7/16 | 5 1/16 | 1.19 |
| | 1 x 8 | 7⅛ | 6¾ | 1.19 |
| | 1 x 10 | 9⅛ | 8¾ | 1.14 |
| | 1 x 12 | 11⅛ | 10¾ | 1.12 |
| **BEVEL SIDING** | 1 x 4 | 3½ | 3½ | 1.60 |
| | 1 x 6 | 5½ | 5½ | 1.33 |
| | 1 x 8 | 7¼ | 7¼ | 1.28 |
| | 1 x 10 | 9¼ | 9¼ | 1.21 |
| | 1 x 12 | 11¼ | 11¼ | 1.17 |

*Allowance for trim and waste should be added.

## *Paneling/Siding Sizes*

| Product | Description | Nominal Size: Thickness In. | Nominal Size: Width In. | Dressed Dimensions: Thickness In. | Dressed Dimensions: Width In. | Dressed Dimensions: Lengths Ft. |
|---|---|---|---|---|---|---|
| **SELECTS AND COMMONS S-DRY** | S1S, S2S, S4S, S1S1E, S1S2E... | 4/4<br>5/4<br>6/4<br>7/4<br>8/4<br>9/4<br>10/4<br>11/4<br>12/4<br>16/4 | 2<br>3<br>4<br>5<br>6<br>7<br>8 and wider | ¾<br>1 5/32<br>1 13/32<br>1 19/32<br>1 13/16<br>2 3/32<br>2⅜<br>2 9/16<br>2¾<br>3¾ | 1½<br>2½<br>3½<br>4½<br>5½<br>6½<br>¾ Off nominal | 6 ft. and longer in multiples of 1′ except Douglas Fir and Larch Selects shall be 4′ and longer with 3% of 4′ and 5′ permitted. |
| **FINISH AND BOARDS S-DRY** | S1S, S2S, S4S, S1S1E, S1S2E ...<br>Only these sizes apply to Alternate Board Grades. | ⅜<br>½<br>⅝<br>¾<br>1<br>1¼<br>1½<br>1¾<br>2<br>2½<br>3<br>3½<br>4 | 2<br>3<br>4<br>5<br>6<br>7<br>8 and wider | 5/16<br>7/16<br>9/16<br>⅝<br>¾<br>1<br>1¼<br>1⅜<br>1½<br>2<br>2½<br>3<br>3½ | 1½<br>2½<br>3½<br>4½<br>5½<br>6½<br>¾ off nominal | 3′ and longer. In Superior grade, 3% of 3′ and 4′ and 7% of 5′ and 6′ are permitted. In Prime grade, 20% of 3′ to 6′ is permitted. |
| **RUSTIC AND DROP SIDING** | (D & M) ........................<br>If ⅜″ or ½″ T & G specified, same over-all widths apply.<br>(Shiplapped, ⅜-in. or ½-in. lap) .. | 1 | 6<br>8<br>10<br>12 | 23/32 | 5⅜<br>7⅛<br>9⅛<br>11⅛ | 4 ft. and longer in multiples of 1′ |
| **PANELING AND SIDING** | T&G or Shiplap................. | 1 | 6<br>8<br>10<br>12 | 23/32 | 5 7/16<br>7⅛<br>9⅛<br>11⅛ | 4 ft. and longer in multiples of 1′ |
| **CEILING AND PARTITION** | T&G .......................... | ⅝<br>1 | 4<br>6 | 9/16<br>23/32 | 3⅜<br>5⅜ | 4 ft. and longer in multiples of 1′ |
| **BEVEL SIDING** | Bevel or Bungalow Siding........<br>Western Red Cedar Bevel Siding available in ½″, ⅝″, ¾″ nominal thickness. Corresponding thick edge is 15/32″, 9/16″ and ¾″. Widths for 8″ and wider, ½″ off nominal. | ½<br><br><br>¾ | 4<br>5<br>6<br>8<br>10<br>12 | 15/32 butt, 3/16 tip<br><br><br>¾ butt, 3/16 tip | 3½<br>4½<br>5½<br>7¼<br>9¼<br>11¼ | 3 ft. and longer in multiples of 1′<br>3 ft. and longer in multiples of 1′ |
| | | | | Surfaced Dry / Green | Surfaced Dry / Green | |
| **STRESS RATED BOARDS** | S1S, S2S, S4S, S1S1E, S1S2E.... | 1<br>1¼<br>1½ | 2<br>3<br>4<br>5<br>6<br>7<br>8 and Wider | ¾ / 25/32<br>1 / 1 1/32<br>1¼ / 1 9/32 | 1½ / 1 9/16<br>2½ / 2 9/16<br>3½ / 3 9/16<br>4½ / 4⅝<br>5½ / 5⅝<br>6½ / 6⅝<br>Off ¾ / Off ½ | 6 ft. and longer in multiples of 1′ |

See coverage estimator chart above for dressed Shiplap and Tongue and Groove (T&G) widths.

**MINIMUM ROUGH SIZES Thicknesses and Widths Dry or Unseasoned All Lumber**

80% of the pieces in a shipment shall be at least ⅛″ thicker than the standard surfaced size, the remaining 20% at least 3/32″ thicker than the surfaced size. Widths shall be at least ⅛″ wider than standard surfaced widths.

When specified to be full sawn, lumber may not be manufactured to a size less than the size specified.

## Light Framing and Studs

| LIGHT FRAMING and STUDS—2" to 4" Thick, 2" to 4" Wide  Recommended Design Values in Pounds Per Square Inch[1] | | Extreme Fiber Stress in Bending "Fb" | | Tension Parallel to Grain "Ft" | Hori- zontal Shear "Fv" | Compression | | Modulus of Elasticity "E" |
|---|---|---|---|---|---|---|---|---|
| Species or Group | Grade | Single | Repetitive | | | Perpen- dicular "Fc⊥" | Parallel to Grain "Fc" | |
| DOUGLAS FIR-LARCH | Construction[2] | 1050 | 1200 | 625 | 95 | 385 | 1150 | 1,500,000 |
| | Standard[2] | 600 | 675 | 350 | 95 | 385 | 925 | 1,500,000 |
| | Utility[2] | 275 | 325 | 175 | 95 | 385 | 600 | 1,500,000 |
| | Stud | 800 | 925 | 475 | 95 | 385 | 600 | 1,500,000 |
| DOUGLAS FIR SOUTH | Construction[2] | 1000 | 1150 | 600 | 90 | 335 | 1000 | 1,100,000 |
| | Standard[2] | 550 | 650 | 325 | 90 | 335 | 850 | 1,100,000 |
| | Utility[2] | 275 | 300 | 150 | 90 | 335 | 550 | 1,100,000 |
| | Stud | 775 | 875 | 450 | 90 | 335 | 550 | 1,100,000 |
| HEM-FIR | Construction[2] | 825 | 975 | 500 | 75 | 245 | 925 | 1,200,000 |
| | Standard[2] | 475 | 550 | 275 | 75 | 245 | 775 | 1,200,000 |
| | Utility[2] | 225 | 250 | 125 | 75 | 245 | 500 | 1,200,000 |
| | Stud | 650 | 725 | 375 | 75 | 245 | 500 | 1,200,000 |
| MOUNTAIN HEMLOCK | Construction[2] | 875 | 1000 | 525 | 95 | 370 | 900 | 1,000,000 |
| | Standard[2] | 500 | 575 | 275 | 95 | 370 | 725 | 1,000,000 |
| | Utility[2] | 225 | 275 | 125 | 95 | 370 | 475 | 1,000,000 |
| | Stud | 675 | 775 | 400 | 95 | 370 | 475 | 1,000,000 |
| MOUNTAIN HEMLOCK- HEM-FIR | Construction[2] | 825 | 975 | 500 | 75 | 245 | 900 | 1,000,000 |
| | Standard[2] | 475 | 550 | 275 | 75 | 245 | 725 | 1,000,000 |
| | Utility[2] | 225 | 250 | 125 | 75 | 245 | 475 | 1,000,000 |
| | Stud | 650 | 725 | 375 | 75 | 245 | 475 | 1,000,000 |
| WESTERN HEMLOCK | Construction[2] | 925 | 1050 | 550 | 90 | 280 | 1050 | 1,300,000 |
| | Standard[2] | 525 | 600 | 300 | 90 | 280 | 850 | 1,300,000 |
| | Utility[2] | 250 | 275 | 150 | 90 | 280 | 550 | 1,300,000 |
| | Stud | 700 | 800 | 425 | 90 | 280 | 550 | 1,300,000 |
| ENGELMANN SPRUCE- ALPINE FIR (Engelmann Spruce- Lodgepole Pine) | Construction[2] | 700 | 800 | 400 | 70 | 195 | 675 | 1,000,000 |
| | Standard[2] | 375 | 450 | 225 | 70 | 195 | 550 | 1,000,000 |
| | Utility[2] | 175 | 200 | 100 | 70 | 195 | 375 | 1,000,000 |
| | Stud | 525 | 600 | 300 | 70 | 195 | 375 | 1,000,000 |
| LODGEPOLE PINE | Construction[2] | 775 | 875 | 450 | 70 | 250 | 800 | 1,000,000 |
| | Standard[2] | 425 | 500 | 250 | 70 | 250 | 675 | 1,000,000 |
| | Utility[2] | 200 | 225 | 125 | 70 | 250 | 425 | 1,000,000 |
| | Stud | 600 | 675 | 350 | 70 | 250 | 425 | 1,000,000 |
| PONDEROSA PINE- SUGAR PINE (Ponderosa Pine- Lodgepole Pine) | Construction[2] | 725 | 825 | 425 | 70 | 235 | 775 | 1,000,000 |
| | Standard[2] | 400 | 450 | 225 | 70 | 235 | 625 | 1,000,000 |
| | Utility[2] | 200 | 225 | 100 | 70 | 235 | 400 | 1,000,000 |
| | Stud | 550 | 625 | 325 | 70 | 235 | 400 | 1,000,000 |
| IDAHO WHITE PINE | Construction[2] | 675 | 775 | 400 | 70 | 190 | 775 | 1,200,000 |
| | Standard[2] | 375 | 425 | 225 | 70 | 190 | 650 | 1,200,000 |
| | Utility[2] | 175 | 200 | 100 | 70 | 190 | 425 | 1,200,000 |
| | Stud | 525 | 600 | 300 | 70 | 190 | 425 | 1,200,000 |
| WESTERN CEDARS | Construction[2] | 775 | 875 | 450 | 75 | 265 | 850 | 900,000 |
| | Standard[2] | 425 | 500 | 250 | 75 | 265 | 700 | 900,000 |
| | Utility[2] | 200 | 225 | 125 | 75 | 265 | 450 | 900,000 |
| | Stud | 600 | 675 | 350 | 75 | 265 | 450 | 900,000 |
| WHITE WOODS (Western Woods) | Construction[2] | 675 | 775 | 400 | 70 | 190 | 675 | 900,000 |
| | Standard[2] | 375 | 425 | 225 | 70 | 190 | 550 | 900,000 |
| | Utility[2] | 175 | 200 | 100 | 70 | 190 | 375 | 900,000 |
| | Stud | 525 | 600 | 300 | 70 | 190 | 375 | 900,000 |

*Grades Described In Sections 40.00 and 41.00 WWPA 1970 Grading Rules*

[1] These design values apply to lumber when used at a maximum moisture content of 19% such as in most covered structures. For other conditions of use, see Section 140.00 of WWPA Grading Rules.
[2] Fb, Ft and Fc recommended design values apply only to 4" widths of these grades.

## stresses illustrated

When loads are applied, structural members bend, producing tension in the fibers along the faces farthest from the applied load and compression in the fibers along the face nearest to the applied load. These induced stresses in the fibers are designated as "extreme fiber stress in bending." ("Fb").

Single member "Fb" design values are used in design where the strength of an individual piece, such as a beam, girder, post or truss chord, is or may be solely responsible for carrying a specific design load.

Repetitive member "Fb" design values are used in design when three or more load sharing members such as joists, rafters, or beams are spaced no more than 24 inches apart and are joined by flooring, sheathing or other load distributing elements. Repetitive members are also used where pieces are adjacent, such as in decking.

## extreme fiber stress in bending "Fb"

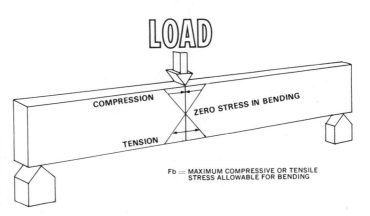

Fb = MAXIMUM COMPRESSIVE OR TENSILE STRESS ALLOWABLE FOR BENDING

## Trusses

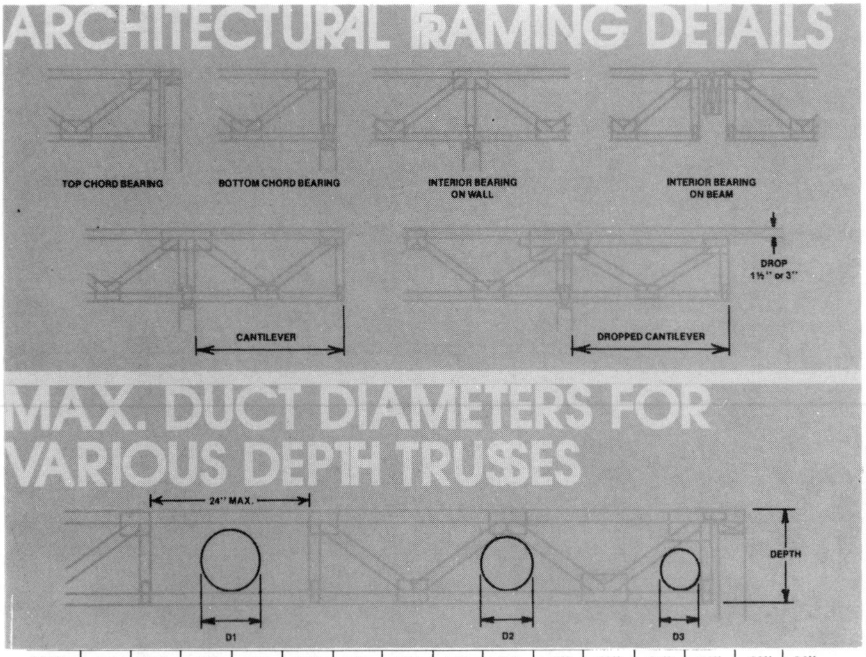


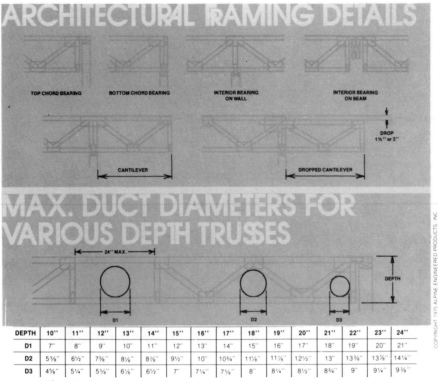

| DEPTH | 10" | 11" | 12" | 13" | 14" | 15" | 16" | 17" | 18" | 19" | 20" | 21" | 22" | 23" | 24" |
|---|---|---|---|---|---|---|---|---|---|---|---|---|---|---|---|
| D1 | 7" | 8" | 9" | 10" | 11" | 12" | 13" | 14" | 15" | 16" | 17" | 18" | 19" | 20" | 21" |
| D2 | 5⅝" | 6½" | 7⅜" | 8⅛" | 8⅞" | 9½" | 10" | 10¾" | 11⅛" | 11⅞" | 12½" | 13" | 13⅜" | 13⅞" | 14¼" |
| D3 | 4⅝" | 5¼" | 5⅝" | 6⅛" | 6½" | 7" | 7¼" | 7⅝" | 8" | 8¼" | 8½" | 8¾" | 9" | 9¼" | 9⅜" |

All "System 42" truss depths are O/A depth



## Maximum Spans for Headers

In this table, headers consist of two pieces of nominal 2-inch framing lumber set on edge and nailed together. The span for the two pieces is expressed as a percentage of the maximum allowable span for floor joists of the same species and grade spaced 16 inches on centers and subjected to a live load of 40 pounds per square foot.

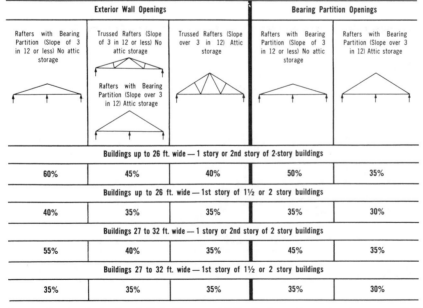

| Exterior Wall Openings | | | Bearing Partition Openings | |
|---|---|---|---|---|
| Rafters with Bearing Partition (Slope of 3 in 12 or less) No attic storage  | Trussed Rafters (Slope of 3 in 12 or less) No attic storage 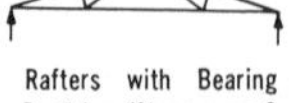 Rafters with Bearing Partition (Slope over 3 in 12) Attic storage 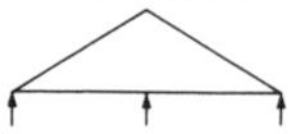 | Trussed Rafters (Slope over 3 in 12) Attic storage 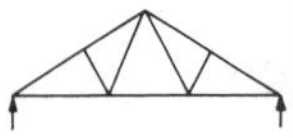 | Rafters with Bearing Partition (Slope of 3 in 12 or less) No attic storage 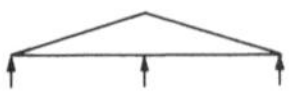 | Rafters with Bearing Partition (Slope over 3 in 12) Attic storage 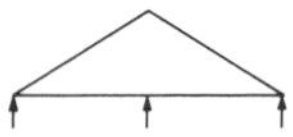 |
| **Buildings up to 26 ft. wide — 1 story or 2nd story of 2-story buildings** | | | | |
| 60% | 45% | 40% | 50% | 35% |
| **Buildings up to 26 ft. wide — 1st story of 1½ or 2 story buildings** | | | | |
| 40% | 35% | 35% | 35% | 30% |
| **Buildings 27 to 32 ft. wide — 1 story or 2nd story of 2 story buildings** | | | | |
| 55% | 40% | 35% | 45% | 35% |
| **Buildings 27 to 32 ft. wide — 1st story of 1½ or 2 story buildings** | | | | |
| 35% | 35% | 35% | 35% | 30% |

Note 1 — Span for a header of two 2x4's should not exceed 2′-6″ in bearing partitions under attic storage nor 3′-0″ elsewhere.

## Span Tables

# SPAN TABLES

6.4/AL

**COMMON**

SIMPLE KINGPOST
DOUBLE HOWE
QUEEN
FINK
HOWE
FAN
MULTIPLE PANEL
BELGIAN (WW)

**MONO PITCH**

2 PANEL
3 PANEL
4 PANEL
5 PANEL
6 PANEL

**SCISSORS**

HOWE
MULTIPLE PANEL
DOUBLE HOWE (KK)

**FLAT**

2 PANEL
3 PANEL
4 PANEL
5 PANEL
6 PANEL
7 PANEL
8 PANEL
Flat roof truss depths are O/A.

| LOAD | 55 psf with 15% Duration Factor (For 40 psf snow load and shingle roof or 30 psf heavy roof, such as tile) | | | 55 psf with 33% Duration Factor or 47 psf with 15% Duration Factor (For 30 psf wind load with tile roof or 30 psf snow load with shingle roof) | | | 47 psf with 33% Duration Factor or 40 psf with 15% Duration Factor (For psf wind load or 20 psf snow load and shingle roof. Meets FHA-Minimum Property Standards.) | | |
|---|---|---|---|---|---|---|---|---|---|
| | CHORD SIZE | | | CHORD SIZE | | | CHORD SIZE | | |
| PITCH | 2×4 Top 2×4 Bot. | 2×6 Top 2×4 Bot. | 2×6 Top 2×6 Bot. | 2×4 Top 2×4 Bot. | 2×6 Top 2×4 Bot. | 2×6 Top 2×6 Bot. | 2×4 Top 2×4 Bot. | 2×6 Top 2×4 Bot. | 2×6 Top 2×6 Bot. |
| 2/12 | 22' | 23' | 34' | 25' | 25' | 39' | 28' | 28' | 44' |
| 3/12 | 29' | 31' | 44' | 33' | 34' | 50' | 37' | 38' | 56' |
| 4/12 | 33' | 39' | 49' | 37' | 42' | 55' | 41' | 46' | 62' |
| 5/12 | 35' | 45' | 53' | 39' | 48' | 59' | 44' | 52' | 66' |
| 6/12 | 37' | 51' | 55' | 41' | 53' | 62' | 44' | 57' | 68' |
| **PITCH** | | | | | | | | | |
| 2/12 | 22' | 23' | 34' | 25' | 25' | 38' | 28' | 28' | 44' |
| 3/12 | 30' | 31' | 45' | 33' | 35' | 51' | 38' | 39' | 57' |
| 4/12 | 33' | 39' | 50' | 37' | 42' | 56' | 42' | 46' | 63' |
| 5/12 | 35' | 45' | 53' | 40' | 48' | 60' | 44' | 53' | 67' |
| 6/12 | 37' | 51' | 56' | 41' | 53' | 62' | 45' | 57' | 68' |
| 6/2* | 32' | 38' | 48' | 36' | 42' | 54' | 40' | 46' | 61' |
| 6/3 | 28' | 30' | 42' | 31' | 34' | 48' | 35' | 38' | 54' |
| 6/4 | 21' | 22' | 32' | 24' | 24' | 36' | 27' | 27' | 42' |
| 16" | 23' | — | — | 24' | — | — | 26' | — | — |
| 18" | 24' | — | — | 26' | — | — | 28' | — | — |
| 20" | 26' | 27' | — | 28' | 28' | — | 30' | 30' | — |
| 24" | 29' | 30' | 34' | 31' | 31' | 37' | 33' | 33' | 39' |
| 28" | 31' | 32' | 38' | 33' | 34' | 40' | 36' | 36' | 43' |
| 30" | 32' | 33' | 39' | 34' | 35' | 42' | 37' | 37' | 45' |
| 32" | 33' | 34' | 41' | 35' | 36' | 43' | 38' | 38' | 47' |
| 36" | 35' | 36' | 43' | 37' | 38' | 46' | 40' | 40' | 50' |
| 42" | 37' | 38' | 47' | 39' | 41' | 50' | 43' | 44' | 54' |
| 48" | 39' | 41' | 49' | 41' | 43' | 53' | 45' | 47' | 57' |
| 60" | 42' | 46' | 54' | 45' | 49' | 59' | 49' | 52' | 64' |
| 72" | 44' | 50' | 58' | 48' | 53' | 63' | 52' | 57' | 68' |

* 6/12 = Top chord pitch, 2/12 = bottom chord pitch

**NOTE:** These safe loads are based upon 24" o.c. spacing, a live load deflection limited to L/360 maximum, and use of lumber with the following properties.

2×4   $f_b$ = 1750 psi   $f_t$ = 1000 psi   $f_c$ = 1250 psi   E = 1.8 × 10⁶
2×6   $f_b$ = 1500 psi   $f_t$ = 1000 psi   $f_c$ = 1250 psi   E = 1.8 × 10⁶

## *Minimum Opening Dimensions for Doors*

**SUGGESTED SPECIFICATIONS**

| Door Size | Opening Type | Wood Frame-Door Only Width-Height* | | Steel Frame-Door Only Width-Height* | Widths For Doors With Sidelights | | | | | |
|---|---|---|---|---|---|---|---|---|---|---|
| | | | | | One 6" | Two 6" | One 14" | Two 14" | One 24" | Two 24" |
| 2′ 6″<br>Single | Rough<br>Brick | 2′ 8¼″<br>2′10″ | 6′ 9⅞″<br>6′10¾″ | Rough Stud Opening: | 3′ 3¾″<br>3′ 5½″ | 3′11¼″<br>4′ 1″ | 3′11¾″<br>4′ 1½″ | 4′ 3¼″<br>5′ 5″ | 4′ 9¾″<br>4′11½″ | 6′11¼″<br>7′ 1″ |
| 2′ 8″<br>Single | Rough<br>Brick | 2′10¼″<br>3′ 0″ | 6′ 9⅞″<br>6′10¾″ | W = Nom. frame width + 4⅜″ min. to 4¾″ max. (i.e., 3′0″ = | 3′ 5¾″<br>3′ 7½″ | 4′ 1¼″<br>4′ 3″ | 4′ 1¾″<br>4′ 3½″ | 5′ 5¼″<br>5′ 7″ | 4′11¾″<br>5′ 1½″ | 7′ 1¼″<br>7′ 3″ |
| 3′ 0″<br>Single | Rough<br>Brick | 3′ 2¼″<br>3′ 4″ | 6′ 9⅞″<br>6′10¾″ | 40⅜″ min. to 40¾″ max.) | 3′ 9¾″<br>3′11½″ | 4′ 5¼″<br>4′ 7″ | 4′ 5¾″<br>4′ 7½″ | 5′ 9¼″<br>5′11″ | 5′ 3¾″<br>5′ 5½″ | 7′ 5¼″<br>7′ 7″ |
| 3′ 6″<br>Single | Rough<br>Brick | 3′ 8¼″<br>3′10″ | 6′ 9⅞″<br>6′10¾″ | H = Nom. frame height + 2⅛″ min. (i.e., 6′8″ = 82⅛″ min.) | 4′ 3¾″<br>4′ 5½″ | 4′11¼″<br>5′ 1″ | 4′11¾″<br>5′ 1½″ | 6′ 3¼″<br>6′ 5″ | 5′ 9¾″<br>5′11½″ | 7′11¼″<br>8′ 1″ |
| 5′ 0″<br>Double | Rough<br>Brick | 5′ 2¾″<br>5′ 4½″ | 6′ 9⅞″<br>6′10¾″ | For Drywall Opening: W = Nom. frame | 5′10¼″<br>6′ 0″ | 6′ 5¾″<br>6′ 7½″ | 6′ 6¼″<br>6′ 8″ | 7′ 9¾″<br>7′11½″ | 7′ 4¼″<br>7′ 6″ | 9′ 5¾″<br>9′ 7½″ |
| 5′ 4″<br>Double | Rough<br>Brick | 5′ 6¾″<br>5′ 8½″ | 6′ 9⅞″<br>6′10¾″ | width + 2″, ± ¼″ (i.e., 3′0″ = 38″, ± ¼″) | 6′ 2¼″<br>6′ 4″ | 6′ 9¾″<br>6′11½″ | 6′10¼″<br>7′ 0″ | 8′ 1¾″<br>8′ 3½″ | 7′ 8¼″<br>7′10″ | 9′ 9¾″<br>9′11½″ |
| 6′ 0″<br>Double | Rough<br>Brick | 6′ 2¾″<br>6′ 4½″ | 6′ 9⅞″<br>6′10¾″ | H = Nom. frame height + 1″, + ¼″ – 0″ | 6′10¼″<br>7′ 0″ | 7′ 5¾″<br>7′ 7½″ | 7′ 6¼″<br>7′ 8″ | 8′ 9¾″<br>8′11½″ | 8′ 4¼″<br>8′ 6″ | 10′ 5¾″<br>10′ 7½″ |
| Sidelight<br>Only | Rough<br>Brick | S/Light<br>S/Light | 6′ 9⅞″<br>6′10¾″ | (i.e., 6′8″ = 81″, + ¼″ – 0″) | 8′ ¼″<br>10″ | | 1′ 4¼″<br>1′ 6″ | | 2′ 2¼″<br>2′ 4″ | |

*Height—Distance From Finish Floor

Patents Pending

# PLYWOOD SPECIFICATIONS

## Plywood Product Coding

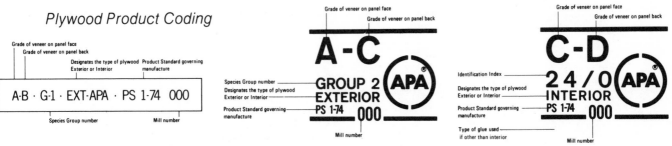

Grade of veneer on panel face
Grade of veneer on panel back
Designates the type of plywood Exterior or Interior
Product Standard governing manufacture

A-B · G-1 · EXT-APA · PS 1-74 000

Species Group number     Mill number

---

Grade of veneer on panel face
Grade of veneer on panel back

**A-C** GROUP 2 EXTERIOR PS 1-74 000 (APA)

Species Group number
Designates the type of plywood Exterior or Interior
Product Standard governing manufacture
Mill number

---

Grade of veneer on panel face
Grade of veneer on panel back

**C-D** 24/0 INTERIOR PS 1-74 000 (APA)

Identification Index
Designates the type of plywood Exterior or Interior
Product Standard governing manufacture
Type of glue used if other than interior
Mill number

## Guide to Engineered Grades of Plywood

Specific grades and thicknesses may be in locally limited supply. See your dealer for availability before specifying.

### Interior Type

| Use these terms when you specify plywood | Description and Most Common Uses | Typical Grade-trademarks | Face | Back | Inner Plies | Most Common Thicknesses (inch) (1) | | | | |
|---|---|---|---|---|---|---|---|---|---|---|
| C-D INT-APA (2) (3) | For wall and roof sheathing, subflooring, industrial uses such as pallets. Also available with intermediate glue or exterior glue. Specify intermediate glue for moderate construction delays; exterior glue for better durability in somewhat longer construction delays and for treated wood foundations. | C-D 32/16 APA INTERIOR PS 1-74 000 | C | D | D | 5/16 | 3/8 | 1/2 | 5/8 | 3/4 |
| STRUCTURAL I C-D INT-APA and STRUCTURAL II C-D INT-APA | Unsanded structural grades where plywood strength properties are of maximum importance: structural diaphragms, box beams, gusset plates, stressed skin panels, containers, pallet bins. Made only with exterior glue. | STRUCTURAL I C-D 24/0 APA INTERIOR PS 1-74 000 EXTERIOR GLUE | C (6) | D (7) | D (7) | 5/16 | 3/8 | 1/2 | 5/8 | 3/4 |
| UNDERLAYMENT INT-APA (3) (2) (9) | For underlayment or combination subfloor underlayment under resilient floor coverings, carpeting in homes, apartments, mobile homes. Specify exterior glue where moisture may be present, such as bathrooms, utility rooms. Touch-sanded. Also available in tongue-and-groove. | UNDERLAYMENT GROUP 1 APA INTERIOR PS 1-74 000 | C Plugged | D | (8) C & D | 1/4 | 3/8 | 1/2 | 5/8 | 3/4 |
| C-D PLUGGED INT-APA (3) (2) (9) | For built-ins, wall and ceiling tile backing, cable reels, walkways, separator boards. Not a substitute for Underlayment, as it lacks Underlayment's punch-through resistance. Touch-sanded. | C-D PLUGGED GROUP 2 APA INTERIOR PS 1-74 000 | C Plugged | D | D | 5/16 | 3/8 | 1/2 | 5/8 | 3/4 |
| 2·4·1 INT-APA (2) (5) | Combination subfloor underlayment. Quality base for resilient floor coverings, carpeting, wood strip flooring. Use 2·4·1 with exterior glue in areas subject to moisture. Unsanded or touch-sanded as specified. | 2·4·1 GROUP 1 APA INTERIOR PS 1-74 000 | C Plugged | D | C & D | (available 1-1/8" or 1-1/4") | | | | |

### Exterior Type

| | | | | | | | | | | |
|---|---|---|---|---|---|---|---|---|---|---|
| C-C EXT-APA (3) | Unsanded grade with waterproof bond for subflooring and roof decking, siding on service and farm buildings, crating, pallets, pallet bins, cable reels. | C-C 42/20 APA EXTERIOR PS 1-74 000 | C | C | C | 5/16 | 3/8 | 1/2 | 5/8 | 3/4 |
| STRUCTURAL I C-C EXT-APA and STRUCTURAL II C-C EXT-APA | For engineered applications in construction and industry where full Exterior type panels are required. Unsanded. See (9) for species group requirements. | STRUCTURAL I C-C 32/16 APA EXTERIOR PS 1-74 000 | C | C | C | 5/16 | 3/8 | 1/2 | 5/8 | 3/4 |
| UNDERLAYMENT C-C Plugged EXT-APA (3) (9) C-C PLUGGED EXT-APA (3) (9) | For Underlayment or combination subfloor underlayment under resilient floor coverings where severe moisture conditions may be present, as in balcony decks. Use for tile backing where severe moisture conditions exist. For refrigerated or controlled atmosphere rooms, pallets, fruit pallet bins, reusable cargo containers, tanks and boxcar and truck floors and linings. Touch-sanded. Also available in tongue-and-groove. | UNDERLAYMENT C-C PLUGGED GROUP 2 APA EXTERIOR PS 1-74 000 / C-C PLUGGED GROUP 3 APA EXTERIOR PS 1-74 000 | C Plugged | C | C (8) | 1/4 | 3/8 | 1/2 | 5/8 | 3/4 |
| B-B PLYFORM CLASS I & CLASS II EXT-APA (4) | Concrete form grades with high reuse factor. Sanded both sides. Mill oiled unless otherwise specified. Special restrictions on species. Also available in HDO. | B-B PLYFORM CLASS I APA EXTERIOR PS 1-74 000 | B | B | C | | | | 5/8 | 3/4 |

(1) Panels are standard 4x8 foot size. Other sizes available.
(2) Also available with exterior or intermediate glue.
(3) Available in Group 1, 2, 3, 4 or 5.
(4) Also available in STRUCTURAL I.
(5) Available in Group 1, 2 or 3 only.
(6) Special improved C grade for structural panels.

(7) Special improved D grade for structural panels.
(8) Ply beneath face a special C grade which limits knotholes to 1 inch or in Interior Underlayment, D under Group 1 or 2 faces 1/6 inch thick.
(9) Also available in STRUCTURAL I (all plies limited to Group 1 species) and STRUCTURAL II (all plies limited to Group 1, 2 or 3 species).

## Plywood Woods and Grades

| Group 1 | Group 2 | Group 3 | Group 4 | Group 5 |
|---------|---------|---------|---------|---------|
| Apitong | Cedar, Port | Alder, Red | Aspen | Basswood |
| Beech, | Orford | Birch, Paper | Bigtooth | Fir, Balsam |
| American | Cypress | Cedar, Alaska | Quaking | Poplar, |
| Birch | Douglas | Fir, | Cativo | Balsam |
| Sweet | Fir 2[a] | Subalpine | Cedar | |
| Yellow | Fir | Hemlock, | Incense | |
| Douglas | California | Eastern | Western | |
| Fir 1[a] | Red | Maple, | Red | |
| Kapur | Grand | Bigleaf | Cottonwood | |
| Keruing | Noble | Pine | Eastern | |
| Larch, | Pacific | Jack | Black | |
| Western | Silver | Lodgepole | (Western | |
| Maple, Sugar | White | Ponderosa | Poplar) | |
| Pine | Hemlock, | Spruce | Pine | |
| Caribbean | Western | Redwood | Eastern | |
| Ocote | Lauan | Spruce | White | |
| Pine, South. | Almon | Black | Sugar | |
| Loblolly | Bagtikan | Engelmann | | |
| Longleaf | Mayapis | White | | |
| Shortleaf | Red Lauan | | | |
| Slash | Tangile | | | |
| Tanoak | White Lauan | | | |
| | Maple, Black | | | |
| | Mengkulang | | | |
| | Meranti, Red[b] | | | |
| | Mersawa | | | |
| | Pine | | | |
| | Pond | | | |
| | Red | | | |
| | Virginia | | | |
| | Western | | | |
| | White | | | |
| | Spruce | | | |
| | Red | | | |
| | Sitka | | | |
| | Sweetgum | | | |
| | Tamarack | | | |
| | Yellow- | | | |
| | poplar | | | |

(a) Douglas Fir from trees grown in the states of Washington, Oregon, California, Idaho, Montana, Wyoming, and the Canadian Provinces of Alberta and British Columbia shall be classed as Douglas Fir No. 1. Douglas Fir from trees grown in the states of Nevada, Utah, Colorado, Arizona and New Mexico shall be classed as Douglas Fir No. 2.

(b) Red Meranti shall be limited to species having a specific gravity of 0.41 or more based on green volume and oven dry weight.

| | |
|---|---|
| **N** | Smooth surface "natural finish" veneer. Select, all heartwood or all sapwood. Free of open defects. Allows not more than 6 repairs, wood only, per 4 x 8 panel, made parallel to grain and well matched for grain and color. |
| **A** | Smooth, paintable. Not more than 18 neatly made repairs, boat, sled, or router type, and parallel to grain, permitted. May be used for natural finish in less demanding applications. |
| **B** | Solid surface. Shims, circular repair plugs and tight knots to 1 inch permitted. Wood or synthetic patching material may be used. Some minor splits permitted. |
| **C** | Tight knots to 1-1/2 inch. Knotholes to 1 inch and some to 1-1/2 inch if total width of knots and knotholes is within specified limits. Synthetic or wood repairs. Discoloration and sanding defects that do not impair strength permitted. Limited splits allowed. |
| **C** (Plugged) | Improved C veneer with splits limited to 1/8 inch width and knotholes and borer holes limited to 1/4 x 1/2 inch. Admits some broken grain. Synthetic repairs permitted. |
| **D** | Knots and knotholes to 2-1/2 inch width and 1/2 inch larger within specified limits. Limited splits are permitted. |

## Plywood Subflooring

| Panel Identification Index | Plywood Thickness (inches) | Maximum Span (inches) |
|---|---|---|
| 30/12 | 5/8 | 12* |
| 32/16 | 1/2, 5/8 | 16** |
| 36/16 | 3/4 | 16** |
| 42/20 | 5/8, 3/4, 7/8 | 20** |
| 48/24 | 3/4, 7/8 | 24 |
| 1-1/8" Groups 1 & 2 | 1-1/8 | 48 |
| 1-1/4" Groups 3 & 4 | 1-1/4 | 48 |

*May be 16" if 25/32" wood strip flooring is installed at right angles to joists.
**May be 24" if 25/32" wood strip flooring is installed at right angles to joists.

## Plywood Underlayment

| Plywood Grades and Species Group | Application | Minimum Plywood Thickness (inch) |
|---|---|---|
| Groups 1, 2, 3, 4, 5 UNDERLAYMENT INT-APA (with interior, intermediate or exterior glue), or UNDERLAYMENT EXT-APA (C-C Plugged) | over plywood subfloor | 1/4 |
| | over lumber subfloor or other uneven surfaces | 3/8 |
| Same grades as above, but Group 1 only | over lumber floor up to 4" wide. Face grain must be perpendicular to boards | 1/4 |

## Exterior Plywood Panel Siding, Over Sheathing

| Description | Nominal Thickness (inch) | Maximum Stud Spacing (inches) | |
|---|---|---|---|
| | | Face Grain Vertical | Face Grain Horizontal |
| MDO EXT-APA | 5/16 | 16* | 24 |
| A-C EXT-APA** B-C EXT-APA** | 3/8 | 16* | 24 |
| C-C Plugged EXT-APA** MDO EXT-APA | 1/2 and thicker | 24 | 24 |
| 303-T 1-11 EXT-APA | 5/8 | 16* | 24 |
| 303-16 o.c. Siding EXT-APA | 5/16 and thicker | 16* | 24 |
| 303-24 o.c. Siding EXT-APA | 7/16 and thicker | 24 | 24 |

*May be 24" with 1/2" plywood or lumber sheathing, if panel is also nailed 12" o.c. midway between studs and if joints fall over studs.
**Only APA Qualified Coatings recommended for quality finish.

## Plywood Roof Decking—maximum allowable uniform live loads

**(5 psf dead load assumed. Live load is applied load, like snow. Dead load is weight of plywood and roofing.)**

| Panel Ident. Index | Plywood thickness (inch) | Max. span (inches) | Unsupported edge-max. length (inches) [d] | Allowable live loads (psf) [e] | | | | | | | | | | |
|---|---|---|---|---|---|---|---|---|---|---|---|---|---|---|
| | | | | (Spacing of supports [inches] center to center) | | | | | | | | | | |
| | | | | 12 | 16 | 20 | 24 | 30 | 32 | 36 | 42 | 48 | 60 | 72 |
| 12/0 | 5/16 | 12 | 12 | 135 | | | | | | | | | | |
| 16/0 | 5/16, 3/8 | 16 | 16 | 165 | 80 | | | | | | | | | |
| 20/0 | 5/16, 3/8 | 20 | 20 | 210 | 115 | 65 | | | | | | | | |
| 24/0 | 3/8, 1/2 | 24 | 24 | 275 | 155 | 105 | 60 | | | | | | | |
| 30/12 | 5/8 | 30 | 26 | 450 | 250 | 175 | 100 | 50 | | | | | | |
| 32/16 | 1/2, 5/8 | 32 | 28 | 420 | 235 | 160 | 100 | 55 | 45 | | | | | |
| 36/16 | 3/4 | 36 | 30 | | 320 | 220 | 140 | 75 | 60 | 45 | | | | |
| 42/20 | 5/8, 3/4, 7/8 | 42 | 32 | | 360 | 250 | 155 | 95 | 75 | 55 | 35 | | | |
| 48/24 | 3/4, 7/8 | 48 | 36 | | | 320 | 200 | 130 | 110 | 85 | 50 | 35 | | |
| 2-4-1 | 1-1/8 | 72 | 48 | | | | 390 | 250 | 215 | 170 | 100 | 75 | 45 | 30 |
| 1-1/8" Grp. 1 & 2 | 1-1/8 | 72 | 48 | | | | 315 | 200 | 175 | 140 | 80 | 60 | 35 | 25 |
| 1-1/4" Grp. 3 & 4 | 1-1/4 | 72 | 48 | | | | 340 | 215 | 190 | 150 | 85 | 65 | 40 | 25 |

NOTES:

(a) These values apply for STANDARD C-D INT-DFPA, C-C EXT-DFPA, STRUCTURAL I C-D INT-DFPA, and STRUCTURAL I C-C EXT-DFPA grades only. Plywood continuous over 2 or more spans; grain of face plies across supports.

(b) Use 6d common, smooth, ring-shank, or spiral-thread nails for 1/2" thick or less and 8d common, smooth, ring-shank, or spiral-thread for plywood 1" thick or less. Use 8d ring-shank or spiral-thread or 10d common smooth-shank nails for 2-4-1, 1-1/8" and 1-1/4" panels. Space nails 6" at panel edges and 12" at intermediate supports, except that where spans are 48" or more, nails shall be 6" at all supports. Space panel ends 1/16", and panel edges 1/8". Where wet or humid conditions prevail, double these spacings.

(c) Special conditions, such as heavy concentrated loads, may require construction in excess of these minimums.

(d) Provide adequate blocking, tongue and grooved edges or other suitable edge support such as Plyclips when spans exceed indicated value. Use two Plyclips for 48" or greater spans and one for lesser spans.

(e) Uniform load deflection limit: 1/180th span under live load plus dead load, 1/240th under live load only.

## Recommended Minimum Stapling Scheduling for Plywood

| Plywood Thickness (inch) | Staple Leg Length (inches) | Spacing Around Entire Perimeter of Sheet (inches) | Spacing at Intermediate Members (inches) |
|---|---|---|---|
| **Plywood Wall Sheathing** / Without diagonal bracing | | | |
| 5/16 | 1-1/4 | 4 | 8 |
| 3/8 | 1-3/8 | 4 | 8 |
| 1/2 | 1-1/2 | 4 | 8 |
| **Plywood Roof Sheathing** | | | |
| 5/16 | 1-1/4 | 4 | 8 |
| 3/8 | 1-3/8 | 4 | 8 |
| 1/2 | 1-1/2 | 4 | 8 |
| **Plywood Subfloors** | | | |
| 1/2 | 1-5/8 | 4 | 7 |
| 5/8 | 1-5/8 | 2-1/2 | 4 |
| **Plywood Underlayment** | | | |
| 1/4* | 7/8 | 3 | 6 each way |
| 3/8 | 1-1/8 | 3 | 6 each way |
| 1/2 | 1-5/8 | 3 | 6 each way |
| 5/8 | 1-5/8 | 3 | 6 each way |
| **Asphalt Shingles to Plywood** / Staples to have crown width of 3/4" min. | | | |
| 5/16 and thicker | 3/4 | | According to shingle manufacturer, but not less than 6 staples for 36" section, or 2 staples for each individual shingle. |

*18 gauge staples with 3/16" crown width may be used for 1/4" Underlayment.

## Plywood Siding Direct to Studs

| Plywood Siding | | | Max. Stud Spacing (inches) | |
|---|---|---|---|---|
| Type | Description | Nominal Thickness (inch) | Face Grain Vertical | Face Grain Horizontal |
| Panel Siding | A-C EXT APA* B-C EXT-APA* C-C Plugged* EXT-APA MDO EXT-APA | 3/8 | 16 | 24 |
| | | 1/2 & thicker | 24 | 24 |
| | 303T 1-11 EXT-APA | 5/8 | 16 | 24 |
| | 303-16 o.c. Siding EXT-APA | 5/16 & thicker | 16 | 24 |
| | 303-24 o.c. Siding EXT-APA | 7/16 & thicker | 24 | 24 |
| Lap Siding | A-C EXT-APA* B-C EXT-APA* C-C Plugged* EXT-APA MDO EXT-APA | 3/8 | -- | 16 |
| | | 1/2 & thicker | -- | 24 |
| | 303-16 o.c. Siding EXT-APA | 5/16 or 3/8 | -- | 16 |
| | 303-16 o.c. Siding EXT-APA 303-24 o.c. Siding EXT-APA | 7/16 & thicker | -- | 24 |

*Only APA Qualified Coatings recommended for quality finish.

## Typical Asphalt Prepared Roofing Products

| 1 PRODUCT | 2 Approx. Shipping Weight Per Square | 3 Packages Per Square | 4 Length | 5 Width | 6 Units Per Square | 7 Side or End Lap | 8 Top Lap | 9 Head Lap | 10 Exposure |
|---|---|---|---|---|---|---|---|---|---|
| Saturated Felt | 15 lb. | 1/4 | 144' | 36" | | 4"to 6" | 2" | | 34" |
| | 30 lb. | 1/2 | 72' | 36" | | 4"to 6" | 2" | | 34" |
| Smooth Roll | 65 lb. | 1 | 36' | 36" | | 6" | 2" | | 34" |
| | 50 lb. | 1 | 36' | 36" | | 6" | 2" | | 34" |
| Mineral Surfaced Roll | 90 lb. | 1.0 | 36' | 36" | 1.0 | 6" | 2" | | 34" |
| | 90 lb. | | | | 1.075 | 6" | 3" | | 33" |
| | 90 lb. | | | | 1.15 | 6" | 4" | | 32" |
| Pattern Edge Roll | 105 lb. | 1 | 42' | 36" | | | 2" | | 16" |
| | 105 lb. | 1 | 48' | 32" | | | 2" | | 14" |
| 19" Selvage Double Coverage | 110 lb. to 120 lb. | 2 | 36' | 36" | | | 19" | 2" | 17" |

| 1 | 2 | 3 | 4 | 5 | 6 | 7 | 8 | 9 | 10 |
|---|---|---|---|---|---|---|---|---|---|
| PRODUCT | Approx. Shipping Weight Per Square | Packages Per Square | Length | Width | Shingles Per Square | Side or End Lap | Top Lap | Head Lap | Exposure |
| 3 Tab Self Sealing Strip Shingle | 205 lb. 235 lb. 300 lb. 380 lb. | 3, 4 & 5 | 36" | 12" to 15" | 67 to 81 | | 7" to 10" | 2" to 5" | 5" to 6" |
| 2 and 3 Tab Hex Strip | 195 lb. | 3 | 36" | 11-1/3" | 86 | | 2" | 2" | 5" |
| Individual Lock Down | 145 lb. | 2 | 16" | 16" | 80 | $2\frac{1}{2}$" | | | |
| Individual Staple Down | 145 lb. | 2 | 16" | 16" | 80 | $2\frac{1}{2}$" | | | |
| Giant Individual American | 330 lb. | 4 | 16" | 12" | 226 | | 11" | 6" | 5" |
| Giant Individual Dutch Lap | 165 lb. | 2 | 16" | 12" | 113 | 3" | 2" | | 10" |

Columns 4 and 5 - State the over-all dimensions of one unit of the product in length and width.

Column 6 - States the number of units or shingles required to cover a square. When the speed with which the average workman can apply the shingles is known, this figure will be a help in computing the labor cost of a job.

Column 7 - Indicates the side or end lap; this is defined as the shortest distance in inches which horizontally adjacent elements of roofing
overlap each other.  See Figs. 4 and 5.

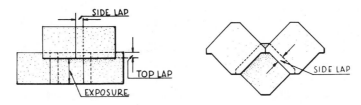

Fig. 4 - Dutch Lap          Fig. 5 - Individual Hex

Column 8 - Indicates top lap.  Top lap is defined as the shortest distance in
inches from the lower edge of an overlapping shingle or sheet to
the upper edge of the lapped unit in the first course below.  See
Figs. 4 and 6.

Column 9 - Indicates head lap.  Head lap is defined as the shortest distance
in inches from the lower edge of an overlapping shingle or sheet,
to the upper edge of the unit lapped in the second course below.
See Fig. 6.

   NOTE - Cut outs, slits, slots or abutted vertical side edges are
        not considered in figuring laps or coverage.

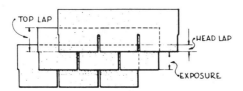

Fig. 6

Column 10 - Indicates the exposure of the unit.  Exposure is defined as the
shortest distance in inches between exposed edges of overlapping
courses of roofing.  See Fig. 6.

The data given in Table I are typical of the groups illustrated but it should be
understood that there are products within each group that differ as to weight,
dimension and design.  For instance, the weight of 3 tab square butt strips
ranges from 205 to 380 pounds per square.


## Typical Accessories for Asphalt Prepared Roofing Products

### 1. ASPHALT COATINGS AND CEMENTS

(a) Asphalt coatings and cements are asphaltic materials combined with
special ingredients and either mixed with suitable solvents (cut-back
type) or emulsified in water.  These materials are processed to
various consistencies, dependent upon the purpose for which they are
to be used.

(b) The materials may be classified into several groups among which are:

            Plastic Asphalt Cements
            Lap Cements
            Quick Setting Asphalt Adhesives
            Roof Coatings
            Asphalt Water Emulsions
            Asphalt Primers

(c) Method of Softening

The materials are flammable, and should never be warmed over an open fire, or placed in direct contact with a hot surface. If necessary, they may be softened by placing the container, unopened, in hot water, or by storing in a warm place.

(d) General Application Practice

All cut-back asphalt coatings and cements should be applied to a dry clean surface, and trowelled or brushed vigorously so that air bubbles are eliminated, the material being forced into all cracks and openings Emulsions may be applied to damp or wet surfaces, but should never be applied in an exposed location if rain is anticipated within 24 hours after completion of the job.

2. PRINCIPAL USES AND RECOMMENDATIONS

(a) Plastic Asphalt Cements

These materials are generally designated as plastic asphalt cements or flashing cements. They are so processed that they will not flow at summer temperatures. They are sufficiently elastic after setting to compensate for normal expansion and contraction of the roof deck or movement between the deck and other elements of the structure. They will not become brittle at low temperatures.

Plastic asphalt cement is used as part of a flashing assembly at points where the roof meets a wall, chimney, vent pipe or other vertical intersection.

(b) Lap Cements

These cements are of various consistencies and should be used for the purpose for which they were designed and sold by the manufacturer.

## Minimum Pitch Requirements for Asphalt Roofing Products

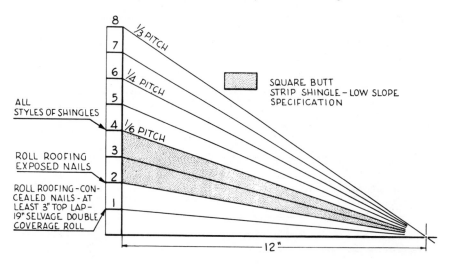

## Estimating Roofing Coverage

Your estimating should become a tidy routine. Here are some steps you can take to get going: Measure the roof in feet, get area in square feet, and then divide that area by 100 — that's how many squares of shingles or shakes you'll need to cover it at standard exposures. Don't forget to allow for double-coursing at the eaves — with shingles, one square will provide about 240 lineal feet of starter course; with shakes, one square will cover about 120 lineal feet. Also, allow about one extra square of shingles for every 100 lineal feet of valleys, and about two squares of shakes.

If you are estimating from a plan or blueprint rather than actual job measurement, don't forget to include all eave overhang. And then you can get the roof area by adding the following percentages for the various roof pitches:

4-in-12  Add 5½% of area     6-in-12  Add 12% of area
5-in-12  Add 8½% of area     8-in-12  Add 20% of area

HIP AND RIDGE — One bundle will cover 16⅔ lineal feet, both shingle ridge and shake ridge.

FELT — Figure 1½ rolls of 15-lb. minimum felt, 18" wide, for each square of shakes at 10" exposure.

NAILS — It takes 2 lbs. per square at standard exposures — 6d nails for 24" shakes @ 10" exposure; 3d nails for 16" shingles @ 5" exposure or 18" shingles @ 5½" exposure, and 4d nails for 24" shingles @ 7½" exposure.

Don't forget that a square of shingles or shakes will cover 100 sq. ft. of roof area only when applied at the standard weather exposure. These are 10" for 24" shakes, 5" for 16" shingles, 5½" for 18" shingles and 7½" for 24" shingles. Proportionately more material, and labor, are required when these weather exposures are reduced. Never increase them, except on walls!

## Red Cedar Shingles and Shakes

### CERTIGRADE RED CEDAR SHINGLES

| GRADE | Length | Thickness (at Butt) | No. of Courses Per Bundle | Bdls/Cartons Per Square | | Description |
|---|---|---|---|---|---|---|
| No. 1 BLUE LABEL | 16" (Fivex) 18" (Perfections) 24" (Royals) | .40" .45" .50" | 20/20 18/18 13/14 | 4 bdls. 4 bdls. 4 bdls. | |  The premium grade of shingles for roofs and sidewalls. These top-grade shingles are 100% heartwood. 100% clear and 100% edge-grain. |
| No. 2 RED LABEL | 16" (Fivex) 18" (Perfections) 24" (Royals) | .40" .45" .50" | 20/20 18/18 13/14 | 4 bdls. 4 bdls. 4 bdls. | |  A good grade for many applications. Not less than 10" clear on 16" shingles, 11" clear on 18" shingles and 16" clear on 24" shingles. Flat grain and limited sapwood are permitted in this grade. |
| No. 3 BLACK LABEL | 16" (Fivex) 18" (Perfections) 24" (Royals) | .40" .45" .50" | 20/20 18/18 13/14 | 4 bdls. 4 bdls. 4 bdls. | |  A utility grade for economy applications and secondary buildings. Not less than 6" clear on 16" and 18" shingles, 10" clear on 24" shingles. |
| No. 4 UNDER-COURSING | 16" (Fivex) 18" (Perfections) | .40" .45" | 14/14 or 20/20 14/14 or 18/18 | 2 bdls. 2 bdls. 2 bdls. 2 bdls. | |  A utility grade for undercoursing on double-coursed sidewall applications or for interior accent walls. |
| No. 1 or No. 2 REBUTTED-REJOINTED | 16" (Fivex) 18" (Perfections) 24" (Royals) | .40" .45" .50" | 33/33 28/28 13/14 | 1 carton 1 carton 4 bdls. | |  Same specifications as above for No. 1 and No. 2 grades but machine trimmed for exactly parallel edges with butts sawn at precise right angles. For sidewall application where tightly fitting joints are desired. Also available with smooth sanded face. |

| PITCH | Maximum exposure recommended for roofs: | | | | | | | | |
|---|---|---|---|---|---|---|---|---|---|
| | NO. 1 BLUE LABEL | | | NO. 2 RED LABEL | | | NO. 3 BLACK LABEL | | |
| | 16" | 18" | 24" | 16" | 18" | 24" | 16" | 18" | 24" |
| 3 IN 12 TO 4 IN 12 | 3¾" | 4¼" | 5¾" | 3½" | 4" | 5½" | 3" | 3½" | 5" |
| 4 IN 12 AND STEEPER | 5" | 5½" | 7½" | 4" | 4½" | 6½" | 3½" | 4" | 5½" |

| LENGTH AND THICKNESS | Approximate coverage of one square (4 bundles) of shingles based on following weather exposures | | | | | | | | | | | | | | | | | | | | | | | | | |
|---|---|---|---|---|---|---|---|---|---|---|---|---|---|---|---|---|---|---|---|---|---|---|---|---|---|---|
| | 3½" | 4" | 4½" | 5" | 5½" | 6" | 6½" | 7" | 7½" | 8" | 8½" | 9" | 9½" | 10" | 10½" | 11" | 11½" | 12" | 12½" | 13" | 13½" | 14" | 14½" | 15" | 15½" | 16" |
| 16" x 5/2" | 70 | 80 | 90 | 100* | 110 | 120 | 130 | 140 | 150‡ | 160 | 170 | 180 | 190 | 200 | 210 | 220 | 230 | 240† | .... | .... | .... | .... | .... | .... | .... | .... |
| 18" x 5/2¼" | .... | 72½ | 81½ | 90½ | 100* | 109 | 118 | 127 | 136 | 145½ | 154½‡ | 163½ | 172½ | 181½ | 191 | 200 | 209 | 218 | 227 | 236 | 245½ | 254½† | .... | .... | .... | .... |
| 24" x 4/2" | .... | .... | .... | .... | .... | 80 | 86½ | 93 | 100* | 106½ | 113 | 120 | 126½ | 133 | 140 | 146½ | 153‡ | 160 | 166½ | 173 | 180 | 186½ | 193 | 200 | 206½ | 213† |

NOTES: * Maximum exposure recommended for roofs.     ‡ Maximum exposure recommended for single-coursing No. 1 and No. 2 grades on sidewalls.
† Maximum exposure recommended for double-coursing No. 1 grades on sidewalls.

### CERTIGROOVE GROOVED RED CEDAR SIDEWALL SHAKES

| GRADE | Length | Thickness (at Butt) | No. Courses Per Carton | Cartons Per Square* | | Description |
|---|---|---|---|---|---|---|
| No. 1 BLUE LABEL | 16" 18" 24" | .40" .45" .50" | 16/17 14/14 12/12 | 2 ctns. 2 ctns. 2 ctns. | |  Machine-grooved shakes are manufactured from shingles and have striated faces and parallel edges. Used exclusively double-coursed on sidewalls. |

NOTE: *Also marketed in one-carton squares.

## CERTI-SPLIT RED CEDAR HANDSPLIT SHAKES

| GRADE | Length and Thickness | 18" Pack** | | Description |
|---|---|---|---|---|
| | | Courses Per Bdl. | Bdls. Per Sq. | |
| No. 1 HANDSPLIT & RESAWN | 15" Starter-Finish<br>18" x ½" Mediums<br>18" x ¾" Heavies<br>24" x ⅜"<br>24" x ½" Mediums<br>24" x ¾" Heavies | 9 9<br>9 9<br>9 9<br>9 9<br>9 9<br>9 9 | 5<br>5<br>5<br>5<br>5<br>5 |  These shakes have split faces and sawn backs. Cedar logs are first cut into desired lengths. Blanks or boards of proper thickness are split and then run diagonally through a bandsaw to produce two tapered shakes from each blank. |
| No. 1 TAPERSPLIT | 24" x ½" | 9 9 | 5 |  Produced largely by hand, using a sharp-bladed steel froe and a wooden mallet. The natural shingle-like taper is achieved by reversing the block, end-for-end, with each split. |
| No. 1 STRAIGHT-SPLIT | 18" x ⅜" True-Edge*<br>18" x ⅜"<br>24" x ⅜" | 20" Pack<br>14 Straight<br>19 Straight<br>16 Straight | 4<br>5<br>5 |  Produced in the same manner as tapersplit shakes except that by splitting from the same end of the block, the shakes acquire the same thickness throughout. |

NOTE: * Exclusively sidewall product, with parallel edges.
    ** Pack used for majority of shakes.

| SHAKE TYPE, LENGTH AND THICKNESS | Approximate coverage (in sq. ft.) of one square, when shakes are applied with ½" spacing, at following weather exposures, in inches (h): | | | | | |
|---|---|---|---|---|---|---|
| | 5½ | 7½ | 8½ | 10 | 11½ | 16 |
| 18" x ½" Handsplit-and-Resawn Mediums (a) | 55(b) | 75(c) | 85(d) | 100 | . . . . | . . . . |
| 18" x ¾" Handsplit-and-Resawn Heavies (a) | 55(b) | 75(c) | 85(d) | 100 | . . . . | . . . . |
| 24" x ⅜" Handsplit | . . . . | 75(e) | 85 | 100(f) | 115(d) | . . . . |
| 24" x ½" Handsplit-and-Resawn Mediums | . . . . | 75(b) | 85 | 100(c) | 115(d) | . . . . |
| 24" x ¾" Handsplit-and-Resawn Heavies | . . . . | 75(b) | 85 | 100(c) | 115(d) | . . . . |
| 24" x ½" Tapersplit | . . . . | 75(b) | 85 | 100(c) | 115(d) | . . . . |
| 18" x ⅜" True-Edge Straight-Split | . . . . | . . . . | . . . . | . . . . | . . . . | 112(g) |
| 18" x ⅜" Straight-Split | 65(b) | 90 | 100(d) | . . . . | . . . . | . . . . |
| 24" x ⅜" Straight-Split | . . . . | 75(b) | 85 | 100 | 115(d) | . . . . |
| 15" Starter-Finish Course | Use supplementary with shakes applied not over 10" weather exposure. | | | | | |

(a) 5 bundles will cover 100 sq. ft. roof area when used as starter-finish course at 10" weather exposure; 6 bundles will cover 100 sq. ft. wall area at 8½" exposure; 7 bundles will cover 100 sq. ft. roof area at 7½" weather exposure; see footnote (h).

(b) Maximum recommended weather exposure for 3-ply roof construction.

(c) Maximum recommended weather exposure for 2-ply roof construction.

(d) Maximum recommended weather exposure for single-coursed wall construction.

(e) Maximum recommended weather exposure for application on roof pitches between 4-in-12 and 8-in-12.

(f) Maximum recommended weather exposure for application on roof pitches of 8-in-12 and steeper.

(g) Maximum recommended weather exposure for double-coursed wall construction.

(h) All coverage based on ½" spacing between shakes.

### Exterior Finishes for Wood Products

| Type of Finish | Preparation of Surface | Sealers and Primers | Application of Finish | Characteristics |
|---|---|---|---|---|
| General Use (Lumber, Siding and Panel Products) | | | | |
| Penetrating Finishes | | | | |
| —Preservatives | | | Brush one coat of water repellent preservative onto surface. | Imparts mildew and decay resistance; some protection from ultra-violet light destruction depending on pigment content; easy to maintain. |
| | | | Brush a solution of fungicide onto surface; best method is to add fungicide to finish. | May tend to leach out with rain. |
| —Pigmented Stains | Sand or scrape wood to flat, clean surface; if new wood, no preparation required. | None required. | Brush latex or oil-based stain onto surface; working area should be small enough to maintain a wet edge; one or two coats applied according to manufacturer's recommendations. | Easy to apply; attractive finish for even rough surfaces; easy to maintain; choice of semi-transparent or opaque finish. |
| —Madison Formula | | | Brush one coat of Madison Formula onto new wood. | Semi-transparent oil-based stain intended for western red cedar; imparts water repellency and mildew and decay resistance; contains wax which leads to refinish problems. |
| —Oil | | | One coat of oil, applied by brush. | Not recommended; oil remains tacky on surface, collecting insects and dirt. |
| Surface Finishes | | | | |
| —Solvent-Based Paints (Including Alkyds) | Sand or scrape off badly deteriorated finish; if new wood, no preparation is required. | Apply knot sealer or shellac to knots and pitch streaks; apply oil-based primer to new wood. | Painting should be done in dry weather with temperatures above 45° F; paint following sun around house, staying one side behind sun; apply one or two coats (depending on colour) by brush. | Alkyd paints overcome blistering and excessive chalking associated with traditional oil-based paints; only white traditional oil-based paint is recommended; alkyd paints are recommended if colour is required; alkyd trim paints should be used above masonry; solvent-based paints with other synthetic resins are available. |

| Type of Finish | Preparation of Surface | Sealers and Primers | Application of Finish | Characteristics |
|---|---|---|---|---|
| General Use (Lumber, Siding and Panel Products) | | | | |
| Surface Finishes<br><br>—Latex Paints | | Apply knot sealer or shellac to knots and pitch streaks; apply oil-based primer as under-coat or special latex primer over previous coats of oil-based paints. | Follow application instructions above for solvent-based paints; apply two coats of latex paint by brush over primer. | Easy to apply; adhere well to damp surface; dry rapidly; easy equipment clean up; chalk-resistant; slower to erode than oil-based paints; thinner surface film, therefore less levelling off of surface irregularities. |
| —Synthetic Varnishes | For refinishing, scrape off loose flaking materials, sand area, wash wood surface and stain bleached areas to match the rest of the wood; if new wood, no preparation required. | None required. | Three coats of synthetic varnish are applied by brush to new wood; fewer coats required for refinishing. | Refinishing required about every two years; finish allows penetration of ultra-violet which degrades film and wood surface; results in darkening of wood colour. |
| Shingles and Shakes (Western Red Cedar) | | | | |
| Penetrating Finishes<br><br>—Pigmented Stains | | | Immersing shingles or shakes in stain (semi-transparent or opaque) is best technique; re-finishing done with a brush. | See section on General Use; rough surface of shingles and shakes readily absorbs stain. |
| —Madison Formula | Same as for General Use. | None required. | Apply as for other pigmented stains. | Madison formula specifically formulated for western red cedar. |

| Type of Finish | Preparation of Surface | Sealers and Primers | Application of Finish | Characteristics |
|---|---|---|---|---|
| Shingles and Shakes (Western Red Cedar) | | | | |
| **Penetrating Finishes** —Preserv- atives | | | Pentachlorophenol (5% to 10% solution) may be added to stain; alterna- tively, wood may be pres- sure treated with pre- servatives. | Preservatives desired but not absolutely necessary for western red cedar. |
| **Surface Finishes** —Alkyd Paints | None required. | None required. | Two coats of specially formulated shingle and shake alkyd paint applied by brush. | Flat finish; covers all but extreme surface irregularities. |
| —Latex Paints | | Specially formulated sealer required; factory primed shin- gles and shakes are available. | Two coats of latex paint applied by brush. | Covers all but extreme surface irregularities. |
| —Weathering and Bleaching Agents | | None required. | Follow manufacturer's directions. | |
| —Synthetic Varnishes | | None required. | Same as for General Use. | Not recommended; see General Use. |

## PENETRATING FINISHES

### Preservatives

Water repellent preservative finishes contain waxes, oils, resins, preservatives and, optionally, pigments. The waxes, oils and resins make the wood surface repellent to water while the preservatives impart mildew and decay resistance to the wood. Pigments add colour and protect the wood surfaces from destruction by ultra-violet light; finish life is related to the pigmentation and ranges from two to four years. One application of a preservative finish is usually sufficient. Maintenance is simple; the surface is cleaned and washed before another coat of finish is applied.

Fungicides such as pentachlorophenol or toxic metallic salts (copper and zinc naphthenates) may be used alone, but they often leach out with rain, depending on the vehicle. A better approach is to mix the fungicide with a good penetrating finish. Products containing fungicides or mildewcides carry a Department of Agriculture registration number and active ingredient description.

## Pigmented Stains

Pigmented stains are popular exterior finishes. They are easy to apply and provide an attractive finish that is easy to maintain. They penetrate into the wood without forming a surface film, so even rough wood, such as sawn-textured siding, can be easily stained. Most pigmented stains are oil-based, but, recently, latex stains have become available.

Semi-transparent stains are often used on new wood or on surfaces with an existing semi-transparent finish (not a surface finish) of similar colour. The natural grain and texture of the wood are not hidden by such a stain.

Opaque stains have greater covering qualities due to their pigmentation and somewhat higher volume of solids; they hide the grain well. They can be used on new wood or previously stained surfaces.

Stains should be applied to clean, dry wood. Brush application is best. The working area should be small so that a wet edge can be maintained, i.e., the stain should be wet enough along the edges of a previously brushed area to allow rebrushing without streaking. A stain containing fungicide should be used where wood may be subject to mildew or decay such as in continually moist areas. Stain should not be applied over a sealer.

A stain finish can be expected to last up to five years depending on climatic conditions. Stain is not subject to peeling, cracking or blistering because the surface film is extremely thin and flexible. Small cracks may occur on the wood product itself, especially on plywood.

Stain finishes are relatively simple to maintain; a new coat of stain should be applied about every two years. Usually it is sufficient to hose the surface down before applying the new stain, but, if the old stain has deteriorated badly, the surface should be sanded before refinishing.

## Madison Formula

The Madison formula is a modified, semi-transparent, oil-based stain developed by the Forest Products Laboratories of the Canadian Department of the Environment and the U.S. Department of Agriculture. Table 4 lists components and gives specific instructions for preparation of the U.S. version of the Madison formula. It is also produced commercially. The mixture is intended for western red cedar; the pigments in the stain give a natural cedar colour. The Madison formula contains paraffin wax to increase the water-repellency of the linseed oil and pentach-

lorophenol to inhibit mildew. Because the formula includes wax, no other finish can be successfully applied over it. Only one coat of the U.S. formula need be applied, preferably to new wood. The Canadian version does not contain zinc stearate and normally requires two coats for proper coverage.

## Madison Formula

| | |
|---|---|
| Boiled Linseed Oil | 3 gallons |
| Mineral Spirits | 1 gallon |
| Burnt Sienna Colour-In-Oil | 1 pint * |
| Raw Umber Colour-In-Oil | 1 pint * |
| Paraffin Wax | 1 pound |
| Pentachlorophenol Concentrate 10:1 | ½ gallon |
| Zinc Stearate | 2 ounces |

Pour the mineral spirits into an open-top 5 gallon can. Heat paraffin and zinc stearate in the top of a double boiler and stir until the mixture is uniform. Pour this into mineral spirits, stirring vigorously. *This should be done outside to avoid the risk of fire.*

Add pentachlorophenol and linseed oil to the cooled solution. Stir in the colours until the mixture is uniform.

One gallon covers 400—500 square feet on a smooth surface and 200—250 square feet on a sawn-textured surface.

\* This colour mixture gives a natural cedar colour.

## Oils

Oil finishes tend to darken wood and perform best in dry areas. Boiled linseed oil may remain soft or tacky so insects and dirt particles tend to stick to it, raw linseed oil even more so. As well, mildew may form. Penetrating stains offer the same protection and provide a better appearance.

## SURFACE FINISHES — GENERAL USE

Paint protects against weather, adds beauty and is easy to apply. There is a large selection of high quality solvent-based and latex paints that give excellent service in exterior applications. Poor paint performance, such as blistering, peeling and cracking, is rarely a result of faulty paint or poor wood performance. Failures are usually caused by improper selection of paint for the intended application, poor construction (allowing moisture to move into the finished wall), haphazard surface preparation or poor paint application.

Painting should be done in dry weather when the temperature is above 45° Fahrenheit (7° Centigrade). After the morning dew has evaporated, it is best to paint following the sun around the house. Stay on one side behind the sun because direct sunlight drys the film surface too quickly and can result in blistering.

Good paint performance requires a clean, dry, sanded surface. For best results, knot sealer or shellac should be applied to knots and pitch streaks to prevent exudation of resin into the paint. On bare wood, a primer is usually required.

Sound construction practices and good surface preparation, which lead to better finish performance, are outlined in a separate section of this publication. The importance of proper surface preparation cannot be overemphasized. Time spent in washing, scraping or sanding a surface before applying the finish is amply rewarded by a longer service life and more satisfactory performance.

### Solvent-Based Paints

Solvent-based paints are widely used, the most common system being an appropriate primer under one or two topcoats, depending on the colour. To avoid problems, ensure that the topcoat and primer are compatible.

The binder in oil-based paints eventually degrades on exposure to sun and water, resulting in erosion of the paint surface. This erosion carries off surface dirt and reduces the paint film thickness. The surface should be repainted before the paint film becomes too thin to protect the underlying wood.

The deterioration of oil-based paint generally follows five stages:
- Soiling stage, when the coating becomes dirty.
- Flatting stage, when the coating loses its gloss.
- Chalking stage, when the surface erodes, carrying off dirt and preventing the build-up of a thick paint coat.
- Fissure stage, when the surface checks or cracks. Generally, cracking occurs later than checking although one may occur without the other.
- Disintegration stage, when the surface becomes exposed by erosion, crumbling (from checking) or flaking (from cracking). Flaking is the quickest type of disintegration.

The surface should be repainted with a solvent-based paint when checking or cracking appears. Before refinishing, the surface should be clean and free from flaking paint. If badly deteriorated, the surface should be scraped or sanded smooth before washing. Even if scraping is unnecessary, the entire surface should be washed down with water to remove all loose chalking material, especially the eaves that are not normally exposed to rain.

House paint is supplied as a chalking or non-chalking type. Chalking types are restricted to whites and are intended to provide self-cleaning. In colours, chalking is undesirable and leads to "white facing". Tinting oil-based paints or alkyd paints have good chalk-resistance and are recommended if a coloured exterior oil-based paint is desired. Alkyd trim enamels are intended for wood areas above masonry to prevent staining.

### Latex Paints

Latex (water-thinned) paints became popular in the 1960's because they are easy to apply, dry rapidly, adhere well to damp surfaces and perform well. Latex paints are also known for their good colour retention. Latex paints are permeable to water vapour because the surface film contains microscopic voids. However, latex paints cannot form an adequate film in cold weather, and should be applied at temperatures of 45°F (7°C) or higher for the paint to dry properly.

Latex paints should not be applied over an old chalking surface. The chalking layer remains unbound and leads to early failure of the new paint, unless special latex primers, modified to bind the chalk, are used. Alternately, the chalking layer can be completely removed before applying an oil-based primer, followed by two coats of finish latex paint.

Usually, a three-coat latex paint system provides a thinner film due to the volume of solids in the paint; therefore, the latex system will not conceal surface irregularities as well. However, latex is less likely to chalk and is slower to erode than oil-based paint, due to the polymers in the emulsion. Deterioration of latex paints follows only the first three of the five steps of deterioration that oil-based paints go through: soiling, flatting and chalking.

### Varnishes

Clear exterior finishes allow the penetration of ultra-violet light, causing a degradation of the film and wood surface. The net result is early failure. Good quality exterior varnishes contain ultra-violet absorbers, but they are of limited effectiveness. A three-coat varnish finish may remain intact for more than two years, but eventually the film cracks and fails. Often the varnish darkens much earlier. Refinishing is required approximately every two years for even the best varnishes and should be carried out before the film cracks. If cracking and peeling have occurred, the old finish must be removed to bare wood. Bleached areas should be stained to match the rest of the wood before more varnish is applied.

## Interior Finishes for Wood Products

| Type of Finish | Preparation of Surface | Sealers and Primers | Application of Finish | Characteristics |
|---|---|---|---|---|
| General Use (Lumber, Boards, Planks and Panelling) | | | | |
| Pigmented Stains<br><br>— Water Stains | Sand or scrape wood to flat, clean surface; for some hardwoods, fill pores with filler before sanding (see Table 1); if new wood, should already be flat and clean. | One coat of sealer often brushed into softwoods before finishing to reduce depth of penetration between springwood and summerwood; also used to reduce prominence of grain; no primers required for pigmented stains and most clear finishes. | Water stains are brushed onto surface; one coat is usually sufficient. | Easy to apply; water can raise wood grain making sanding necessary after stain has dried; fabric dyes in water are typical water stain. |
| — Spirit Stains | | | Spirit stains are brushed onto wood rapidly and evenly; one coat is usually sufficient. | Quick drying so apply evenly; little time to restroke spots; little tendency to raise wood grain. |
| — Oil Stains | | | Oil stains are brushed onto wood, all strokes made along the grain; one coat is usually sufficient; sometimes used under varnishes. | Penetrate well; do not raise grain; dry slowly so easy to distribute evenly. |
| Clear Finishes<br><br>— Waxes | | | Two coats of paste wax can be applied over shellac in methanol sealer; surface damage repaired by spot cleaning with mineral spirits and applying more wax. | Low gloss finish; rarely used because of excellent performance of synthetic varnishes; great refinish problems if wax allowed to penetrate wood. |
| — Synthetic Varnishes (such as polyurethane) | | | Three coats of synthetic varnish brushed onto surface (two coats if filler used); can be polished with wax but not necessary. | Varying gloss finishes, synthetics give hard, tough finish, resistant to oil, water and alcohol; dries quickly by reaction with moisture in air. |
| — Shellacs | | | Two coats of shellac are brushed onto surface (used as methanol solution); patched in spots using methanol remover and applying more shellac. | Brittle finish; water spots easily; not recommended because synthetic varnishes do better job. |
| — Boiled Linseed Oil | | | Two coats of boiled linseed oil are spread evenly onto surface using brush or rag; 24-hour drying period is required between coats. | Seldom used; long drying time required so surface susceptible to marking. |
| Paints<br><br>— Alkyd Enamels | Sand or dust wood to ensure good paint adhesion. | Apply alkyd or oil-based primer with good enamel holdout or an enamel undercoat. | Two coats of alkyd-based enamel are brushed or rolled onto surface. | High- or semi-gloss finish; resistant to solvents; good colour retention; optimum results using enamel undercoater. |
| — Latexes | | Recommend application of latex primer; not absolutely necessary. | Two coats of latex are brushed or rolled onto surface; may be used without primer but primer recommended. | Full range of glosses available; high- or semi-gloss recommended for kitchens and bathrooms; fast drying; little yellowing; easy clean up with water; no solvent vapour; spot touch up without patch effect; reduced fire hazard. |

| Type of Finish | Preparation of Surface | Sealers and Primers | Application of Finish | Characteristics |
|---|---|---|---|---|
| Plywood | | | | |
| Pigmented Stains | Hardwood and softwood plywood are usually factory sanded on face to be finished; require no surface preparation other than filling and sanding surface blemishes. | Priming and edge sealing not necessary; sealer will subdue grain contrast if dark stain preferred. | One coat of combined wax and stain are applied; after a few minutes wipe with rag to desired shade, then apply a coat of self-polishing wax and buff surface.<br><br>Pigmented stains can be used alone as described under General Use. | Wax penetrates wood making surface unsuitable for refinishing.<br><br>Features listed under General Use. |
| Clear Finishes<br>— Synthetic Varnishes<br><br>— Blond Finish<br><br>— Waxes | Fill nail holes with tinted filler, sand smooth and spot prime. | Apply coat of sealer. | Brush two coats of varnish onto prepared surface; semi-gloss varnish often applied over flat varnish.<br><br>Apply one coat of interior white undercoat (thinned so grain shows through) under one coat of flat synthetic varnish.<br><br>Wax systems commercially available but not recommended; if used, follow manufacturer's instructions closely. | Features listed under General Use.<br><br>Easy and inexpensive; offers features of synthetic varnishes.<br><br>Not recommended because wax imbedded in wood fibres cannot be removed; this wax will interfere with alternative refinishing. |
| Paints<br>— Alkyd Enamels<br><br>— Latexes | Sand or scrape wood to smooth, clean surface. | Apply one coat of enamel undercoat.<br><br>Apply one coat of latex-based check-retardant primer. | Apply either one coat of undercoater tinted to finish colour and one coat of alkyd enamel or two coats of alkyd enamel (for better gloss).<br><br>Apply two coats of latex paint. | Good washable finish; checking and cracking may become problem.<br><br>Primer effectively eliminates cracking and checking on new wood. |
| Particleboard | | | | |
| Pigmented Stains | Surfaces available smooth or porous depending on type of particleboard; porous surfaces must be filled and sanded; some boards available with resin impregnated fibrous sheet applied in factory. | A primer or sealer may be necessary to isolate additives from the finish; finish a scrap to determine if primer or sealer is needed. | Apply stains as described under General Use. | Interesting decorative effects can be achieved with stains or clear finishes; shape and colour contrast of wood particles is emphasized. |
| Clear Finishes | | | Apply any clear finish as described under General Use. | |
| Paints | | | Apply alkyd or latex paints as described under General Use. | Paint is most common finish for particleboard. |
| Hardboard | | | | |
| Paints<br>— Alkyd Enamels<br><br>— Latexes | Nailheads should be countersunk and puttied, or treated with anti-corrosive primer; surface should be smooth and clean. | Apply one coat of primer unless hardboard has been factory primed. | Apply alkyd enamels or latexes as described under General Use. | Hardboard is usually painted because it has no grain, or natural characteristics to be emphasized. |

| Type of Finish | Preparation of Surface | Sealers and Primers | Application of Finish | Characteristics |
|---|---|---|---|---|
| Floors (Hardwood and Softwood) | | | | |
| Pigmented Stains | Sand floor with power sander, first cut across the grain and successive cuts with the grain; after sanding, vacuum off dust; apply finish as soon as possible; some hardwoods, such as oak, require filler before sanding (Table 1). | Not required unless sealer used alone as finish for industrial occupancies. | One coat of stain (oil stain if synthetic varnish is used) is brushed onto surface. | Stains change colour of the wood and emphasize grain; often used under varnish. |
| Clear Finishes<br>— Synthetic Varnishes (Polyurethane)<br>— Floor Sealers<br><br><br><br>— Shellac | | | Two coats of synthetic varnish are brushed onto stained or filled floor; bubbles should be removed by brushing back area lightly.<br><br>Apply sealer across grain as a spray or with a brush; buff with steel wool and vacuum off dust; apply second coat of sealer with the grain; sealed floor may be waxed or varnished for greater gloss.<br>Three coats of shellac are applied by brush, following wood grain. | Varying degrees of gloss; extremely wear-resistant; no wax needed for protection; difficult to spot refinish.<br><br>Inexpensive; provides protection against water damage and warping in industrial occupancies.<br><br>Easily repaired; water staining becomes chronic problem so shellac not recommended. |
| Paints<br>— Alkyd Floor of Deck Enamels | | Sealer may be required for softwood floors unless enamel is self-sealing. | Three coats of floor or deck enamel brushed onto surface. | Good wear resistance; wide colour range; softwood and hardwood floors are easily painted. |

## Pigmented Stains

Pigmented stains are classified by the solvent in which they are dispersed. Common solvents are water, spirits (alcohol) and oil.

Water stains perform satisfactorily, but the grain tends to be raised and sanding may be required after the stain has dried. A weak solution of fabric dyes in water is a typical water stain.

Spirit stains also give good service. They dry rapidly so care should be taken to apply them evenly; little time is available for touch-up.

Oil stains do not raise the grain appreciably and penetrate well. They dry more slowly than the spirit type and thus are easier to apply evenly. All strokes should be made along the grain. Oil stains may be added to wood filler to tint it to the desired colour. They may also be used under varnishes to control colour.

## Clear Finishes

### Waxes

Waxes used to be popular as flat finishes for interior wood surfaces, but are rarely used today because of the excellent water and abrasion resistance of synthetic varnishes. The major advantage of waxes was that surface damage could be repaired by spot cleaning with mineral spirits and applying more wax.

If wax is used and is allowed to penetrate the wood, it is virtually impossible to remove and serious refinish problems will be encountered. Sealers (or oil-based filler for hardwoods) can be used under wax finishes to minimize this problem.

### Varnishes

Three coats of clear, synthetic varnish such as polyurethane are recommended for floors, but two coats may be sufficient if a filler is applied first. Polyurethane varnishes are available in the full range of glosses and give a hard, tough finish that is resistant to oil, water, alcohol and heat. Often advertised as "plastic" finishes, polyurethane varnishes are usually one-component, moisture-cured products or the oil-modified type. Moisture-cured means the varnish dries by reacting with moisture in the air. The oil-modified type dries like an alkyd. The long drying time that used to be a problem with traditional varnishes has been eliminated.

Brushing shellac gives a brittle finish that water spots easily (water leaves a white mark that disappears in time); it is not recommended as a wood finish. Shellac is a natural resin dissolved in methanol (methyl hydrate or methyl alcohol). After drying, it remains soluble in methanol and worn spots can be easily patched with fresh shellac. This property was important when shellac was an inexpensive finish, but now varnishes do a better job of protecting wood.

## Boiled Linseed Oil

Boiled linseed oil is an old-fashioned wood finish seldom used today because of the time required to produce a good finish. The oil should be spread evenly with a brush or rag. A 24-hour drying period is required between successive coats, but, unfortunately, the oil finish takes much longer than this to dry completely. Until dry, the surface is susceptible to marking. Raw linseed oil can also be used, but takes even longer to dry.

## PAINTS — GENERAL USE

Walls should be sanded and dusted before painting to ensure good paint adhesion. It is advisable to use a primer or sealer on "open grain" hardwoods before sanding. Any paint finish from the full range of glosses may be selected for softwoods and hardwoods.

### Alkyd Enamel Paints

Alkyd interior enamels are often used for semi-gloss and high-gloss finishes. Two coats are usually sufficient to properly cover the wood surface. A suitable primer or enamel undercoater should be used before topcoating.

### Latex Paints

The full range of gloss finishes is now available in latex paints. High-gloss or semi-gloss latex paints are often chosen for kitchens or bathrooms, although slightly better performance may be obtained from alkyd enamels. Latex paints are frequently used as a self-priming two coat system, but use of a primer yields a smoother finished surface. The advantages of these water-based paints include no solvent vapour, fast drying, little yellowing after application, easy equipment clean-up with water, spot touch-up without patch effects and reduced fire hazard.

## PLYWOOD FINISHES

Any good quality interior finish can be applied successfully to softwood plywood. For a decorative effect, the butted joints of softwood plywood can be covered with battens or mouldings to emphasize the panels. Hardwood plywood is available in the wide colour range offered by various species. Both softwood and hardwood plywood are factory sanded; surface priming and edge sealing are not necessary for interior uses.

One of the easiest methods to stain plywood is to apply one coat of combined wax and stain and, after a few minutes, wipe the surface with a rag to the desired shade. A coat of self-polishing wax is then applied and the surface is buffed for better appearance. Regular pigmented stains used alone are also suitable.

To obtain a clear, natural finish, a prime coat of sealer is applied and allowed to dry. Then nail holes should be filled with tinted putty, sanded and spot-primed. Two coats of varnish of the desired gloss are then applied. A blond finish can be obtained by applying a thinned interior white undercoat before the synthetic varnish.

Wax finishing systems are available commercially, but subsequent paint or varnish cannot be applied over a waxed surface because wax imbedded in the wood fibres will prevent adhesion of the paint film. Some of the surface wax can be removed with mineral spirits, but, generally, wax systems are not recommended.

Plywood can also be painted. Cracking and checking often associated with painted plywood can be minimized by using a special latex-based, check-retardant primer. These primers should only be used on new or bare wood.

## PARTICLEBOARD FINISHES

Particleboard is a panel product made up of small wood pieces and an adhesive binder. The product is compacted under heat and pressure to cure the adhesive and form a rigid panel. The wood pieces in particleboard come from a variety of wood residue sources; these pieces vary in size throughout the panel. Flakeboard, such as aspenite, is a type of particleboard made entirely from flakes of predetermined dimensions cut along the direction of the grain.

Particleboard has a surface free of knots and grain, but surface porosity and texture vary among the various types of particleboard. These surface characteristics influence the treatment required before a finish is applied; all particleboard should be finished in some manner as it soils easily, is difficult to clean and may give off an odour.

Some surfaces are sanded smooth, but other more porous surfaces such as flakeboard require a wood filler or sanding sealer prior to applying finishes. Alternately, panels are available that already have the voids filled in the factory. Some manufacturers apply a resin impregnated fibrous sheet to particleboard faces to provide a base for painting. Some particleboards may contain additives that can react with some finishes. If this is the case, a specific primer or sealer should be used to isolate the finish from additives (such as wax).

**Wood Finishing Characteristics**

| Name | Relative Hardness | Grain | Finish |
|------|-------------------|-------|--------|
| Ash | Hard | Open | Requires filler. |
| Alder | Soft | Close | Stains readily. |
| Aspen | Soft | Close | Paint. |
| Basswood | Soft | Close | Paints well. |
| Beech | Hard | Close | Poor for paint, takes varnish well. |
| Birch | Hard | Close | Stains and varnishes well. |
| Cedar | Soft | Close | Paints well. Finishes well with varnish. |
| Cherry | Hard | Close | Requires filler. |
| Chestnut | Hard | Open | Must be filled. Not suitable for paint finish. |
| Cottonwood | Soft | Close | Good for paint finish. |
| Cypress | Hard | Close | Takes paint or varnish. Finishes well. |
| Elm | Hard | Open | Not suitable for paint. Requires filler. |
| Fir | Soft | Close | Can be painted, stained or finished natural. |
| Gum | Soft | Close | Can be finished with variety of finishes. |
| Hemlock | Soft | Close | Paints fairly well. |
| Hickory | Hard | Open | Requires filler. |
| Mahogany | Hard | Open | Requires filler. |
| Maple | Hard | Close | Takes any type finish. |
| Oak | Hard | Open | Requires filler. |
| Pine | Soft | Close | Takes any type finish. |
| Spruce | Soft | Close | Can be painted, stained or finished natural. |
| Teak | Hard | Open | Requires filler. |
| Walnut | Hard | Open | Requires filler. Takes all finishes well. |

Notes: (1) "Open grain" is associated with varying pore sizes between springwood and summerwood.
(2) "Close grain" is associated with woods having overall uniform pore sizes.
(3) "Hard" and "soft" are relative hardness of wood; no relation to hardwoods or softwoods.

# SIZE OF COMMON WIRE NAILS

**GAGE**

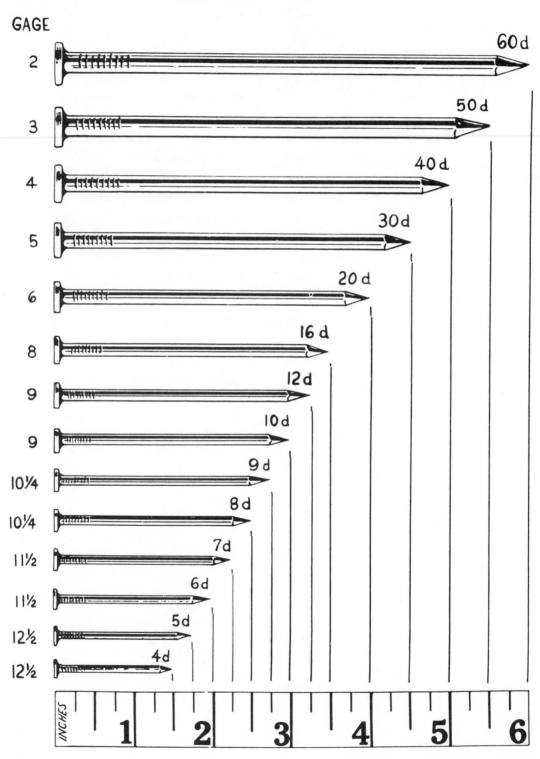

| GAGE | Nail Size |
|------|-----------|
| 2 | 60 d |
| 3 | 50 d |
| 4 | 40 d |
| 5 | 30 d |
| 6 | 20 d |
| 8 | 16 d |
| 9 | 12 d |
| 9 | 10 d |
| 10¼ | 9 d |
| 10¼ | 8 d |
| 11½ | 7 d |
| 11½ | 6 d |
| 12½ | 5 d |
| 12½ | 4 d |

INCHES  1  2  3  4  5  6

# THERMAL PROPERTIES AND "U" VALUES _____

## "U" Values and Insulation Requirements

### All-Weather Comfort Standard

| | U-Value | Insulation "R" Number |
|---|---|---|
| Ceilings | 0.05 | R19 |
| Walls | 0.07 | R11 |
| Floors over unheated spaces | 0.07 | R13 |

### Moderate Comfort and Economy Standard

| | U-Value | Insulation "R" Number |
|---|---|---|
| Ceilings | 0.07 | R13 |
| Walls | 0.09 | R8 |
| Floors over unheated spaces | 0.09 | R9 |

### Minimum Comfort Standard

| | U-Value | Insulation "R" Number |
|---|---|---|
| Ceilings | 0.10 | R9 |
| Walls | 0.11 | R7 |
| Floors over unheated spaces | 0.11 | R7 |

## Thermal Properties of Various Building Materials per Inch of Thickness

| Material | Thermal Conductivity K | Thermal Resistance R | Efficiency as an insulator Percent |
|---|---|---|---|
| Wood | 0.80 | 1.25 | 100.0 |
| Air Space[1] | 1.03 | 0.97 | 77.6 |
| Cinder Block | 3.6 | 0.28 | 22.4 |
| Common Brick | 5.0 | 0.20 | 16.0 |
| Face Brick | 9.0 | 0.11 | 8.9 |
| Concrete (Sand and Gravel) | 12.0 | 0.08 | 6.4 |
| Stone (Lime or Sand) | 12.5 | 0.08 | 6.4 |
| Steel | 312.0 | 0.0032 | 0.25 |
| Aluminum | 1416.0 | 0.00070 | 0.06 |

[1] Thermal properties are for air in a space and apply for air spaces ranging from 3/4 to 4 inches in thickness.

## *Coefficients of Heat Transmission "U" Values*

**FRAME WALLS\***

| Exterior | Type of Sheathing | No Insul. | Type of Balsam-Wool | | | |
|---|---|---|---|---|---|---|
| | | | REGULAR | | REFLECTIVE | |
| | | | STD. | D–T | STD. | D–T |
| Asbestos-Cement Siding or Stucco (1") | Gypsum – 1/2" | .34 | .13 | .083 | .083 | .062 |
| | Wood – 25/32" | .28 | .12 | .079 | .079 | .060 |
| | Nu-Wood – 1/2" | .26 | .11 | .077 | .077 | .059 |
| | Nu-Wood – 25/32" | .22 | .10 | .073 | .073 | .056 |
| Face Brick Veneer (4") | Gypsum – 1/2" | .32 | .12 | .082 | .082 | .062 |
| | Wood – 25/32" | .27 | .11 | .078 | .078 | .059 |
| | Nu-Wood – 1/2" | .25 | .11 | .076 | .076 | .058 |
| | Nu-Wood – 25/32" | .21 | .10 | .072 | .072 | .056 |
| Wood Lap Siding (1/2" × 8") | Gypsum – 1/2" | .29 | .12 | .079 | .079 | .060 |
| | Wood – 25/32" | .24 | .11 | .075 | .075 | .058 |
| | Nu-Wood – 1/2" | .22 | .11 | .074 | .074 | .057 |
| | Nu-Wood – 25/32" | .19 | .10 | .070 | .070 | .055 |
| Wood Lap Siding (3/4" × 10") | Gypsum – 1/2" | .27 | .11 | .078 | .078 | .059 |
| | Wood – 25/32" | .23 | .11 | .074 | .074 | .057 |
| | Nu-Wood – 1/2" | .21 | .10 | .073 | .073 | .056 |
| | Nu-Wood – 25/32" | .18 | .10 | .069 | .069 | .054 |
| Wood Shingles and Nu-Wood Shingle Backer | Gypsum – 1/2" | .25 | .11 | .076 | .076 | .058 |
| | Wood – 25/32" | .21 | .10 | .072 | .072 | .056 |
| | Nu-Wood – 1/2" | .20 | .10 | .071 | .071 | .055 |
| | Nu-Wood – 25/32" | .17 | .09 | .067 | .067 | .053 |

\*Wall interior finish: 1/2" gypsum wallboard or 3/8" gypsum lath and 1/2" sand aggregate plaster.

"U" values for walls with 1/2" Nu-Wood sheathing would also apply if 1/2" Nu-Wood Nail-Bond and 1/2" Nu-Wood Super SS products were used.

"U" values for walls with 1/2" gypsum sheathing would also apply if 5/16" or 3/8" plywood sheathing were used.

Small air space between brick veneer and sheathing is neglected.

---

Calculated "U" values of insulated structure between framing members are based on data in ASHRAE Guide and are expressed in Btu per sq. ft. per hour per F. degree temperature difference.

Balsam-Wool abbreviations: Regular or Reg. indicates asphalt kraft liners. Reflective or Refl. indicates aluminum reflective liners. Std. = Standard (1"). D–T = Double-Thick (2"). Type "E" = Blanket 5/8" with regular liners.

## FRAME CEILINGS*

| Type of Ceiling | Type of Balsam-Wool | | | | | | | | | |
|---|---|---|---|---|---|---|---|---|---|---|
| | HEAT FLOW UP (WINTER) | | | | HEAT FLOW DOWN (SUMMER) | | | | | |
| | REGULAR | | REFLECTIVE | | REGULAR | | REFLECTIVE** | | | |
| | STD. | D–T | STD. | D–T | STD. | D–T | STD. | | D–T | |
| | | | | | | | Air Space | | Air Space | |
| | | | | | | | 3/4" | 1–1/2" | 3/4" | 1–1/2" |
| Gypsum Wallboard, 3/8" | .16 | .096 | .12 | .080 | .14 | .091 | .088 | .075 | .065 | .058 |
| 1/2" | .15 | .095 | .12 | .079 | .14 | .090 | .087 | .075 | .064 | .057 |
| Gypsum Lath, 3/8" & | | | | | | | | | | |
| 1/2" pl. – sand aggr. | .15 | .095 | .12 | .079 | .14 | .090 | .087 | .075 | .065 | .058 |
| 1/2" pl. – lt. wt. aggr. | .15 | .093 | .11 | .078 | .14 | .088 | .085 | .074 | .064 | .057 |
| Metal Lath | | | | | | | | | | |
| 3/4" pl. – sand aggr. | .16 | .098 | .12 | .081 | .15 | .092 | .089 | .076 | .066 | .059 |
| 3/4" pl. – lt. wt. aggr. | .15 | .095 | .12 | .079 | .14 | .090 | .088 | .075 | .064 | .057 |
| Nu-Wood Acoustical Tile | | | | | | | | | | |
| 1/2" on gypsum lath | .13 | .085 | .10 | .073 | .12 | .082 | .079 | .069 | .060 | .054 |
| 1/2" on furring | .14 | .088 | .11 | .075 | .13 | .084 | – | .071 | – | .055 |
| 3/4" on gypsum lath | .12 | .082 | .10 | .070 | .11 | .078 | .076 | .066 | .058 | .052 |
| 3/4" on furring | .13 | .084 | .10 | .072 | .12 | .080 | – | .068 | – | .054 |

*Attic space above ceiling assumed ventilated so roof construction is disregarded.

**When heat flow is down, an air space faced with a reflective surface has greater thermal resistance as the depth is increased. This results in better performance and lower "U" values as illustrated in the 1–1/2" air space columns. Depth of air space makes very little difference when faced with regular materials or when heat flow is up (even with reflective surfaces).

## FRAME FLOORS*

| Type of Floor Finish | No Insul. | Type of Balsam-Wool | | | |
|---|---|---|---|---|---|
| | | REGULAR | | REFLECTIVE | |
| | | STD. | D–T | STD. | D–T |
| Hardwood – 3/4" | .28 | .12 | .080 | .063 | .050 |
| Plywood – 5/8" and floor tile or linoleum – 1/8" | .27 | .11 | .078 | .062 | .050 |
| Nu-Wood Board – 5/16", Tuff-Wood (1/4") and Floor tile or linoleum – 1/8" | .26 | .11 | .078 | .062 | .050 |

*Subfloor is 25/32" wood and building paper.

Insulation is assumed to be applied near bottom of floor joist so air space of 4" or more is provided between it and subfloor. Space between ends of joists at perimeter of building should also be insulated.

## SOLID MASONRY WALLS*

| Exterior Construction | | No Insulation | | Type of Balsam-Wool | | | |
| --- | --- | --- | --- | --- | --- | --- | --- |
| MATERIAL | THICK | PLASTER ON MASONRY | INTERIOR ON 1 x 2 FURRING | TYPE "E" 1 x 2 FURRING | STD–REG 2 x 2 FURRING | D–T–REG 2 x 3 FURRING | STD–REFL 2 x 3 FURRING |
| Brick | 8" | .45 | .29 | .16 | .13 | .087 | .079 |
| (4" Face & Common) | 12" | .33 | .23 | .15 | .12 | .081 | .075 |
| Stone | 8" | .62 | .34 | .18 | .14 | .091 | .083 |
| (Lime & Sand) | 12" | .52 | .31 | .17 | .14 | .089 | .081 |
| Hollow Clay Tile | 8" | .35 | .24 | .15 | .12 | .082 | .076 |
| | 12" | .29 | .21 | .14 | .11 | .078 | .072 |
| Poured Concrete | 8" | .62 | .34 | .18 | .14 | .091 | .083 |
| (140 lb. cu. ft.) | 12" | .52 | .31 | .17 | .14 | .089 | .081 |
| Concrete Block | | | | | | | |
| Gravel Aggregate | 8" | .48 | .30 | .17 | .13 | .087 | .080 |
| Gravel Aggregate | 12" | .44 | .27 | .16 | .13 | .086 | .079 |
| Cinder Aggregate | 8" | .37 | .25 | .15 | .12 | .083 | .076 |
| Cinder Aggregate | 12" | .35 | .24 | .15 | .12 | .082 | .075 |
| Lt. wt. Aggregate | 8" | .34 | .24 | .15 | .12 | .081 | .075 |
| Lt. wt. Aggregate | 12" | .31 | .22 | .14 | .12 | .079 | .073 |

## MASONRY WALLS WITH 4" FACE BRICK*

| Type of Backing | Thick-ness | No Insulation | | Type of Balsam-Wool | | | |
| --- | --- | --- | --- | --- | --- | --- | --- |
| | | PLASTER ON MASONRY | INTERIOR ON 1 x 2 FURRING | TYPE "E" 1 x 2 FURRING | STD–REG 2 x 2 FURRING | D–T–REG 2 x 3 FURRING | STD–REFL 2 x 3 FURRING |
| Concrete Block | 4" | .46 | .29 | .17 | .13 | .087 | .080 |
| Gravel Aggregate | 8" | .39 | .26 | .16 | .13 | .084 | .077 |
| | 12" | .36 | .25 | .15 | .12 | .083 | .076 |
| Cinder Aggregate | 4" | .39 | .26 | .16 | .13 | .084 | .077 |
| | 8" | .31 | .22 | .14 | .12 | .080 | .074 |
| | 12" | .30 | .21 | .14 | .11 | .079 | .073 |
| Lt. wt. Aggregate | 4" | .35 | .23 | .15 | .12 | .082 | .075 |
| | 8" | .29 | .21 | .14 | .11 | .078 | .072 |
| | 12" | .28 | .20 | .13 | .11 | .077 | .071 |
| Hollow Clay Tile | 4" | .39 | .26 | .16 | .13 | .084 | .077 |
| | 8" | .30 | .22 | .14 | .11 | .079 | .073 |

*Interior finish on furring is 1/2" gypsum wallboard or 3/8" gypsum lath and sand aggregate plaster. When plastered direct, 5/8" sand aggregate plaster is assumed.

2" x 3" furring is assumed to be 2" x 6" ripped.

## MASONRY

| | Resistance |
|---|---|
| **Brick** — common, 4" | 0.80 |
| face, 4" | 0.44 |
| **Cement mortar,** per 1" | 0.20 |
| **Concrete** — sand & gravel aggregate — 140 lb. density per 1" | 0.08 |
| lightweight aggregate — 100 lb. density per 1" | 0.28 |
| lightweight aggregate — 60 lb. density per 1" | 0.59 |
| lightweight aggregate — 30 lb. density per 1" | 1.11 |
| **Hollow clay tile** — 1 cell deep — 4" | 1.11 |
| 2 cells deep — 8" | 1.85 |
| 3 cells deep — 12" | 2.50 |
| **Concrete blocks** — (3 oval core) — sand & gravel aggregate, 8" | 1.11 |
| sand & gravel aggregate, 12" | 1.28 |
| cinder aggregate, 8" | 1.72 |
| cinder aggregate, 12" | 1.89 |
| lightweight aggregate, 8" | 2.00 |
| lightweight aggregate, 12" | 2.27 |
| **Stone,** limestone or sandstone, per 1" | 0.08 |

The above thermal resistance values are based on data in the ASHRAE Guide.

*Air space resistances shown are commonly used values. The emissivity values for polished aluminum flake and aluminum foil surfaces are .17 and .05, respectively. Resistance values in column "Alum. Flakes" are based on data in Guide but are interpolated between values listed for surfaces having emissivity values (e) of .05 and .20. For other spaces, such as sloping (45°) and for other temperature conditions, see Table #3 of Chapter 9 of the 1960 ASHRAE Guide.

**Air space of insulated wall usually has approximately 10° temperature difference between the two ordinary surfaces (use 1.02 value). In uninsulated wall, the temperature difference is usually about 20° (use 0.97 value). For more accurate results, air space temperature differences should be calculated and proper resistance values used as explained in the Guide.

***The U.S. Department of Commerce, "Simplified Practice Recommendation for Thermal Conductance Factors for Preformed Above-Deck Roof Insulation," No. R257-55, recognizes the specification of roof insulation on the basis of the "C" values shown. Roof insulation is made in thicknesses to meet these values. The thicknesses supplied by different manufacturers may vary depending on the conductivity value of the particular material. Where certification of thermal insulation value of roof insulation is required, the "C" factor to be certified must appear on face of order.

*"U" Values of Doors, Glass Blocks, and Windows*

## SOLID WOOD DOORS*

| Thickness | | "U" | |
|---|---|---|---|
| NOMINAL | ACTUAL | EXPOSED DOOR | WITH GLASS STORM DOOR |
| 1–1/2" – 1–3/4" | 1–5/16" – 1–3/8" | 0.49 | 0.32 |
| 2" | 1–5/8" | 0.43 | 0.28 |

## VERTICAL GLASS SHEETS*

| Number of Sheets | One | Two | | | Three | |
|---|---|---|---|---|---|---|
| Air Space – inches | None | 1/4" | 1/2" | 1" | 1/4" | 1/2" |
| "U" | 1.13 | 0.61 | 0.55 | 0.53 | 0.41 | 0.36 |

## APPLICATION FACTORS FOR WINDOWS*
*Multiply Flat Glass "U" Values by These Factors*

| Window Description | Single Glass | | Double Glass | | Windows With Storm Sash | |
|---|---|---|---|---|---|---|
| | % GLASS | FACTOR | % GLASS | FACTOR | % GLASS | FACTOR |
| Sheets | 100 | 1.00 | 100 | 1.00 | | |
| Wood sash | 80 | 0.90 | 80 | 0.95 | 80 | 0.90 |
| Steel sash | 80 | 1.00 | 80 | 1.20 | 80 | 1.00 |
| Aluminum | 80 | 1.10 | 80 | 1.30 | 80 | 1.10 |

*Data from ASHRAE Guide

## Thermal Resistance Values of Building Insulations

| | Resistance |
|---|---|
| **BALSAM-WOOL*** | |
| Panel Insulation (nom. 5/8") | 2.50 |
| Type "E" (5/8") | 2.50 |
| Standard (1") | 4.00 |
| Double Thick (2") | 8.00 |
| Full-Thick (3 5/8") | 14.50 |
| Super-Thick (nom. 6") | 24.00 |
| **CONWED BLOWING INSULATION** | |
| 4" thickness | 16.00 |
| 6" thickness | 24.00 |
| 8" thickness | 32.00 |
| 10" thickness | 40.00 |
| **NU-WOOD TILE and PANELS** | |
| Non Acoustical (1/2") | 1.43 |
| Acoustical (1/2") | 1.19 |
| **NU-WOOD STA-LITE BOARD** | |
| Board (1/2") | 1.43 |
| Thin Board (nom. 3/8") | 1.07 |
| **NU-WOOD SHEATHING** | |
| Regular (25/32") | 2.06 |
| Regular (1/2") | 1.32 |
| Super SS (1/2") | 1.22 |
| Nail-Bond (1/2") | 1.14 |
| **NU-WOOD SHINGLE BACKER** | |
| 5/16" plus 1 course of wood shingles | 1.40 |
| **NU-WOOD ROOF INSULATION** | |
| Nom. 1/2" C = .72** | 1.39 |
| Nom. 1" C = .36** | 2.78 |
| Nom. 1 1/2" C = .24** | 4.17 |
| Nom. 2" C = .19** | 5.26 |
| Nom. 2 1/2" C = .15** | 6.67 |
| Nom. 3" C = .12** | 8.33 |

* Resistance values shown are for the insulating mat only. Products having reflective liners have additional thermal resistance values due to the reflective air spaces. See "Air Spaces" section.

** The U.S. Department of Commerce, "Simplified Practice Recommendation for Thermal Conductance Factors for Preformed Above-Deck Roof Insulation," No. R257-55, recognizes the specification of roof insulation on the basis of the "C" values shown. Roof insulation is made in thicknesses to meet these values. The thicknesses supplied by different manufacturers may vary depending on the conductivity value of the particular material. Where certification of thermal insulation value of roof insulation is required, the "C" factor to be certified must appear on face of order.

Note — Balsam-Wool and Nu-Wood are registered trade-marks.

## Thermal Resistance Values of Building Materials

### AIR SPACES *

| | | | | | RESISTANCE FACED ONE SIDE WITH | | |
|---|---|---|---|---|---|---|---|
| Position | Heat Flow | Mean Temp. | Temp. Diff. | Thickness | Reg. Matl. | Alum. Flakes* | Alum. Foil |
| Vertical | Horiz. (Winter) | 50° | 10° | 3/4" – 4" | 1.02** | 2.56 | 3.52 |
| " | " " | 50° | 20° | " | 0.97** | 2.31 | 3.08 |
| " | " (Summer) | 90° | 10° | " | 0.86 | 2.38 | 3.49 |
| Horizontal | Up (Winter) | 50° | 10° | 3/4" – 4" | 0.90 | 1.92 | 2.44 |
| " | " (Summer) | 90° | 10° | " | 0.78 | 1.85 | 2.47 |
| Horizontal | Down (Winter) | 50° | 20° | 3/4" | 1.02 | 2.56 | 3.57 |
| " | " " | 50° | 20° | 1–1/2" | 1.15 | 3.57 | 5.56 |
| " | " " | 50° | 20° | 4" | 1.23 | 4.76 | 8.94 |
| Horizontal | Down (Summer) | 90° | 20° | 3/4" | 0.85 | 2.27 | 3.23 |
| " | " " | 90° | 20° | 1–1/2" | 0.93 | 3.22 | 5.00 |
| " | " " | 90° | 20° | 4" | 0.99 | 3.84 | 7.82 |

### AIR SURFACES

| | RESISTANCE | | |
|---|---|---|---|
| | Reg. Matl. | Alum. Flakes | Alum. Foil |
| Inside – still air, vertical | 0.68 | 1.41 | 1.70 |
| horizontal, heat flow up | 0.61 | 1.14 | 1.32 |
| heat flow down | 0.92 | 2.94 | 4.55 |
| Outside – 15 m.p.h. wind, horiz. or vertical | 0.17 | | |

### EXTERIOR

| | Resistance |
|---|---|
| Brick – common, 4" | 0.80 |
| face, 4" | 0.44 |
| Building paper | 0.06 |
| Roofing – asphalt roll | 0.15 |
| built up, 3/8" | 0.33 |
| Roof deck – wood, 1" (25/32") | 0.98 |
| 2" (1–5/8") | 2.03 |
| Sheathing – fir or yellow pine, 25/32" | 0.98 |
| insulating board, 1/2" | 1.32 |
| insulating board, 25/32" | 2.06 |
| Plywood – (see "Interior") | – |
| Shingles – asbestos-cement | 0.21 |
| asphalt | 0.44 |
| wood (roof) | 0.94 |
| Siding – asbestos – cement board, 1/8" | 0.03 |
| asbestos – cement, 1/4" lapped | 0.21 |
| wood drop siding, 1" × 8" | 0.79 |
| wood lap siding, 1/2" × 8" | 0.81 |
| wood lap siding, 3/4" × 10" | 1.05 |

| | Resistance |
|---|---|
| **EXTERIOR (continued)** | |
| Shingles, wood, double — 12" exposure | 1.19 |
| wood plus insulating shingle backer | 1.40 |
| Stucco, 1" | 0.20 |

## INSULATION BATTS AND BLANKETS

| | |
|---|---|
| Cotton Fiber (per inch) | 3.85 |
| Mineral Fiber (per inch) | 3.70 |
| Wood Fiber (per inch) | 4.00 |
| Wood Fiber, multilayer, stitched (per inch) | 3.70 |

## INSULATION, LOOSE FILL

| | |
|---|---|
| Macerated paper and pulp products (per inch) | 3.57 |
| Redwood bark, shredded (per inch) | 3.33 |
| Mineral wool (per inch) | 3.33 |
| Vermiculite (expanded ) — (per inch) | 2.08 |

## INSULATION — ROOF

| | |
|---|---|
| All types — Approx. 1/2", C = .72*** | 1.39 |
| 1", C = .36 | 2.78 |
| 1-1/2" C = .24 | 4.17 |
| 2", C = .19 | 5.26 |
| 2-1/2" C = .15 | 6.67 |
| 3", C = .12 | 8.33 |

## INTERIOR

| | |
|---|---|
| Gypsum plaster — Sand aggregate, 1/2" | 0.09 |
| Sand aggregate, 1/2" on 3/8" gypsum lath | 0.41 |
| Sand aggregate, 3/4" on metal lath | 0.13 |
| Lightweight aggregate, 1/2" | 0.32 |
| Lightweight aggregate, 1/2" on 3/8" gypsum lath | 0.64 |
| Lightweight aggregate, 3/4" on metal lath | 0.47 |
| Gypsum wallboard, 3/8" | 0.32 |
| 1/2" | 0.45 |
| Tile — wood or cane fiber acoustical tile, 1/2" | 1.19 |
| wood or cane fiber acoustical tile, 3/4" | 1.78 |
| wood or cane fiber interior finish, 1/2", plank tile | 1.43 |
| Plywood, 1/4" | 0.31 |
| 3/8" | 0.47 |
| 1/2" | 0.63 |
| Plywood or wood panels, 3/4" | 0.94 |
| Floor — maple or oak, 3/4" | 0.68 |
| fir or yellow pine, 25/32" | 0.98 |
| linoleum, 1/8" | 0.08 |
| terrazzo, 1" | 0.08 |
| carpet or fibrous pad | 2.08 |
| cork tile, 1/8" | 0.28 |
| floor tile — asphalt, plastic, rubber (av. value) | 0.05 |

# BATHROOM FIXTURES AND PLANS _____

## Bathtubs

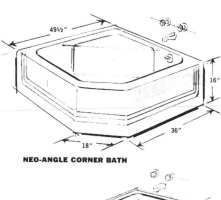

**NEO-ANGLE CORNER BATH**

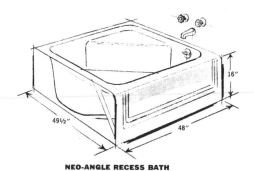

**NEO-ANGLE RECESS BATH**

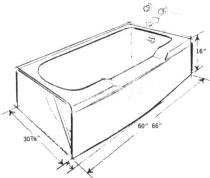

**BUCKINGHAM RECESS BATH**

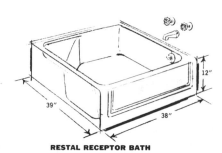

**RESTAL RECEPTOR BATH**

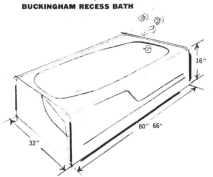

**CONTOUR RECESS BATH**

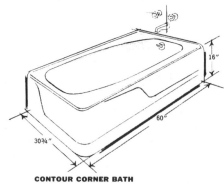

**CONTOUR CORNER BATH**

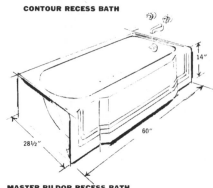

**MASTER BILDOR RECESS BATH**

**SALEM RECESS BATH**

# Cabinets, Mirrors, and Lighting

## CABINET STYLES

**1.** Economy single apron or single drawer depth.

**2.** Knee high cabinet off the floor installation for ease of maintenance.

**3.** Three quarter cabinet height provides space for baseboard heating strips.

**4.** Full height cabinet affords ample storage with "furniture" appeal.

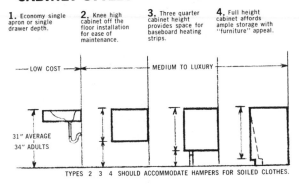

— LOW COST — — MEDIUM TO LUXURY —

31" AVERAGE
34" ADULTS

TYPES 2 3 4 SHOULD ACCOMMODATE HAMPERS FOR SOILED CLOTHES.

## MEDICINE CABINETS

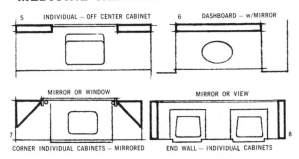

5    INDIVIDUAL — OFF CENTER CABINET      6    DASHBOARD — w/MIRROR

MIRROR OR WINDOW        MIRROR OR VIEW

7    CORNER INDIVIDUAL CABINETS — MIRRORED      END WALL — INDIVIDUAL CABINETS    8

Medicine Cabinet location is basically important for ease of use and storage capacity. Don't center cabinets directly over the lavatory. Note the various possibilities shown in the chart above as well as in the thumbnail sketches. Flexibility of location permits larger expanse of mirrors and possible captivating landscape views.

## LIGHTING DETAILS

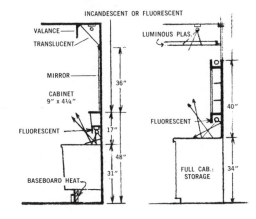

INCANDESCENT OR FLUORESCENT

VALANCE
TRANSLUCENT

LUMINOUS PLAS.

MIRROR

36"

CABINET
9" x 4¼"

FLUORESCENT    17"

FLUORESCENT    40"

48"

31"

BASEBOARD HEAT

FULL CAB.:
STORAGE    34"

Lighting is a very important factor in bathrooms. A variety of lighting effects in high and low intensities produces variables in emotional as well as aesthetic values.

**Mirrors** should be used to create pleasant and emotional space illusions in addition to their grooming use. Lighting can also be dramatic with good use of mirrors and further add to emotional grandeur.

## Water Closets

### CONVENTIONAL TYPE—FLOOR-MOUNTED WATER CLOSETS

For Budget Housing          Recommended for all housing          For Deluxe and Luxury Installations

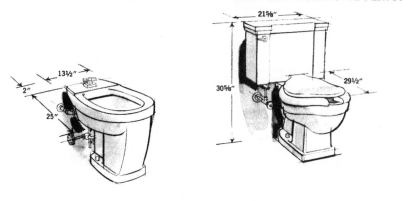

20½″          20⅝″          21½″

27½″          29″          29½″

29¾″          29⅜″          23¾″

### SPECIALIZED FIXTURES...WITH EMPHASIS ON SANITARY AND CLEANSING FEATURES

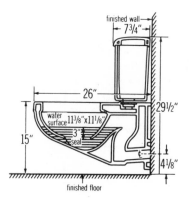

13½″          21⅝″

2″          29½″

25″          30⅝″

### WALL-HUNG WATER CLOSET

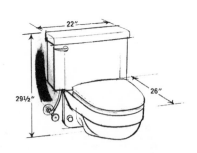

22″

26″

29½″

finished wall

7¾″

26″

29½″

water surface 11⅜″x11⅛″

3″ seal

15″

4⅛″

finished floor

## Fixtures and Space Planning Standards

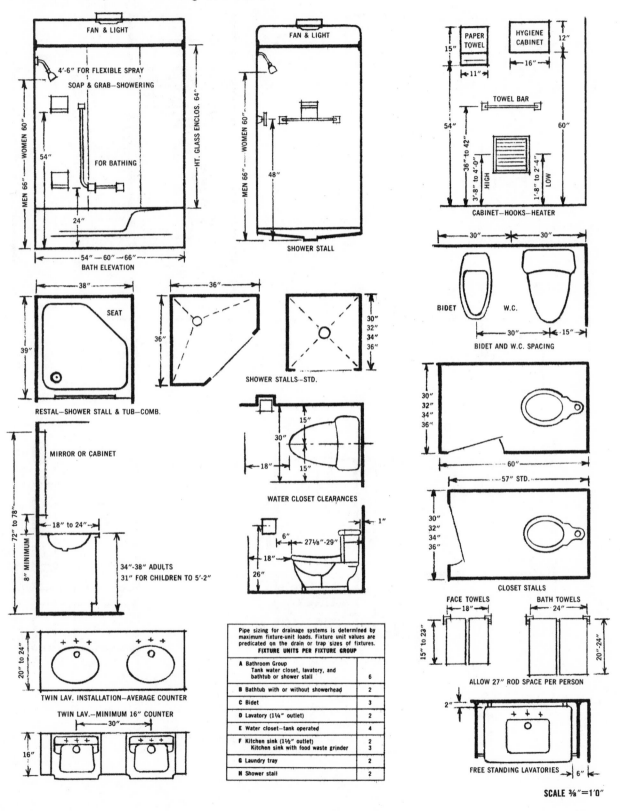

FAN & LIGHT

4'-6" FOR FLEXIBLE SPRAY
SOAP & GRAB—SHOWERING

WOMEN 60"
MEN 66"

54"

FOR BATHING

HT. GLASS ENCLOS. 64"

24"

54"   60"   66"

BATH ELEVATION

FAN & LIGHT

WOMEN 60"
MEN 66"

48"

SHOWER STALL

PAPER TOWEL
15"
11"

HYGIENE CABINET
12"
16"

TOWEL BAR

54"
36" to 42"
3'-8" to 4'-0" HIGH
1'-8" to 2'-4" LOW

60"

CABINET—HOOKS—HEATER

30"   30"

BIDET    W.C.

30"   15"

BIDET AND W.C. SPACING

38"
SEAT
39"

RESTAL—SHOWER STALL & TUB—COMB.

36"
36"

30"
32"
34"
36"

SHOWER STALLS—STD.

30"
32"
34"
36"

60"

57" STD.

30"
32"
34"
36"

CLOSET STALLS

MIRROR OR CABINET

72" to 78"
8" MINIMUM

18" to 24"

34"-38" ADULTS
31" FOR CHILDREN TO 5'-2"

15"
30"
18"
15"

WATER CLOSET CLEARANCES

1"
6"
27⅛"-29"
18"
26"

FACE TOWELS
18"

BATH TOWELS
24"

15" to 23"

20"-24"

ALLOW 27" ROD SPACE PER PERSON

2"
6"

FREE STANDING LAVATORIES

20" to 24"

TWIN LAV. INSTALLATION—AVERAGE COUNTER

TWIN LAV.—MINIMUM 16" COUNTER
30"
16"

Pipe sizing for drainage systems is determined by maximum fixture-unit loads. Fixture unit values are predicated on the drain or trap sizes of fixtures.

**FIXTURE UNITS PER FIXTURE GROUP**

| | |
|---|---|
| A Bathroom Group<br>   Tank water closet, lavatory, and<br>   bathtub or shower stall | 6 |
| B Bathtub with or without showerhead | 2 |
| C Bidet | 3 |
| D Lavatory (1¼" outlet) | 2 |
| E Water closet—tank operated | 4 |
| F Kitchen sink (1½" outlet)<br>   Kitchen sink with food waste grinder | 2<br>3 |
| G Laundry tray | 2 |
| H Shower stall | 2 |

**SCALE ⅜"=1'0"**

## Typical Plans

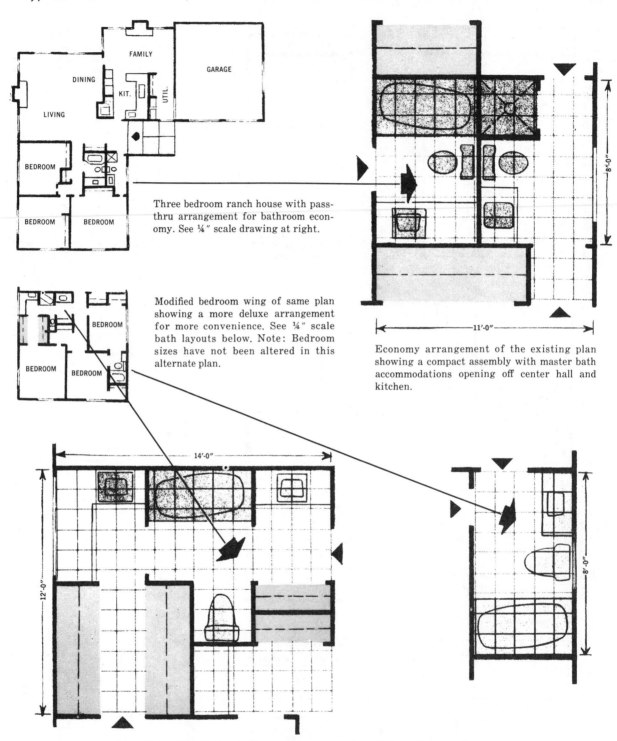

Three bedroom ranch house with pass-thru arrangement for bathroom economy. See ¼" scale drawing at right.

Modified bedroom wing of same plan showing a more deluxe arrangement for more convenience. See ¼" scale bath layouts below. Note: Bedroom sizes have not been altered in this alternate plan.

Economy arrangement of the existing plan showing a compact assembly with master bath accommodations opening off center hall and kitchen.

Note: The Master Bath now has a convenient clothes storage and dressing area and doubles as a powder room.

**BATHROOM PLANS ¼" SCALE**

# CABINET DETAILS AND DIMENSIONS

## ACCESSORIES

**CUTLERY DIVIDER**

**CHOP BLOCKS***

1824
2424
(with backsplash)
*All blocks — 1½" thick
edgegrain, select hardwood

**BREAD BOX SLIDER**

Use in

| SIZE | BD | D |
|------|----|----|
| 15" | 15 | 15 |
| 18" | 18 | 18 |
| 21" | 21 | — |
| 24" | 24 | 24 |

## OVEN UNITS

Height 84" oven platforms adjustable
— screwed to sides

**OU24-27**
Min. 21"  Max. 25½"
Width 27"

**OUA-33S**
Min. 29"
Max. 31½"

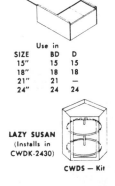

Min. 24½"  Max. 60⅝"

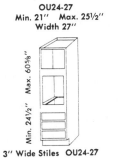

Mt. Vernon only
Min. 29"  Max. 38¼"

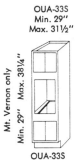

3" Wide Stiles  OU24-27

OUA-33S

**SLIDING TRAY KIT**
Fits  B-18
B-24
BC-1824
BC-2424
Note — Specify 18" & 24"
sizes when ordering.

**LINEN SHELF KIT**

LK shelf 18
LK shelf 24
Installs in
BC-1824
BC-2424

(Kit includes
3 shelves and rests)
Specify 18" or 24" unit

**LAZY SUSAN**
(Installs in
CWDK-2430)

CWDS — Kit

## DESK UNIT

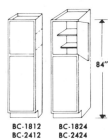

21"    5"
V-27
(Drawer)
27"

21"
30"
4"
4"

BDB-18

## UTILITY STORAGE CABINETS

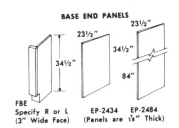

**CANNED GOODS
BROOMS
LINEN**
The walls of the Broom Units
are bored to receive LK-18
and LK-24 shelf kits.
Sliding 18" and 24" tray kits
can be used in BC-1824 and
BC-2424 for canned goods
storage, and for a variety of
other household supplies.
SEE ACCESSORIES

84"

BC-1812    BC-1824
BC-2412    BC-2424

## MISCELLANEOUS

**PREFINISHED PANEL**
48"x36" x 1⅛"

**BLACK TOE BOARD**
⅛"x4"x8'
Inexpensive
Toe Space Cover
Not available
in Country Estate

**BASE FILLER STRIPS**

K/D

4"    4"

4"    4"

BFS-384    BFS-2    BCF-3
BFS-3    Complete
BFS-6
BFS-2 Not available
in Country Estate

**BASE END PANELS**

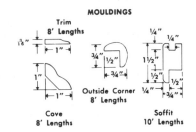

23½"    23½"

23½"

34½"

34½"

84"

FBE
Specify R or L
(3" Wide Face)

EP-2434    EP-2484
(Panels are 1⅛" Thick)

**RANGE FRONT**

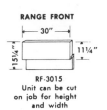

30"
15¼"    11¼"

RF-3015
Unit can be cut
on job for height
and width

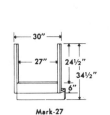

30"
27"    24½"
34½"
6"

Mark-27

**MOULDINGS**

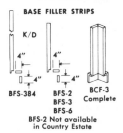

Trim
8' Lengths
1⅛"    1"

¾"  ½"
¾"

Outside Corner
8' Lengths

¼"    ¼"
1½"
½"    ½"
¼"    ¾"

1"

1"

Cove
8' Lengths

Soffit
10' Lengths

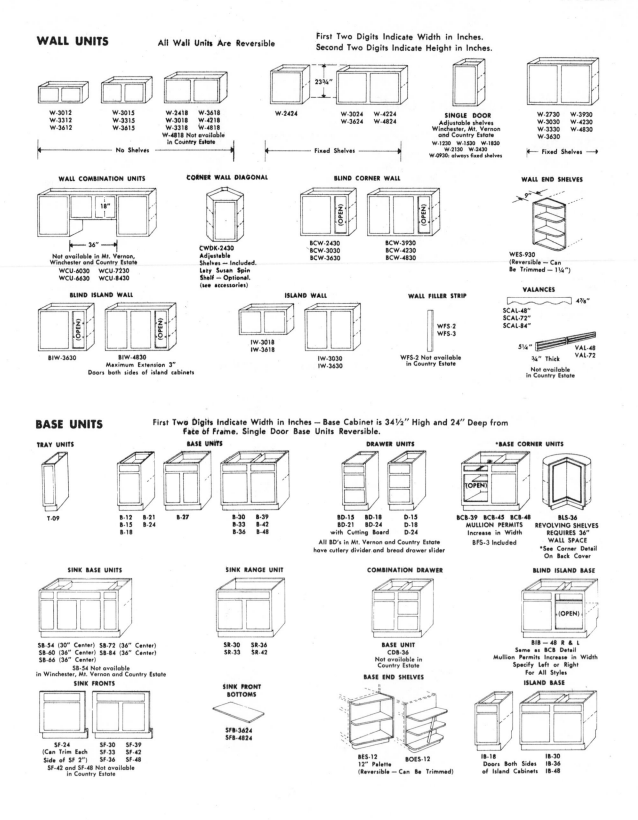

## WALL UNITS

All Wall Units Are Reversible

First Two Digits Indicate Width in Inches.
Second Two Digits Indicate Height in Inches.

| W-3012 | W-3015 | W-2418 | W-3618 |
|---|---|---|---|
| W-3312 | W-3315 | W-3018 | W-4218 |
| W-3612 | W-3615 | W-3318 | W-4818 |

W-4818 Not available
in Country Estate

←————— No Shelves —————→

W-2424

23¾"

| W-3024 | W-4224 |
|---|---|
| W-3624 | W-4824 |

←———— Fixed Shelves ————→

**SINGLE DOOR**
Adjustable shelves
Winchester, Mt. Vernon
and Country Estate

W-1230  W-1530  W-1830
W-2130  W-2430
W-0930: always fixed shelves

| W-2730 | W-3930 |
|---|---|
| W-3030 | W-4230 |
| W-3330 | W-4830 |
| W-3630 | |

←— Fixed Shelves —→

**WALL COMBINATION UNITS**

18"

←— 36" —→

Not available in Mt. Vernon,
Winchester and Country Estate

WCU-6030   WCU-7230
WCU-6630   WCU-8430

**CORNER WALL DIAGONAL**

CWDK-2430
Adjustable
Shelves — Included.
Lazy Susan Spin
Shelf — Optional.
(see accessories)

**BLIND CORNER WALL**

(OPEN)      (OPEN)

| BCW-2430 | BCW-3930 |
|---|---|
| BCW-3030 | BCW-4230 |
| BCW-3630 | BCW-4830 |

**WALL END SHELVES**

9"

WES-930
(Reversible — Can
Be Trimmed — 1¼")

**BLIND ISLAND WALL**

(OPEN)      (OPEN)

BIW-3630      BIW-4830
           Maximum Extension 3"
Doors both sides of island cabinets

**ISLAND WALL**

IW-3018
IW-3618

IW-3030
IW-3630

**WALL FILLER STRIP**

WFS-2
WFS-3

WFS-2 Not available
in Country Estate

**VALANCES**

SCAL-48"      4⅞"
SCAL-72"
SCAL-84"

5¼"          VAL-48
¾" Thick     VAL-72

Not available
in Country Estate

## BASE UNITS

First Two Digits Indicate Width in Inches — Base Cabinet is 34½" High and 24" Deep from
Face of Frame. Single Door Base Units Reversible.

**TRAY UNITS**

T-09

**BASE UNITS**

| B-12 | B-21 | B-27 | B-30 | B-39 |
|---|---|---|---|---|
| B-15 | B-24 | | B-33 | B-42 |
| B-18 | | | B-36 | B-48 |

**DRAWER UNITS**

| BD-15 | BD-18 | D-15 |
|---|---|---|
| BD-21 | BD-24 | D-18 |
| with Cutting Board | | D-24 |

All BD's in Mt. Vernon and Country Estate
have cutlery divider and bread drawer slider

**\*BASE CORNER UNITS**

(OPEN)

BCB-39  BCB-45  BCB-48
MULLION PERMITS
Increase in Width
BFS-3 Included

BLS-36
REVOLVING SHELVES
REQUIRES 36"
WALL SPACE
\*See Corner Detail
On Back Cover

**SINK BASE UNITS**

SB-54 (30" Center)  SB-72 (36" Center)
SB-60 (36" Center)  SB-84 (36" Center)
SB-66 (36" Center)
SB-54 Not available
in Winchester, Mt. Vernon and Country Estate

**SINK RANGE UNIT**

SR-30  SR-36
SR-33  SR-42

**COMBINATION DRAWER**

BASE UNIT
CDB-36
Not available in
Country Estate

**BLIND ISLAND BASE**

(OPEN)

BIB — 48 R & L
Same as BCB Detail
Mullion Permits Increase in Width
Specify Left or Right
For All Styles

**SINK FRONTS**

| SF-24 | SF-30 | SF-39 |
|---|---|---|
| (Can Trim Each | SF-33 | SF-42 |
| Side of SF 2") | SF-36 | SF-48 |

SF-42 and SF-48 Not available
in Country Estate

**SINK FRONT
BOTTOMS**

SFB-3624
SFB-4824

**BASE END SHELVES**

BES-12      BOES-12
12" Palette
(Reversible — Can Be Trimmed)

**ISLAND BASE**

IB-18      IB-30
Doors Both Sides   IB-36
of Island Cabinets IB-48

# CONVERSION TABLES

## CONVERSION OF FRACTIONS OF AN INCH TO MILLIMETERS

| Fraction | mm | Fraction | mm | Fraction | mm | Fraction | mm | Fraction | mm | Fraction | mm |
|---|---|---|---|---|---|---|---|---|---|---|---|
| 1/64 | 0.40 | 3/16 | 4.76 | 23/64 | 9.13 | 17/32 | 13.49 | 11/16 | 17.46 | 27/32 | 21.43 |
| 1/32 | 0.79 | 13/64 | 5.16 | 3/8 | 9.53 | 35/64 | 13.89 | 45/64 | 17.86 | 55/64 | 21.83 |
| 3/64 | 1.19 | 7/32 | 5.56 | 25/64 | 9.92 | 9/16 | 14.29 | 23/32 | 18.26 | 7/8 | 22.23 |
| 1/16 | 1.59 | 15/64 | 5.95 | 13/32 | 10.32 | 37/64 | 14.68 | 47/64 | 18.65 | 57/64 | 22.62 |
| 5/64 | 1.98 | 1/4 | 6.35 | 27/64 | 10.72 | 19/32 | 15.08 | 3/4 | 19.05 | 29/32 | 23.02 |
| 3/32 | 2.38 | 17/64 | 6.75 | 7/16 | 11.11 | 39/64 | 15.48 | 49/64 | 19.45 | 59/64 | 23.42 |
| 7/64 | 2.78 | 9/32 | 7.14 | 29/64 | 11.51 | 5/8 | 15.88 | 25/32 | 19.84 | 15/16 | 23.81 |
| 1/8 | 3.18 | 19/64 | 7.54 | 15/32 | 11.91 | 41/64 | 16.27 | 51/64 | 20.24 | 61/64 | 24.21 |
| 9/64 | 3.57 | 5/16 | 7.94 | 31/64 | 12.31 | 21/32 | 16.67 | 13/16 | 20.64 | 31/32 | 24.61 |
| 5/32 | 3.97 | 21/64 | 8.33 | 1/2 | 12.70 | 43/64 | 17.07 | 53/64 | 21.03 | 63/64 | 25.00 |
| 11/64 | 4.37 | 11/32 | 8.73 | 33/64 | 13.10 | | | | | | |

## CONVERSION OF MILLIMETERS INTO INCHES

Millimeters / Fractions of an inch

| mm | 0 | 1 | 2 | 3 | 4 | 5 | 6 | 7 | 8 | 9 |
|---|---|---|---|---|---|---|---|---|---|---|
| 0  in. | | 3/64 | 5/64 | 1/8 | 5/32 | 13/64 | 15/64 | 9/32 | 5/16 | 23/64 |
| 10 | 25/64 | 7/16 | 15/22 | 33/64 | 35/64 | 19/32 | 5/8 | 43/64 | 45/64 | 3/4 |
| 20 | 25/32 | 53/64 | 55/64 | 29/32 | 15/16 | 63/64 | | | | |
| 1 | | | | | | | 1/32 | 1/16 | 7/64 | 9/64 |
| 30 | 3/16 | 7/32 | 17/64 | 19/64 | 11/32 | 3/8 | 27/64 | 29/64 | 1/2 | 17/32 |
| 40 | 37/64 | 39/64 | 21/32 | 11/16 | 47/64 | 49/64 | 18/16 | 27/32 | 57/64 | 59/64 |
| 50 | 31/32 | | | | | | | | | |
| 2 | | 1/64 | 3/64 | 3/32 | 1/8 | 11/64 | 13/64 | 1/4 | 9/32 | 21/64 |
| 60 | 23/64 | 13/32 | 7/16 | 31/64 | 33/64 | 9/16 | 19/32 | 41/64 | 43/64 | 23/32 |
| 70 | 3/4 | 51/64 | 53/64 | 7/8 | 29/32 | 61/64 | 63/64 | | | |
| 3 | | | | | | | | 1/32 | 5/64 | 7/64 |
| 80 | 5/32 | 3/16 | 15/64 | 17/64 | 5/16 | 11/32 | 25/64 | 27/64 | 15/32 | 1/2 |
| 90 | 35/64 | 37/64 | 5/8 | 21/32 | 45/64 | 47/64 | 25/32 | 13/16 | 55/64 | 57/64 |
| 100 | 15/16 | 31/32 | | | | | | | | |
| 4 | 4/64 | 1/16 | 3/32 | 9/64 | 11/64 | 7/32 | 1/4 | 19/64 | | |

Example 38 mm = 1-1/2 in., 65 mm = 2-9/16 in.

## CONVERSION OF METERS INTO FEET

| m | 0 | 1 | 2 | 3 | 4 | 5 | 6 | 7 | 8 | 9 |
|---|---|---|---|---|---|---|---|---|---|---|
| 0 | | 3.28 | 6.56 | 9.84 | 13.12 | 16.40 | 19.69 | 22.97 | 26.25 | 29.53 |
| 10 | 32.81 | 36.09 | 39.37 | 42.65 | 45.93 | 49.21 | 52.49 | 55.77 | 59.06 | 62.34 |
| 20 | 65.62 | 68.90 | 72.18 | 75.46 | 78.74 | 82.02 | 85.30 | 88.58 | 91.86 | 95.14 |
| 30 | 98.43 | 101.71 | 104.99 | 108.27 | 111.55 | 114.83 | 118.11 | 121.39 | 124.67 | 127.95 |
| 40 | 131.23 | 134.51 | 137.80 | 141.08 | 144.36 | 147.64 | 150.92 | 154.20 | 157.48 | 160.76 |
| 50 | 164.04 | 167.32 | 170.60 | 173.88 | 177.17 | 180.45 | 183.73 | 187.01 | 190.29 | 193.57 |
| 60 | 196.85 | 200.13 | 203.41 | 206.69 | 209.97 | 213.25 | 216.54 | 219.82 | 223.10 | 226.38 |
| 70 | 229.66 | 232.94 | 236.22 | 239.50 | 242.78 | 246.06 | 249.34 | 252.62 | 255.91 | 259.19 |
| 80 | 262.47 | 265.75 | 269.03 | 272.31 | 275.59 | 278.87 | 282.15 | 285.43 | 288.71 | 291.99 |
| 90 | 295.28 | 298.56 | 301.84 | 305.12 | 308.40 | 311.70 | 314.96 | 318.24 | 321.52 | 324.80 |

## CONVERSION OF FEET INTO METERS

| ft. | 0 | 1 | 2 | 3 | 4 | 5 | 6 | 7 | 8 | 9 |
|---|---|---|---|---|---|---|---|---|---|---|
| 0 | | 0.30 | 0.61 | 0.91 | 1.22 | 1.52 | 1.83 | 2.13 | 2.44 | 2.74 |
| 10 | 3.05 | 3.35 | 3.66 | 3.96 | 4.27 | 4.57 | 4.88 | 5.18 | 5.49 | 5.79 |
| 20 | 6.10 | 6.40 | 6.71 | 7.01 | 7.32 | 7.62 | 7.92 | 8.23 | 8.53 | 8.84 |
| 30 | 9.14 | 9.45 | 9.75 | 10.06 | 10.36 | 10.67 | 10.97 | 11.28 | 11.58 | 11.89 |
| 40 | 12.19 | 12.50 | 12.80 | 13.11 | 13.41 | 13.72 | 14.02 | 14.33 | 14.63 | 14.94 |
| 50 | 15.24 | 15.54 | 15.85 | 16.15 | 16.46 | 16.76 | 17.07 | 17.37 | 17.68 | 17.98 |
| 60 | 18.29 | 18.59 | 18.90 | 19.20 | 19.51 | 19.81 | 20.12 | 20.42 | 20.73 | 21.03 |
| 70 | 21.34 | 21.64 | 21.95 | 22.25 | 22.56 | 22.86 | 23.16 | 23.47 | 23.77 | 24.08 |
| 80 | 24.38 | 24.69 | 24.99 | 25.30 | 25.60 | 25.91 | 26.22 | 26.52 | 26.82 | 26.21 |
| 90 | 27.43 | 27.74 | 28.04 | 28.35 | 28.65 | 28.96 | 29.26 | 29.57 | 29.87 | 30.18 |

## CONVERSION OF CENTIMETERS INTO INCHES

| cm | 0 | 1 | 2 | 3 | 4 | 5 | 6 | 7 | 8 | 9 |
|---|---|---|---|---|---|---|---|---|---|---|
| 0 | | 0.394 | 0.787 | 1.181 | 1.575 | 1.969 | 2.362 | 2.756 | 3.150 | 3.543 |
| 10 | 3.937 | 4.331 | 4.724 | 5.118 | 5.512 | 5.906 | 6.299 | 6.693 | 7.087 | 7.480 |
| 20 | 7.874 | 8.268 | 8.661 | 9.005 | 9.449 | 9.842 | 10.236 | 10.630 | 11.024 | 11.417 |
| 30 | 11.811 | 12.205 | 12.598 | 12.992 | 13.386 | 13.780 | 14.173 | 14.567 | 14.961 | 15.354 |
| 40 | 15.748 | 16.142 | 16.535 | 16.929 | 17.323 | 17.717 | 18.110 | 18.504 | 18.898 | 19.291 |
| 50 | 19.685 | 20.079 | 20.472 | 20.866 | 21.260 | 21.654 | 22.047 | 22.441 | 22.835 | 23.228 |
| 60 | 23.622 | 24.016 | 24.410 | 24.803 | 25.197 | 25.591 | 25.984 | 26.378 | 26.772 | 27.165 |
| 70 | 27.559 | 27.953 | 28.346 | 28.740 | 29.134 | 29.528 | 29.921 | 30.315 | 30.709 | 31.102 |
| 80 | 31.496 | 31.890 | 32.283 | 32.677 | 33.071 | 33.465 | 33.858 | 34.252 | 34.646 | 35.039 |
| 90 | 35.433 | 35.827 | 36.220 | 36.614 | 37.008 | 37.402 | 37.795 | 38.189 | 38.583 | 38.976 |

## CONVERSION OF INCHES INTO CENTIMETERS

| inch | 0 | 1 | 2 | 3 | 4 | 5 | 6 | 7 | 8 | 9 |
|---|---|---|---|---|---|---|---|---|---|---|
| 0 | | 2.54 | 5.08 | 7.62 | 10.16 | 12.70 | 15.24 | 17.78 | 20.32 | 22.86 |
| 10 | 25.40 | 27.94 | 30.48 | 33.02 | 35.56 | 38.10 | 40.64 | 43.18 | 45.72 | 48.26 |
| 20 | 50.80 | 53.34 | 55.88 | 58.42 | 60.96 | 63.50 | 66.04 | 68.58 | 71.12 | 73.66 |
| 30 | 76.20 | 78.74 | 81.28 | 83.82 | 86.36 | 88.90 | 91.44 | 93.98 | 96.52 | 99.06 |
| 40 | 101.60 | 104.14 | 106.68 | 109.22 | 111.76 | 114.30 | 116.84 | 119.38 | 121.92 | 124.46 |
| 50 | 127.00 | 129.54 | 132.08 | 134.62 | 137.16 | 139.70 | 142.24 | 144.78 | 147.32 | 149.86 |
| 60 | 152.40 | 154.94 | 157.48 | 160.02 | 162.56 | 165.10 | 167.64 | 170.18 | 172.72 | 175.26 |
| 70 | 177.80 | 180.34 | 182.88 | 185.42 | 187.96 | 190.50 | 193.04 | 195.58 | 198.12 | 200.66 |
| 80 | 203.20 | 205.74 | 208.28 | 210.82 | 213.36 | 215.90 | 218.44 | 220.98 | 223.52 | 226.06 |
| 90 | 228.60 | 231.14 | 233.68 | 236.22 | 238.76 | 241.30 | 243.84 | 246.38 | 248.92 | 251.46 |

## TABLE FOR FINDING SQUARE FEET

|     | 5 | 6 | 7 | 8 | 9 | 10 | 11 | 12 | 13 | 14 | 15 | 16 | 17 | 18 | 19 | 20 | 21 | 22 | 23 | 24 | 25 | 26 | 27 | 28 | 29 | 30 |
|-----|---|---|---|---|---|----|----|----|----|----|----|----|----|----|----|----|----|----|----|----|----|----|----|----|----|----|
| 12 | 0.4 | 0.5 | 0.6 | 0.7 | 0.8 | 0.8 | 0.9 | 1.0 | 1.1 | 1.2 | 1.3 | 1.3 | 1.4 | 1.5 | 1.6 | 1.7 | 1.8 | 1.8 | 1.9 | 2.0 | 2.1 | 2.2 | 2.3 | 2.3 | 2.4 | 2.5 |
| 13 | 0.5 | 0.5 | 0.6 | 0.7 | 0.8 | 0.9 | 1.0 | 1.1 | 1.2 | 1.3 | 1.4 | 1.4 | 1.5 | 1.6 | 1.7 | 1.8 | 1.9 | 2.0 | 2.1 | 2.2 | 2.3 | 2.3 | 2.4 | 2.5 | 2.6 | 2.7 |
| 14 | 0.5 | 0.6 | 0.7 | 0.8 | 0.9 | 1.0 | 1.1 | 1.2 | 1.3 | 1.4 | 1.5 | 1.6 | 1.7 | 1.8 | 1.8 | 1.9 | 2.0 | 2.1 | 2.2 | 2.3 | 2.4 | 2.5 | 2.6 | 2.7 | 2.8 | 2.9 |
| 15 | 0.5 | 0.6 | 0.7 | 0.8 | 0.9 | 1.0 | 1.1 | 1.3 | 1.4 | 1.5 | 1.6 | 1.7 | 1.8 | 1.9 | 2.0 | 2.1 | 2.2 | 2.3 | 2.4 | 2.5 | 2.6 | 2.7 | 2.8 | 2.9 | 3.0 | 3.1 |
| 16 | 0.6 | 0.7 | 0.8 | 0.9 | 1.0 | 1.1 | 1.2 | 1.3 | 1.4 | 1.6 | 1.7 | 1.8 | 1.9 | 2.0 | 2.1 | 2.2 | 2.3 | 2.4 | 2.6 | 2.7 | 2.8 | 2.9 | 3.0 | 3.1 | 3.2 | 3.3 |
| 17 | 0.6 | 0.7 | 0.8 | 0.9 | 1.1 | 1.2 | 1.3 | 1.4 | 1.5 | 1.7 | 1.8 | 1.9 | 2.0 | 2.1 | 2.2 | 2.4 | 2.5 | 2.6 | 2.7 | 2.8 | 3.0 | 3.1 | 3.2 | 3.3 | 3.4 | 3.5 |
| 18 | 0.6 | 0.8 | 0.9 | 1.0 | 1.1 | 1.3 | 1.4 | 1.5 | 1.6 | 1.8 | 1.9 | 2.0 | 2.1 | 2.3 | 2.4 | 2.5 | 2.6 | 2.8 | 2.9 | 3.0 | 3.1 | 3.3 | 3.4 | 3.5 | 3.6 | 3.8 |
| 19 | 0.7 | 0.8 | 0.9 | 1.1 | 1.2 | 1.3 | 1.5 | 1.6 | 1.7 | 1.8 | 2.0 | 2.1 | 2.2 | 2.4 | 2.5 | 2.6 | 2.8 | 2.9 | 3.0 | 3.2 | 3.3 | 3.4 | 3.6 | 3.7 | 3.8 | 4.0 |
| 20 | 0.7 | 0.8 | 1.0 | 1.1 | 1.3 | 1.4 | 1.5 | 1.7 | 1.8 | 1.9 | 2.1 | 2.2 | 2.4 | 2.5 | 2.6 | 2.8 | 2.9 | 3.1 | 3.2 | 3.3 | 3.5 | 3.6 | 3.8 | 3.9 | 4.0 | 4.2 |
| 21 | 0.7 | 0.9 | 1.0 | 1.2 | 1.3 | 1.5 | 1.6 | 1.8 | 1.9 | 2.0 | 2.2 | 2.3 | 2.5 | 2.6 | 2.8 | 2.9 | 3.1 | 3.2 | 3.4 | 3.5 | 3.6 | 3.8 | 3.9 | 4.1 | 4.2 | 4.4 |
| 22 | 0.8 | 0.9 | 1.1 | 1.2 | 1.4 | 1.5 | 1.7 | 1.8 | 2.0 | 2.1 | 2.3 | 2.4 | 2.6 | 2.8 | 2.9 | 3.1 | 3.2 | 3.4 | 3.5 | 3.7 | 3.8 | 4.0 | 4.1 | 4.3 | 4.4 | 4.6 |
| 23 | 0.8 | 1.0 | 1.1 | 1.3 | 1.4 | 1.6 | 1.8 | 1.9 | 2.1 | 2.2 | 2.4 | 2.6 | 2.7 | 2.9 | 3.0 | 3.2 | 3.4 | 3.5 | 3.7 | 3.8 | 4.0 | 4.2 | 4.3 | 4.5 | 4.6 | 4.8 |
| 24 | 0.8 | 1.0 | 1.2 | 1.3 | 1.5 | 1.7 | 1.8 | 2.0 | 2.2 | 2.3 | 2.5 | 2.7 | 2.8 | 3.0 | 3.2 | 3.3 | 3.5 | 3.7 | 3.8 | 4.0 | 4.2 | 4.3 | 4.5 | 4.7 | 4.8 | 5.0 |
| 25 | 0.9 | 1.0 | 1.2 | 1.4 | 1.6 | 1.7 | 1.9 | 2.1 | 2.3 | 2.4 | 2.6 | 2.8 | 3.0 | 3.1 | 3.3 | 3.5 | 3.6 | 3.8 | 4.0 | 4.2 | 4.3 | 4.5 | 4.7 | 4.9 | 5.0 | 5.2 |
| 26 | 0.9 | 1.1 | 1.3 | 1.4 | 1.6 | 1.8 | 2.0 | 2.2 | 2.3 | 2.5 | 2.7 | 2.9 | 3.1 | 3.3 | 3.4 | 3.6 | 3.8 | 4.0 | 4.2 | 4.3 | 4.5 | 4.7 | 4.9 | 5.1 | 5.2 | 5.4 |
| 27 | 0.9 | 1.1 | 1.3 | 1.5 | 1.7 | 1.9 | 2.1 | 2.3 | 2.4 | 2.6 | 2.8 | 3.0 | 3.2 | 3.4 | 3.6 | 3.8 | 3.9 | 4.1 | 4.3 | 4.5 | 4.7 | 4.9 | 5.1 | 5.3 | 5.4 | 5.6 |
| 28 | 1.0 | 1.2 | 1.4 | 1.6 | 1.8 | 1.9 | 2.1 | 2.3 | 2.5 | 2.7 | 2.9 | 3.1 | 3.3 | 3.5 | 3.7 | 3.9 | 4.1 | 4.3 | 4.5 | 4.7 | 4.9 | 5.1 | 5.3 | 5.4 | 5.6 | 5.8 |
| 29 | 1.0 | 1.2 | 1.4 | 1.6 | 1.8 | 2.0 | 2.2 | 2.4 | 2.6 | 2.8 | 3.0 | 3.2 | 3.4 | 3.6 | 3.8 | 4.0 | 4.2 | 4.4 | 4.6 | 4.8 | 5.0 | 5.2 | 5.4 | 5.6 | 5.8 | 6.0 |
| 30 | 1.0 | 1.3 | 1.5 | 1.7 | 1.9 | 2.1 | 2.3 | 2.5 | 2.7 | 2.9 | 3.1 | 3.3 | 3.5 | 3.8 | 4.0 | 4.2 | 4.4 | 4.6 | 4.8 | 5.0 | 5.2 | 5.4 | 5.6 | 5.8 | 6.0 | 6.3 |
| 31 | 1.1 | 1.3 | 1.5 | 1.7 | 1.9 | 2.2 | 2.4 | 2.6 | 2.8 | 3.0 | 3.2 | 3.4 | 3.7 | 3.9 | 4.1 | 4.3 | 4.5 | 4.7 | 5.0 | 5.2 | 5.4 | 5.6 | 5.8 | 6.0 | 6.2 | 6.5 |
| 32 | 1.1 | 1.3 | 1.6 | 1.8 | 2.0 | 2.2 | 2.4 | 2.7 | 2.9 | 3.1 | 3.3 | 3.6 | 3.8 | 4.0 | 4.2 | 4.4 | 4.7 | 4.9 | 5.1 | 5.3 | 5.6 | 5.8 | 6.0 | 6.2 | 6.4 | 6.7 |
| 33 | 1.1 | 1.4 | 1.6 | 1.8 | 2.1 | 2.3 | 2.5 | 2.8 | 3.0 | 3.2 | 3.4 | 3.7 | 3.9 | 4.1 | 4.4 | 4.6 | 4.8 | 5.0 | 5.3 | 5.5 | 5.7 | 6.0 | 6.2 | 6.4 | 6.6 | 6.9 |
| 34 | 1.2 | 1.4 | 1.7 | 1.9 | 2.1 | 2.4 | 2.6 | 2.8 | 3.1 | 3.3 | 3.5 | 3.8 | 4.0 | 4.3 | 4.5 | 4.7 | 5.0 | 5.2 | 5.4 | 5.7 | 5.9 | 6.1 | 6.4 | 6.6 | 6.8 | 7.1 |
| 35 | 1.2 | 1.5 | 1.7 | 1.9 | 2.2 | 2.4 | 2.7 | 2.9 | 3.2 | 3.4 | 3.6 | 3.9 | 4.1 | 4.4 | 4.6 | 4.9 | 5.1 | 5.3 | 5.6 | 5.8 | 6.1 | 6.3 | 6.6 | 6.8 | 7.0 | 7.3 |
| 36 | 1.3 | 1.5 | 1.8 | 2.0 | 2.3 | 2.5 | 2.8 | 3.0 | 3.3 | 3.5 | 3.8 | 4.0 | 4.3 | 4.5 | 4.8 | 5.0 | 5.3 | 5.5 | 5.8 | 6.0 | 6.3 | 6.5 | 6.8 | 7.0 | 7.3 | 7.5 |
| 37 | 1.3 | 1.5 | 1.8 | 2.1 | 2.3 | 2.6 | 2.8 | 3.1 | 3.3 | 3.6 | 3.9 | 4.1 | 4.4 | 4.6 | 4.9 | 5.1 | 5.4 | 5.7 | 5.9 | 6.2 | 6.4 | 6.7 | 6.9 | 7.2 | 7.5 | 7.7 |
| 38 | 1.3 | 1.6 | 1.8 | 2.1 | 2.4 | 2.6 | 2.9 | 3.2 | 3.4 | 3.7 | 4.0 | 4.2 | 4.5 | 4.8 | 5.0 | 5.3 | 5.5 | 5.8 | 6.1 | 6.3 | 6.6 | 6.9 | 7.1 | 7.4 | 7.7 | 7.9 |
| 39 | 1.4 | 1.6 | 1.9 | 2.2 | 2.4 | 2.7 | 3.0 | 3.3 | 3.5 | 3.8 | 4.1 | 4.3 | 4.6 | 4.9 | 5.1 | 5.4 | 5.7 | 6.0 | 6.2 | 6.5 | 6.8 | 7.0 | 7.3 | 7.6 | 7.9 | 8.1 |
| 40 | 1.4 | 1.7 | 1.9 | 2.2 | 2.5 | 2.8 | 3.1 | 3.3 | 3.6 | 3.9 | 4.2 | 4.4 | 4.7 | 5.0 | 5.3 | 5.6 | 5.8 | 6.1 | 6.4 | 6.7 | 6.9 | 7.2 | 7.5 | 7.8 | 8.1 | 8.3 |
| 41 | 1.4 | 1.7 | 2.0 | 2.3 | 2.6 | 2.8 | 3.1 | 3.4 | 3.7 | 4.0 | 4.3 | 4.6 | 4.8 | 5.1 | 5.4 | 5.7 | 6.0 | 6.3 | 6.5 | 6.8 | 7.1 | 7.4 | 7.7 | 8.0 | 8.3 | 8.5 |
| 42 | 1.5 | 1.8 | 2.0 | 2.3 | 2.6 | 2.9 | 3.2 | 3.5 | 3.8 | 4.1 | 4.4 | 4.7 | 5.0 | 5.3 | 5.5 | 5.8 | 6.1 | 6.4 | 6.7 | 7.0 | 7.3 | 7.6 | 7.9 | 8.2 | 8.5 | 8.8 |
| 43 | 1.5 | 1.8 | 2.1 | 2.4 | 2.7 | 3.0 | 3.3 | 3.6 | 3.9 | 4.2 | 4.5 | 4.8 | 5.1 | 5.4 | 5.7 | 6.0 | 6.3 | 6.6 | 6.9 | 7.2 | 7.5 | 7.8 | 8.1 | 8.4 | 8.7 | 9.0 |
| 44 | 1.5 | 1.8 | 2.1 | 2.4 | 2.8 | 3.1 | 3.4 | 3.7 | 4.0 | 4.3 | 4.6 | 4.9 | 5.2 | 5.5 | 5.8 | 6.1 | 6.4 | 6.7 | 7.0 | 7.3 | 7.6 | 7.9 | 8.3 | 8.6 | 8.9 | 9.2 |
| 45 | 1.6 | 1.9 | 2.2 | 2.5 | 2.8 | 3.1 | 3.4 | 3.8 | 4.1 | 4.4 | 4.7 | 5.0 | 5.3 | 5.6 | 5.9 | 6.3 | 6.6 | 6.9 | 7.2 | 7.5 | 7.8 | 8.1 | 8.4 | 8.8 | 9.1 | 9.4 |
| 46 | 1.6 | 1.9 | 2.2 | 2.6 | 2.9 | 3.2 | 3.5 | 3.8 | 4.2 | 4.5 | 4.8 | 5.1 | 5.4 | 5.8 | 6.1 | 6.4 | 6.7 | 7.0 | 7.3 | 7.7 | 8.0 | 8.3 | 8.6 | 8.9 | 9.3 | 9.6 |
| 47 | 1.6 | 2.0 | 2.3 | 2.6 | 2.9 | 3.3 | 3.6 | 3.9 | 4.2 | 4.6 | 4.9 | 5.2 | 5.5 | 5.9 | 6.2 | 6.5 | 6.9 | 7.2 | 7.5 | 7.8 | 8.2 | 8.5 | 8.8 | 9.1 | 9.5 | 9.8 |
| 48 | 1.7 | 2.0 | 2.3 | 2.7 | 3.0 | 3.3 | 3.7 | 4.0 | 4.3 | 4.7 | 5.0 | 5.3 | 5.7 | 6.0 | 6.3 | 6.7 | 7.0 | 7.3 | 7.7 | 8.0 | 8.3 | 8.7 | 9.0 | 9.3 | 9.7 | 10.0 |

# INDEX